JEHOVAH'S WITNESSES AND THE THIRD REICH: SECTARIAN POLITICS UNDER PERSECUTION

Since the end of the Second World War, leaders of the Jehovah's Witness movement in Germany and elsewhere have steadfastly argued that Witnesses were united in their opposition to Nazism and did not collude with the Third Reich. Documents have been uncovered, however, that prove otherwise. Using materials from Witness archives, the U.S. State Department, Nazi files, and other sources, M. James Penton demonstrates that while many ordinary German Witnesses were brave in their opposition to Nazism, their leaders were quite prepared to support the Hitler government.

Penton begins his study with a close reading of the 'Declaration of Facts' released by the Witnesses at a Berlin convention in June 1933. Witness leaders have called the document a protest against Nazi persecution; however, closer examination shows it contained bitter attacks on Great Britain and the United States (jointly referred to as 'the greatest and most oppressive empire on earth'), the League of Nations, big business, and, above all, Jews, who are referred to as 'the representatives of Satan the Devil.' Later that year – when the Nazis would not accept Witness blandishments – leader J.F. Rutherford called on Witnesses to seek martyrdom by carrying on a campaign of passive resistance. Many ultimately died in prisons and concentration camps, and postwar Witness leaders have attempted to use this fact to assert that Jehovah's Witnesses stood consistently against Nazism.

Based on extensive archival material and years of research, *Jehovah's Witnesses and the Third Reich* separates fact from fiction and sheds new light on this dark period in history.

M. JAMES PENTON is a professor emeritus in the Department of History at the University of Lethbridge.

JEHOVAH'S WITNESSES AND THE THIRD REICH

Sectarian Politics under Persecution

M. James Penton

UNIVERSITY OF TORONTO PRESS
Toronto Buffalo London

Toronto Buffalo London
Printed in the U.S.A.

Reprinted 2013

ISBN 0-8020-8927-5 (cloth)
ISBN 0-8020-8678-0 (paper)

Printed on acid-free paper

Library and Archives Canada Cataloguing in Publication

Penton, M. James, 1932–
Jehovah's Witnesses and the Third Reich :
sectarian politics under persecution/M. James Penton.

Includes bibliographical references and index.
ISBN 0-8020-8927-5 (bound). ISBN 0-8020-8678-0 (pbk.)

1. Jehovah's Witnesses – Nazi persecution. 2. Jehovah's Witnesses – History. 3. Russell, C.T. (Charles Taze), 1852–1916. 4. Rutherford, J.F. (Joseph Franklin), 1869–1942. 5. Jehovah's Witnesses – History – Sources. I. Title.

BX8525.8.G3P46 2004 289.9'2'094309043 C2004-903230-5

This book has been published with the help of a grant from the Canadian Federation for the Humanities and Social Sciences, through the Aid to Scholarly Publications Programme, using funds provided by the Social Sciences and Humanities Research Council of Canada.

University of Toronto Press acknowledges the financial assistance to its publishing program of the Canada Council for the Arts and the Ontario Arts Council.

University of Toronto Press acknowledges the financial support for its publishing activities of the Government of Canada through the Book Publishing Industry Development Program (BPIDP).

In memory of my mother, Ida Emily Hanson Penton; my mother-in-law and second mother, Myrtle Anna Ley Kling; my uncle, Marvin Everett Penton; and with deep appreciation to all of those who walked with me spiritually through times that tried my soul. With William Penn they understood, 'No pain, no palm; no thorns, no throne; no gall, no glory; no cross, no crown.'

Wenn ich mit Menschen- und Engelszungen rede, aber nicht Liebe habe, bin ich ein tönendes [Stück] Erz oder eine schallende Zimbel geworden. Und wenn ich die Gabe des Prophezeiens habe und mit allen heiligen Geheimnissen und aller Erkenntnis vertraut bin und wenn ich alle Glauben habe, um Berge zu versetzen, aber nicht Liebe habe, so bin ich nichts. Und wenn ich alle meine Habe austeile, um andere zu speizen, und wenn ich meinen Lieb hingebe, um mich zu rühmen, aber nicht Liebe habe, so nützt es mir nichts.

1 Korinther 13:1-3, *Neue-Welt-Übersetzung der Heiligen Schrift*

If I speak in the tongues of men and of angels but do not have love, I have become a sounding [piece of] brass or a clashing cymbal. And if I have the gift of prophesying and am acquainted with all the sacred secrets and all knowledge, and if I have all the faith so as to transplant mountains, but do not have love, I am nothing. And if I give all my belongings to feed others, and hand over my body, that I may boast, but do not have love, I am not profited at all.

1 Corinthians 13:1–3, *New World Translation of the Holy Scriptures*

Contents

Illustrations

Foreword

Carl Thornton

James Penton and I have a number of things in common. We were both raised as Jehovah's Witnesses. We both obtained PhDs, although our religion strongly discouraged education beyond high school. It considered advanced education bad for one's spiritual health. Despite that fact, Dr Penton's family had such a long tradition of respect for education that he was able to obtain a BA at the University of Arizona and an MA and PhD in history, with a minor in religious studies, at the University of Iowa. In my case, I was the son of a blue-collar worker and the first in my family to go on to postgraduate, academic studies. After working for a year after graduating from high school, I talked my mother into letting me study further. I completed two years of college while living at home and paid for all of my tuition and books. After I married, I continued my education and eventually obtained a PhD in organizational psychology with a minor in clinical psychology. Because both of us were raised in the same faith and because of my profession as a psychologist, Dr Penton has asked me to compose this foreword.

Jehovah's Witnesses and the Third Reich begins with the year 1933. Dr Penton first analyses the importance of two documents: the *Declaration of Facts* produced by the Witnesses at a general convention in Berlin on 25 June 1933, and a Watch Tower letter sent directly to Adolf Hitler. He then discusses the Witnesses' long-held assertion that at no time did their leaders ever attempt to compromise with Nazism or show any signs of anti-Semitism. Starting from his contention that these claims are bogus, he gives a detailed history of the Witness movement in Germany until 1945. He then demonstrates why we must know their history in America during the era of the Watch Tower Society's second president, Judge Joseph Franklin Rutherford, before we can understand how they behaved in Nazi Germany. In the final chapters of this book, he provides an overview of the ongoing history of Jehovah's Witnesses to the present and how their leaders are exploiting accounts of their persecution during the Nazi Holocaust to protect themselves from governmental actions and criticism in the Europe of today.

In his earlier book, *Apocalypse Delayed: The Story of Jehovah's Witnesses,* Dr Penton documented thoroughly the religion's history from its earliest days and showed how the first two presidents of the Watch Tower Bible and Tract Society, C.T. Russell and J.F. Rutherford, fashioned that history. He demonstrated how Rutherford, in particular, shaped events in Germany. So I believe it important to discuss briefly some of the earlier history of what was originally called the Bible Student movement, which became Jehovah's Witnesses in 1931. I also want to briefly analyse Rutherford's behaviour based largely on material found in *Apocalypse Delayed.*

C.T. Russell was born in 1852 into a very comfortable home – comfortable both financially and spiritually. Religion was of utmost importance to him from boyhood on. He did have a brief period of doubt when he was sixteen, but after that he immersed himself in religious study, both privately and with close friends. In his twenties he became associated with a number of Second Adventists (those groups and private individuals who believed Christ's second advent was at hand) and contributed articles to their literature. However, in 1879, at the age of twenty-seven, he broke with an older associate, Nelson Barbour, and started his own independent ministry.

The year 1879 was a pivotal one for Russell. He married, began printing his own literature, and organized thirty congregations across seven American states. When he began this work he had no intention of forming an organized religion. He mistrusted all denominations; in fact, he believed that in just two years, true Christians – members of the 144,000 of Revelation 7 and 14 – would be taken to heaven. He therefore saw his mission as one of reaching people and helping them become sanctified. Thus they would receive a 'higher' or heavenly calling to become part of the bride of Christ.

Russell and his associates did not go to heaven in 1881, but this did not dispel his enthusiasm for spreading his message. He became a prolific writer and kept establishing new congregations. He also founded an organization for the purpose of printing religious literature. This non-profit organization was incorporated in 1884 as Zion's Watch Tower Tract Society.

In the early years of his ministry, Russell showed a permissive attitude toward fellow believers. When they organized their own congregations, he did not try to control them. Furthermore, they could differ in their beliefs, except for the most fundamental ones. They were expected to elect their elders democratically. If some members of a congregation wanted to, they could form their own separate congregation without any interference or objections from Russell or from other congregations. Fellowship was ordinarily maintained.

Over the years, Russell began to change. In 1894 some of his associates accused him of being domineering. A year later his wife answered these criticisms by declaring that he was the 'faithful and wise servant' spoken of in Matthew 24:45–7. Russell did not refer to himself openly as such, but neither did he contradict his wife, and his followers came to recognize him as 'that servant.' The same year, 1895, Russell recommended that Bible Student congregations study his books instead of studying the Bible directly, as they had in the past. In 1905 he recommended that local Bible Student 'class studies' be organized by subject, with scriptures drawn from all parts of the Bible. Before this, his brethren had read large sections of scripture and discussed the meaning of single passages within their broader context.

Some years later, after a bitter divorce trial, Russell asked all believers to take a 'vow' he had written and to send him written notice that they had done so. He then proceeded to print a list of all those who had taken this vow. In effect, he was trying to extend his authority rather dramatically over the Bible Student community. This is shown clearly by the fact that in 1910 he asserted that the reading and study of his books was more important than the study of the Bible itself.

Russell gradually gained more control over his brethren, yet generally speaking he was not dictatorial. Rather, he tried through kindness to persuade those who trusted him. The following passage from *Apocalypse Delayed* best sums it up: 'He was basically an honest man even when he was thoroughly misguided. In fact, his personal life was generally free from blemish. Furthermore, he was generally an attractive, kindly man, who was completely devoted to the stewardship which he believed to be his. But there is no doubt that he had a streak of arrogant pride and that he was sometimes guileless to the point of naivete.'[1]

1 M. James Penton, *Apocalypse Delayed: The Story of Jehovah's Witnesses*, 2nd ed. (Toronto: University of Toronto Press, 1997), 43–4.

The second Watch Tower president, J.F. Rutherford, was born in 1869 into a poor Missouri family. He was raised as a Southern Baptist, a religion that emphasized man's inherent sinfulness and that instilled fear of God's wrath. Not much is known about Rutherford's early religious life, but it does not appear that religion was central to his early adult life. He became a lawyer and grew active in politics, which seems to have been his main interest for some years.

When Rutherford was twenty-five, he obtained some Watch Tower Society literature, but he was not baptized into the Bible Student religion until he was thirty-seven. He quickly became prominent in it, however, since his legal skills came in highly useful in defending Russell and the Watch Tower Society in various lawsuits. Furthermore, he was a dynamic orator with a gift for defending his newfound faith. Although prominent in the religion, he was not one of those favoured by Russell to be a part of the future leadership. Rutherford obtained the position of Watch Tower president by staging what amounted to a political coup.

After becoming president, Rutherford behaved much like a corporate executive bent on reshaping the organization in his own image. He set in motion a series of dramatic doctrinal changes that would reshape the religion and diminish the legacy and importance of its founder. Thus, between 1917 and 1933 the religion's doctrine and structure were transformed. During those years, Rutherford's control over his brethren became complete. Elders were no longer democratically elected; they were replaced by appointees – Watch Tower 'service directors' and 'servants.' All members of congregations were required to turn in time sheets to show how much time they had spent proselytizing. The mode of study was no longer an option: all congregations were required to study from assigned Watch Tower literature. Many differences of belief had been accepted under Russell; they were not tolerated under Rutherford. Russell despised denominational labels and simply called his brethren Bible Students; Rutherford adopted the striking denominational name, Jehovah's Witnesses, to separate the Watch Tower movement from dissident Bible Students. While these changes were being dictated, dissenters who did not leave of their own accord were forced out.

To understand Rutherford's mindset, it is useful to compare and contrast his writings with those of Russell. Russell distrusted religious denominations and other societal institutions, yet this distrust was not central to his writings. Besides his eschatology, his writings focused mainly on matters of Christian charity, morality, love, and mercy.

Rutherford's major written themes were quite different. Through them he transformed Watch Tower religion into one of hatred and paranoia. His world view demonstrated a militant animosity to what he regarded as Satan's world, which included everything outside the movement he dominated. Thus he preached a message of antipathy toward all 'worldly' institutions, and he constantly vilified organized religion, politics, and big business. He scoffed at Russell's notion of Christian 'character building' as being of no consequence. People were no longer honoured for quietly manifesting 'the fruits of the Spirit.' Rather, they were respected for regular meeting attendance and for the amount of time they spent trying to make converts.

This makes Rutherford's conciliatory *Declaration of Facts* to Nazi governmental officials – discussed by Dr Penton in chapter 1 – especially deceitful. In that document he condemned Great Britain, the United States, the League of Nations, the churches, the business community, and especially the Jews, in order to curry favour with Hitler and the Nazis; yet the fact is that he also hated the *Führer* and the German government as a whole. This is apparent in his later, bitter attacks on them after they refused his blandishments.

So, from a psychological standpoint, what sort of man was Rutherford? Simply stated, he was a ruthless, hedonistic dictator. His ruthlessness and his dictatorial methods are obvious in the brief history I have presented here. But why the term hedonistic? The answer is that while Russell had lived in modest comfort, Rutherford lived in semiroyal splendour. During the Great Depression he spent his winters in a mansion in San Diego. During summers he took extensive trips to Europe. While at Watch Tower headquarters in Brooklyn, he spent weekends at a country retreat. He had two top-of-the-line Cadillacs, one in Brooklyn and one in San Diego. Even during Prohibition he drank heavily of the finest whiskeys, brandies, and wines. And all the while, most ordinary Jehovah's Witnesses were living in dire poverty.

Is it possible that despite his personal behaviour, Rutherford truly believed he was the leader of the one true Christian faith. If so, he used the mental mechanism called *projection*. According to J.P. Chaplin's *Dictionary of Psychology*, projection is 'attributing one's own traits or attitudes to others' and, more specifically, 'the process of attributing to others one's own faults.'[2] This was certainly the case with Rutherford. He was harsh in castigating other leaders both verbally and in

2 Rev. ed. (New York: Dell, 1975), 411.

writing, yet often what he said of them could accurately have been applied to him as well. At one point he stated, 'The men who rule are few in number, harsh, arrogant, cruel and oppressive.' At another, he described certain political leaders who came to power after the First World War as 'ambitious men, void of conscience.' He called Mussolini 'a gang leader, who bluffed himself into office.' Then, in a blanket condemnation of all political leaders, he declared: 'The selfish ruling element adopt all manner of means to keep the people from learning the inside workings of the political gang.'[3] But if anyone had bluffed himself into office, it was Rutherford, and he did his best to keep ordinary Jehovah's Witnesses 'from learning the inside working of the political gang' – his closest associates – at Watch Tower headquarters.

How did Rutherford become himself? It is possible to guess, but at this remove, I am reluctant to do so. It is difficult enough to diagnose a living patient, never mind someone who is dead. But whatever the roots of his personality were, he was the man who made the religion of Jehovah's Witnesses what it is today – a religion that Russell would not recognize.

What has changed since Rutherford's death in 1942? Central control over the Witness faithful has grown even stronger. Elders now have a secret instruction manual they must follow. If they are unsure how to handle a situation, they are to call Watch Tower headquarters immediately. Individual latitude in giving sermons has been reduced to nearly zero. At one time, those assigned to deliver sermons were given one page outlines and had to do research to develop the content of what they were to preach. Now, Witness elders are given very detailed outlines of what to say with very little latitude for individual expression. At conventions, speakers receive manuscripts they must read word for word. Senior officials sit in audiences with copies of those manuscripts and note any deviations from the text. The extemporaneous enthusiasm of the past is gone, and Witness talks now tend to have a dull, robot-like quality to them. This allows the Governing Body of Jehovah's Witnesses and its corporate entities to carry on the propaganda campaigns that Dr Penton describes in the latter part of this book.

3 J.F. Rutherford, *Enemies* (Brooklyn, NY: Watch Tower Society and IBSA, 1937), 9, 12, 13, 18.

Preface

I know well what it is like to suffer religious persecution. Born in 1932, I was raised a Jehovah's Witness on the Canadian Prairies and experienced a ban on my family religion during the years 1940 to 1943. I remember how Witness family and friends had to hide Watch Tower literature in straw stacks and coal mines. It was even a crime to possess a King James Bible printed by one of the Witnesses' publishing societies. I recall vividly how the police came to my parents' home to interrogate my mother about membership in an illegal organization and how my father, a veteran of the First World War, received a threatening, unsigned letter that attacked him as unpatriotic. For me the most difficult part was having to agonize constantly over whether to participate in patriotic exercises. Like other Jehovah's Witness schoolchildren, in my heart I felt it wrong to salute the flag or sing the National Anthem. Fortunately, the Minister of Education in my home province, Saskatchewan, had issued a directive to school boards and teachers that no Witness child was to be forced to participate in such exercises. So unlike schoolchildren in the United States and Ontario, I was in no danger of being expelled from school or taken from my parents. Yet I was under intense pressure to do what my classmates did, and that was especially hard on an eight- to eleven-year-old boy. I cannot forget my third grade teacher's diatribe to the effect that my parents ought to be sent to prison for their lack of patriotism. To this day when I remember that woman, I do so with *angst* and disgust.

Years later, when I was proselytizing from door to door as an active Jehovah's Witness, people who regarded themselves as 'Christians' reviled me on many occasions. In a few instances I was pummeled, I was shot at once while distributing tracts, and on another occasion was attacked and beaten. So I have a great deal of sympathy for the men, women, and children who suffered terrible persecution as Jehovah's Witnesses in Nazi Germany. Nothing in this book is intended in any way to impugn the bravery and integrity of those ordinary German Jehovah's Witnesses.

My sympathy for them is not just because of my own experiences; I still agree strongly with some of the positions that they took at the time. They refused openly to engage in the state worship that has so sickened modern societies. They would not give the Hitler salute, vote in forced elections, or serve in the *Führer's* war machine. They therefore deserve the greatest credit for refusing to bow to one of the most evil regimes in human history. As Jehovah's Witnesses say, and as others acknowledge today, had the major churches of Germany taken stands similar to theirs, it would have been difficult if not impossible for Hitler to carry out his monstrous policies.

During the early 1970s I researched and wrote *Jehovah's Witnesses in Canada: Champions of Freedom of Speech and Worship,* which detailed the Canadian Witnesses' struggle to defend and legally establish their activities, especially during the two world wars and in Quebec after the Second World War. However, as I continued to do research on the history of my faith and saw what was happening within the Witness community itself, I came to realize fully the totalitarian nature of my religious community. Jehovah's Witness lawyers made much of the libertarian tradition when arguing for freedom of worship, speech, and the press in courts of law; yet Witness leaders and most Jehovah's Witnesses had no respect for those freedoms within the Witness community itself. Over and over again I beheld serious injustices in the treatment of various brethren. I came to feel a sense of being betrayed by the men who had governed my religion for many years. After trying without success to discuss my concerns with members of the Governing Body of Jehovah's Witnesses, I left the movement in a bitter parting.

Although I felt that there was much wrong with Witness doctrines and practices when I broke with the community, I still believed that, however misguided, its leadership was honest. With further investigation, I came to realize that even that was not the case, nor had it been during most of the movement's history. It became clear that Witness leaders had been guilty of false prophecy, duplicity, and the cruel treatment of members and former members. Despite the claim that they were politically 'neutral,' it was evident that they and their Bible Student predecessors had practised a militant form of sectarian politics. They were guilty of violating their own stated principles in relation to the 'world,' and through incredible tactlessness and fanaticism had caused persecution to fall unnecessarily on ordinary members of their community in many nations of the earth. Besides this, I became deeply disturbed by the Witness leadership's distortion of history. It is now almost twenty-five years since I broke with the Jehovah's Witness community, yet its leaders' false descriptions of its history still trouble me. Through their biased accounts, they continue to deceive ordinary Witnesses and make converts to a movement that is less than honest about its past. As a person who is both a professional historian and a practising Christian, I do not feel that any religion that claims to have a monopoly on salvation – as Jehovah's Witnesses do – and yet promotes a series of historical falsehoods can in any sense represent the God taught by Jesus of Nazareth. Thus after my earlier study, *Apocalypse Delayed: The Story of Jehovah's Witnesses,* I decided to write the present work. For despite their denials, the Witnesses have been strongly political, at least since the First World War.

For helping me with this book, I have many people to thank, some of whom were colleagues at my long-time academic home, the University of Lethbridge in Alberta, Canada. Among these, Ted Orchard and Timothy Pope were of especially great assistance. So too were Elizabeth Boumans, for years secretary of the University of Lethbridge Physics Department, and Roman Scholdra, a former member of the University's Board of Governors. Also in Lethbridge, but not at the university, my long-time friends John and Doris Poole have given me ongoing assistance and encouragement.

Many people in Europe and the United Kingdom have helped me a great deal. A number of German friends and associates provided important help without which this work would never have seen the light of day. In particular, my thanks go to Helmut Lasarcyk, Mehmet Aslan, Manfred Gebhard, and, above all, Hans Mahrla. He assisted me in obtaining a great deal of data, including the very important 'Harbeck letter,' which shows clearly what Jehovah's Witness leaders were doing in the summer of 1933. In Sweden, Rud Persson and Carl Olof Jonsson served as inspirations for my work. Rud, in particular, deserves credit for obtaining a copy for me of Dr Dietrich Hellmund's dissertation at the University of Hamburg. In Norway, Kent Steinhaug's ongoing research and willingness to provide information were very helpful. In the Netherlands, Richard Singelenberg made a number of important suggestions and gave me a number of references to helpful sources. In Spain, José Luis Gil Álvarez provided me with many documents and various published works that are extremely valuable. In addition, I cannot thank him enough for his constant interest and psychological support. In Italy, Achille Aveta and Sergio Pollina were equally supportive and show interest in translating my work into Italian. In England Anthony Bowyer was a source of solid information.

Friends in the United States and Mexico provided ongoing help with my research and writing as well. Among these, Ray and Larry Mattera were the most important. Both contributed much direct information, and made suggested improvements for the text. Ray was also a faithful proofreader despite suffering serious health problems. As will be noted, I have taken useful information from his master's thesis at Northern Baptist Seminary and from a major paper of his that ought to be published. Carl Thornton deserves my deep appreciation for writing a foreword for this book and providing important information on the private life of Joseph F. Rutherford. Buddy Carlton, Edmond Gruss, Guntram Anders, Norbert Rieder, Ken Raines, my brother- and sister-in-law, Jim and Mary Kling, and my nephew, Nathaniel Kling all deserve honourable mention here also for the ways in which they assisted me.

Besides these people, there are others that are still technically associated with the Jehovah's Witness movement whom I would like to thank by name but cannot. In a sense they are captives of that movement, for in many cases if their families or marriage mates knew they had assisted me in any way, they would have them 'disfellowshipped' and would break all relations with them. So I want them to know how much I appreciate the help they gave me at the risk of their ties with Witness family members and their personal happiness.

At the University of Toronto Press, I want to thank Virgil Duff, who has edited three of my books, and all of the friends I have made there over the years.

As always, I want to express my deepest appreciation to my dear wife Marilyn, who along with our large family, has continued to support me in so many ways. Her love and assistance and that of our children, grandchildren, nephews, and nieces have made it possible to bring this book to completion.

As is customary and proper, I take full responsibility for any errors of omission or commission in what appears in the following pages.

MJP
Ajijic, Jalisco
Mexico
14 July 2004

A Note on Titles, Sources, and Terminology

The publishing organization through which Jehovah's Witnesses and their spiritual predecessors, the Bible Students, were given spiritual guidance from its establishment in 1881, and through which they have been governed from the 1930s to the present, was originally called Zion's Watch Tower and Tract Society. Although most Jehovah's Witnesses' publications are now printed under the direction of the Watchtower Bible and Tract Society of New York, Inc., or various other incorporated societies throughout the world, because the Watch Tower Society of Pennsylvania is the senior organization that has been used by all the men who have led and governed the Bible Student – Jehovah's Witnesses throughout their history, except in a few cases I have chosen to use the name of that society rather than that of the New York or other corporations.

The journal that is now *The Watchtower Announcing Jehovah's Kingdom* was first called *Zion's Watch Tower and Herald of Christ's Presence*. It was known under that name until January 1909, when it became *The Watch Tower and Herald of Christ's Presence.* On 15 October 1931 it became *The Watchtower and Herald of Christ's Presence.* On 1 January 1939 it became *The Watchtower and Herald of Christ's Kingdom.* Finally, on 1 March of that year, it assumed its present title. Despite the name changes, this journal, which was first published in July 1879, is the same publication. Therefore, to simplify references to it in notes, I have designated it by the letters WT. When I refer to the German editions of this journal, I call it *Der Wachtturm*.

Over the years, the Watch Tower Society's other journals have been *The Golden Age* (1919–37), *Consolation* (1937–46), and *Awake!* (1946 to the present). In German, the respective names of these publications have been *Das Goldene Zeitalter, Trost,* and *Erwachet!*.

Like most religious communities, Jehovah's Witnesses have developed their own distinctive terminology that marks their members as part of a special in-group. For years the Watch Tower Society insisted on writing the name of the denomination, Jehovah's witnesses, with the first letter of witnesses in lower case. The Society argued, rather strangely, that they were not a religious organization but simply people who testified to the name of the only true God, Jehovah. Eventually, however, the Society recognized that since the movement's title is a proper noun in English, it should be written as Jehovah's Witnesses.

Jehovah's Witness terms that may not be familiar to the general reader are 'publisher,' 'pioneer,' 'anointed remnant,' 'other sheep,' and 'disfellowship.' In Watch Tower parlance, a 'publisher' is a Jehovah's Witness who engages in part-time public preaching and proselytizing, usually in a door-to-door ministry. A 'pioneer' is a Witness evangelist whose main vocation is carrying on this public work. Those described as the 'anointed remnant' are Jehovah's Witnesses yet living who believe they have been called to join Christ in heaven as the last remaining members of the 144,000 'spiritual' Israelites of Revelation 7 and 14. Until 1935, most Witnesses believed they were members of this elite group of 144,000 chosen by the Holy Spirit over the centuries. Since then, however, the vast majority have looked forward to everlasting life in paradise on a material earth. The title given to this latter group is 'other sheep.' 'Disfellowship' means excommunicate. Those disfellowshipped are shunned.

JEHOVAH'S WITNESSES AND THE THIRD REICH

Introduction

What follows is in part a case study of the history of Jehovah's Witnesses at a time when they were under intense Nazi persecution. As such, it focuses on their relations with the Hitler regime. However, unlike most historians of the Witnesses under Nazi rule, I include a much more general analysis of their movement and history in other parts of the world, especially the United States. It is impossible to understand what took place in Nazi Germany, and how those events are viewed today, without that broader perspective. Thus, chapters 4 and 7 in particular deal with Witness history and other events outside the Third Reich.

Jehovah's Witnesses assert today that they were politically neutral when Hitler came to power in January 1933. They hold that the Nazis began to persecute them in the spring of that year because of an alliance between Adolf Hitler and the Catholic Church. They boast that despite repeated attempts by the *Sturmabteilung* (SA), the *Geheime Staats Pollizei* (Gestapo), and the *Schutzstaffel* (SS) to suppress them, the Witnesses – and they alone as a religious community – took a firm stand against Nazism. Witness publications and Witness spokespeople emphasize strongly that their German brethren would not *Heil Hitler*, would not vote in Nazi-controlled elections, and would not serve in the German *Wehrmacht*. These publications and spokespeople make much of the fact that many ordinary Jehovah's Witnesses became martyrs because they continued to preach to the German people, because they exposed the crimes of the Nazis throughout Germany and the world, and because they refused to be conscripted for military service. They often claim that roughly 10,000 out of a total Witness community of around 25,000 were imprisoned or sent to concentration camps and that an indeterminate number of them (between 838 and 2,000) lost their lives through execution or terrible physical mistreatment.

Many non-Witness survivors of the concentration camps have testified to their bravery, their integrity, and their kindness. Various scholars have praised them highly for their conduct. Thus, contemporary Jehovah's Witnesses have been able to create what amounts to a martyrology surrounding those Witnesses who suffered and died in Nazi Germany and in the many lands it came, briefly, to control.

The Witnesses have their critics as well. In general, those critics – among whom I count myself – claim that Witness leaders at first tried to compromise with Nazism, and that only when the Nazis refused their blandishments did those leaders take a strong stand against them. Jehovah's Witnesses then began door-to-door preaching with Bibles, Watch Tower literature, and portable phonographs in the face of an all-out ban. Most significantly, they also distributed anti-Nazi tracts throughout the country. These actions, which were directed by American Watch Tower president Joseph Franklin Rutherford, were foolhardy in the extreme and resulted in much unnecessary suffering. Angered by what they regarded as an obstreperous sect, the German government launched a severe persecution of members of the German movement.

As I point out in chapter 1, I long ago concluded that Witness leaders tried to ingratiate their movement with the Nazis in 1933 and attempted to scapegoat the Jews. Today's Witness leaders, and some non-Witness scholars as well, have vehemently denied this. In order to determine whether my earlier contentions about these matters were correct, I set out to examine many additional sources, both primary and secondary. Among the most important of the former are Jehovah's Witnesses' own publications. They tell what the Witnesses were thinking, saying, and doing at the time of their persecution in Germany rather than what later generations state or even what those who went through that persecution might emphasize in retrospect. In order to evaluate those primary Witness sources, I have had to place them in a broader historical context by examining them in relation to what others – both friend and foe – were saying at the same time. Thus I have looked at contemporary newspaper accounts, Nazi documents, and U.S. State Department documents, to name but a few of the other sources I have used.

Besides examining the history of Jehovah's Witnesses at the time and since, I have found it necessary to evaluate many of the positions I have taken in the light of what both the Witnesses and certain non-Witness scholars have said and written. For example, was I right in assuming that the Witnesses really attempted to compromise with the Hitler government in the spring and summer of 1933? Did they really indulge in anti-Semitism in an attempt to protect themselves? How valid were (and are) Witness charges that the churches – especially the Catholic Church – supported Hitler and were largely responsible for their persecution? Is it true, as both the Witnesses and certain non-Witness scholars contend, that they were 'forgotten victims' in Germany for many years? Why have non-Witness scholars been so divided over Witness conduct in Nazi Germany? And finally, why is it that in the past two decades Jehovah's Witnesses and others have focused so much attention on what happened to them during the dark years of the Third Reich? All of these questions deserve answers, which I will attempt to provide in this book.

Since many of the sources I use are in other languages, I have tried to give most of them as they appear in the original, with English translations either in the text or footnotes or appendixes. The reason for doing this is that translations are by necessity always interpretations – or as an Italian expression has it, *traduttori traditori* (translators are traitors). Thus whenever there may be questions about my translations, I provide the originals to avoid the charge that I have been unfair.

The Watch Tower Society's Attempted Compromise with Hitler

> Instead of being against the principles advocated by the government of Germany, we stand squarely for such principles, and point out that Jehovah God through Christ Jesus will bring about the full realization of these principles and will give the people peace and prosperity and the greatest desire of every honest heart.
>
> J.F. Rutherford, *Declaration of Facts*, June 1933

Jehovah's Witnesses loudly proclaim that among all the Christian movements in Germany during the dark days of the Third Reich, only their German brethren stood solidly against Nazism. Because of the courageous stands taken by thousands of ordinary German Witnesses, many non-Witnesses have showered praise on them.

As pointed out earlier, many former concentration-camp prisoners, including Eugen Kogon, Bruno Bettelheim, and Geneviève de Gaulle (Charles de Gaulle's niece), have noted their outstanding courage. So too have many historians, such as Friedrich Zipfel, Michael H. Kater, John S. Conway, Christine Elizabeth King, and Detlef Garbe.[1] But the bravery shown by those Witnesses stands in sharp contrast to that demonstrated by their leaders during the first year of the Third Reich – a fact those leaders and their successors and some non-Witness apologists have tried to keep hidden and falsely deny to this day.

During the first half of their history, the Bible Student–Jehovah's Witnesses were notable for their philo-Judaism. Like many late-nine-

1 See *Jehovah's Witnesses in the Divine Purpose* (Brooklyn, NY: Watchtower Society and IBSA, 1959), 172–4; Eugen Kogon, *The Theory and Practice of Hell* (New York: Berkley

teenth- and twentieth-century premillennialists, Charles T. Russell, the founder of what is now known as the Watch Tower Bible and Tract Society and the Bible Student movement, was a thoroughgoing supporter of Zionist causes. He believed strongly in the Jewish resettlement of Palestine, he denied that Jews should be converted to Christianity,[2] and in 1910 he led a New York Jewish audience in singing the Zionist anthem, 'Hatikva.'[3] Furthermore, under the influence of Paul S.L. Johnson, a Bible Student of Jewish origin and one-time Lutheran clergyman, between 1907 and 1909 Russell went so far as to proclaim that Christians were not under the New Covenant mentioned in Jeremiah 31:31. According to him, that covenant would apply fully only to natural Jews at the end of Christ's future millennial reign over the earth.[4] Russell held this belief until his death even though it and several closely linked doctrines caused a major schism in the Bible Student movement.[5]

For a time, Russell's immediate successor, Judge Joseph Franklin Rutherford, followed in his footsteps. In 1926 he wrote a short book, *Comfort for the Jews,* in which he claimed that Jewish migration to the Holy Land was a fulfilment of biblical prophecy. A year later he pro-

---

Medallion Books, 1958), 43; Bruno Bettelheim, *The Informed Heart* (Glencoe, IL: The Free Press of Glencoe, 1961), 122–3; Friedrich Zipfel, *Kirchenkampf in Deutschland - 1933–1945: Religionsverfolgung und Selbsbehauptung der Kirchen in der Nationalsozialistischen Zeit* (Berlin: Walter de Gruyter, 1961), 175–203; Michael H. Kater, 'Die Ernsten Bibelforscher im Dritten Reich,' *Vierteljahrshefte für Zeitgeschichte* 17:2 (April 1969): 181–218; John S. Conway, *The Nazi Persecution of the Churches – 1933–1945* (New York: Basic Books, 1968) 196–9; Christine Elizabeth King, *The Nazi State and the New Religions: Five Case Studies in Non-Conformity* (New York and Toronto: Edwin Mellon Press, 1982), 147–79, 246–50; Detlef Garbe, *Zwischen Widerstand und Martyrium: Die Zeugen Jehovas im 'Dritten Reich,'* 4th ed. (Munich: R. Oldenbourg Verlag, 1993); and Hans Hesse, ed., *Persecution and Resistance of Jehovah's Witnesses during the Nazi Regime 1933–1945* (Bremen: Edition Temmen, 2001).

2 C.T. Russell, 'Jews Not to Be Converted to Christianity,' *Overland Monthly* 58 (August 1911): 171–5.

3 'Pastor Russell Cheered by an Audience of Hebrews,' *New York American* (10 October 1909). This article, which includes Russell's sermon 'Zionism in Prophecy,' has been reprinted by the Chicago Bible Students in an undated volume titled *Convention Report Sermons* (see 134–42).

4 Russell, 'Jews Not to Be Converted,' 171–5.

5 For a brief discussion of what has come to be known as the 'New Covenant Schism,' see M. James Penton, *Apocalypse Delayed: The Story of Jehovah's Witnesses,* 2nd ed. (Toronto: University of Toronto Press, 1997), 40–2.

duced *Restoration,* another short book on the same subject. Then, in 1929, he published a similar but longer book called *Life,* in which he proclaimed: 'God promised to restore Palestine to the Jews. The rebuilding of Palestine is now beginning and is well under way. This is being done clearly in fulfillment of prophecy uttered as promises from Jehovah.'[6] In an attempt to prove this assertion, in the same volume he discussed at great length the importance of the British conquest of Palestine in 1917, the Balfour Declaration,[7] the British Palestinian Mandate, and the settlement and development of Palestine by Jewish *chaluzim* (pioneers). Rutherford enthused: 'Have these things come about by chance? Can any Jew who is familiar with the history of his people, and particularly with God dealing with that people, have any doubt about what the present activities in Palestine mean? The return of the Jews to that land, the building of houses and roads and waterways, planting vineyards and trees, and otherwise improving the land, is but in fulfillment of prophecy.'[8]

Yet only three years later, in an emphatic doctrinal shift, the second Watch Tower president suddenly repudiated his beliefs respecting the Jews without offering anything like a reasoned explanation for so doing. *Life* was withdrawn from circulation, and in 1932 Rutherford proclaimed that 'fleshly Israel' had no specific role to play in salvation history. In the three-volume set *Vindication,* he wrote:

> The Jews were evicted from Palestine and 'their house left unto them desolate' because they rejected Christ Jesus, the beloved and anointed King of Jehovah. To this day the Jews have not repented of this wrongful act committed by their forefathers. Many of them have been returned to the land of Palestine, but they have been induced to go there because of selfish and for sentimental reasons. During the long period elapsing from the time of their expulsion to the present day the Jews have not 'borne the shame of the heathen' for Jehovah's sake, nor the name of Christ. During all this period of time, and particularly during the World War, the true followers of Christ Jesus devoted to God, and to his kingdom, have been bearing the shame of the heathen and have been hated by all nations for Christ's sake and for the sake of Jehovah's name. (Matt. 24:9; Mark 13:13) In contrast to

6 J.F. Rutherford, *Life* (Brooklyn, NY: IBSA and Watch Tower Society, 1929), 54.

7 On 2 November 1917, Lord Arthur James Balfour, then British Foreign Secretary, issued the declaration that bears his name. It called for the establishment of a Jewish homeland in Palestine.

8 See Rutherford, *Life,* 130–44. The quotation found above is taken from page 141.

this, during the World War the Jews received recognition of the heathen nations. In 1917 the Balfour Declaration, sponsored by the heathen governments of Satan's organization, came forth, recognized the Jews, and bestowed upon them great favors. In this the seventh world power [the British Empire and the United States] took the lead. Now Big Business and other wings of Satan's organization place the Jews along side of and in the same category as the Gentiles. Heretofore even God's people have overlooked the fact that the affairs of God's kingdom with reference to the things of the earth are of far greater importance than the rehabilitation of that little strip of land on the eastern side of the Mediterranean sea. The Jews have received more attention at their hands than they really have deserved.[9]

In another place in the same volume, Rutherford was more blunt. Referring to the commercial organizations of Great Britain and America, which collectively he called 'a special division or part of Satan's organization,' he wrote:

While most of these organizations and powers operate within the borders of the land called 'Christendom', yet many of them do not even pretend to be of 'organized Christianity'. Among the powerful men who control the commerce of the sea are many Jews, so called, yet who are against God and against Christ and the kingdom of God. This is probably the reason why God by his prophet speaks of them separately and distinctly from Jerusalem, both ancient and modern. All are representatives of the Devil, to be sure, and form a part of his organization, but the Lord is pointing them out as separate and integral parts of Satan's organization and gives his people a vision of them from different standpoints.[10]

Today the Watch Tower Society asserts that Rutherford was simply publishing 'new light' and that he wanted to make it clear that Jehovah's Witnesses were the 'true Israel of God.'[11] It seems apparent

9 J.F. Rutherford, *Vindication* (Brooklyn, NY: Watch Tower Society and IBSA, 1932), 2: 257–8.

10 Ibid., 54–5.

11 After speaking of Rutherford's earlier teachings, the Watch Tower's most recent official history states: 'But it gradually [*sic*] became evident that what was taking place in Palestine with regard to the Jews was not the fulfillment of Jehovah's grand restoration prophecies. Desolation came on first-century Jerusalem because the Jews had rejected God's son, the Messiah, the one sent in Jehovah's name. (Dan. 9:25–27; Matt. 23:38, 39). It was becoming increasingly obvious that *as a people* they had not

to the sceptical eye, however, that he had other reasons for making such a dramatic doctrinal switch. Unlike Russell, Rutherford really did not like Jews. Although he followed Russell in publicly supporting Zionism for many years after Russell's death, he had disdain for all but Orthodox Jews. Even while supporting Zionist causes, he made it plain that he had contempt for irreligious Jews and Jewish 'clergy.'[12] But his strongest animosity was directed at Jewish businessmen. In the early 1920s, while addressing a Canadian Bible Student convention in Winnipeg, Manitoba, he explained, 'I'm speaking of the Palestine Jew, not that stoop-shouldered, hook-nosed little individual who meets you on the street corner and tries to gyp you out of every nickel you've got.'[13] Unfortunately, this statement is not documented in written form, but there can be little doubt that it is accurate at least in substance. This is evident from another of Rutherford's typically belligerent remarks, this one broadcast in 1927 over the New York Watch Tower radio station, WBBR: 'Doubtless many of you have heard that the Jews shall again rule the earth. This has been much misunderstood. Not every man who is a descendant of Abraham is a Jew, by any means. Be it known once and for all that those profiteering, conscienceless, selfish men who call themselves Jews, and who control the greater portion of the finances of the world, will never be the rulers in this new earth. God would not risk such selfish men with such an important position.'[14]

It is quite probable that Rutherford would not have received 'new light' in 1932 regarding the role of the Jews in Jehovah's divine plan had it not been for the rising tide of anti-Semitism then engulfing the Western world. During the late 1920s and early 1930s, anti-Semitism was growing rapidly in the United States and Canada with the rise of a variety of movements both political and religious.[15] Once the Great

---

changed their attitude. There was no repentance over the wrongful act committed by their forefathers. The return of some to Palestine was not motivated by any love for God or desire for his name to be magnified by fulfillment of his Word.' *Jehovah's Witnesses: Proclaimers of God's Kingdom* (Brooklyn, NY: Watchtower Society and IBSA, 1993), 141.

12 Rutherford, *Life*, 49–51.

13 My father, Levis Penton, who died a Jehovah's Witness in 'good standing' in 1972, was present at the Winnipeg convention and reported Rutherford's words to me on several occasions.

14 *The Golden Age*, 23 February 1927, 343.

15 The racist, anti-Catholic Ku Klux Klan, which was also anti-Semitic, was active in most parts of both the United States and Canada. Certain Catholic movements in both countries, and especially in the province of Quebec, were equally anti-Semitic.

Depression began in 1929, it became evident that Adolf Hitler and the violently racist and anti-Jewish Nazis might well come to power in Germany – which they in fact did, on 30 January 1933. So it seems likely that Rutherford was anxious to dissociate Jehovah's Witnesses from the Jewish community in any way possible. However, that cannot excuse what the Watch Tower president and his subordinates were to do shortly afterwards, in the first year of the Third Reich.

Early in April 1933, authorities in Prussia, Germany's largest *Land* (state), moved against Jehovah's Witnesses. The Nazis seized their branch offices at Magdeburg, and the Prussian government temporarily outlawed their religious activities. But on 28 April those authorities returned the Magdeburg properties to the Watch Tower Society at the behest of the U.S. State Department. Still, Witness leaders and Jehovah's Witnesses in general knew they were unpopular. They remained banned in many of the *Länder* of the Reich and were harassed constantly by the police.[16] According to standard Watch Tower accounts, Rutherford and the German Witness community decided shortly afterwards to take a bold stand against the Hitler dictatorship. The Watch Tower Society's first official history, *Jehovah's Witnesses in the Divine Purpose,* states:

> Judge Rutherford had been watching the German situation closely and was well acquainted with its development as it affected the witness work. With this serious turn of events he lost no time in going to Germany, accompanied by N. H. Knorr, to see what could be done. On June 25 ... a convention was called in Berlin. There a prepared Declaration of Facts was presented to the 7,000 in attendance in protest against the Hitler government for their highhanded interference with the witness work of the Society, and was unanimously adopted. The declaration was mailed to every high officer of the government from the president down to the members of the council, and 2,500,000 copies were given public distribution. Retaliation came quickly. Three days later, on June 28, for the second time the Society's property was seized and occupied, and by government decree its printing plant was closed.[17]

Did the German government seize Watch Tower property and completely ban Jehovah's Witnesses for the second time because the *Decla-*

16 *1974 Yearbook of Jehovah's Witnesses,* 109–10; King, 150–1. For a detailed chronology of these and future events, see Appendix A.

17 *Jehovah's Witnesses in the Divine Purpose,* 130.

ration of Facts (in German, *die Erklärung*) was a bold protest against Nazi actions? No, quite the contrary. In the first place, the Nazis had already moved to outlaw the Witnesses in Prussia for a second time – on 24 June, a day before the declaration was adopted. More important, that document was nothing short of a cowardly, self-serving statement in which Rutherford and his German associates attempted to ingratiate the Witness community with the Hitler government. As already indicated, the U.S. State Department had acted on behalf of the Watch Tower Society in demanding that Germany return its properties at Magdeburg to the Witnesses. Despite that fact, Rutherford showed no hesitation in condemning what he called the 'Anglo-American empire' in the harshest terms to the Nazis. At the same time, he attacked the League of Nations and, above all, the Jews. In a subsection titled 'Jews,' the *Declaration of Facts* reads:

> It is falsely charged by our enemies that we have received financial support for our work from the Jews. Nothing is farther from the truth. Up to this hour there never has been the slightest bit of money contributed to our work by Jews. We are the faithful followers of Christ Jesus and believe upon Him as the Savior of the world, whereas the Jews entirely reject Jesus Christ and emphatically deny he is the Savior of the world sent of God for man's good. This of itself should be sufficient proof to show that we receive no support from Jews and therefore the charges against us are maliciously false and could proceed only from Satan, our great enemy.
>
> The greatest and most oppressive empire on earth is the Anglo-American empire. By this is meant the British Empire, of which the United States of America forms a part. It has been the commercial Jews of the British-American Empire that have built up and carried on Big Business as a means of exploiting and oppressing the peoples of many nations. This fact particularly applies to the cities of London and New York, the stronghold of Big Business. This fact is so manifest in America that there is a proverb concerning the city of New York which says: 'the Jews own it, the Irish Catholics rule it, and the Americans pay the bills.' We have no fight with any of these persons mentioned but, as witnesses for Jehovah and in obedience to his commandment set forth in the Scriptures, we are compelled to call attention to the truth concerning the same in order that the people may be enlightened concerning God and his purpose.[18]

18 The quotation that appears here is taken from the *Declaration of Facts* as it appears on page 134 of the English-language *1934 Year Book of Jehovah's Witnesses.*

Besides damning Great Britain, the United States, the League of Nations, and the Jews, the declaration censured the churches and attacked 'Big Business.' Regarding the latter, it stated: 'The present government of Germany has declared against Big Business oppressors and in opposition to the wrongful religious influence in the political affairs of the nation. Such is exactly our position.' Then it proclaimed: 'Instead of being against the principles advocated by the government of Germany, we stand squarely for such principles, and point out that Jehovah God through Christ Jesus will bring about the full realization of these principles and will give the people peace and prosperity and the greatest desire of every honest heart.'[19] As Jehovah's Witnesses were soon to discover, the Nazis were not impressed by their declaration, nor by a fawning letter sent to Adolf Hitler. In fact, German authorities unleashed a wave of persecution against them almost immediately.[20] Yet it was not until four months later that Rutherford and the Watch Tower Society decided to oppose Nazi policies in an uncompromising and extreme manner.

Ever since 1939 the Watch Tower Society has done its best to keep the real nature of the *Declaration of Facts* and the Hitler letter hidden from loyal Jehovah's Witnesses and the general public.[21] At the same

19 Ibid., 135, 136.

20 *1974 Yearbook of Jehovah's Witnesses,* 111–12.

21 *Der Wachtturm* (the German edition of *The Watchtower,* published in Switzerland) of 1 May 1939 states on page 134: 'Am 25. Juni 1933 kamen siebentausend deutsche Christen auf einer Hauptversammlung in Berlin zusammen und faßten öffentlich eine Resolution gegen das ungerechtfertige Vorgen der Hitler-Regierung, wonach die Zeugen Jehovas am Zeugniswerk gehindert werden; und eine Million Exemplare jenes Protestes wurden in ganz Deutschland verbreitet.'

In translation, this statement reads: 'On 25 June 1933 seven thousand German Christians met in a general convention in Berlin and adopted a resolution against the unjustified persecution of the Hitler government by which Jehovah's Witnesses were prevented from carrying on their witness work; and one million copies of that protest were spread all over Germany.'

More recently, an undated booklet, *Memoria de un Testimonio,* which is printed and published in Madrid by the Círculo europeo de antiguos deportados e internados Testigos de Jehová (The European Circle of Former Deported and Interned Jehovah´s Witnesses) passes over the 1933 Berlin-Wilmersdorf convention with *leger de main*. Its statement reads: 'Ya en 1933, el juez Rutherford, presidente de la sociedad Watch Tower Bible and Tract, fue a Berlin. La sociedad protestó por el cierre de sus oficinas y, ante la falta de pruebas acusatorias, las pudo recuperar en abril de 1933. A pesar de la evidente hostilidad del régimen, el 25 de junio de 1933 se celebró una asamblea en Berlin que reunió a 7.000 Testigos de Jehová. La represión aumentó inmediatamente.'

time, it has poured verbal vitriol over the churches for having compromised with the Nazis. But seemingly embarrassing facts began to come out about one of the Watch Tower's principal German leaders, Erich Frost, as early as 1961. In that year *The Watchtower* published an autobiographical statement by Frost, the Society's former, postwar German branch overseer, in which he recounted his persecution by the Nazis. This article was titled 'Deliverance from Totalitarian Inquisition through Faith in God.'[22] Not surprisingly, in it Frost portrayed himself as totally faithful to both his religious principles and his brethren. In his own words, he was like 'Daniel in the lions' den.' Shortly thereafter, however, the German newsmagazine *Der Spiegel* claimed that after his arrest in March 1937 he had betrayed a number of his Witness subordinates and their secret meeting places to the Gestapo.[23] The Watch Tower Society has chosen to ignore the allegations found in *Der Spiegel* and continues to revere Frost as a Jehovah's Witness hero.[24]

In 1970 a book titled *Die Zeugen Jehovas: Eine Dokumentation über die Wachtturmgesellschaft* (The Jehovah's Witnesses: A Documentation about the Watch Tower Society)[25] was published in East Germany. Although Manfred Gerhard was listed as its author, in fact it was produced by a ghostwriter, Dieter Pape, under the direction of the Ministry of State Security.[26] Its obvious purpose was to discredit Jehovah's Witnesses as allies of the United States and enemies of communism. Undoubtedly,

---

In English, this statement reads: 'Already in 1933, Judge Rutherford, the president of the Watch Tower Bible and Tract Society, went to Berlin. The Society protested the closing of its offices, and, because of the lack of proof of accusations, it was able to reoccupy them in April 1933. Despite the evident hostility of the [Nazi] regime, it held an assembly in Berlin on 25 June 1933 that brought 7,000 Jehovah's Witnesses together. Repression increased immediately.'

22 WT, 15 April 1961, 244–9. For Frost's article in German, 'Befreiung von Totaliärer Inquisition durch Glauben an Gott,' see *Der Wachtturm,* 1 July 1961. Interestingly, Frost's comments regarding the 1933 Berlin convention are a paraphrase of what was published in the 1 May 1939 issue of *Der Wachtturm.* He remarks on page 245 of the 15 April 1961 *Watchtower:* 'In June [1933] seven thousand Witnesses assembled in Berlin and passed a resolution protesting the highhanded action of the Hitler government.' It seems rather evident from this statement that Frost was repeating a 'party line' rather than giving an account from memory.

23 'Väterchen Frost,' *Der Spiegel,* No. 30 (19 July 1961): 38, 39.

24 For more information on this matter, see page ? below.

25 Leizig, Jena, Berlin: Urania-Verlag, 1970.

26 See pages 50, 51, 56, 94, and 95 below.

some of the statements in it are exaggerations or outright distortions. For example, it tries nonsensically to tie the Watch Tower Society and Jehovah's Witnesses to Western imperialism, capitalism, and psychological warfare against communism. In addition, instead of simply arguing that the Witnesses were trying to mollify the Nazis at their Berlin convention in 1933 by attacking Great Britain, the United States, the League of Nations, and the Jews, it suggests that Witnesses were outright racists and profascists.[27] Nonetheless, it is impossible to deny some of the information in the book. It presents evidence from Gestapo records that three senior German Watch Tower officials – Fritz Winkler, Erich Frost, and Konrad Franke – gave up information about their brethren and the Witnesses' underground activities after being apprehended by the Gestapo.[28] Also included in *Die Zeugen Jehovas* are photocopies of a portion of the *Declaration of Facts*, the Watch Tower letter to Hitler, and an anti-Semitic statement from the Society's magazine *Trost* (Consolation) as published by the Watch Tower's Swiss branch in 1938.[29] Strikingly, the book's documentation includes several paragraphs from Frost's 1961 *Watchtower* article in German, *Der Spiegel's* attempted exposé of Frost, and photocopies of Gestapo documents that verify some of the statements made in that exposé.[30] Unfortunately, because of its pro-Marxist interpretation of much of the Witnesses' behaviour and because it fails to concede that Watch Tower officials such as Winkler, Frost, and Franke may have divulged information only under torture or at least extreme duress, it has been regarded as an unfair piece of propaganda even by many ex-Jehovah's Witnesses who are otherwise highly critical of the Watch Tower Society. It was therefore not difficult for the Society to ignore it. So for some years after its publication, almost nothing appeared in the West outside Germany that revealed the hidden facts of the Society's attempted compromise with Nazism or the fact that high Watch Tower officials in Germany had sometimes broken down under Gestapo interrogation. Regardless of the propagandistic nature of *Die Zeugen Jehovas*, the documents it provides demonstrate the Society's willingness to compromise with 'the world' when facing severe pressure. It is also true that many of its officials bent under persecution in the

27 Gebhard, 66–8, 164.
28 Ibid., 171–94.
29 Ibid., 160–70.
30 Ibid., 173–87.

same way that other religious leaders have often done in similar circumstances.

The Watch Tower wanted to bury the facts about the actions of some of its officials, but there were people in Germany who knew what had happened in 1933 at the Berlin convention, which is often called the Berlin-Wilmersdorf convention after the district of the capital where it was held. Copies of the *Declaration of Facts* and the Hitler letter were still extant. So in 1973 the Society took a new tack. Indirectly, it admitted that the declaration was much less than it had claimed, quite falsely, in *Jehovah's Witnesses in the Divine Purpose*. Yet it still felt it had to justify Rutherford for having written such a compromising document. To that end, it now blamed the *Declaration of Facts* on Paul Balzereit, the German Watch Tower branch office manager at the time, who in 1935 had dissociated himself from the Witness movement after being disfellowshipped by Rutherford. Hence the following statement appears in the *1974 Yearbook of Jehovah's Witnesses* on pages 110 and 111 as part of a history of Jehovah's Witnesses in Germany:

> By the summer of 1933 the work of Jehovah's witnesses had been banned in the majority of German states. The brothers' homes were being searched regularly and many brothers had been arrested. The flow of spiritual food was partially hampered, although only for a time; still many brothers were asking how long it would be possible to continue the work. In this situation the congregations were invited on very short notice to a convention to be held in Berlin on June 25. Since it was expected that many would be unable to attend because of the various bans, the congregations were encouraged to send at least one or several delegates. But, as it turned out, 7,000 brothers got there. For many of them it took three days, some riding bicycles the entire distance, whereas others went by truck, since bus companies refused to rent buses to a banned organization.
>
> Brother Rutherford, who together with Brother Knorr, had come to Germany just a few days before in order to see what could be done to ensure the safety of the Society's property, had prepared a declaration with Brother Balzereit to be presented to the convention delegates for adoption. It was a protest against the meddling of the Hitler government into the preaching work we were doing. All high government officials, from the Reich's president on down, were to receive a copy of the declaration, if possible, by registered mail. Several days before the convention started Brother Rutherford returned to America.

Many in attendance were disappointed in the 'declaration,' since in many points it failed to be as strong as the brothers had hoped. Brother Mütze from Dresden, who had worked closely with Brother Balzereit up until that time, accused him later of having weakened the original text. It was not the first time that Brother Balzereit had watered down the clear and unmistakable language of the Society's publications so as to avoid difficulties with government agencies.

A large number of brothers refused to adopt it just for this reason. In fact, a former pilgrim brother by the name of Kipper refused to offer it for adoption and another brother substituted. It could not be rightfully said that the declaration was unanimously adopted, even though Brother Balzereit notified Brother Rutherford that it had been.

The conventioners returned home tired and many were disappointed. They took 2,100,000 copies of the 'declaration' home with them, however, and made fast work of distributing them and sending them to numerous persons in positions of responsibility. The copy sent to Hitler was accompanied by a letter that, in part, read:

'The Brooklyn presidency of the Watch Tower Society is and always has been *exceedingly friendly to Germany*. In 1918 the president of the Society and seven members of the Board of Directors in America were sentenced to 80 years' imprisonment for the reason that the president *refused to let two magazines* in America, which he edited, *be used in war propaganda against Germany*.'

Even though the declaration had been weakened and many of the brothers could not wholeheartedly agree to its adoption, yet the government was enraged and started a wave of persecution against those who had distributed it.

This attempt to blame Balzereit does not square with the facts, as the Watch Tower's German *Awake!* correspondent has recently admitted[31] and as has long been apparent to anyone willing to look at the

31 His statement reads: 'According to the account of the *1974 Yearbook of Jehovah's Witnesses,* some German Witnesses were disappointed that the language of the "Declaration" was not more explicit in tone. Had the branch office manager, Paul Balzereit, weakened the text of the document? No, for a comparison of the text of the German and English texts shows that this is not the case. Evidently, an impression to the contrary was based on the subjective observations of some who were not directly involved in the preparation of the "Declaration." Their conclusions may also have been influenced by the fact that Balzereit renounced his faith only two years later.' 'Jehovah's Witnesses Courageous in the Face of Nazi Peril,'

evidence. For the Society published a copy of the *Declaration of Facts* in the German and English editions of the *1934 Year Book of Jehovah's Witnesses* with only a few changes from the text of the German leaflet that had been sent to public officials throughout the Reich.[32] In so doing it was indicating clearly that it was an official statement of the Society and its president. Furthermore, its style is unmistakably that of Judge Joseph Franklin Rutherford.

The letter written to Hitler was extremely obsequious and contained some outright falsehoods. As the extract from it in the *1974 Yearbook* makes clear, the letter claimed that the Brooklyn administration of the Watch Tower Society had always been friendly to Germany. It also asserted that Rutherford and his colleagues had been sent to prison in 1918 after *The Watch Tower* magazine and the '*Bible Student*' (i.e., *The Bible Students Monthly*) refused to print anti-German propaganda.[33] In fact, the Society was no more friendly to Germany than to any other nation and had printed attacks on it and its government. It had done so in the spring of 1918 in order to try to keep J.F. Rutherford and other high Watch Tower officials from being sent to prison under the American Espionage Act.[34] The Hitler letter was evidently the work of Paul Balzereit alone (the *1974 Yearbook of Jehovah's Witnesses* implies as much); that, or Balzereit wrote it with the assistance of German colleagues (which is what Detlef Garbe speculates).[35] Whether it had the direct approval of Rutherford or not is impossible to say at this time.

Awake! 8 July 1998, 14. Had anyone at the Watch Tower Society's German branch offices or its Brooklyn headquarters taken the time to make an examination of the texts in 1973, when the *1974 Yearbook* was being prepared, this would have been obvious. The failure to do so, which blackened Balzereit's reputation unfairly, is a typical example of the low level of Watch Tower 'scholarship' and its thoroughgoing untrustworthiness.

32 For a comparison of the texts of the *Declaration of Facts* as published originally in English and German, see Appendix C.

33 For the original text of the Hitler letter in German and an English translation thereof, see Appendix C.

34 During the First World War, the Watch Tower Society was as hostile to Germany and its Kaiser as it was to any nation and its head of state. In fact, in a strikingly pro-American statement, it called on Bible Students to pray for an Allied victory over German 'autocracy'; It stated specifically: 'Let there be praise and thanksgiving to God for the promised glorious outcome of the war, the breaking of the shackles of autocracy, the freeing of the captives (Isaiah 61:1) and the making of the world safe for the common people – blessings all assured by the Word of God to the people of this country and of the whole world of mankind.' WT, 1 June 1918, 174.

35 Garbe, *Widerstand und Martyrium,* 107n89.

But there is certainly no evidence to suggest that the Society's officers in Brooklyn ever repudiated it or even mentioned it prior to 1974. Even with the misinformation found in it, there is every reason to believe that it represented Watch Tower policy at the time. Its tone is in full harmony with the *Declaration of Facts*.

Despite these facts and the additional one that scholars were gradually becoming aware of the Watch Tower's efforts to ingratiate itself with the Nazi state by attacking Great Britain, the United States, and the League of Nations, and by scapegoating the Jews, the Society continued to maintain that Jehovah's Witnesses had never been guilty of compromise with one of 'Satan's organizations.' In fact, it lifted favourable information and quotes from scholarly studies to buttress its assertions, although, following Watch Tower practice, it failed to give proper citations so that readers could check the original sources for themselves. For example, *The Watchtower* of 1 October 1984 reported on page 8 the supposed findings of Christine E. King and Michael Kater to the effect that the number of Witness imprisonments and deaths brought about by Nazi persecution had been greatly underestimated by Jehovah's Witnesses.[36] Yet it is evident from the article itself that its anonymous author had made no attempt to verify King's assertions or to check her sources.[37] Then, in order to try to substantiate the Society's long-time boast that Jehovah's Witnesses had

36 In *The Nazi State and the New Religions*, King states that '10,000 were imprisoned, and together they received sentences totaling 20,000 years. One out of every two German Witnesses was imprisoned, and one in four lost their lives.' King, 169. The sources King gives to support her assertions are Kater, 181, and Kurt Hutten, *Seher, Grübler, Enthusiasten* (Stuttgart: Quell-Verlag, 1954), 69. Although she cites Kater as her source for saying that 10,000 were imprisoned and Hutten to the effect that half were imprisoned and that half of those imprisoned lost their lives, she need not have cited Hutten. Kater says specifically that if one sets the membership of the Bible Students at a constant 20,000 between 1933 and 1945, it can be reckoned that half of them were imprisoned and that of those, half lost their lives. Although Kater quotes Friedrich Zipfel's *Kirchenkampf in Deutschland* (Berlin: Walter de Gruyter, 1965), 176n5, to say that over 2,000 died, he notes that Zipfel claims that only 5,911 were imprisoned. Thus, neither King nor Kater was reporting anything new. Furthermore, the numbers of Witnesses who died from persecution in Germany during the Third Reich were far smaller than those held by King, Kater, and the sources on which they relied – something already known by the Watch Tower Society. This is evident from the statistics published in the *1974 Yearbook of Jehovah's Witnesses* on page 212.

37 Besides the fact that the article in question relies entirely on King's assertions, it wrongly refers to Michael Kater's article as 'a volume.'

never compromised with Nazism in any way, the article's author quoted a statement from King. It reads: 'Theological principles were adhered to; Witnesses remained "neutral," they were honest and completely trustworthy and as such, ironically, often found themselves employed as servants of the S.S.' Of course at that point, King was discussing the behaviour of Jehovah's Witnesses in the Nazi concentration camps, not the policy of the Watch Tower Society.[38]

What is significant about this account is that the individual who produced the *Watchtower* article of 1 October 1984 just discussed must have been aware that King knew that Watch Tower leaders had not been entirely faithful to their principles in 1933. Although he had taken the statement quoted immediately above from Christine King's *The Nazi State and the New Religions*, page 8, he failed to note what she had written about the Society's *Declaration of Facts*. For clearly, in what is a brief and somewhat superficial evaluation of that document, she makes what, from a Jehovah's Witness standpoint, are some rather damning observations:

> A *Declaration of Facts* was thus sent to every high ranking government officer in June 1933, representing the results of deliberations at a Berlin convention. The document indicates the nature of attacks they [Jehovah's Witnesses] are experiencing, explains the group's teaching, asserts the law-abiding character of its members, denies any links with Communism, Freemasonry [*sic*] or Jewry and expresses support for the 'parallel goals' [*sic*] of the new national government.[39] The document is a master of its kind and worthy of the other four sects [the Christian Scientists, the Latter-day Saints, the Seventh-day Adventists, and members of the New Apostolic Church, all of whom supported, in one way or another, the Nazi state]. It explains, flatters and offers just a hint of compromise.[40]

In her next paragraph following the above quotation, King goes on to say: 'Having attempted to assure the authorities by the *Declaration of Facts,* of their good citizenship, having interpreted and explained their teachings in a way, which given the preoccupations of the regime, was designed to ally fears and offer a hint of compromise, the

38 King's statement appears on page 169 of *The Nazi State and the New Religions*.

39 Ibid., 151. I find no reference to Freemasonry in the *Declaration of Facts*. The words 'parallel goals,' which appear in quotation marks in King's account, clearly represent her interpretation. These words do not appear in the declaration.

40 King, 151.

Witnesses seemed to have expected little further harassment. Had the *Declaration* not condemned with the Nazis, the League of Nations, had it not described National Socialism as standing out against the injustices Germans had suffered since 1919, and had it not ended with a personal appeal to the *Führer?*'[41]

In another place, King writes: 'In many ways the Nazis drove the sect into an extreme position, for the sectarians had been willing to offer some initial compromise.'[42] She notes too how Heinrich Himmler had recognized their 'anti-semitism and fanaticism,'[43] which in his eyes were good qualities. Later, she says: 'It has been seen that there were high ranking Nazis who openly admitted that the Witnesses were anti-semitic and that they were no more than "harmless cranks" whose teaching had admirable effects on the moral behavior of its members.'[44] Despite making these remarks, she credits the Witnesses with a continuing degree of philo-Judaism. Although she is aware of the 1932 change in the Watch Tower Society's teachings with respect to the Jews, in one place she remarks: 'The Witnesses saw a special role for the Jewish nation as the once chosen people. They believed that this role would be fulfilled in the new age. There is little however, outside this teaching, to link the Witnesses with the "world Zionist conspiracy" feared by the Nazis.'[45] Then she goes on to state: 'There are cases of individual Witnesses helping Jews, but there are also cases of Witnesses condemning the Jews as "murderers of Christ."'[46]

41 Ibid., 152. Evidently, in writing 'a personal appeal to the *Führer*,' King must be referring to the Society's letter to him. There is no direct appeal to Hitler in the declaration.

42 Ibid., 166.

43 Ibid., 168.

44 Ibid., 175.

45 Ibid., 174, 286n135. In the just cited end note, King states: 'In the "continuous revelation" of the movement, the teaching of the "gathering" of the Jews to Palestine which had once been important was abandoned after 1932. Nevertheless, in popular opinion, the Witnesses were frequently still believed to hold this view.' While it is true that that idea may have been the 'popular opinion' about the Witnesses among most other Germans, as fed by Nazi propaganda, it certainly was not one held by the Witnesses themselves. After 1929, when Rutherford had purged most of his critics from the Bible Student movement, unless forced by extreme circumstances to question, the Bible Student-Witnesses accepted (and accept) the last dictum from the Watch Tower Society as 'the Truth.' Thus Rutherford's most recent view of the Jews was certainly held among them 'to be from Jehovah.'

46 Ibid., 174.

Michael Kater is clearer and more damning in his assessment of Jehovah's Witnesses' attitudes under the Third Reich, arguing that their anti-Semitism arose out of the totalitarian nature of their community. He states, regarding Nazi attitudes toward the Witnesses and Witness attitudes toward the Jews:

> Indoctrinated in this fashion [by previous propaganda], the Justice Department, the police, and the SS always sought to brand the sect of the Earnest Bible Students as a 'Jewish' organization. In that way they propagated the ideological basis for the persecution of Jehovah's Witnesses. Yet in high Nazi circles it was known quite accurately that the Bible Students cherished no pro-Jewish bias. In 1944, SS Reichsführer Himmler even stated that he knew that Jehovah's Witnesses were 'intensely anti-Jewish'; and Rudolf Höss related that in Auschwitz he had observed that the Earnest Bible Students let Jews suffer and die 'because their forefathers had once betrayed Jehovah.' Actually, Höss's remark is basically correct: Jehovah's Witnesses were never anti-Semites for racial reasons; they have, however, always [*sic*] manifested a religiously motivated anti-Semitism, as is clearly evident from their writings. Intolerance against the Jews certainly coincided with the Bible Students' over-all totalitarian concept of the world.[47]

47 The original German of Kater's statement reads: 'Auf diese Weise indoktriniert, versuchten Justiz, Polizei und SS immer wieder, die Sekte der Ernsten Bibelforscher als "jüdische" Organisation zu brandmarken. Sie verbreiteten dadurch die ideologische Grundlage für die Verfolgung der Zeugen Jehovas. In hohen nationalsozialistischen Kreisen wußte man jedoch sehr genau, daß die Bibelforscher keine pro-jüdischen Neigungen hegten. Reichsführer-SS Himmler gab 1944 sogar vor zu wissen, die Zeugen Jehovas seien "schärfstens gegen die Juden" eingestellt, und auch Rudolf Höß will in Auschwitz beobachtet haben, daß Ernste Bibelforscher die Juden leiden und sterben ließen, "weil ihre Vorväter einst Jehova verrieten". Tatsächlich kommt die Bemerkung Höß der Wahrheit ziemlich nahe: die Zeugen Jehovas waren niemals Antisemiten aus rassischen Gründen, doch haben sie einen religiös motivierten Antisemitismus stets vertreten, wie aus ihren Schriften klar hervorgeht. Intoleranz gegenüber Juden vertrug sich durchaus mit dem totalitären Weltbild der Bibelfoscher.' Kater, 186–87. Kater is of course wrong in stating that the Bible Students were *always* anti-Semitic. But when referring to the attitude of the Bible Student–Jehovah's Witnesses during the time of the Third Reich, he is absolutely correct. In making his assessment, on page 187, in footnote 37, of 'Die Ernsten Bibelforsher im Dritten Reich,' Kater cites both the *Declaration of Facts* and Franz Zürcher's *Kreuzzug gegen das Christentum* (Zurich and New York: Europa-Verlag, 1938), 18, to support his allegation. Kater also quotes Bruno Bettelheim, who says about the Witnesses: 'Their anti-Semitism ... was a mild one and took the form that they resented that the Jews denied the Godship of Christ.'

The present-day leadership of the Watch Tower Society cannot possibly be ignorant of the true nature of the *Declaration of Facts* and its compromising, anti-Semitic tone. Despite this, the 8 June 1985 *Awake!* – after damning the clergy of Catholicism and Protestantism in the harshest terms for supporting Nazism – proclaimed on page 10: 'However, there was one group in Germany that courageously championed Christian principles. That group was Jehovah's Witnesses. Unlike the clergy and their followers, the Witnesses refused to compromise with Hitler and the Nazis. They refused to violate God's commandments. They would not break their Christian neutrality in political affairs. (See Isaiah 2:2–4; John 17:16; James 4:4.) They did not attribute Heil, or salvation, to Hitler, as did the overwhelming majority of the clergy and their flocks.'

About the same time that the 8 June 1985 *Awake!* was making these assertions, the University of Toronto Press published the first edition of *Apocalypse Delayed: The Story of Jehovah's Witnesses*, in which I made the facts concerning the Watch Tower's attempted compromise with Nazism known to the English-speaking world.[48] Shortly thereafter the *Toronto Star* published an article based on my findings,[49] which forced the Watch Tower Society to air the matter publicly for the first time.

Spokesmen for the Watch Tower's Canadian branch offices tried to deny the nature of the *Declaration of Facts* by attacking me personally. The Society's public relations spokesman for Canada, Walter Graham, claimed that 'the declaration was neither to placate Hitler nor anti-Semitic.' He said respecting me: 'Penton does have an axe to grind. He has been trying to discredit the Jehovah's Witnesses ever since he was removed from the society.'[50] However, remarkably, he had not read the evidence I had presented in *Apocalypse Delayed*: 'We haven't read the book. We are not interested in reading it. We're not interested in what James Penton does, writes or thinks, because he has chosen not to be one of us.'[51] In a similar vein, Eugene Rosam, another official then at the Canadian Watch Tower branch office, refused to comment on what I had written in *Apocalypse Delayed*: 'We have no comment on the publication. Anybody can write a book and get it published. It's just surprising some people refer to it as if it were Gospel.'[52]

48 Pages 147–9.

49 *The Toronto Star,* 20 July 1985, L12.

50 *Spokane Chronicle,* 10 August 1985, 11.

51 Ibid.

52 *Hamilton Spectator,* 7 September 1985, D12.

For the Watch Tower Society in the United States and Germany, what I had uncovered in *Apocalypse Delayed* had little immediate impact. *Awake!* published several articles on the Holocaust in its 8 April 1989 issue in which it argued, rightly, that many others besides Jews had died as a result of Nazi extermination policies. Regarding the persecution of Jehovah's Witnesses from 1933 to the collapse of the Third Reich in 1945, one of those articles, 'The Holocaust: Victims or Martyrs?' stated on page 12: 'They [Jehovah's Witnesses] were of many nationalities but were misconstrued as a pacifist threat to Germany's National Socialist regime because of their Christian stand of neutrality and refusal to be incorporated into the war effort of any nation. Hitler called them a "brood to be exterminated."' Significantly, this article also quoted Christine King but made no mention of either the *Declaration of Facts* or the Watch Tower letter to Hitler. Just after the publication of the 8 April 1989 *Awake!*, a series of articles appeared in the 1 and 15 April and 1 and 15 May 1989 issues of *The Watchtower* on the subject of 'Babylon the Great.' Referring to the great 'harlot' described at Revelation 17, these articles identified her as the worldwide empire of false religion – which includes all faiths but the Witnesses' own – that has 'committed fornication with the kings of the earth.' Accordingly, *The Watchtower* censured both Catholicism and Protestantism in the harshest terms for having supported various European governments in past centuries and, especially, for having been in league with Nazism during the Second World War. For example, *The Watchtower* of 15 April stated on page 12: 'If there had been no love affair between the Vatican and the Nazis, the world might have been spared the agony of having scores of millions of soldiers and civilians killed in the war, of six million Jews murdered for being non-Aryan, and – most precious in Jehovah's sight – of thousands of his Witnesses, both of the anointed and of the other sheep, suffering great atrocities, with many Witnesses dying in the Nazi concentration camps.' Speaking of Protestantism, the same magazine remarked on page 22: 'In fact, Protestantism sold itself out to Nazi nationalism and became its handmaiden, just as the Catholic Church had done.' Yet not once in these articles did the anonymous author of them admit that from the standpoint of their own teachings, what had been done by Watch Tower president J.F. Rutherford and his subalterns in 1933 was nothing short of an attempt to get into bed – to 'commit spiritual fornication' – with the Nazis at the expense of the Jews.

As a result of the Watch Tower Society's continuing refusal to recognize that it had tried to placate the Nazis in 1933, I determined to do further research on the history of Jehovah's Witnesses in Germany during that period. Fortunately, an ex-Witness in Germany, Helmut Lasarcyk, supplied me with a portion of a word-for-word transcript of a recorded, two-part lecture given by the late German Watch Tower branch overseer Konrad Franke. In that talk, 'The History of Jehovah's Witnesses in Germany,' Franke made the following revealing statement about the Berlin-Wilmersdorf Witness convention of 1933:

> At the last moment, therefore, we were invited to a special assembly in Prussia, thus Berlin, [to be held] in the Tennis Hall, where a 'Declaration' was to be presented. Many were now unable to come [to the convention], but I had the privilege of traveling with Brother Albert Wandres from Wiesbaden to Berlin on a motorcycle through torrential rain.
>
> But we were shocked when we arrived at the Tennis Hall the next morning and did not find the atmosphere that we ordinarily found at [Jehovah's Witness] conventions. When we entered, we found the hall bedecked with swastika flags! But not only that: when the meeting started, it was begun with a song that we had not sung for years, especially not in Germany, because of the melody. Though the lyrics were fine, the melody – well, the musicians who are here will recognize that the notes were [taken from] the melody of 'Deutschland, Deutschland über alles'!
>
> Can you imagine how we felt? Many could not join in the singing. It was just as though their throats were throttled. What kind of leaders did we have who brought us [into] such dangers – and the danger of faltering under these circumstances – instead of helping and supporting us, so that we could take a fearless stand [against Nazism]. May all elders who are here among us learn something from these examples, and may they recognize their responsibilities in such matters in the near future.
>
> Now the Declaration, which Brother Rutherford had prepared, was approved, and every person was instructed to take 250 copies home if he possibly could. If he then had the courage to do so, he was to send copies of it by registered mail to judges, lawyers, mayors, etc.
>
> At the time I sent fifty-two registered letters [with the Declaration], and the result was that a few days later I found myself in a concentration camp for the first time when most people had no idea what a concentration camp was.[53]

53 The above translation was made by Mr Lasarcyk. The original German from the transcript reads:

'So wurden wir dann noch im letzten Moment für den 25. Juni zu einer besonderen Versammlung nach Preußen, also nach Berlin, eingeladen, in die Tennishallen, zu einer besonderen Versammlung, wo eine Erklärung angenommen

Using this new information, copies of the original *Declaration of Facts* in German, and the English version thereof as published in the *1934 Year Book of Jehovah's Witnesses*, in the spring of 1990 I published a short article, with full documentation, in *The Christian Quest*.[54] This article gave full details of what happened at the Berlin-Wilmersdorf Witness convention in 1933. In it I asserted that Judge J.F. Rutherford clearly had been the author of the declaration and that Paul Balzereit had not 'weakened it.' However, because *The Christian Quest* had a small circulation,[55] that article had little impact on Jehovah's Witnesses or anyone else for several years. But in the mid-1990s a Norwegian ex-Witness, Kent Steinhaug, posted a copy of it on his website, 'Watchtower Observer.' Shortly thereafter the article was translated into sev-

---

werden sollte. Viele konnten schon nicht mehr kommen. Aber ich hatte das Vorrecht, mit Bruder Albert Wandres auf dem Motorrad von Wiesbaden bis Berlin bei strömendem Regen zu fahren. Aber das hat uns nicht viel ausgemacht. Aber wir waren erschüttert, als wir am nächsten Morgen in die Tennishallen kamen und nicht diese Stimmung vorfanden, wie wir sie sonst bei Kongressen vorfinden. Als wir hereinkamen, waren die Hallen mit Hakenkreuzfahnen geschmückt. Aber nicht nur das. Als jetzt nun die Versammlung eingeleitet wurde, wurde sie mit einem Lied eingeleitet, was wir jahrelang und überhaupt in Deutschland nie gesungen hatten, wegen seiner Melodie. Der Text war wohl gut, aber die Melodie ... Nun, Musiker, die hier sind, die werden an den Noten sofort erkennen, daß es die Melodie war "Deutschland, Deutschland, über alles". Könnt ihr euch vorstellen, wie es uns zumute war? Viele könnten nicht mitsingen. Es war gerade, als wenn ihnen die Kehle zugeschnürt wurde. Was hatten wir denn bloß jetzt für eine Führung, die uns in diese Gefahren brachte und in die Gefahr, jetzt unter diesen Umständen zu straucheln, statt uns zu helfen, uns beizustehen, damit wir eine furchtlose Stellung einnahmen? Mögen alle Ältesten, die unter uns sind, aus diesen Beispielen etwas lernen und mögen sie ihre Verantwortung in diesem Zusammenhang in der nahen Zukunft erkennen.

'Nun wurde diese Erklärung, die Bruder Rutherford noch vorbereitet hatte, angenommen. Uns wurde der Auftrag gegeben, jeder sollte 250 Stück mit nach Hause nehmen und soweit es ist moglich ist, sofern er mutig dazu war, per Einschreiben an Richter, Staatsanwälte, Oberbürgermeister usw. senden.

'Ich habe damals 52 solcher Briefe weggeschickt per Einschreiben. Die Folge war, daß ich wenige Tage später das erste Mal schon dafür im KZ saß, wo die meisten noch gar nicht wußten, was das war.'

54 'A Story of Attempted Compromise: Jehovah's Witnesses, Anti-Semitism, and the Third Reich,' *The Christian Quest* 3:1 (Spring 1990): 33–45. In addition to the article itself, I published the *Declaration of Facts*, the Watch Tower letter to Hitler, and Konrad Franke's testimony regarding the 1933 Berlin-Wilmersdorf convention, all of which were printed in both German and English. These documents appear on pages 49–75 of the same issue of *The Christian Quest*.

55 *The Christian Quest* was published for members of the small Free Bible Student community and ex-Jehovah's Witnesses only.

eral languages, including German, and posted on various websites. In Italy it was translated and published in print, and according to one of its translators, Achille Aveta, 'it caused quite a stir.'[56] In addition, it was cited – albeit incorrectly – in the first two editions of Detlef Garbe's study of the Witnesses' *via dolorosa* under Nazism, *Zwischen Wiederstand und Martyrium*.[57] As a result, it came to the attention of many ordinary Jehovah's Witnesses and to Watch Tower officials as well.

At the time this was happening, others – particularly in Germany – began to publish statements on the Internet that supported what I had written in *The Christian Quest* and added additional information embarrassing to the Watch Tower Society and Jehovah's Witnesses. This was especially true of the German ex–Jehovah's Witness website, Infolink. In addition, in 1999 Manfred Gebhard published his well-documented book, *Geschichte der Zeugen Jehovas,* which offers a clear picture of Witness conduct under the Third Reich. Yet the Watch Tower's response to all of this unflattering information has been one of complete denial and bitter attacks on anyone who dares to expose the facts surrounding its attempted compromise with Nazism.

This is clearly shown by the fact that the Italian Witness Internet website 'Triangolo Viola' (Purple Triangle) has published a letter from one Sandra Malakovich under the title '*Una docente risponde*' (A teacher replies). That letter attacks Kent Steinhaug for posting my article from *The Christian Quest,* and says of him and of me:

> The post by Mr. Steinhaug on the Jehovah's Witnesses and the Holocaust contains an old argument that scholars already debunked several years ago. In English sources, I found some good material in the book, 'Persecution and Resistance of Jehovah's Witnesses During the Nazi-Regime, 1933–1945,' edited by Hans Hesse. A number of scholars have discussed the Berlin 1933 convention mentioned by Mr. Steinhaug. For instance, historian Sybil Milton, religious scientist Gabriele Yonan, noted German church historian Gerhard Besier, and religious historian Christine King all analyze the response of the Jehovah's Witnesses both in the early and later years of National Socialist control. They come to a very different conclusion than Mr. Steinhaug or Mr. Penton, whose writing seems to be an emotional polemic more than an academic historical treatment. In fact, Professor Besier shows that much of the material that Penton repeats was actually recycled propa-

56 Comment by Achille Aveta to author.

57 See discussions of this matter on pages 47 and 69 below.

> ganda generated by the Stasi (East German Police) to discredit leaders among the Witness movement. If he is a scholar, Mr. Penton should be more careful of his sources.

Sadly, Ms Milakovich's letter and its appearance on 'Triangolo Viola' indicates nothing less than a willingness on the part of a Jehovah's Witnesses outlet to use false statements openly in defence of the Witness religion. I did not take any information from Stasi sources for my article in *The Christian Quest*. My conclusions in that article were drawn entirely from Jehovah's Witness publications and from Konrad Franke's tape-recorded statement. King does not disagree with me regarding the nature of the *Declaration of Facts,* and she recognizes that some Jehovah's Witnesses were anti-Semitic. Milton does not discuss the 1933 Berlin convention or the documents generated at it, at least in Hesse's *Persecution and Resistance of Jehovah's Witnesses*. Only Yonan takes a stand clearly in opposition to the one I presented in *The Christian Quest* as reproduced by Kent Steinhaug. Also, Ms Malakovich's reference to Gerhard Besier raises a serious question: To which publication of his does she refer? No article by him appears in Hans Hesse's *Persecution and Resistance of Jehovah's Witnesses*. So in the circumstances, what Sandra Malakovich has written is simply out of harmony with the facts.

Of course it is not particularly strange that Ms Malakovich and a Witness Internet outlet such as 'Triangolo Viola' would attempt to deny my charges and to condemn Steinhaug's airing of them. What *is* surprising is that a number of non-Witness historians have supported the Watch Tower Society in its denial that Rutherford and German Witness leaders were guilty of Jew baiting and of trying to ingratiate their movement with the Nazis. Because of this fact, their comments are presented and discussed in chapters 2 and 3.

2

Watch Tower Holocaust Propaganda and Responses to Charges of Compromise and Anti-Semitism

Talking much about oneself may be a way of hiding oneself.
Friedrich Nietzsche, *Beyond Good and Evil*

Since the Second World War the Watch Tower Society has never wavered in its assertion that Jehovah's Witnesses opposed Nazism consistently. In an attempt to prove this point the Society has taken four different tacks. First, it often has referred to the many anti-Nazi articles that appeared in its literature from at least 1934 to the end of the war and beyond. Second, it has often recounted the faithfulness of Jehovah's Witnesses under terrible persecution in Germany and throughout the Nazis' wartime empire. Third, it has argued that Jehovah's Witnesses in the Nazi concentration camps were notably supportive of Jewish prisoners. Fourthly, it has 'exposed' the activities of the German churches, both Catholic and Protestant, during those years, claiming that they were pro-Nazi. In fact, the Watch Tower Society has repeatedly claimed that many of Hitler's and the Nazis' crimes are directly attributable to the *Führer's* background as a Catholic. In addition – as is evident from the Berlin *Declaration of Facts* – the Society has blamed the persecution of the Witnesses in Germany primarily on the Catholic Church and its clergy.

Regarding the first point, there can be no doubt that after the late autumn of 1933, Judge J.F. Rutherford and the Watch Tower Society in America became stridently anti-Nazi. From that point on, Watch Tower literature offered a drumfire of articles damning Nazism in Germany and Fascism in Italy and Spain as of the Devil. The Witnesses came to regard the Hitler regime as the 'wild beast' of Revelation,[1] and eventually they came to see Germany in particular as 'the King of the North' mentioned in the biblical book of Daniel. Accordingly, the Watch Tower Society prophesied that Germany would fall before the might of the 'King of the South,' the 'Anglo-American world power.'[2] More important, however, the Witnesses tried to awaken the outside world to the terrible oppressiveness of the Hitler regime. The Society's magazines *The Golden Age* and *Consolation* provided regular reports about the persecution of Jehovah's Witnesses in Germany; they also told what was happening to others, including the Jews. In 1938, Franz Zürcher, a senior Watch Tower official who later became the Society's Swiss branch overseer, produced *Kreuzzug gegen das Christentum* (Crusade against Christianity),[3] which gave a detailed account of the sufferings of the Witnesses in the Third Reich. The German novelist Thomas Mann, by then a refugee from Nazism, was so moved by Zürcher's account that he wrote an introduction to it.

With respect to the second point, again it must be said that the Watch Tower Society's assertions and those of many others are generally quite true: of all the prisoners in the concentration camps, none were as faithful to their beliefs, and none withstood persecution better, than Jehovah's Witnesses. There were many defections and compromises, especially in prisons (i.e., rather than in the concentration camps), and some Witnesses broke under persecution either temporarily or permanently; that said, many were amazingly loyal and deserve great respect. For example, Eugen Kogon has written about Witnesses' bravery in Nazi concentration camps and has remarked: 'One cannot escape the impression that, psychologically speaking, the SS was never quite equal to the challenge offered them by Jehovah's Witnesses.'[4]

1 As noted by Johannes Wrobel, the Watch Tower's German archivist, this was brought out in *Das Goldene Zeitalter* (*The Golden Age*), published in Switzerland on 1 February 1937. See Johannes Wrobel, 'The Video Documentary "Jehovah's Witnesses Stand Firm against Nazi Assault,"' in Hans Hesse, ed., *Persecution and Resistance during the Nazi Regime: 1933–1945,* (Bremen: Edition Temmen, 2001), 312, 326n52.

2 WT, 15 February 1942, 51, 54; 15 September 1943, 275–6.

3 Franz Zücher, *Kreuzzug gegen das Christentum* (Zurich and New York: Europa-Verlag, 1938). Editions were published in French and Polish as well as German. It has never been translated into English.

4 Eugen Kogon, *The Theory and Practice of Hell* (New York: Berkley, 1964), 43.

Regarding Witness attitudes toward the Jews, the Watch Tower Society has claimed that it exposed the Nazi persecution of them and that Jehovah's Witnesses were consistently helpful to them. Speaking of the Witnesses at the time, the *Awake!* issue of 8 May 1964 made the following assertion:

> From 1933 onward in particular their international magazine, *The Golden Age,* kept exposing the Nazi terror, year after year. Thus in its October 9, 1935, issue, reporting on 'One Year of Nazi Terror,' it gave the numbers murdered, imprisoned and sent to concentration camps. The following year it had such articles as 'All Germany Worships a Murderer,' and 'Nazi Robbery of the Jews.' In 1937 it featured, among other things, an article headed 'German Jews Law-abiding.' In 1938 it told of discrimination against Jews throughout Germany, of intolerance, and the persecution of the Jews. In 1939 articles told of 'Fiendishness at Sachsenhausen,' where Jews were being clubbed to death. Among other articles to appear in subsequent years were 'Abuse of Jews,' 'End of Jews in Germany,' 'Terrible Plight of Hungarian Jews.' More than that, so long as Jehovah's witnesses in Germany were able to do so they went out of their way to befriend Jews, ignoring the ordered boycotts and sharing their food with them.[5]

While there can be no doubt that Watch Tower publications did expose the Nazi persecution of the Jews, the Watch Tower's claim that the Witnesses regularly 'went out of their way to befriend the Jews' is – as has been shown earlier – open to question. It is equally questionable whether the exposé of the Nazis' crimes against the Jews was primarily out of concern for them or more out of hatred of the Third Reich. After all, a year after the war the Watch Tower Society published the first edition of *'Let God Be True,'* a book that blamed the Jews for 'much of their suffering.' This book, which was for eight years thereafter the primary Jehovah's Witness doctrinal tool for making converts, stated:

> The facts and prophecies prove that the natural Jews will never again be a chosen, regathered people. They have as a people flagrantly rejected the Messiah, his truth and his kingdom. It is a false hope that they must be regathered to Palestine and be converted in mass to Jesus Christ prior to his second coming as a sign of the early establishment of his kingdom. God's

5 Page 16.

> kingdom was established in A. D. 1914, and Christ Jesus came into Kingdom power at his Father's right hand, and this without any mass conversion of natural Jews to Christ. *Much of their suffering has been brought on themselves by their commercial, rebellious course of action.* They will ever be a target of assault by Satan and his agents until Armageddon cleanses the earth of all opposers of Messiah-Christ. Therefore, their only hope is to accept Jehovah's Messiah, Christ Jesus, and come under the protection of his kingdom.[6] [Italics mine]

The second edition of *'Let God Be True'* did not contain this statement; however, the first edition's words were never specifically repudiated by the Watch Tower Society, and *The Watchtower* issue of 1 November 1975 stated: 'To this day the natural circumcised Jews are suffering the sad consequences from the works of darkness that were done within their nation nineteen hundred years ago. This illustrates what can happen to a whole nation that comes under the influence of that unseen superhuman intelligence, Satan the Devil.'

Although the Watch Tower Society has damned the German Protestant clergy over the years,[7] Witness leaders and publications have held the Catholic Church primarily responsible for Hitler and the Nazis' crimes. A few examples taken from Watch Tower publications from the 1930s to the present illustrate this dramatically. Writing in 1937, Rutherford proclaimed: 'In Germany, which is outwardly ruled by the fanatic Hitler, but which is secretly ruled by the Roman Catholic Hierarchy and the Devil, thousands of faithful and true witnesses for the Lord are imprisoned, cruelly beaten and some of them foully murdered because they have in possession a Bible or books which explain the Bible.'[8] The following year, *Consolation* took up the same theme in a slightly less extreme manner. In an article titled 'The Tragedy of Germany' it stated: 'While there has been persecution of members of the Roman Catholic organization, to which considerable publicity has been given, the Hierarchy has nevertheless made substantial progress. The Protestant system, on the other hand, has suffered many reverses, but the persecution of Jehovah's witnesses is far greater. The thought, therefore, that the Hierarchy is essentially in harmony with the Nazis

6 Pages 208–9.

7 See for example *Awake!*, 8 July 1975, 30; 22 August 1995, 12–15; and WT, 1 April 1978, 7; 1 June 1979, 20. In almost all cases the Watch Tower Society has used the device of quoting outside sources regarding Protestant cooperation with Nazism.

8 J.F. Rutherford, *Enemies* (Brooklyn, NY: Watch Tower Society, 1937), 323.

'Merely Political Differences'
(from *The Golden Age*, 8 April 1936, 421)

is justified.'[9] In the same vein, the anonymous author of 'The Tragedy of Germany' provided evidence that the number of Catholic churches and priests had actually grown in the Reich under Hitler. He added: 'As a further evidence of co-operation between the Hierarchy and Hitler, note that German Freemasonry has been destroyed, buildings and property confiscated, and the members are forbidden to communicate one with another, under penalty of arrest and imprisonment.'[10]

After Rutherford's death the Watch Tower Society continued to claim that the Catholic hierarchy – in particular Pope Pius XII – was behind Hitler and all forms of fascism. Just before the war's end, *Consolation* published an article titled 'When Hitler Lost the War.' At the beginning of this article, which shows a great deal of admiration for Russia and for Joseph Stalin, *Consolation* trumpeted: 'Adolf Hitler, Jesuit trained, was making rapid progress toward the re-establishment of the "Holy Roman Empire". He, and his fellow Jesuits, had destroyed the German republic, shortly after he became chancellor, January 30, 1933.'[11] However, although Hitler was born a Catholic, he was not Jesuit trained, and it was nonsense to call him a Jesuit.

Later, in 1945, immediately after the end of the war in the Pacific and some months after the defeat of Germany, *Consolation* published the article 'Jehovah's witnesses Triumph over Concentration Camps.' Although devoted mainly to accounts of Witness suffering in Nazi concentration camps, it began with a long diatribe against the Catholic Church. Among other things, it stated: 'Within the borders of Germany itself, was it not the Catholic bishop of Fulda who pledged loyalty to Hitler and expressed gratitude and indebtedness to the then-victorious German troops? Was not Hitler a Catholic? a concordat partner of the pope? and was he ever excommunicated, in accord with numerous requests from honest and liberal groups of Catholic laymen? Who, then, were the Nazi collaborationists, sympathizers, and fifth-columnists? Anyone who knows anything about what has gone on in this battered old world for the past dozen years need not be told that it was the Roman Catholic Hierarchy and her dupes.'[12] This article was mild, however, compared to another that followed in *Consolation* only a few weeks later. In 'Has Nazism Been Destroyed?' it was claimed over and over again that Roman Catholicism was National Socialism's

9 'The Tragedy of Germany' (Part 1), *Consolation*, 4 May 1938, 6.
10 Ibid.
11 *Consolation*, 31 January 1945, 3.
12 *Consolation*, 12 September 1945, 3.

Restorers of the Holy(!) Roman Empire
(from *The Golden Age*, 9 September 1936, 771)

greatest supporter. It ended with this statement: 'Therefore do not be deceived; the Hierarchy is Nazism's greatest promoter and exponent. As long as she exists Nazism will be forcefully represented.'[13]

It would be tiresome to repeat all of the Watch Tower's constant denunciations since 1945 of the Roman Catholic clergy for their support of Hitler and Nazi Germany.[14] While it is true that these attacks have become slightly more scholarly over the years – the approach they take now is to argue that the Catholic Church cooperated with the Third Reich but was not its instigator or its spiritual godmother – the Watch Tower Society nonetheless has continued its barrage of attacks. For instance, *The Watchtower* of 1 January 1980 stated on page 5:

> During World War II the pope refused to excommunicate such Catholic leaders as Adolf Hitler and Hermann Göring, or millions of Church members in their armies. It is a well-known fact of history that the Catholic Church in Germany blessed the Nazi war effort, as is shown by news clippings shown below.[15]
>
> Why was there almost total German support for the Nazi war effort? Catholic scholar and educator Gordon Zahn explains why, stating: 'The German Catholic who looked to his religious superiors for spiritual guidance and direction regarding service in Hitler's wars received virtually the same answers he would have received from the Nazi ruler himself.'

While carrying on a ceaseless campaign against the German churches for their involvement in politics, the Watch Tower Society has created a martyrology of those German and other European Jehovah's Witnesses who suffered under Hitler. As described in chapter 1, it has denied that it made any attempt to compromise with the Nazis either on its own part or on that of Jehovah's Witnesses who lived under Nazi rule. For example, the *Awake!* issue of 22 November 1987 published an article on page 14 which discussed an American Jewish Congress letter to the pope that pointed out Catholic failings during the Nazi Holocaust. This article went on to assert that others besides the

13 *Consolation,* 26 September 1945, 14.

14 For some examples, see the consecutive articles '"The Deputy" Stirs Consciences and Opposition' and 'The Nazi-Vatican Concordat,' *Awake!* 8 May 1964, 9–21.

15 The article shows partial clippings from the *New York Post,* 27 August 1940,15; the *New York Times*, 25 September 1939, Late City Edition, 6; and the *New York Times,* 7 December 1942, Late City Edition, 337.

Jews had suffered under the Third Reich, including Jehovah's Witnesses. Less than eighteen months later it began a strong campaign to enhance the prestige of those Witnesses by contrasting them with others who had been persecuted by the Nazis. In an article titled 'The Holocaust: The Forgotten Victims,' the *Awake!* issue of 8 April 1989 again stressed the fact that the Nazis had murdered others in great numbers who were not Jews. It pointed out quite legitimately that the German Army and Heinrich Himmler's SS had executed Poles, other Slavs, and Gypsies by the millions. Then it asked, 'What is the difference between those who were victims of the Holocaust and those who were martyrs?'[16]

The point of this question became clear in 'The Holocaust: Victims or Martyrs?' published in the same issue of the Witness journal. Paraphrasing Gordon Zahn, it asserted that there were three types of Nazi victims: '(1) those who suffered *for what they were* – Jews, Slavs, Gypsies; (2) those who suffered for what they did – homosexuals, political activists, and resisters; (3) and those who suffered *for what they refused to do* – conscientious objectors, Jehovah's Witnesses and others.' Then, without recognizing that Zahn's categories were somewhat artificial, since Jehovah's Witnesses' widely published attacks on the Nazi state could be considered political, and that the Witnesses were clearly *resisters, Awake!* went on to argue that the Witnesses were 'neutral.' The article had a further point to make, however. In contrast to most others, the Witnesses were *true martyrs.* Unlike the Jews, Slavs, and Gypsies, they could have escaped their fate simply by bowing to the demands of Hitler's National Socialists – after all, most of them were so-called Aryans.[17] Finally, *Awake!* argued that the sufferings of the Witnesses had largely been ignored: they were 'forgotten victims.'

As a sidebar to this article, *Awake!* reprinted a letter written by concentration camp survivor Martin Poetzinger and published in the *New York Times* of 14 May 1985:

> Your recent letters telling of ordinary Germans who suffered under Hitler's Nazi regime ... provoke me to mention one minority group, usually ignored, that was persecuted ferociously by the Gestapo. They were known as Ernste Bibelforscher (Earnest Bible Students) or Jehovas Zeugen (Jehovah's Witnesses).

16 'The Holocaust: The Forgotten Victims,' *Awake!* 8 April 1989, 9–16.
17 Ibid., 12–13.

> As soon as Hitler came to power in 1933, he commenced a systematic persecution of Jehovah's Witnesses because of their stand of neutrality in politics and war. As a result, thousands of German Witnesses, many of whom were friends of mine, became not only victims of the Holocaust but also martyrs. Why the subtle difference? Because we could have left the concentration camps at any time if we had been willing to sign a paper renouncing our religious beliefs.[18]

Following the publication of the above article, the theme of Witness martyrdom began to appear more frequently in Witness publications. In promoting this theme the Watch Tower Society was not above using data that clearly exaggerated Witness sufferings. For example, *The Watchtower* of 1 February 1990 quoted Friedrich Zipfel in *Kirchenkampf in Deutschland* (Church Struggle in Germany) regarding the persecution of Jehovah's Witnesses in the Third Reich. There, Zipfel is recorded as having written: 'Ninety-seven percent of the members of this small religious group were victims of National Socialistic [Nazi] persecution. One third of them were killed, either by execution, other violent acts, hunger, sickness or slave labor. The severity of this subjection was without precedent and was the result of uncompromising faith which could not be harmonized with National Socialistic ideology.' Following this quotation and a claim that 'in Austria, 25 percent of Jehovah's Witnesses were executed, beaten to death, or died from disease or exhaustion in Nazi camps,' the Witness journal stated: 'Those martyred for obeying the law of love were confident that "God is not unrighteous so as to forget [their] work and the love [they] showed for his name."'[19] Yet sixteen years earlier, the Society's own account of Nazi persecution in the *1974 Yearbook of Jehovah's Witnesses* had demonstrated that Zipfel's statistics were overblown.[20]

Another Watch Tower account – rather, series of accounts – of the Witnesses' sufferings in Nazi Germany appeared in 1993 in *Jehovah's Witnesses: Proclaimers of God's Kingdom.* This 750-page, badly organized, and extremely biased book fails in general to divulge anything new. But it does quote statistical figures only slightly higher than those which appear in the *1974 Yearbook* – figures that cast doubt on those of Friedrich Zipfel as trumpeted in the 1 February 1990 *Watchtower* re-

18 Ibid.
19 WT, 1 February 1990, 22.
20 Page 212.

garding the number of Witnesses who suffered from Nazi persecution. In a chronological list of 'noteworthy events' on page 720, this Witness history remarks for the year 1933: 'Jehovah's Witnesses are banned in Germany. During the intense persecution down to the end of World War II, 6,263 are arrested, and their combined time of imprisonment totals 14,332 years; 2,074 are sent to concentration camps, where their confinement totals 8,332 years.' So if the statistics in this most recent Witness history are correct, both Zipfel's and most earlier Watch Tower Society numbers were greatly inflated.[21]

The Watch Tower Society has evidently never been bothered by such inconsistencies. In order to make Witness martyrdom seem more real, it began printing personal histories of Jehovah's Witness individuals and families who had gone through the Holocaust.[22] It also began publishing more quotations from various historians and other scholars on both the plight and faith of the Witnesses under the Third Reich. Quoted besides Zipfel were Bruno Bettelheim, Ana Pawelczynska, John Conway, and, above all, Christine Elizabeth King.[23] Without giving any further bibliographical data, in 1992 it quoted a book with the mixed French-German title *Les Bibelforscher et le nazisme* as follows: 'Despite all the beatings, threats, and bans, despite the public humiliations, the imprisonments and detention in concentration camps, Bible Students [Jehovah's Witnesses] never allowed themselves to be "reeducated."'[24] Curiously, at the very time that it was able to dredge up so much evidence from outside testimonies concerning what had happened to Jehovah's Witnesses in the concentration camps, the Watch Tower Society began to play on the theme that Jehovah's Witnesses' sufferings had been largely ignored and largely forgotten.

21 For a discussion of Watch Tower Holocaust statistics, see Appendix I.

22 A list of these accounts can be found in Wolfram Slupina, 'Persecuted and Almost Forgotten,' in Hesse, *Persecution and Resistance,* 279–82.

23 WT, 1 August 1990, 19; 1 November 1991, 12; 1 February 1992, 32; 1 February 1993, 5; 15 September 1993, 15; 15 January 1996, 4; 1 February 1996, 6. *Awake!,* 8 May 1993, 5; 22 August 1995, 12, 15; 8 November 1993, 19; 8 November 1995, 23; 8 September 1996, 30.

24 WT, 2 February 1992, 32. The quotation is in fact taken from Sylvie Graffard and Leo Tristan, *Les Bibelforscher et le nazism 1933–1945* (Paris: Editions Tirésias, 1990). A new edition of this excellent work has been produced in English by Michel Reynaud and Sylvie Graffard, titled *The Jehovah's Witnesses and the Nazis: Persecution, Deportation, and Murder 1933–1945.* Translated from the French by James A. Moorhouse with an introduction by Michael Berenbaum, it was published by Cooper Square Press of New York in 2001.

Jehovah's Witnesses took other tacks to advertise their position with regard to what had happened in Germany under the Nazis. They held various meetings and produced videos that emphasized Witness faithfulness in the face of persecution. On 29 September 1994, at the Holocaust Museum in Washington, D.C., a conference was held on the role of Jehovah's Witnesses under the Third Reich. Following this event, large commemorative reunions of concentration camp survivors were held under the auspices of the Cercle Européen des Témoins de Jéhovah Anciens Déportés et Internés (the European Circle of Formerly Deported and Interned Jehovah's Witnesses): in Strasbourg on 28 March 1995, in Paris on 30 March, and near Berlin on 27 April of the same year. Concerning these gatherings and what followed, the *Awake!* of 8 June 1996 reported on page 18:

> At these reunions, an exhibition with the theme 'Mémoire de Témoins' (Witness Testimony) was presented. From May 1995 to April 1996, it toured 42 cities in France and various cities in Belgium and French-speaking Switzerland. Above all, the men and women in the exhibition are Witnesses of Jehovah God. But they are also witnesses of the suffering that they and others endured in the concentration camps. They are living proof of an ideology of intolerance that caused the suffering and death of millions of people because of their race or religion. The testimony of the Witnesses, furthermore, exposes how so-called Christians preferred a pseudo-messiah, Hitler, to Jesus Christ; hate to love of neighbor; and violence to peace.

On pages 18 and 19 in the same article, *Awake!* stated:

> A short ceremony opened each presentation of the exhibition, during which a representative of the former deportees [from countries conquered by Nazi Germany] explained the spiritual resistance of Jehovah's Witnesses to Nazism. Non-Witness deportees as well as several historians and officials, including a former French government minister, also kindly accepted invitations to speak.
>
> A former deportee who knew Jehovah's Witnesses in Buchenwald said regarding them: 'I am unaware of any category of deportees, apart from the Jews, who were treated as ignominiously, beaten, humiliated, insulted, given the vilest tasks. Without their faith, they could not have withstood. I have the greatest admiration for them.'

That same year, 1995, the German branch offices of the Watch Tower Society produced an interesting and informative brochure on the Witnesses in Germany. Titled *Jehovas Zeugen: Menschen aus der Nachbarschaft. Wer sind sie?* (Jehovah's Witnesses: People in the Neighborhood. Who Are They?), this brochure includes a section called *'Zahlt Cäsars Dinge Cäsar zurück, Gottes Dinge aber Gott'* (Give Back Caesar's Things to Caesar, but God's Things to God), in which it gives a far more conservative statistic than it had in the past regarding the number of Witnesses who died from persecution under Hitler. After claiming that 'circa 10,000' had been imprisoned, it states that only some 1,200 lost their lives.[25] Yet at the same time, the brochure continues to play on old themes. It states that the Witnesses were 'neutral in every land of the earth,' and in another short article following *'Zahlt Cäsars Dinge Cäsar zurück,'* it presents a series of pictures along with brief statements from ten elderly Witnesses who had survived Nazi persecution.[26]

In 1996 the Watch Tower Society produced its most important piece of propaganda to date on the Witnesses under Nazism: the video 'Jehovah's Witnesses Stand Firm against Nazi Assault.' In 1991 Starlock Pictures of Great Britain had produced a twenty-five-minute program for television called 'Purple Triangles' (the insignias worn by Jehovah's Witness concentration inmates). This video focussed on the Kusserows, a German Jehovah's Witness family whose eleven members all suffered terrible persecution under the Nazis. This program, which simply tells a factual human story of great courage, did of course throw much favourable light on the Witnesses' stand against Hitler and on the martyrdom of two Kusserow brothers who were executed for refusing to serve in the *Wehrmacht* (German Army). Realizing this, the Watchtower Bible and Tract Society obtained the rights to produce and distribute this program as a video for the Witness faithful. However, 'Purple Triangles' said nothing about the stand that Jehovah's Witnesses in general took under the Third Reich. Therefore, the Watch Tower Society decided to produce the 'Stand Firm' video.

What is interesting and remarkable about 'Stand Firm' is that, as the back of its sleeve states, it includes the remarks of '10 historians from Europe and North America, and more than 20 Witness survivors.' These people have nothing but praise for the Witnesses, and nothing but condemnation for the German churches with regard to their rela-

25 Page 16. This statement is based on a brochure produced by the German Federal Central for Political Organizations at Bonn called *Informationen zur politischen Bildung* (Nr. 243, 2. Quartal 1994.). The above quoted information is given on page 21 under the title 'Deutscher Widerstand 1933–1945.'

26 Ibid., 16–19.

tionships to the Nazi state. Most important from a historical standpoint are the comments of three of the historians: Christine King, now the vice-chancellor of Staffordshire University in England; Detlef Garbe, director of the Neuengamme Concentration Camp Memorial in Germany; and the late Sybil Milton of the Holocaust Museum in Washington, D.C. Significantly, King comments in the video to the effect that the Witnesses never compromised with the Nazis; this is not what she had suggested earlier.[27] Specifically, she states: 'Jehovah's Witnesses did speak out [against Nazism]. They spoke out from the beginning. They spoke out with one voice. And they spoke out with tremendous courage, which has a message for all of us.' Equally significantly, Garbe claims that Jehovah's Witnesses were not anti-Semitic: 'Anti-Semitism bears characteristics of racism, and the last thing Jehovah's Witnesses would do was regard the Jews as being of less worth simply because of their origin. For them, all persons were of the same worth, were equal.' As for Milton, she asks rather leading questions that contrast what she considers to be the firm stand of Jehovah's Witnesses against Nazism with the position taken by members of other Christian religions.

As indicated above, 'Stand Firm' also contains a good deal of first-hand testimony from Jehovah's Witnesses who were jailed, or sent to concentration camps, or both. As in 'Purple Triangles,' the Kusserow family is highlighted as an example of Witness faithfulness. But in keeping with Watch Tower tradition, the video ignores all criticisms of Jehovah's Witnesses and Witness leaders. For example, it says not a word about the documents drawn from Gestapo records by *Der Spiegel* or about the book attributed to Manfred Gebhard which declares that, regardless of the circumstances, Erich Frost and other high German Watch Tower officials divulged information to the Gestapo, to the serious detriment of their Witness brethren. In fact, 'Stand Firm' has a Witness woman hum a few bars of the 'kingdom song' or hymn, 'Forward You Witnesses,' and points out that Frost composed it.

The production of 'Stand Firm' demonstrated the Watch Tower Society's effective use of other media besides print to spread its message and to blunt criticisms from both inside and outside the community. It also showed that the Witnesses were, for the first time, prepared to take a tack that has been employed consistently in recent decades by such new religious movements as the Unification Church

27 See pages 20 and 21 above.

(the Moonies) and the Church of Scientology. That is, it was now mobilizing the support of non-Witness scholars, notably historians, to support its position regarding the Witnesses' rôle in Nazi Germany and to blunt critics' attacks.

The Watch Tower Society has used 'Stand Firm' as the basis of a major propaganda campaign. In Europe, that video has been shown many times in tandem with first-hand accounts by concentration camp survivors. More recently, Jehovah's Witnesses in the United States have established a 'Stand Firm Organization' with its own website to promote special programs directed especially at judges, lawyers, and historians. It has successfully recruited a number of historians, and it has had Jewish Jehovah's Witness concentration camp survivors speak alongside those historians to promote the idea that the Witnesses were supportive of the Jews during the dark days of the Third Reich.

For all its loud claims that the Witnesses never attempted to compromise in any way with the Third Reich, it became obvious from an article published in the *Awake!* magazine of 8 July 1998 that criticisms of the Watch Tower Society's stand in 1933 were beginning to sting. In an article titled 'Jehovah's Witnesses Courageous in the Face of Nazi Peril,' the *Awake!* correspondent – probably Johannes Wrobel,[28] the Watch Tower's German archivist – wrote on page 10 of that issue:

No Compromise with Hitler

It was more than 50 years ago that Hitler's monstrous 12-year reign of racism and murder came to an end. Yet, the Nazi regime inflicted wounds that grieve humanity to this day.

History records that only a few groups courageously stood up and spoke out against Nazi terror. Among them were Jehovah's Witnesses, described as 'a tiny island of unflagging [moral] resistance existing in the bosom of a terrorized nation.' Their courageous stand is well documented by respected historians.

A few critics, however, including some former associates of Jehovah's Witnesses, charge that the Witnesses attempted to compromise with the Hitler regime in its early days. They claim that representatives of the Watch Tower Society tried unsuccessfully to curry favor with the new government

28 Wrobel makes statements in his article 'The Video Documentary "Jehovah's Witnesses Stand Firm against Nazi Assault": Propaganda or Historical Document?' in Hesse, *Persecution and Resistance,* 306, that are almost identical to those produced in the *Awake!* article 'Jehovah's Witnesses Courageous in the Face of Nazi Peril.'

and, that at least for a time, they endorsed the racist ideology of the Nazis, which eventually led to the murder of six million Jews.

These serious allegations are absolutely false. The following is a frank examination of the events in question, based on available documentation and historical context.

To buttress this argument, Wrobel (or whoever wrote this article) attacks 'critics' of the Watch Tower and Jehovah's Witnesses: 'For instance, critics claim that the Witnesses decorated the Wilmersdorf Tennishallen with swastika flags.'[29] He then asserts: 'Photographs of the 1933 convention show clearly that they displayed no swastikas in the hall. Eye witnesses confirm that there were no flags inside.'[30] He also states: 'Critics further state that the Witnesses opened the convention with the German National Anthem.'[31] Of course, in typical Watch Tower fashion, he does not name the critics, nor does he quote or cite them directly. Regarding the hymn the Witnesses used to open their 1933 convention, the anonymous author of the *Awake!* article says:

> Actually, the convention was opened with 'Zion's Glorious Hope,' Song 64 in the Witnesses religious songbook. The words of the song were set to music composed by Joseph Haydn in 1797. Song 64 had been in the Bible Student's songbook since at least 1905. In 1922 the German government adopted Haydn's melody with words by Hoffmann von Fallersleben as their national anthem. Nevertheless, the Bible students in Germany still sang their song 64 occasionally, as did Bible Students in other countries. The singing of a song about Zion could hardly be construed as an effort to placate the Nazis. Under pressure from anti-Semitic Nazis, other churches removed Hebrew terms such as 'Judah,' 'Jehovah,' and 'Zion' from their hymnals and liturgies. Jehovah's Witnesses did not. The convention organizers, then, certainly did not expect to win favor with the government by singing a song extolling Zion. Possibly, some delegates were reluctant to sing 'Zion's Glorious Hope,' since the melody of this composition by Haydn was the same as that of the national anthem.[32]

It is amazing how the author of the 'Courageous in the Face of Nazi Peril' deals with the *Declaration of Facts*. He quotes the following state-

29 *Awake!* 8 July 1998, 12.
30 Ibid.
31 Ibid.
32 Ibid., 12–13.

ment from that declaration: '*It has been the commercial Jews of the British-American Empire that have built up and carried on Big Business as a means of exploiting and oppressing the peoples of many lands*'[33] (italics in original). Then he asserts that this statement was in no way anti-Semitic:

> This statement clearly did not refer to the Jewish people in general, and it is regrettable if it has been misunderstood and has given any cause for offense. Some have claimed that Jehovah's Witnesses shared the hostility toward Jews that was commonly taught in the German churches at the time. This is absolutely untrue. By their literature and conduct during the Nazi era, the Witnesses rejected anti-Semitic views and condemned the Nazi mistreatment of the Jews. Certainly, the kindness toward Jews who shared in their lot in the concentration camps provides a resounding rebuttal to this false accusation.[34]

As was pointed out earlier, this *Awake!* author concedes that J.F. Rutherford, rather than the German Watch Tower branch director, Paul Balzereit, was the author of the *Declaration of Facts*. Furthermore, he is forced to confront the statement that appears in the *1974 Yearbook of Jehovah's Witnesses* to the effect that many present at the Berlin convention were unhappy with the declaration and regarded it as weak. To clear Rutherford of any blame, he tries a new approach: he suggests that the second Watch Tower president did not know how vicious the Nazis really were and that he was simply trying to deal with what he thought was a legitimate government. Thus, 'Courageous in the Face of Nazi Peril' states:

> On January 30, 1933, Adolf Hitler was appointed Germany's new chancellor. In the beginning, the Hitler government worked to conceal its violent and extremist nature. Hence, the Witnesses, along with millions of other Germans in early 1933, viewed the National Socialist Party as the legitimate ruling authority of the time. The Witnesses hoped that the National Socialist (Nazi) government would realize that this peaceable, lawabiding Christian group posed no subversive threat to the State. This was no offer to compromise Bible principles. As has been the case in other lands, the Witnesses wanted to inform the government of the true nonpolitical nature of their religion.[35]

33 Ibid., 13–14.
34 Ibid., 14.
35 Page 11.

'Courageous in the Face of Nazi Peril' deserves far more analysis, which it will receive in chapters 3 and 4. At this point it is important to note that it reflects not only the position of the Watch Tower Society but also that of several Witness and non-Witness historians. Detlef Garbe, Johannes Wrobel, Gabriele Yonan, and Guy Canonici are among those who take similar positions, in whole or in part.

Dr Detlef Garbe is by far the best known of these historians. His book *Zwischen Widerstand und Martyrium: Die Zeugen Jehovas in 'Dritten Reich'* (Between Opposition and Martyrdom: Jehovah's Witnesses in the 'Third Reich') gives the most complete, overall history of Jehovah's Witnesses during the Third Reich and contains a wealth of excellent information.[36] Originally written as a doctoral dissertation at the University of Hamburg in 1989, it has already been reprinted three times. Significantly, the two latest editions of the book have become more favourable to Jehovah's Witnesses. In those editions he now claims that a statement he made in the first two editions was based on a 'misunderstanding.' In those earlier editions he asserted – on the basis of what Konrad Franke said in his public talk on the history of Jehovah´s Witnesses in Germany – that there were swastika flags in the Wilmersdorf Tennis Hall when Jehovah's Witnesses held their 1933 convention, and that they opened their meeting with the German National Anthem. But in the latest edition of his book, on pages 103–4, footnote 71, he denies that this was the case:

> The assertion found in the first two editions of this book that the convention was 'opened with the German National anthem' is based on a misunderstanding. Also, the affirmation that the convention hall was draped with swastika flags cannot and should not be tolerated in the future. The reason for this is that in that [earlier] version, I based my [statements] on an audiotaped copy of a speech (partially published in the magazine 'Christian Quest,' 3, 1990, N. 1, P. 46f) by the former German branch servant Konrad Franke about which there are some doubts that do not allow further publication of that version. Pictures taken during the Bible Student convention in the Wilmersdorf Tennis Hall do not show any draped swastika flags, at least in the interior room. This is proved also by reports of Witnesses who were present on that day (based on information from Johannes Wrobel). Nevertheless, it is possible that the sports hall, rented by the Watch Tower Society for this event, was still draped outside with those flags because the

36 Garbe, *Zwischen Widerstand,* 4th ed. (Munich: R, Oldenbourg Verlag, 1999).

day before the summer solstice was celebrated in its immediate surroundings by the SA, the SS, and other National Socialist groups.[37]

Garbe has been strongly influenced by Johannes Wrobel in coming to these conclusions. This is evident from two facts: he goes into the same explanation with respect to the origin of the song 'Zion's Glorious Hope' (as does the *Awake!* magazine of 8 July 1998), and he attributes this information to Wrobel.[38]

Garbe also states that both Michael Kater and I are wrong in asserting that the Witnesses were anti-Semitic. He says regarding the *Declaration of Facts*:

> The fact that [allegations] can be found in the literature that Jehovah's Witnesses were representatives of a 'religiously motivated' (Kater, Jehovas Zeugen, page 187) 'clear anti-Semitism' (Penton Story, page 42 'outright anti-Semitism'), nevertheless misjudges the true nature of the statement that, although not free from polemic and verbal gaffes, cannot, however, be considered as part of the concept of racial hatred and anti-Semitism. In any case, at the level of ordinary plain religious folk [among Jehovah's Witnesses] the proclaimed admiration for the Jews was still effective until the beginning of the 1930s. During the Third Reich's persecution [of the Jews] that was similar to their own, Jehovah's Witnesses even felt sympathy for the Jews' situation, which was manifested, for example, by their shopping in Jewish stores despite the [Nazi] boycott.[39]

37 Ibid., 103–4, n71. The original German: 'Die in den beiden ersten Auflagen dieses Buches getroffene Feststellung, daß der Kongreß, "mit dem Deutschlandlied eingeleitet wurde", beruht auf einem Mißverständnis. Auch die Behauptung, "daß der Veranstaltungsort mit Hakenkreuzfahnen versehen war", kann und soll hier nicht mehr aufrechterhalten werden, da gegenüber dieser Darstellung, bei der ich mich auf eine Tonbandmitschrift eines (in der Zeitschrift "Christian Quest", 3, 1990, N. 1, S. 46f., auszugsweise publizierten) Vortrages des ehemaligen deutschen Zweigdieners Konrad Franke gestützt habe, zumindest Zweifel bestehen, die eine weitere Kolportage der Darstellung nicht angezeigt sein lassen. So weisen Fotos, die augenscheinlich von dem IBV-Kongreß in der Wilmersdorfer Tennishalle stammen, zumindest für den Innenraum keine Hakenkreuzbeflaggung auf, was auch durch weitere Zeitzeugenberichte gestüzt wird (UaP Johannes Wrobel). Allerdings ist es sehr wohl möglich, daß die von der WTG angemietete Sporthalle, in deren unmittelbarer Umgebung noch am Vortag SA, SS und andere NS-Formationen Sonnenwendfeier zelebrierten (vgl Christofffel Wilmersdorf, S. 269) von außen mit Hakenkreuzfahnen versehen war.'

38 Ibid., 103, especially n70.

39 Garbe states in German: 'Die gelegentlich in Literatur zu findende Feststellung, die

As already mentioned, he has made the same assertion in the 'Stand Firm' video.

In a recent article titled 'Social Disinterest, Governmental Disinformation, Renewed Persecution, and Now Manipulation of History,'[40] Garbe asserts that Jehovah's Witnesses 'are among the so-called forgotten victims of the Nazi regime.'[41] Unlike the Watch Tower Society, he has also attempted to rehabilitate Erich Frost's reputation – and, indirectly, that of Konrad Franke – in relation to the charge that they 'treasonably' gave information to the Gestapo at the expense of their Witness brethren. On the basis of information – no doubt supplied by Johannes Wrobel – that will be discussed later, he attacks the 1961 article in *Der Spiegel*. That article stated that Frost was briefly released from prison after his initial arrest in 1936, even though he clearly was not. According to Garbe, *Der Spiegel* was insinuating that Frost's consignment to a work camp in the Elmslandmoor – where life was supposedly somewhat less trying than in prison – was because he had divulged information to the Gestapo. Thus Garbe charges *Der Spiegel* with using 'cynical language' in describing Frost's imprisonment.[42] He also censures the East German book attributed to Manfred Gebhard for claiming that Frost gave information to the Gestapo voluntarily; Garbe himself asserts that according to Frost, he was severely interrogated, beaten, and roused from unconsciousness by being doused with buckets of water.[43]

Some former Jehovah's Witnesses in Germany believe that Garbe has become a convert to the Witness movement. That seems far-fetched,

---

Zeugen Jehovas seien Vertreter eines "religiös motivierten" (Kater, Bibelforscher, S. 187) bzw. "Klaren Antisemitismus" (Penton, Story, S. 42 "outright anti-Semitism") gewesen, verkennt allerdings den Charakter der Auseinandersetzung, die zwar nicht frei von Polemik und verbalen Entgleisungen war, sich aber deswegen gleichwohl nicht unter dem Rassenhass implizierenden Begriff "Antisemitismus" subsumieren läßt. Auf der Ebene der einfachen Glaubensangehörigen wirkte ohnehin noch die bis Anfang der dreißiger Jahre verkündete Wertschätzung der Juden nach; in der Verfolgungssituation des "Dritten Reiches" äußerte sich bei Zeugen Jehovas aufgrund gleichartiger Ehrfahrungen eher Mitgefühl für deren Lage, das sich beispielsweise in Einkauf bei jüdischen Geschäfen trotz Boycott zeigen konnte.' Garbe, *Zwischen Widerstand und Martyrium*, 105n80.

40 Published in Hesse, *Persecution and Resistance*, 251–65.

41 Ibid., 251.

42 Ibid., 260.

43 Ibid., 260, 265n55. See also Manfred Gebhard, *Geschichte der Zeugen Jehovas: Mit Scherpunkt der deutschen Geschichte* (Berlin: Libri Books on Demand, 1999), 182.

however, for Garbe has recently stated: 'As a non-Witness, I have engaged myself academically over ten years with the history of Jehovah's Witnesses. My critical reserve toward ... the doctrinal and organizational structure of the Watchtower Society remains unaltered.'[44] Additionally, in both *Zwischen Widerstand und Martyrium* and the article just quoted, Garbe makes a number of criticisms of Jehovah's Witness conduct during the Third Reich that no loyal Jehovah's Witness would willingly make. Nevertheless, it is quite clear that on certain issues he has become an important albeit naive apologist for the Witnesses and for the Watch Tower Society in particular. For example, besides parroting Watch Tower claims that the *Declaration of Facts* was not anti-Semitic, he has adopted the Witnesses' unfounded assertion that they were long 'forgotten victims' of the Nazi Holocaust.[45] He has collaborated rather uncritically with Johannes Wrobel, the Watch Tower Society's German archivist, as can be seen from the way that Wrobel has influenced him with regard to the Berlin-Wilmersdorf convention and from the fact that the two regularly quote and cite each other in their works.

Wrobel's article 'The Video Documentary "Stand Firm against Nazi Assault": Propaganda or Historical Document?'[46] is an extremely pro-Jehovah's Witness apologia and quite evidently was written for the academic community. The first sections of this article are devoted to defending the video against its critics. Perhaps, however, the most relevant sections of it come later.

In one of these later sections, subheaded 'Falsification of History or Historical Accuracy,' Wrobel uses Garbe's denial that the Witnesses draped the Wilmersdorf Tennis Hall with swastikas and that they opened the June 1933 convention with the German National Anthem as a basis for denying that the Witnesses were less than 'neutral' at the time. He points out that in the third edition of *Zwischen Widerstand und Martyrium,* Garbe corrected a statement he had made in the first two editions of that work. However, Wrobel does not blame Garbe for admittedly having given 'misinformation' that had been repeated by American historian, Francis L. Carsten: he blames it on *Gegner* (opposers). Furthermore, in the same note he points directly to my article in *The Christian Quest,* which in the original German edition of

44 Garbe, 'Social Disinterest, Governmental Disinformation, Renewed Persecution, and Now Manipulation of History,' 262.

45 For an evaluation of this assertion, see pages 95–9 below.

46 This article appears in Hesse, *Persecution and Resistance,* on pages 306–31.

his article he haughtily dismisses as an 'ominous English publication' (*einer ominösen englischen Veröffentlichung*).[47] In the rather poor English translation of the note, he states:

> Francis L. Carsten wrote, in his otherwise remarkable essay about the religious association that, 'among the opponents of the Nazi regime pride of place in many ways belongs to the religious sect which called itself Jehovah's Witnesses': 'A mass meeting held in Berlin in June [1933] with five or six thousand [Jehovah's Witness] participants began with the singing of the German national anthem and the hall was decorated with swastika flags.' (Carsten, *Widerstand gegen Hitler: Die deutsche Arbeiter und die Nazis*, Frankfurt and Leipzig, 1996 [English in 1995], ch. 7, 'Jehovah's Witnesses.') F.L. Carsten based this statement on the first edition of Detlef Garbe's book *Zwischen Widerstand und Martyrium* (Munich, 1993), pp. 84f. Garbe, on the other hand, refers to an article in *The Christian Quest*, a dubious publication which is, undoubtedly, published by opponents of Jehovah's Witnesses but which could not be established as a publication in any North American library.[48]

Under the same subheading, Wrobel also attempts to discredit completely what is published in the work attributed to Manfred Gebhard, *Die Zeugen Jehovas: Eine Dokumentation über die Wachtturmgesellschaft*. He points to certain exaggerations and false statements in what is often called 'the Urania book,' such as its claim that the 1933 Wilmersdorf-Berlin convention was an 'antisemitic and pro-fascist convention' and the statement that J.F. Rutherford really did not take a stand against Nazism until 1938. He quotes Detlef Garbe as stating: '"This book, published under the name of Manfred Gebhard, but compiled by anonymous authors with the assistance of the [East German Communist] Ministry for State Security, clearly takes prescribed ideological conclusions into account" and is characterized by a "selective use of sources" and "distorted quotations."'[49] Wrobel then quotes briefly

47 For the German original see Johannes Wrobel, 'Die Videodokumentation "Stadhaft trotz Verfolgung" – Propaganda oder zeitgeschichtliches Dokument?' in Hans Hesse, ed., *'Am mutigsten waren immer wieder die Zeugen Jehovas: Verfolgung und Widerstand der Zeugen Jehovas in Nationalsozialismus,'* (Bremen: Edition Temmen, 1998), 375n32.

48 Wrobel, 'Video Documentary,' 322n32.

49 Ibid., 310.

from a letter by Gebhard to Dieter Pape, who had evidently served as a ghostwriter for *Die Zeugen Jehovas.* Gebhard is quoted as having written to Pape: 'I have already stated elsewhere that my role in the Urania book was mainly as editor (which is not identical to author). I let you know this as you are frankly also concerned. Based on what I know today, I would *not* give my name for it again. [*sic*] I am accusing you of distorting history (probably because of the worst kind of toadying to your bosses) ... But also your citations on "anti-Communism" also seem questionable to me.'[50] Significantly, however, Wrobel makes no attempt to deal with the many specific documents published in *Die Zeugen Jehovas.*

Perhaps Wrobel's strangest arguments relate to his efforts to clear the Witnesses of charges of anti-Semitism. After quoting those portions of the *Declaration of Facts* and the Watch Tower letter to Hitler which seem clearly to indicate that Jehovah's Witnesses – at the very least, their leaders – had a negative attitude toward the Jews – he goes on to assert that these comments applied only to Jewish businessmen and not to all Jews. Because these remarks undoubtedly served as the basis for similar claims in the *Awake!* article 'Courageous in the Face of Nazi Peril,' they deserve careful analysis.

The portion from the *Declaration of Facts* that Wrobel quotes reads:

> It is falsely charged by our enemies that we have received financial support for our work from the Jews. Nothing is farther from the truth. Up to this hour there never has been the slightest bit of money contributed to our work by Jews. We are the faithful followers of Christ Jesus and believe upon Him as the Savior of the world, whereas the Jews entirely reject Jesus Christ and emphatically deny that he is the Savior of the world sent of God for man's good. This of itself should be sufficient proof to show that we receive no support from Jews and that therefore the charges against us are maliciously false and could proceed only from Satan, our great enemy.
>
> The greatest and most oppressive empire on earth is the Anglo-American empire. By that is meant the British Empire, of which the United States of America forms a part. It has been the *commercial Jews* of the British-American empire that have built up and carried on Big Business as a means of exploiting and oppressing the peoples of many nations. This fact particularly applies to the cities of London and New York, the stronghold of Big Business. This fact is so manifest in America that there is a proverb

50 Ibid.

> concerning the city of New York which says: 'The Jews own it, the Irish Catholics rule it, and the Americans pay the bills.' We have no fight with any of these persons mentioned, but, as the witnesses for Jehovah and in obedience to his commandment set forth in the Scriptures, we are compelled to call attention to the truth concerning the same in order that the people may be enlightened concerning God and his purpose.[51]

Wrobel also quotes as follows, with italics added by him, from the Watch Tower letter sent personally to Hitler along with a copy of the declaration:

> In the same manner the President of our Society, during the last months, has not only refused to take part in the propaganda against Germany, but he has taken [a] position even against it, as is also emphasized in the enclosed Declaration by calling attention to the fact that those who, in America, take the lead in the 'German cruelties' propaganda (namely *business Jews* and Catholics) are also the greatest persecutors of the work of our Society and its President in America. *By these and other facts laid down in the Declaration, the slander that the Bible Students are supported by the Jews is refuted.*[52]

To explain these comments away, Wrobel presents a number of arguments. He notes that the Hitler letter was not written by Rutherford but rather by the Watch Tower manager in Magdeburg (Paul Balzereit). He then claims that the latter was not pointing to the Jews in general but to commercial Jews in London and New York. He says this position is underlined by the American maxim to the effect that the Jews own New York.[53] He holds further that by the above statements, the Witnesses were simply trying to dissociate themselves from charges that they were receiving Jewish contributions to help establish a Jewish super-state. He says: 'The vehement attacks on Jehovah's Witnesses through opponents had already led to government prohibitions in Germany. They were accused of being financed by "Jews," so that they could set up a supposed Jewish world power. German Jehovah's Witnesses vehemently responded to this slander and emphatically repudiated it. They used clear language in order to distin-

51 Ibid., 317. This statement, as it appears in Wrobel's article, comes originally from page 134 of the English edition of the *1934 Year Book of Jehovah's Witnesses*. The words 'commercial Jews' are not italicized in the *Year Book*.

52 Wrobel, 317–18. No italics appear in the original Watch Tower letter to Hitler.

53 *1934 Year Book*, 318.

guish between their non-commercial activities and the activities of their alleged Jewish sponsors.'[54]

Wrobel recognizes that the language used in both the declaration and the Hitler letter with respect to the Jews is, in the present era, quite incriminating. He therefore remarks: 'Their statement of that time can today be easily misunderstood as antisemitic, if one ignores the historical context and takes quotations out of context.'[55] So in order to prove that the Witnesses were in no sense anti-Semitic at the time, he claims that the term 'commercial Jews' – *'Handelsjuden,'* in the German version of the declaration – applied only to those Jews who were guilty of exploiting others – such as the commercial Jews of New York, and not to all Jews. He says as well that the term 'business Jews' or *'Geschäftsjuden'* was an anachronism taken from nineteenth-century German that did not imply hostility toward the Jews in general. According to him, neither of these terms signifies anti-Semitism as such, nor was the German word *Geschäftsjuden* taken from the vocabulary of National Socialism.[56] To sum up his argument, the Watch Tower archivist declares: 'It is safe to say that Jehovah's Witnesses had neither hatred nor enmity toward Jews and that they never had any resentment toward them. The video documentary Stand Firm against Nazi Assault is not guilty of misusing history and outlines the relationship of Jehovah's Witnesses to the Jews in a concrete historical context.'[57]

On another issue, Wrobel takes a very strange tack. He argues that there is a misunderstanding regarding the Witnesses' position toward secular governments. Here he is perhaps trying to explain away criticisms respecting the presence of swastikas at the Wilmersdorf Tennis Hall and the alleged singing of the German National Anthem at the 1933 Berlin convention. His comments may also be an attempt to explain away the rather fawning remarks made to the Nazis – and to Hitler in particular – in the *Declaration of Facts* and in the Watch Tower letter to the *Führer.* He says: 'One misunderstanding in connection with the Berlin convention may be due to the notion that Jehovah's Witnesses reject all governments, and believe that all governments originate with the Devil. Jehovah's Witnesses do not and did not hold such a view.'[58] He next asserts that this concept is based on a faulty

54 Ibid.
55 Ibid.
56 Ibid., 317–16, 330n88, 331n89.
57 Ibid., 318.
58 Ibid., 311.

understanding of Bible Student teaching that was promoted by the churches in the 1920s and 1930s and is still extant in the literature.[59] Then, using Watch Tower teaching which was developed in 1962, and which echoed that of C.T. Russell rather than that of J.F. Rutherford,[60] Wrobel holds that the Witnesses taught that Jehovah had given temporal authority to the rulers of the earth, who are to be respected until the full establishment of Christ's kingdom:

> These 'superior authorities' merit their obedience and respect. (Romans, chapter 13, verse 1) But when a government breaks God's law and, for example, initiates the murder of Jews, Jehovah's Witnesses deny it (the authorities) their obedience and instead follow their Christian conscience. This seems to be a valuable lesson in loyalty toward the State. Since this view of relative obedience to the authorities is Biblically founded, it should not be surprising that similar positions can be found also in some Protestant and Catholic biblical commentaries and catechisms. The difference between many members of the major churches and Jehovah's Witnesses is that the Witnesses have lived up to this ethical view by 'standing firm despite persecution.'[61]

Wrobel is aware that in Hitler's time the Watch Tower Society taught that the higher powers of Romans 13:1 were Jehovah God and Christ Jesus rather than the rulers of the nations. Nonetheless, he holds that they still had respect for secular rulers, and he asserts that the fundamental attitude of Jehovah's Witnesses did not change after 1962.[62] In taking this position, he is simply parroting what *The Watchtower,* which he quotes, has said dishonestly.[63]

Finally, in an extended endnote, Wrobel attacks the authors of two negative German reviews of the 'Stand Firm' video. He quotes Hans-Jürgen Twisselmann as claiming in the *Materialdienst* of the Evangelische Zentrale für Weltanschauungsfragen (the Protestant Center for Ideological Questions) that the video conceals the fact that at the time of the 1933 Witness convention, the Berlin-Wilmersdorf Ten-

59 Ibid.

60 For a full discussion of these teachings, see M. James Penton, 'Jehovah's Witnesses and the Secular State: A Historical Analysis of Doctrine,' *Journal of Church and State* 21(1), 1979: 55–72.

61 Wrobel, 'Video Documentary,' 311–12.

62 Ibid., 312, 326n52.

63 WT, 1 October 1966, 608.

nis Hall was decorated with swastikas; and as also claiming that J.F. Rutherford sought accommodation with the Nazis and that when this was not forthcoming he changed course and confronted them. Wrobel also claims that Twisselmann has charged the Watch Tower Society with 'marketing martyrs' by distributing the 'Stand Firm' video, and that the video itself is propaganda. Wrobel also quotes Eckhard Türk in an article in the *Mainzer Bistumsnachrichten.* Therein, Türk stated that the 'Stand Firm' video says nothing about the Watch Tower's efforts to curry favour with Hitler by addressing him as Hochverehreten Reichkanzler Adolf Hitler (Most Honorable Reich Chancellor Adolf Hitler), that the same video intentionally forgets that the Wilmersdorf Tennis Hall was decorated with swastikas, and that after failing to get what he wanted from the Nazis, Rutherford called for the martyrdom of servile German Jehovah's Witnesses.

In answer to these reviews, Wrobel states simply that Twisselmann is 'off course' for having suggested that the 'Stand Firm' video, given away freely, markets martyrs. To Türk, however, he offers a more extended reply. He makes the point, quite rightly – whether it makes much difference or not – that the Watch Tower letter to Hitler opened with the complementary salutation *Sehr verehrter Herr Riechskanzler* (Very Honourable Mr Reich Chancellor) rather than *Hochverehrten Reichkanzler Adolf Hitler.* Then he notes that the Watch Tower letter did not use the title *Führer* in addressing Hitler, which he seems to regard as a major plus in the Witnesses' favour.[64]

In an earlier work, Wrobel does report something quite significant that deserves further analysis. This relates to the supposed 'treason' of Erich Frost while he was under interrogation by the Gestapo. In this publication, which in English translation reads *The Video Documentary 'Stand Firm despite Persecution: Jehovah's Witnesses under the National Socialist Regime.' A Commentary,* he quotes from a letter sent by Ludwig Cyranek to the Swiss branch offices of the Watch Tower Society in Bern dated 2 April 1939. It describes the type of torture to which the Gestapo subjected prisoners under interrogation, especially those being held at Gestapo Central Headquarters in Berlin. He also quotes from an unpublished autobiography written by Frost himself wherein the latter relates how terribly he was treated. According to Frost, he was beaten so severely that on three occasions he lost consciousness and had to be roused by buckets of cold water. A woman was shocked

64 Wrobel, 322–3n35.

by his appearance when the Gestapo presented him to her to ascertain whether she knew him. As a result of the torture, he could neither sit nor stand for a time. He was horrified when he looked at himself in a mirror. He was in so much agony that he cried out to Jehovah to release him from his pain by letting him die. The Nazi police may have spiked his food with a drug to make him unaware of how and when he gave them information concerning the Witnesses' underground activities.[65] All of this Frost claimed.

Most interestingly, Wrobel quotes Frost regarding a conversation he had with Watch Tower president N.H. Knorr. As translated, that account reads: 'I questioned Brother Knorr whether I should do something about these accusations [as they had appeared in *Der Spiegel*]. However, he told me, "No, Brother Frost! Would you believe how many accusations are made against me. We give them no attention. We put them in File D. We set them aside and take no time to read them."'[66]

Dr Gabriele Yonan is another important Watch Tower apologist. She has a doctorate from the University of Haifa in Israel, has published books on Aramaic-speaking Christians (Assyrians) in the Middle East, and is currently reader and counsellor at the Institute of the Max Planck Society for Promoting Science and Education. Besides being an academic defender of Jehovah's Witnesses, she has been active on behalf of the Church of Scientology in its European struggles.[67] None of this, however, bears on what she has to say about Jehovah's Witnesses except that it suggests she has become a regular defender of those whom she regards as oppressed and marginalized. What *is* important is that she has written a book titled *Jehovas Zeugen – Opfer unter zwei deutschen Dictaturen: 1933–1945, 1949–1989* (Jehovah's Witnesses – Victims under Two German Dictatorships: 1933–1945, 1949–1989),[68] an article titled 'History, Past and Present: Jehovah's Witnesses

65 *Die Videodokumentation 'Standhaft troz Verfolgung: Jehovas Zeugen unter dem NS-regime' Eine Stellungnahme* (Stelters/Taunus: self-published, 1997), 13, 14.

66 Ibid. The original of this account reads: 'Ich hatte über diese Anschuldigungen Bruder Knorr befragt, ob ich vielleicht etwas tun sollte. Doch er sagte mir: "Nein, laß das sein, Bruder Frost! Was glaubst du, wie viele Anschuldigungen gegen mich gemacht werden. Wir schenken solchen keine Aufmerksamkeit. We put them in the file, d.h. wir legen sie ab, aber haben keine Zeit, sie zu lesen."'

67 This has been reported on various websites, including those favourable to the Church of Scientology.

68 Gabriele Yonan, *Jehovas Zeugen – Opfer unter zwei deutschen Dictaturen: 1933–45, 1949–1989* (Berlin: Numinos, 1999).

in Germany. An Analysis of the Documentary "Stand Firm against Nazi Assault" from the Perspective of Religious Studies,'[69] and an article in the *Journal of Church and State,* 'Spiritual Resistance of Christian Conviction in Nazi Germany: The Case of the Jehovah's Witnesses.'[70] This last- mentioned article is to all intents and purposes a somewhat shortened version of her earlier article, which appeared in the German edition of Hesse's *Persecution and Resistance.*

In her two articles, Yonan presents many of the same arguments she makes in *Jehovas Zeugen – Opfer unter Zwei deutschen Dictaturen.* Those arguments are virtually identical to those of the Watch Tower Society itself, and they express much the same hostility to the churches. She really differs from the Society only in her description of the now famous (or infamous) *Declaration of Facts.* She calls it 'a petition,' an 'appeal,' and a 'sermon' rather than a 'protest' or an attempt to explain.[71] Otherwise she is a thoroughgoing apologist for the Watch Tower and for Jehovah's Witnesses. She says, for example: 'There was one Christian group which rejected the Nazi state without compromise: Jehovah's Witnesses, or Earnest Bible Students as they were then known.'[72] But more important are her remarks regarding the 1933 Berlin-Wilmersdorf Witness convention and the *Declaration of Facts*:

> As the situation for Jehovah's Witnesses clearly continued to grow worse (on June 24, 1933, Prussia also issued a ban on their activities), the Watch Tower Society, together with its German branch office, decided to hold a large convention in Berlin-Wilmersdorf. The 7,000 delegates in attendance adopted a Declaration which spoke out against the false charges of seditious activity and emphasized the political neutrality of Jehovah's Witnesses. This resolution was addressed to Reich Chancellor Adolf Hitler in the form of a petition, an appeal.
>
> The churches in Germany today criticize the Witnesses that this Declaration represented an attempt by Jehovah's Witnesses to 'curry the favor' of Hitler and the Nazi state, and that it included antisemitic statements. They claim that it was only after the failure of this attempt that Jehovah's Witnesses rebelled against the Nazi regime. The charges climax in the

69 Published in Hesse, *Persecution and Resistance,* 332–42.

70 *Journal of Church and State* (Spring 1999), as posted by the *Encyclopedia Britannica* on www.britannica.com.

71 Yonan, 'History Past and Present,' 339; 'Spiritual Resistance,' 8, 9.

72 Yonan, 'History, Past and Present,' 337.

accusation that the American Watch Tower office and its president, J.F. Rutherford, had knowingly sacrificed the German Jehovah's Witnesses and pushed them onto a road that would inevitably lead to martyrdom.

A textual analysis of the actual document examines these charges:

> The excerpts and passages quoted from the Declaration create the impression that it is primarily a justification, conforming to the Nazi system, and an expression of their anti-Jewish attitude. This, however, is a falsification of the facts. From a secular point of view, the document is a 'sermon' or pronouncement directed to the addressee, Reich Chancellor Hitler himself. [*sic*] It was a clear renunciation of secular power but assumed suggestively that surely even Hitler sought the good, that he had to seek the good. But it also proclaimed that if this should prove not to be the case, then the Reich Chancellor and Führer of the German people belonged to Satan's kingdom. Then Hitler was an enemy of Jehovah and his Witnesses. These straightforward statements left the Reich Chancellor with only two possible conclusions: Either the Declaration was the product of collective delusions by a religious group, or it was a crazy, brazen declaration of war from a Biblical David against a Goliath.[73]

Shortly after this, Yonan goes on to make what can only be described, by those who have read the *Declaration of Facts* and who know something of the history of Jehovah's Witnesses in Germany, as an astonishing statement: 'If Hitler ever read this Declaration personally, the result must certainly have been one of his renowned fits of rage. The words, "This brood will be exterminated in Germany!," which according to the Witnesses he exclaimed in such a moment, have the ring of authenticity.'[74]

In her next paragraph, Yonan continues: 'When the entire text of the Declaration of June 25, 1933, and the letter to Hitler are seen today in the context of the history of Jehovah's Witnesses in Nazi Germany, the history of their religious resistance, and their stand during the Holocaust, then the text does not reveal itself as an "antisemitic statement" or an attempt at "currying Hitler's favor." These accusations emanate from contemporary church circles and are deliberate manipulations and falsifications of history, seemingly motivated by discomfort about their moral mediocrity.'[75]

73 Ibid., 338–9.

74 Ibid., 340. Hitler's statement was not made as a response to the *Declaration of Facts*, but rather to Witness telegrams sent to him in the fall of 1934. For further information on this see pages 166, 167.

75 Ibid.

Finally, there is one important issue that Yonan deals with in her book, *Jehovas Zeugen – Opfer unter zwei deutschen Dictaturen,* that she does not discuss in her two articles. She claims that the article in *Der Spiegel* which 'exposed' Erich Frost was planted by Communists in the former German Democratic Republic (East Germany) and therefore has no basis in fact.[76] It has not been proved that the source of the German newsmagazine's information was someone working for the Communist regime, but it may well have been the case. But whether it was or not, this contention does not weaken the validity of the Gestapo documents, which are evidently quite genuine.

Guy Canonici, a senior Watch Tower official and an officer of the Cercle Européen des Témoins de Jéhovah Anciens Déportés et Internés, has tried to do in French essentially what Garbe, Wrobel, and Yonan have attempted to do in German – and, in the case of Yonan, in English as well. That is, he has tried to clear Jehovah's Witnesses of any and all blame for their conduct during the Third Reich. In his book, *Les Témoins de Jéhovah face à Hitler* (Jehovah's Witnesses Face Hitler),[77] he makes many of the same assertions as found in the 8 July 1998 *Awake!* and in the works of the three German apologists for Jehovah's Witness discussed immediately above. Canonici has done considerable useful, independent research besides relying heavily on Garbe and Wrobel; that said, except in one instance he has slavishly followed Watch Tower interpretations.

Concerning that one issue, he admits that it was Konrad Franke, rather than 'opposers,' who was the first to claim that there were swastika flags in the Wilmersdorf Tennis Hall when Jehovah's Witnesses met there in 1933. Canonici remarks: 'Konrad Franke, in attendance that day, was disturbed by the sight of bent crosses [swastikas] that decorated the halls.' Yet immediately after that statement he says: 'Without doubt, he must have felt better upon noticing that there were none in the room where the meeting took place.'[78] In support of his conclusion, he claims: 'Konrad Franke, who seems to remember one of two flags [*sic*], speaks of *die Hallen,* that is to say the halls, being bedecked with them.' Then he resorts to the argument that photos of the convention room do not show the presence of swastika flags, and

76 Yonan, *Jehovas Zeugen,* 96–9.

77 Guy Canonici, with a Preface by François Bédarida, *Les Témoins de Jéhovah face à Hitler* (Paris: Albin Michel, 1998).

78 'Konrad Franke, présent ce jour-là, éprouve de la gene a la vue des croix gammée qui decorant les halls. Il doute se sentir plus a l'aise en observant qu'il n'y en pas dans la salle où ils reunissent.' Ibid., 122.

reminds us of Detlef Garbe's point that if there had been flags on the exterior of the building, the Witnesses would have accepted their presence there.[79] Finally, he quotes Walter Jurish of Augsburg, who was a Witness worker at the German Watch Tower headquarters in Magdeburg in 1933, and who also denies that there were any swatikas there.[80]

Like Garbe, Wrobel, and the 8 July 1998 *Awake!* Canonici goes into a long and irrelevant explanation of the origins of the Bible Student–Witness hymn, 'Zion's Glorious Hope,' and of 'Deutschland über alles.'[81] Like *Awake!* he notes that Konrad Franke and others present at the Berlin convention had difficulty joining in the singing of this hymn, which for some years in Germany had rarely been heard. Yet he adds that Franke hedged his remarks by stating that the words to it were good. After noting this, he comes to the same conclusion as does the article 'Jehovah's Witnesses Courageous in the Face of Nazi Peril.' He claims that the singing of 'Zion's Glorious Hope' – because of the reference to Zion in its title – was in no way an attempt to placate the Nazis. In fact, he goes even farther than *Awake!* by stating that it was actually 'a challenge.'[82]

Canonici's analysis of the *Declaration of Facts* is fascinating. Following a practice resorted to in many Watch Tower publications, he is liberal with the use of ellipses when statements in a quoted text could be embarrassing. He says: 'Those attending the [1933 Berlin] convention adopted an *Erklärung* (Declaration).' Then he immediately goes on to provide an extremely eviscerated, one-paragraph version of that document, with sentences or partial sentences of the original taken from hither, thither, and yon and divided by numerous ellipses.[83] This

79 'Konrad Franke, qui semble n'avior retenu la présence que d'un seul des deux drapeaux, en parle comme decorant *die Hallen,* cete-à-dire les halls. Les photos de l'intérieur ne revelent pas le presence du svastika ... Garbe précise que si le hall était pavoisé a l'extérieur, les témoins de Jéhovah, en tant que locataires, ont du accepte tacitement ce fait.' Ibid., 415n3.

80 '"Es ist nicht wahr, dass sich Hakenkreutzfahnen sich gegenseitig Zuschwenken in Kongress-Saal befunden hätten." Attestation produite le 4 mars 1990. Document archives WBTG.' Ibid., 414–15n5.

81 Pages 415–16n7.

82 'En pleine période d'antisionisme et d'antisémitisme, ce chant pouvait être interprété comme un défi.' Ibid., 123.

83 The following is Canonici's full, French-language quotation from the *Declaration of Facts:* 'Le but de cette "Declaration" est de donner aux gouvernements et aux gouvernés un témoignage véridique et sincère ... Nous avons êté faussement

gives a false (because incomplete) impression of what the declaration was about. It is true that in an endnote, rather than in the main text of his book, he deals with one of the most clearly compromising statements in the declaration. But he tries to excuse J.F. Rutherford for having written it by saying that it was addressed to a 'coalition' government rather than to the Nazis specifically. Then he asserts that the principles the Witnesses adhered to along with the German government were those touching on Big Business and anticlericalism. Accordingly, Canonici says:

> Some sentences of this Declaration have been quoted outside their context. For example, this quote: 'Instead of being against the principles advocated by the government of Germany, we stand squarely for such principles, and point out that Jehovah God through Christ Jesus will bring about the full realization of these principles and will give the people peace and prosperity and the greatest desire of every honest heart.' This letter [*sic*], addressed to the government of the coalition [*sic*], made reference to the 'principles' which are the struggle against 'the oppression exercised by Big Business oppressors and in opposition to the wrongful religious influence in the political affairs of the nation' concerning which, it said further that ecclesiastical politicians have given more grave inquietude to the German people over recent years than any other group.[84]

---

accusés auprès des autorités gouvernementales du peuple allemand ... Nos ennemis ont faussement prétendu que notre activité était soutenue financièrement par les Juifs ... Nous somme de fidèles deciples de Jésus-Christ, et croyons en lui comme Sauver du monde. Les Juifs, par contre, rejettent complètement Jésus-Christ et nient absolutment qu'il est le Sauveur ... ce fait devrait à lui seul démontrer que nous ne sommes pas soutenus par les Juifs, et que les accusations lancées contre nous sont fausses ... Notre organisation n'est nullement politique ... Nous réclamons le droit d'enseigner et de croire ce que nous prenons pour l'ensiegnement biblique. Il est par conséquent impossible que nos écrits et notre activité puissent mettre en danger l'ordre public et la sûreté du pays ... Nous faisons appel par conséquent à l'esprit de justice des dirigeants du pays, et demandons respectuesement que l'interdiction qui pèse sur notre activité et sur nos imprimés soit levée et que l'occasion nous soit offerte d'être entendus de façon impartiale, avant de être condamnés.' Ibid., 124.

84 'Quelques phrases de cette déclaration ont ete parfois citées hors de leur contexte. Ansi cette citation: "Loin de prendre position contre les princips répresentés par le gouvernment allemand, nous les approuvons entièrement et indiquons que Jéhovah Dieu, par Christ Jésus, apportera la réalisation totale de ces principes, donnera la paiz et la prospérité au peuple et exaucera les voex les plus chers de tous les cours sincères." Cette lettre, adressée au gouvernement du coalition, fait re référence aux "principes" que sont lutte contre "l'oppression exercée par la grand négoce et les

Like the three German Watch Tower apologists, Canonici responds defensively to all criticisms levelled against the Watch Tower Society, in particular with regard to the 1933 Berlin-Wilmersdorf convention. However, instead of trying to defend the Society directly, he chooses to refer to what Garbe has written in recent editions of *Zwischen Widerstand und Martirium.*[85]

Finally, some reference must be made to the fact that others besides the Watch Tower Society and Detlef Garbe have argued that the travails of the Witnesses under the Third Reich have, at least until recently, been practically forgotten. This contention appears in articles by Christopher Daxelmüller,[86] Sybil Milton,[87] and Wolfram Slupina.[88] Naturally, it deserves analysis, which will be provided in chapter 3.

Such then are the positions taken by the Watch Tower Society and its major apologists. What is needed now is a careful analysis of these apologies to determine whether they are defensible.

influences religieuses perverses dans les affairs politiques de l'Etat" à propos desquels il est dit plus loin "que les ecclésiastiques politiques ont donné plus d'inquiétudes au peuple allemand, au cours des dernières annés, que n'importe quel groupment."' Ibid., 416n9.

85 Ibid., 414n2.

86 'Solidarity and the Will to Survive: Religious and Social Behavior of Jehovah's Witnesses in Concentration Camps,' in Hesse, *Persecution and Resistance,* 23.

87 'Jehovah's Witnesses as Forgotten Victims,' in Hesse, *Persecution and Resistance,* 141–8.

88 'Persecuted and Almost Forgotten,' in Hesse, *Persecution and Resistance,* 266–92.

3

Evaluating the Arguments and the Evidence

> Let God be true though every man be false, as it is written, 'That thou mayest be justified in thy words, and prevail when thou art judged.'
> Romans 3:4 RSV

What the information just surveyed indicates is that the Watch Tower Society wants to blunt any and all criticisms respecting the 1933 Berlin-Wilmersdorf convention. In particular, it is anxious to deny that Jehovah's Witnesses were in any way anti-Semitic and that they made any attempt to ingratiate themselves with the Nazi government of Adolf Hitler. The Society has attempted to cloud the issue by emphasizing the later martyrdom of many Witnesses and by arguing that from the beginning they stood four-square and united in their stand against Hitler. In these claims they have been more than happy to use the statements of various scholars. How then, do their assertions and those of their academic apologists stand up?

In the first place, it is obvious that what Christine King states in the 'Stand Fast' video to the effect that Jehovah's Witnesses 'spoke out from the beginning' and 'with one voice' is simply false. Dietrich Hellmund notes: 'Dr. King is *not* correct, when she is quoted on the cover of the blurb of the video stating: "Jehovah's Witnesses spoke out from the beginning. They spoke out with one voice. And they spoke out with tremendous courage." With tremendous courage – yes. With one voice? I am not certain.'[1] King's mistake is evident from the *Decla-*

1 Dietrich Hellmund, 'Critical Reflection on the Video Documentary "Stand Firm against Nazi Assault": Propaganda or Historical Documentation,' in Hans Hesse,

ration of Facts and from the June 1933 Watch Tower letter to Hitler; it is also clear that a great many ordinary German Witnesses did not want to provoke the Nazi authorities by defying the bans on their religious activities. They were therefore opposed to carrying on the preaching work that J.F. Rutherford was soon to demand of them. Proof of this comes from the Watch Tower Society itself, albeit in a highly sanitized version. The history of the movement in Germany offered by the *1974 Yearbook of Jehovah's Witnesses* relates:

> Although in the first year of the Nazis coming to power the underground witness activity went practically unorganized and meetings in small groups were not held everywhere, yet the Gestapo found new reasons to arrest the brothers.
>
> Soon after the first brothers had been arrested and their homes searched, those objective in their thinking began to realize that those measures were simply the beginning of a more severe campaign of persecution. They knew that it would be completely senseless to try to settle these questions at the conference table. The only proper course was to fight for the truth.
>
> But a large number hesitated, feeling it best to wait, for Jehovah would surely do something to prevent this persecution of his people. Whereas this group was wasting time in hesitation, and anxiously trying not to make matters worse by any action on their part, the other publishers were determined to continue the work.[2]

The *1974 Yearbook* goes beyond this when it describes the failure of many Witnesses to maintain their values. According to it, some witnesses voted in Hitler's elections – which was contrary to Watch Tower teachings – and some later served in the German *Wehrmacht*.[3] Most seriously, for some months after June 1933, the Watch Tower leadership itself did not take a strong stand regarding how to deal with the Nazis. German branch overseer Paul Balzereit fled to Czechoslovakia for a time, fearing for his personal safety. There he continued to call for a conciliatory approach toward Nazism, just as he had during the first months of the Nazi government.[4] For a time, Rutherford was of

---

ed., *Persecution and Resistance of Jehovah's Witnesses during the Nazi Regime 1933–1945* (Bremen: Edition Temmen, 2001), 345.

2 Page 113.

3 Pages 129–30.

4 Page 131. Concerning Balzareit's attitude toward the Nazis, it is notable that he had ordered the removal of a particularly bloodthirsty picture from the booklet *The*

much the same mind; he placed the greatest importance on regaining the ownership and use of the Watch Tower's offices and printing plant at Magdeburg after they were seized for a second time on 28 June 1933. He appointed the Swiss branch overseer, Martin Harbeck, an American citizen, to negotiate with the German government on the basis of the argument that the Society's Magdeburg properties were owned by an American corporation, which made them a subject of German-American relations. Harbeck's activities prompted a response from Balzereit and a number of his supporters, who 'accused Brother Harbeck of being negligent in looking after German interests, while others went so far as to telegraph Brother Rutherford in behalf of Brother Balzereit.'[5]

The *1974 Yearbook* says that Balzereit was resentful because his 'pride was hurt.'[6] But there seems more to it than that. It is clear that Harbeck, acting as Rutherford's agent in the fullest sense, was so thoroughly caught up in negotiating for the return of the Magdeburg properties that he was neglecting to do anything significant on behalf of the now severely persecuted German Jehovah's Witnesses. Yet he did not call on them to take a firm stand against Nazism – something that would have exposed them to even harsher persecution. Quite the contrary. The *1974 Yearbook* tells us: 'For the year 1933 drew to a close without any unity being achieved as regards the holding of regular meetings and the carrying on of the preaching work. Brother Poddig describes the situation: "Two groups developed. The fearful ones maintained that we were disobedient and were endangering both them and Jehovah's Work." A letter written by Brother Harbeck in August 1933 was given wide distribution among the German brothers and was used by the fearful ones in their discussions as proof of the rightness of their stand.'[7]

In fact, the situation was much more complex than either 'Brother Poddig' or the *1974 Yearbook* would have us believe. What that year-

---

Crisis that the Witnesses were circulating throughout Germany in the spring of 1933. The *1974 Yearbook,* page 109, reports his action as follows: 'In Magdeburg, government officials had notified the [Watch Tower] office that the picture on the title page (a warrior holding a sword dripping blood) was unacceptable and demanded that it be removed. Brother Balzereit, who had repeatedly shown his willingness to compromise, gave immediate instructions to remove the colored covers from the booklet.'

5 *1974 Yearbook,* 131.

6 Ibid.

7 Ibid., 132–3.

book does not say is that Harbeck had stated forcefully that German Jehovah's Witnesses were to obey the Nazi authorities *in everything* by not meeting, preaching, or circulating Watch Tower literature. Thus it was those German Witnesses who wanted to defy the Nazi bans on them who were out of step with Watch Tower leaders, *including Rutherford*. This will be made abundantly clear in chapter 5.

It must have shocked the 'fearful ones' – who were actually following Watch Tower instructions – when soon after this, Rutherford suddenly published the article 'Fear Them Not' in the 1 November 1933 issue of *The Watchtower*. A translation appeared in the 1 December 1933 German edition of that magazine. This article practically called on all Jehovah's Witnesses to seek martyrdom. The English edition of that journal opened on page 323 with what amounted to a declaration of war: 'JEHOVAH has made it perfectly clear to those who love him that the present is the time for his preparation for war and that war with the enemy will shortly follow, resulting in the complete vindication of Jehovah's name. "To everything there is a season ... A time to love, and a time to hate; a time of war, and a time of peace."' Under the subheading 'FEAR,' on page 328, it stated:

> Some will say: 'If in the face of so much persecution and opposition we continue to go out amongst the people and publicly tell these truths, then I fear we may be killed.' That is true; and probably many of the faithful will be killed because they continue to faithfully proclaim the truth which they have learned in the secret place of the Most High. Jesus, of course, foreknew these facts, and therefore in the prophecy he said further: 'And fear not them which kill the body, but are not able to kill the soul; but rather fear him which is able to destroy both body and soul in [gehenna].' (Verse 28 [of Matthew 10]) The inference to be drawn from these words is that some of the faithful will be killed. Satan and his agents both visible and invisible can kill Jehovah's witnesses, and we know that they are trying to do so; but they cannot destroy the very existence of these faithful ones. Only Jehovah's Great Executioner can do that. The question is put squarely up to the remnant [Jehovah's Witnesses]: Shall we fear man or fear Jehovah God? It is written, in Proverbs 29:25: 'The fear of man bringeth a snare: but whoso putteth his trust in the Lord shall be safe.' The fear of man will certainly bring the remnant into a snare.

Although the *1974 Yearbook* account does not say so in so many words, it is obvious that Rutherford had switched signals on his German brethren. As long as he held out hope of regaining control and use of the Magdeburg properties, he was willing to take a soft line toward the Nazis. When Harbeck sent out his circular letter in August calling on German Witnesses to lie low, he was following Rutherford's instructions. When negotiations over those properties did not resolve matters to his satisfaction,[8] Rutherford called on Jehovah's Witnesses in Germany to defy the Nazis regardless of how this might endanger their well-being and their very lives.[9]

Fear of the Nazis and shifts in Watch Tower policy no doubt disheartened many German Witnesses. Various sources indicate that more than half of the Witness community stopped meeting and preaching. In Dresden, home to the largest Witness congregation in Germany, the number of Witnesses fell rapidly from a peak of some 1,200 door-to-door 'publishers' to 500.[10] The *1974 Yearbook* claims that there *may* have been 10,000 who were willing to continue such preaching despite the dangers involved,[11] but this is probably wishful thinking. It is difficult to say exactly how many continued to preach, but the evidence suggests that it was no more than two-fifths of the total community, and perhaps even fewer.[12] Furthermore, recent evidence indi-

8 As a result of American intervention, the German government returned the Magdeburg properties to the Watch Tower Society on 7 October 1933. But this was a hollow gesture insofar as German Witnesses were concerned. A total of 65,189 kilograms of books, bibles, and pictures worth 92,719.50 marks had already been destroyed. More important, even after the property was 'restored' the Witnesses, as a banned organization, were not allowed to use it to publish Watch Tower literature. *1974 Yearbook,* 112.

9 In a letter dated 5 January 1934, Rutherford wrote to Harbeck: 'I have little hope that we will get anything at all from the German government. I am of the opinion that this wing of Satan's organization will continue to oppress our people till the Lord intervenes.' Evidently he had come to this understanding more than two months earlier. *1974 Yearbook,* 132.

10 Ibid., 141.

11 Ibid.

12 *The 1974 Yearbook,* 109–10, tells that in the spring of 1933, a total of 24,843 persons were present at the Witnesses' annual memorial celebration in comparison with 14,453 the year before, and the number of 'publishers' or door-to-door preachers had risen from 12,484 to 19,268. For a further analysis of German Witness numbers at the time, see Detlef Garbe, *Zwischen Widerstand und Martyrium: Die Zeugen Jehovas im 'Dritten Reich,'* 4th ed. (Munich: Oldenburg, 1999), 81. On the other hand, if the *1974 Yearbook* is correct, the number of Witnesses arrested under the Third Reich totalled only 6,019, and during the period from 16 May through 15 June 1936, before a wave of arrests, only 5,930 publishers or 'workers' reported being engaged in preaching. *1974 Yearbook,* 212.

cates that in 1938 more than 500 renounced their faith while in prison.[13] So although it is true that those who remained faithful to Witness principles generally did so in a way that was truly outstanding and admirable – especially if they stood firm till death – these were a minority. But even when remaining loyal to what they considered Christian principles, they were sometimes divided among themselves and treated one another badly.[14] So much, then, for the assertion that Jehovah's Witnesses spoke out from the beginning and with one voice.

What about the statements in the 8 July 1998 *Awake!* article 'Jehovah's Witnesses Courageous in the Face of Nazi Peril,' and other sources regarding swastika flags at the Berlin-Wilmersdorf convention in 1933? And what about the claims by 'critics' that that convention opened with the German National Anthem? To evaluate these, it is worth recapitulating what *Awake!* and those other sources say. On page 12, the 8 July 1998 *Awake!* states: 'For instance, critics claim that the Witnesses decorated the Wilmersdorfer Tennishallen with swastika flags. Photographs of the 1933 convention clearly show that they displayed no swastikas in the hall. Eyewitnesses confirm that there were no flags inside.' On the same page, it also claims: 'Critics further state that the Witnesses opened the convention with the German National Anthem.' As mentioned earlier, Johannes Wrobel actually asserts that my article in *The Christian Quest* was the basis for saying the Witnesses decked the hall with swastikas and that they opened their convention with the National Anthem or *Deutschlandlied*.[15] The fact is that in making these assertions, both the *Awake!* article and Wrobel are guilty of outright falsehoods.

As Ken Raines has pointed out in a thoughtful article, he has not read 'any critic who claimed the Witnesses decked the halls with Swastika flags.' Furthermore, he notes respecting my article in *The Christian Quest:* 'Penton simply repeated Franke's comments as an eye witness that the hall was decked with Swastika flags when he entered the

13 Report No. 20, 30 June 1938 of the *Informationen des geheimen Staatspolizeiamts* (Reports of the Secret State Police Authority) states that 516 Bible Students were released from investigative detention or from serving their prison sentences as a result of the amnesty of 30 June 1938. Accordingly, 'the released persons have obligated themselves, by written statement, not to become active any more on behalf of the illegal Bible Students Association nor to testify in future any more for the teachings of the same.'

14 *1974 Yearbook,* 174–9.

15 See pages 49–50 above.

building, he didn't claim JWs were the ones responsible. It should be pointed out that this was the testimony of a Witness in good standing who was there, not a "critic."'[16] Thus the information about swastikas at the Berlin-Wilmersdorf convention did not come from 'critics,' as the Watch Tower Society and Johannes Wrobel would have it. *Rather, it came from Konrad Franke, who apparently discussed this matter on a number of occasions at the headquarters of the Watch Tower Society's German branch during the period when he was branch overseer there.*[17]

The *Awake!* account and that of Wrobel to the effect that critics claim the Berlin-Wilmersdorf convention opened with the singing of the German National Anthem is simply false as well. Ken Raines remarks: 'I haven't read any "critic" who has claimed the Society opened their convention with the national anthem of Germany. This was not Konrad Franke's testimony. Nor has anyone claimed that their singing a song about Zion was done to placate the Nazis. What was claimed by Penton in referring to Franke's testimony was that they had no objection to the words [about Zion], but to opening [with] a song that had the melody of the German national anthem with Swastika flags on display.'[18]

From what Franke says, it is difficult to understand how the story originated that 'critics' had claimed that the 1933 convention opened with the National Anthem. It is possible, though, that Wrobel and the Watch Tower Society wanted to cloud matters by drawing attention away from what actually happened and from Konrad Franke's statement. It is true that in earlier versions of *Zwischen Widerstand und Martyrium,* Detlef Garbe stated that the Witnesses opened their convention with the German National Anthem; supposedly this was based on Franke's recorded talk and on what Garbe read in *The Christian Quest.* But Garbe admits in recent editions of *Zwischen Widerstand und Martyrium* that his statement was based on a 'misunderstanding' – something that in itself is difficult to comprehend. After all, the recording was in German and Franke's remarks appear in *The Christian Quest* both in German and in English translation. So one has to wonder how Garbe could have made such an egregious error. Above and beyond that, Wrobel had no reason to assert that Garbe's mistake was

16 Ken Raines, 'JWs and the Nazis: The Watchtower Responds to Critics.' *JW Research Journal,* January–June 1999, 3.

17 Based on the comments of a former worker at the German branch headquarters of the Watch Tower Society who wishes to remain anonymous.

18 Raines, 4.

based on what he had read in *The Christian Quest*. If he did not have personal access to the article in question, he could have obtained it from Garbe or, alternatively, checked to see what was written in it on the 'Watchtower Observer' website out of Norway, where Franke's remarks had been posted for years. It seems rather clear, however, that he did have access to it: as noted earlier, he refers to *The Christian Quest* as an 'ominous English publication' (*einer ominösen Veröffentlichung*) in the original German of his article. No matter, though, whether he saw or did not see it. An honest and competent scholar – which Wrobel seems to want to parade himself as being – does not make damning allegations about others without solid facts to back them up. So it is evident that he does not mind spreading falsehoods when it is in the interests of his religion to do so. It is also apparent that the Watch Tower Society is willing to spread those falsehoods without checking their factual basis.

Can we believe Franke's account? Undoubtedly, for although he may have felt bitterness toward Balzereit, Balzereit's close associates, and even Rutherford for their attempts to placate the Nazis (as his remarks seem to indicate), he had no reason to distort the truth. Furthermore, he must have known that what he was saying about these matters would not place the Watch Tower Society in a positive light. Still, it is difficult to establish whether there actually were swastikas in the main Wilmersdorf convention meeting hall or not. As noted earlier, Guy Canonici says that Konrad Franke must have felt reassured when he saw there were no flags in the main hall. But this is not certain. As Ken Raines indicates, the pictures the 8 July 1998 *Awake!* published are not as conclusive as the Watch Tower Society, Detlef Garbe, Johnnes Wrobel, and Guy Canonici would like to think. Writing about the author of the 8 July 1998 *Awake!* article, 'Jehovah's Witnesses Courageous in the Face of Nazi Peril,' and the photos therein, Ken Raines comments:

> The writer said photos of the convention show no Swastika flags inside and print two such photos in the article. However, the two photos do not decisively refute Franke's testimony. One of the photos is a view of the audience from near or on the stage in front. It looks toward the back wall of the Tennishallen and shows some of the side bleachers or stands filled with attendees. Any flags on the sides would simply have obscured the view of those in the stands, which is why flags are not normally displayed on the sides in stands of stadiums. Flags also are rarely displayed in the back of halls.

> The other picture reproduced as evidence against the Swastika flag testimony is from the left side of the platform (if looking from the front towards the audience) from among those in the orchestra and looking toward the wall on the right side of the platform. It just includes the front of the platform in front where an individual is speaking and [an] other person is sitting next to him (another speaker presumably). It doesn't show the main portion of the platform behind the speaker, this is cut off from view (deliberately?).[19]

There is the testimony of Walter Jurish to the effect that there were no flags in the meeting hall room. However, he was simply one person – not the 'workers' mentioned in *Awake!* – and his testimony must be placed against that of Franke. So it is not possible to take a definitive position on the matter. Regarding the song that was sung to open the convention, there can be no doubt. The lyrics may have been acceptable; even so, it is obvious that many of the Witnesses present were shocked at seeing swastika flags (be they outside or inside the hall, or both) and then hearing a hymn played to the music of the German National Anthem. As Konrad Franke says: 'Can you imagine how we felt? Many could not join in the singing; it was just as though their throats were throttled.'

Witness claims that they were not guilty of anti-Semitism ring hollow as well. When one looks at the *Declaration of Facts* and the Watch Tower letter to Hitler, they clearly indicate efforts to vilify and scapegoat the Jews. Significantly, the declaration was circulated throughout Germany, and the letter was sent to Hitler after individual Jews had been subjected to months of brutal treatment and shortly after the start of the Nazis' first major boycott of Jewish businesses, which had begun on 1 April 1933. At that point, Jewish communities in other countries, notably Britain, France, and the United States, launched a media campaign against the Nazis. This campaign called on governments to refuse to purchase German goods. The Nazis responded by proclaiming that Germany was the victim of *Greuelpropaganda* (atrocity propaganda).[20] Thus it seems evident that Watch Tower leaders were attempting to pander to the Nazis, for the *Declaration of Facts* and the letter to Hitler were in many ways saying exactly what the Nazis

19 Raines, 6, 7.

20 For a full discussion of events surrounding the boycott, see Ian Kershaw, *Hitler 1889–1936: Hubris* (New York and London: W.W. Norton, 1998) 472–4.

themselves were saying both domestically and to the world at large. So how can any reasonable person regard those documents as anything but openly anti-Semitic and, equally, openly anti-British and anti-American as well?[21]

Lutz Lemhöfer outlines clearly how this was the case and just how willing the Witnesses were to bow to the Nazis in the spring and summer of 1933: 'On April 26, 1933, in the name of the *Norddeutsche Bibelforschervereinigung* [North German Bible Students Association] and the *Süddeutsche Bibelforschervereinigung* [South German Bible Students Association], the legal advisor of the Watch Tower Society had already deemed it necessary to point out that in the new name[s] of the association (with the deletion of the title 'International Bible Students Association') "that only German citizens were members and held leading positions."' A few lines later, Lemhöfer quotes Detlef Garbe to the effect that 'it became clear that the course of conformity did not leave their former religious self-image undamaged, but rather affected its substance: Everyone who intended to get on good terms with the high and mighty of the "old world" through such actions had left their self-stated "neutrality" far behind.'[22] It is therefore not surprising that Witness leaders were also willing to scapegoat the Jews.

As pointed out in chapter 2, the *Awake!* of 8 July 1998 argued that the *Declaration of Facts* was not attacking *all* Jews but rather only those who were part and parcel of big business. Indeed, it claims that the Witnesses were friendly toward the Jews and gave them assistance during their time of persecution. Garbe, Wrobel, and Yonan have all stated that the Witnesses were not anti-Semitic despite the clear statements of the declaration and the letter to Hitler. Garbe holds that the Witnesses were not anti-Semitic because they were not racists and because until the early 1930s they believed the Jews were to play a special role in Jehovah's divine plan. In fact, like the Watch Tower

21 Neither the Watch Tower Society nor its non-Witness apologists say very much about Rutherford's foolish exaggeration: 'The greatest and most oppressive empire on earth is the Anglo-American empire. By that is meant the British Empire, of which the United States of America forms a part.' Nor has the Watch Tower ever had the honesty or courtesy to admit that his statement cannot bear historical analysis. But then, the Watch Tower has never cared much about correcting past errors.

22 Lutz Lemhöfer, 'Between Historical Documentation and Public Promotion of One's Image' in Hans Hesse, ed., *Persecution and Resistance,* 352. For Garbe's remarks on the *Norddeutsche Bibelforschervereinigung* and *Süddeutsche Bibelforschervereinigung*, see *Zwischen Widerstand und Martyrium*, 88, 92, 107.

Society, he claims that they were actually friendly toward the Jews. Wrobel asserts much the same thing, but he also claims – in a bizarre analysis – that the terms 'commercial Jews' and 'business Jews' used in the declaration and in the letter to Hitler did not imply anti-Semitism or hostility toward the Jews in the way that Nazi terminology did. Yonan simply claims that the declaration is *not* anti-Semitic and that its publication was *not* an attempt to curry favour with Hitler and the Nazis. To her, it was a 'sermon.' Canonici skirts the issue as far as the declaration itself is concerned. He simply deals with the side issues: whether there were swastikas in the main hall at Wilmersdorf and whether the Witnesses opened their convention with the German National Anthem or a hymn to the same music. As noted, he does argue that critics have taken statements from the declaration out of context.

When we look clearly at these assertions, whether they are official Watch Tower pronouncements or those of its apologists, it is hard to take them seriously. The Nazis and other anti-Semites had long resorted to the argument that the Jews dominated much of the world economy and that they were greedy and exploitative. In *Mein Kampf,* written in the mid-1920s, Hitler made this point over and over.[23] In referring to the United States, he stated in *Mein Kampf*: 'It is Jews who govern the stock exchange forces of the American Union. Every year makes them more and more the controlling masters of the producers in a nation of one hundred and twenty millions; only a single great man, Ford, to their fury, still maintains full independence.'[24] Josef Goebbels's statement '*Wir fordern*' (We Demand), made shortly after the publication of *Mein Kampf,* also attacks the Jewish business community. It states in part: 'While the front soldier was fighting in the trenches to defend the Fatherland, some Eastern Jewish profiteer robbed him of his hearth and home. The Jew lives in the palaces and the proletarian, the front soldier, lives in holes that do not deserve to be called "homes."'[25] At the beginning of the 1 April 1933 boycott of Jewish stores in Germany, Julius Streicher, who was himself in charge of it, lashed out: 'For weeks past the whole of the Jewish Press abroad is inciting its readers, and the people believe its lies ... The Jew earns his money not by honest work, as a peasant or workman, but he lives

23 Adolf Hitler, *Mein Kampf,* trans. Ralph Manheim (Boston and New York: Houghton Mifflin, 1971),148, 243, 314, 453, 600, 622, 623, 624.

24 Ibid., 639.

25 Printed originally in the fourth issue of *Der Angriff,* 25 July 1927. *Der Angriff, Aufsätze aus der Kampfzeit* (Munich: Zentralverlag der NSDAP, 1935), 18.

by profiting by the labours of others. He lives by the sweat of other people who work for him.'[26] Several months later, In response to a Jewish conference in London convened to deal with the German boycott of Jewish businesses, the Nazi paper *Der Stürmer* of July 1933, Number 34, stated (in translation):

> All the leading Jews of the world will come together. The leading rabbis (they are the political leaders of world Jewry) and the Jewish millionaires and billionaires, the bank and stock exchange leaders, the heads of trusts and major Jews in commerce. These are the Jews of whom Walter Rathenau wrote even before the war in the *Neue Freien Presse:*
>
> **'Three hundred men, all of whom know each other, determine the history of the world. Nothing happens against their will. They are the true rulers, the real uncrowned kings.'** (bold in original)
>
> These three hundred men want to continue and intensify Pan-Jewry's boycott war against Germany.

Thus it can be seen that the *Declaration of Facts,* in attacking 'commercial Jews,' was making assertions that clearly reflected the Nazis' anti-Semitic propaganda and that were obviously intended to resonate with the Hitler government.

The Watch Tower letter to Hitler was even more obsequious to the *Führer* and to Nazi values than the *Declaration of Facts*. Besides claiming that J.F. Rutherford was friendly to Germany and had gone to prison in 1918 for refusing to publish anti-German 'atrocity propaganda' (*Gruelpropaganda*), it did several other things to appeal to Hitler. It noted, quite accurately, that the Watch Tower Society had not joined in the atrocity propaganda over Germany's treatment of the Jews, but then it claimed, falsely, that the Society had actually opposed it. Among other things, it lied blatantly when it claimed that commercialistic Jews in the United States were among the most 'eager persecutors' of the Watch Tower's work and leadership.[27] It stated specifically: 'In a similar manner, [to Rutherford's supposedly earlier behaviour] the administration of our Society not only refused to participate in the

26 From the *Münchener Beobachter,* the Daily Supplement to the *Völkisher Beobachter,* Issue No. 91/91, 1/2 April 1933. Partial translation of Document M33. Source: Nazi Conspiracy and Aggression. Volume VIII. USGOP, Washington, 1946, 21–33.

27 There is no evidence that members of the Jewish community, whether commercialistic or otherwise, were major persecutors of Jehovah's Witnesses in America, and no mention of this supposed fact appears in Watch Tower English-language literature.

atrocity propaganda against Germany, but it took a position against it. This is emphasized by the attached Declaration that refers to the fact that the circles that led [in promoting] atrocity propaganda in the United States (commercialistic Jews and Catholics) are also the most eager persecutors of our Society's work and its administration. These and other statements in our Declaration are meant to serve as a rejection of the slanderous claim that the Bible Students are supported by Jews.'[28] Following this statement, the letter went on to deny any relationship to Marxism and to declare the Witnesses' allegiance to Nazi values:

> Further, it was stated at the five-thousand-delegate convention – as expressed in the Declaration – that Bible Students are fighting for the same high, ethical goals and ideals that the National Government of the German Reich proclaimed regarding the relationship of man to God, namely: honesty of the created towards the Creator!
>
> At the convention, it was stated that there are no opposing views in the relationship between German Bible Students and the National Government of the German Reich, but that, to the contrary, respecting the purely religious and apolitical goals and objectives of the Bible Students, it can be said that these are in complete harmony with the similar goals of the National Government of the German Reich.

Then, finally and most shockingly, it specifically endorsed Hitler's own policies as stated in Section 24 of the Nazi Party Platform by quoting that section directly. That section – *which is clearly anti-Semitic* – reads: 'The party as such takes the position of a positive Christianity without being bound to any one confession. The party opposes the Jewish-materialistic spirit within and without and is convinced that a permanent recovery of our people can only be accomplished from within.'[29]

28 For the German original of the Watch Tower letter to Hitler and a full English translation thereof, see Appendix C.

29 The German reads: 'Die Partei als solche vertritt den Standpunkt eines positiven Christentums, ohne sich konfessionell an ein bestimmtes Bekenntnis zu binden. Sie bekämpft den jüdisch-materialistischen Geist in und außer uns und ist überzeugt, daß eine dauernde Genesung unseres Volkes nur erfolgen kann von innen heraus.' A full quotation of Section 24 appears in Friedrich Zipfel, *Kirchenkampf in Deutschland 1933–1945* (Berlin Walter de Gruyter, 1965), 1.

As Garbe asserts, this letter was written by Paul Balzereit, perhaps along with close Witness associates, rather than by J.F. Rutherford. Even so, it is an official Watch Tower statement. It is difficult to believe that it did not have the approval or at least the passive acceptance of Rutherford, who was in Germany just before the Berlin-Wilmersdorf convention. Its tone is in full harmony with the *Declaration of Facts* and with much of what Rutherford himself was preaching and writing. Just as Rutherford was soon to do through Harbeck, it signalled that Jehovah's Witnesses would not defy bans placed on them by Nazi governments. It stated to Hitler: 'We will continue to conform to the regulations of prohibition issued [against us] because we are confident that you, Mr. Chancellor, or the governments of the *Länder,* will lift these measures – by which tens of thousands of Christian men and women would fall victim to a martyrdom reminiscent of that of the original Christians – once the true state of affairs is known.'

With regard to Garbe's statement that since the Witnesses were not racists, they could not be anti-Semitic, we can only gape at his apparent lack of knowledge of the history of anti-Semitism. Non-racist anti-Semitism existed as long ago as the ancient Persian Empire; this is evident in the biblical book of Esther. It was certainly present at the time of Antiochus Epiphanes in the second century before Christ.[30] It existed in both pre-Christian and Christian Roman times.[31] Many suggest that it is found in the New Testament[32] and in the writings of the post-apostolic Fathers of the Christian Church.[33] It was present in many

30 Maccabbees 1:20–61.

31 See J.G. Gager, *The Origins of Anti-Semitism: Attitudes towards Judaism in Pagan and Christian Antiquity* (New York: Oxford University Press, 1983), and J.N. Sevenster, *The Roots of Pagan Anti-Semitism in the Ancient World* (Leiden: E.J. Brill, 1975). On pages 36–56, Sevenster holds that ancient anti-Semitism was never based on race.

32 Whether this is the case or not is difficult to ascertain. It is now generally held that most of the New Testament was written by Jewish Christians. For a discussion of this matter, see Richard N. Longnecker, *The Christology of Early Jewish Christianity* (Grand Rapids: Baker Book House, 1970), passim. For this reason, the polemic against 'the Jews' in the Johannine writings, for example, may be no more than a reflection of what amounts to a bitter internal Jewish debate. There can be no doubt, however, that later generations of Christians used New Testament attacks on 'the Jews' as a basis for their own anti-Semitic attitudes.

33 For a short discussion of both New Testament and post-apostolic Christian attitudes toward Judaism, see 'Judaism and Christianity,' in *The Encyclopedia of Early Christianity.* For a more detailed account see J. Parker, *The Conflict of the Church and the Synagogue: A Study in the Origins of Antisemitism* (New York: Atheneum, 1974).

medieval societies and resulted in pogroms and Jewish edicts.[34] The Jews were driven from England under Edward I in 1270, from France under Philip the Fair in 1306, from Castile under Isabella the Catholic in 1492, and from Portugal under Manoel I in 1496. Martin Luther was thoroughly bigoted in his remarks about the Jews,[35] and Shakespeare has given us a remarkably anti-Semitic view of the Merchant of Venice with his desire for 'a pound of flesh.' There was the terrible anti-Semitism of the Spanish Inquisition[36] and that of eastern Europe over the centuries.[37] In the nineteenth and twentieth centuries this spirit of hostility toward the Jews continued for religious reasons, especially in Catholic and Eastern Orthodox countries. The Dreyfus case in France was certainly a case in point, as was the circulation of the bogus *Protocols of the Learned Elders of Zion,* and wild tales to the effect that Jews used the blood of Christian children to make Passover matzohs.[38] Significantly, even up to the eve of the Second World War, Catholic clerics and lay organizations in Quebec regularly petitioned the Canadian government to bar German-Jewish refugees from Canada.[39]

34 This was especially true with the Justinian Code. For an account of medieval Catholic Christian discrimination and persecution of the Jews, see Paul Johnson, *A History of the Jews* (London: Phoenix, 1998), 207–17, 231–2.

35 For an excellent discussion of Luther's rabid anti-Semitism, which some have compared to Nazi attitudes toward the Jews, see Heinrich Bornkamm, *Luther's World of Thought,* trans. Martin H. Bertram (Saint Louis: Concordia Publishing House, 1965), 226–33. Bornkamm argues that Luther was motivated by religious rather than racial prejudice.

36 For a study of the subject, see Henry Kamen, *Inquisition and Society in Spain in the Sixteenth and Seventeenth Centuries* (London: Weidenfeld and Nicolson, 1958), 219–21.

37 This continued well into the twentieth century. Following the creation of the Polish Republic in November 1918, 'newly established Poland celebrated its independence with pogrom after pogrom against Jews within its territory, and the Poles were joined by the Ukrainians, who historically had been in the forefront of a savage anti-Semitism that had butchered thousands of victims.' Eugene Davidson, *The Making of Adolf Hitler: The Birth and Rise of Nazism* (Columbia and London: University of Missouri Press, 1997), 127.

38 See John Cornwell, *Hitler's Pope: The Secret History of Pius XII* (New York: Viking Penguin, 1999), 27–8.

39 An article in *L'Action Catholique* of Quebec of 29 November 1938 by Louis-Philippe Roy virtually parrots Nazi arguments against the Jews in opposition to Jewish refugee immigration to Canada. This article shows just how anti-Semitic Catholic, French Canada was. See also Irving Abella and Harold Troper, *None Is too Many: Canada and the Jews of Europe, 1933–1948* (Toronto: Lester & Orpen Dennys, 1982).

Almost none of this was motivated by racism as such. Racial anti-Semitism only developed in the late nineteenth century, in Europe. Promoted by the French Count Joseph Arthur de Gobineau and by the Englishman Houston Stewart Chamberlain (the son-in-law of Richard Wagner), racism grew into a strong force in Germany and resulted in an especially virulent form of anti-Semitism.[40] But it should be noted that even that racist anti-Semitism developed and grew out of a long tradition of religious hostility to the Jews, the so-called Christ killers.

It is true, of course, that the Spaniards used the concept of *limpieza de sangre* (purity of blood) to discriminate against 'New Christians' of Jewish or Moorish ancestry by prohibiting them from holding certain offices and from immigrating to the Americas. The reason for this was the belief that many Jewish and Moorish *conversos* (converts) had become Christians only under threat of persecution and expulsion from the Iberian Peninsula and were secretly carrying on the practices of their old religions. Thus even *limpieza de sangre* was rooted in religious concerns rather than in anything approaching modern biological racism,[41] which in its biological and sociological forms owes much to Darwinism.

In must be said, then, that Garbe's assertion regarding the Witnesses' supposed lack of anti-Semitism is simply naive. That they were motivated by religious anti-Semitism was admitted by people of very different backgrounds, including Heinrich Himmler, Rudof Höss, many or most other Nazis, and the Jewish psychologist Bruno Bettelheim, all of whom had first-hand knowledge of the attitudes and behaviour of Jehovah's Witnesses in the concentration camps. One may argue that as Nazis, neither Himmler nor Höss were especially good witnesses. The fact is, however, that Himmler's remarks were made to a subordinate in a private letter, and Höss was writing what amounted to a personal confession while awaiting execution in a Polish prison. Thus neither had any reason to lie.

Wrobel's statement that the terms 'commercial Jews' (*Handelsjuden*) and 'business Jews' (*Geschäftsjuden*) in the *Declaration of Facts* and the Watch Tower letter to Hitler respectively did not imply anti-Semitism is absurd. After quoting the most shocking statements about the Jews

40 For a brief discussion of Gabineau and Chamberlain's ideas and their impact on Germany, see William L. Shirer, *The Rise and Fall of the Third Reich* (New York: Fawcett Crest, 1983), 150–9.

41 For the background to the *casta de limpieza de sangre,* see Americo Castro, *La realidad historica de España* (Mexico: Editorial Porrua, 1971), 48–52. See also Kamen, 114–33.

in both the declaration and the Watch Tower letter, he goes on to say: 'The use of the term "commercial Jews" in connection with big business can be traced back to the nineteenth century as part of the standard German vocabulary of those days. The term seems not to have disappeared from German dictionaries until 1933. In any case, it is neither an indication of antisemitism, nor does it appear that Nazi terminology was taken into account.'[42] Regarding the term business Jews, Wrobel says little. He simply argues that it was used to show that Jehovah's Witnesses were not receiving Jewish money. Note once again what he says on this matter: 'The vehement attacks on Jehovah's Witnesses through opponents had already led to government prohibitions in Germany. They were accused of being financed by the "Jews," so that they could set up a supposed Jewish world power. German Jehovah's Witnesses vehemently responded to this slander and emphatically repudiated it. They used clear language in order to distinguish between their non-commercial activities and the activities of their alleged Jewish sponsors.'[43]

Contentions like these simply cannot stand sober analysis. As far as trying to explain away anti-Semitism in the *Declaration of Facts* by a historical study of the German word *Handelsjuden* is concerned, this is quite meaningless. *The declaration was originally written in English, not German, and the term 'commercial Jews' in the context in which it was written clearly implies anti-Semitism.* Besides that, as most modern linguists hold, the meaning of words is determined more by the context in which they are used than by their etymology. Although it is true that the declaration stressed the evils of commercial Jews, it went far beyond that. For one thing, it specifically condemned the Jewish clergy by quoting Jesus' denunciation of the scribes and Pharisees. Second, it dissociated the Witnesses from the Jews by pointing out that they rejected Jesus as the Christ or Messiah. Third, the declaration, as it was circulated in Germany in June 1933, contained a statement that does not appear in reproductions of that document as published in the *1934 Year Book of Jehovah's Witnesses* in both its German and English editions. That statement, which is found at the end of the subsection of the declaration titled 'Our Literature,' reads: 'We would like to be permitted to stress here that in America, where our books were written, Catholics as well as Jews have joined with one another in insult-

42 Wrobel, 318.
43 Ibid.

ing the national government in Germany and in the attempt to boycott Germany because of the National Socialist Party's announced principle.'[44] This 'announced principle' was, clearly, its overt attack on the Jews! So, it is evident that Watch Tower leaders wanted to distance Jehovah's Witnesses from any condemnation of the Nazis for their persecution of the Jews. Rutherford and the Watch Tower Society's officers in Magdeburg obviously knew that the proposed international boycott was directed at stopping the oppression of Jews in Germany, not commercial or business Jews in London or New York.

In the conclusion of his article, Wrobel quotes and criticizes the church paper *Mainzer Bistumsnachrichten* of May 1997 for having stated the following in a critique of the 'Stand Firm' video: 'In a Declaration made at that time, the many common interests of the Watch Tower Society with goals of the Nazi leaders had been affirmed. In this letter [*sic*] the "commercial Jews of the Anglo-American empire" were also held responsible for the exploitation of peoples and had been denounced by Hitler. Jehovah's Witnesses also emphasized the rejection of "commercial Jews and Catholics" in this letter to Hitler. The Declaration of 1933 is, however, mentioned in the film but is played down, and the producers express neither regret nor admission of guilt, despite the renunciation of solidarity with the Jewish people.'[45] After offering this quote, the Watch Tower archivist says: 'I believe that such incorrect polemical criticism will soon be a thing of the past.'[46] In this assumption, as in other previous matters, Wrobel has already proven himself wrong. The evidence demonstrates that the *Mainzer Bistumsnachrichten* is not incorrect, and its remarks are hardly 'polemical.' So despite Wrobel's attempt to deny the obvious in long and detailed footnotes that often attack the assessments of others, the case that the Watch Tower tried to compromise with Nazism stands rock solid.

Above and beyond what can be found in the *Declaration of Facts* and in the Watch Tower letter to Hitler, there is much additional written

44 The original German of this statement reads: 'Man möchte uns gestatten, hier darauf aufmerksam zu machen, daß in Amerika, wo unsere Bücher geschrieben wurden, Katholiken als auch Juden sich miteinander verbunden haben in der Beschimpfung der nationalen Regierung in Deutschland und in dem Versuch, Deutschland zu boykottieren wegen der von der national-sozialistischen Partei verkündigten Grundsätze.' For other changes in the contents of the *Declaration,* see Appendix C.

45 Quoted in Wrobel, 318.

46 Ibid.

evidence from Watch Tower sources which shows that the Witnesses – and especially J.F. Rutherford and his close associates – were displaying anti-Semitic attitudes in the 1930s and 1940s. In 1934, Rutherford produced a booklet that included 'seven Bible treatises,' the first of which was titled 'Jews.' Along with much else in that treatise, the second Watch Tower president wrote:

> The Scriptures furnish an abundance of proof that during the thousand-year reign of Christ Jesus, Jehovah's great King, the peoples of earth who are obedient to the law of that kingdom will be brought to perfect conditions and live on the earth. It has often been said that all who receive the blessings of the kingdom under Christ must become Jews. The Scriptures do not warrant any such conclusion, but, on the contrary, show that the rule is exactly the reverse. The wrongful conclusion has been reached for the reason of not properly applying the Scriptures. The people now on earth and which are called Jews are a commercial people. Among them are some of the richest and most avaricious of men the world has ever known. Some of the men of Big Business are called Jews. Many of these people are very arrogant, self important and extremely selfish. They have little or no faith in God's Word and do not believe at all in the Lord Jesus Christ as the Savior of man. It does not seem at all reasonable that at the beginning of the earthly blessings in the kingdom the Lord would extend his first favors to such people. It is not Scriptural. *On the contrary, the Scriptures show that the people now called Jews will have a harder time during the reign of Christ than many other peoples.*[47] [italics mine]

Some four years later, in 1938, long after the Watch Tower Society itself had exposed the terrors of Nazism and the persecution of the Jews in Germany, Rutherford still summoned the brazenness to write the following:

> The 'Jews' religion' (Galatians 1:13, 14) brought about the foul crucifixion of Jesus Christ, the murder of Stephen, and the wide-spread and malicious persecution of numerous Christians, the disciples of Jesus Christ. (Acts 9:1–13) Jesus Christ denounced the practice of the Jews' religion as a fraud and the practitioners as hypocrites. It was the practice of the Jews' religion that caused the complete destruction of Jerusalem and of the entire nation of

47 J.F. Rutherford, *Favored People* (Brooklyn, NY: Watch Tower Society and IBSA, 1934), 4–5.

> Israel, and that nation has never been and never will be permitted to again exist as a nation. Jew religionists continue to practice their religion, but it is manifest that it holds out no hope for mankind.[48]

But it was in *Enemies*,[49] published a year earlier, that Rutherford outdid himself for thoroughgoing bigotry. On pages 212 and 213 of that book, which was little more than a series of diatribes against everything and everyone not associated with Jehovah's Witnesses, he wrote: 'Today Protestantism is dead so far as the protest against the practitioners of Catholicism is concerned, and the Protestant clergy, together with the practicers of the Jewish religious organization, follow the lead of the Roman Catholic organization and act in harmony therewith. All such practice religion of which the Devil is the author.' On page 222 of the same volume, he continued his caustic remarks about both Protestants and Jews, referring to Jewish rabbis with contempt as 'Yiddish clergy.' There he stated:

> Today the so-called 'Protestants' and the Yiddish clergy openly co-operate with and play into the hands of the Roman Catholic Hierarchy like foolish simpletons and thereby aid the Hierarchy to carry out her commercial, religious traffic and increase her revenue. The Hierarchy takes the lead, and the simpletons follow. The Hierarchy is now taking the lead in compulsory flag-saluting, and in building images or monuments, such as what is now widely advertised to be built at Washington, D.C.; and the clergy of the so-called 'Protestant' and Yiddish organizations fall in line and do what they are told, and when the 'sackbut' sounds they fall down and worship. (Daniel 3:5) Poor simpletons!

In summing up what he considered to be Protestant and Jewish collaboration with Catholicism, Rutherford wrote on page 225: 'Other religious organizations, the Yiddish and Protestants, deal with the Roman Catholic Hierarchy because it appears to them to be to their selfish advantage.'

The Witness community reflected Rutherford's attitudes, for he was regarded as the head of Jehovah's Theocratic Organization on earth. *Consolation* even went so far as to say: 'The Theocracy is at present administered by the Watch Tower Bible and Tract Society, of which

48 J.F. Rutherford, *Cure* (Brooklyn, NY: Watch Tower Society and IBSA, 1938), 6.
49 J.F. Rutherford, *Enemies* (Brooklyn, NY: Watch Tower Society and IBSA, 1937).

Judge Rutherford is the president and general manager.'[50] Hence, because to all intents and purposes he was 'Jehovah's channel,' his teaching authority was more absolute among Jehovah's Witnesses than was that of the pope among Roman Catholics. So we must read other statements in Witness publications in the light of what he taught. His hatred of politics, commerce, and religion[51] *and his anti-Semitism* were taken up with a passion by his followers.

For example, in a mad-hatter attack on the American Medical Association, *The Golden Age* of 26 September 1934 published the following quotation from a quack medical journal with approval: 'The Journal of the A. M. A. Is the vilest sheet that passes the United States mail ... Nothing new and useful in therapeutics escapes its unqualified condemnation. Its attacks are generally ad hominem. Its editorial columns are largely devoted to character assassination ... Its editor [Dr Morris Fishbein] is of the type of Jew that crucified Jesus Christ.'[52] Of course it was Clayton Woodworth, the editor of *The Golden Age* and its later replacement, *Consolation*, who was directly responsible for printing those words, but Woodworth never did anything that Rutherford would not have approved.

The following statement, from Franz Zürcher's *Kreuzzug gegen das Christentum*, should also be understood in the light of Rutherford's teachings regarding the Jews:

> Also, everyone who knows the Bible is familiar with the contrast between the Jewish religion and Christianity.
>
> The adversaries and persecutors of Christ Jesus were religious Jews. Jesus said to them that they were children of the Devil. (John 8:42–4). Paul was, when he still was called Saul, an adherent of the Jewish religion and persecuted Christians. As God revealed the truth to him, however, he became Christian and was immediately converted to serve God in spirit and truth. His own statement in this affair is rich in disclosure: 'For you have heard what my style of life was when I was yet a practicing Jew: how severely I persecuted the church of God and attempted to destroy it; and how in the practice of Judaism [i.e., the Jewish religion] I exceeded many of

50 *Consolation*, 4 September 1940, 25.

51 During much of Rutherford's presidency of the Watch Tower Society and for years thereafter, Jehovah's Witnesses claimed that they were not a religion and that all religion was of the Devil.

52 Page 807.

my contemporaries in the boundless zeal for the ancestral traditions of my forefathers.' (Gal. 1:13–15).

As a practicer of the Jewish religion, Paul was never persecuted; however, when he became a Christian he had to suffer the bitter persecution of the religious Jews because he now told the truth. Jesus predicted that all his true followers would always be persecuted by religionists, and so it has always been. (John 15:19, 20).[53]

The Watch Tower Society's magazine *Trost,* published in Switzerland, took an even more outspoken stance. Its 15 July 1938 issue contained the following:

The Jews in Palestine

For this reason their eyes are blind and their ears are deaf to God's truth. The things that God had his prophets say to his apostate people from time immemorial are today quite up to date. Just as they leaned on the 'Rod of Egypt' instead of on Jehovah, they now lean on England. Quite eloquently, English Jews try to convince the English government just how much England is in need of a Jewish political state in Palestine for English-imperialistic reasons, how very loyal the Jews are to the British Empire, and that today they are again prepared to shed their blood for that empire.

53 Franz Zürcher, *Kreuzzug gegen das Christentum* (Zurich and New York: Europa-Verlag, 1938), 18. What Zürcher says here is practically a direct quote from testimony given by Rutherford in the trial of Martin Harbeck and Zürcher himself at Bern, Switzerland, in 1936. For Rutherford's original testimony, see *The Golden Age,* 21 October 1936, 45. Zürcher's statement reads in German: 'Auch ist jedem Bibelkenner der Gegensatz zwischen der jüdischen Religion und dem Christentum geläufig.

'Die Gegner und Verfolger Christi Jesu waren religiöse Juden. Ihnen sagte Jesus, daß sie Kinder des Teufels seien (Johannes 8:42–4). Paulus war, als er noch Saulus hieß, ein Anhänger der jüdischen Religion und verfolgte die Christen. Als Gott ihm aber die Wahrheit offenbarte, wurde er Christ und bekehrte sich augenblicklich, um Gott in Geist und Wahrheit zu dienen. Seine eigene Aussage in dieser Angelegenheit ist aufschlußreich: "Denn ihr habt von meinem ehemaligen Wandel in dem Judentum gehört, daß ich die Versammlung Gottes über die Maßen verfolgte und sie zerstörte, und in dem Judentum [das ist der jüdischen Religion] zunahm über viele Altersgenossen in meinem Geschlecht, indem ich übermäßig ein Eiferer für meine vaterlichen Überlieferungen war" (Gal. 1:13–15).

'Bei der Ausübung der jüdischen Religion wurde Paulus nie verfolgt; aber als er Christ wurde, mußte er seitens der religiösen Juden bittere Verfolgungen erleiden, weil er nun den Menschen die Wahrheit sagte. Jesus sagte voraus, daß alle seine wahren Nachfolger durch Religionisten verfolgt werden würden, und so ist es auch stets gewesen' (Johannes 15:19, 20).

So, here again in their former native country, this people tread on a path lacking in knowledge of Jehovah and his anointed King Jesus, the Messiah. By human means and thoughts they try to take possession of that country, and they do not see how Jehovah keeps 'making their chariot wheels heavy' so that they do not achieve the ends set by themselves. They cry for more 'religiosity' like all the other allies within the organization of the Devil. The Jews are also blind to the fact that the 'old hag' in Rome devotes all her energy to preventing the Jews from becoming independent. Her priests are the most malicious agitators; their 'holy places' are endangered, they cry, if the Jews become more numerous! This is why England, in her agreement with Italy, has to warrant the 'justified Italian (that is Catholic) interests'; namely, the right for the 'old hag' to further dull poor people's minds by her schools and monasteries in order to ultimately bleed them white.

The Jews are the epitome of the fact of how terrible it is not to be under Jehovah's blessings. Separated from God's grace, they are restless here, too. Sowing the wind they are reaping the whirlwind! Just how long?[54]

54 The German original reads:

'Deshalb sind auch ihre Augen blind und die Ohren taub gegenüber Gottes Wahrheit. Was Gott vor alters durch seine Propheten einem abtrünnigen Volke sagen ließ, ist heute sehr zeitgemäß. So wie man sich vor Jahrtausenden auf den "Stab Ägypten" stützte, anstatt auf Jehova, so stützt man sich auf England. Englische Juden suchen mit aller Beredsamkeit die englische Regierung zu überzeugen, wie sehr England einen jüdischen Staat in Palästina aus englisch-imperialistischen Gründen benötige, und wie loyal die Juden dem englischen Weltreich gegenüber seien, und daß sie auch heute wieder bereit wären für dieses Reich ihr Blut zu vergießen.

'So geht dieses Volk auch hier in seinem ehemaligen Heimatland einen Weg ohne Erkenntnis Jehovas und seines gesalbten Königs Jesus, des Messias. Mit menschlichen Mitteln und menschlichen Gedanken sucht man in den Besitz dieses Landes zu kommen und sieht nicht, wie Jehova "die Räder des Wagens schwer macht", damit er nicht sein selbstgestecktes Ziel erreicht. Manschreit nach mehr "Religiosität", wie die anderen Bundesgenossen in des Teufels Organisation. Blind sind die Juden auch dafür, daß das "alte Weib" in Rom alles daransetzt, zu verhindern, daß die Juden hier selbständig werden. Seine Priester sind die größten Hetzer. Ihre "heiligen Stätten" seien gefährdet, sollten die Juden zahlreicher werden! so schreien sie. Deshalb muß auch England in seiner Abmachung mit Italien "die berechtigten italienischen (lies: katholischen) Interessen" garantieren, d. h. das Recht, daß das "alte Weib" fernerhin durch seine Schulen und Klöster das arme Volk verdummen darf, um es dann auszusaugen.

'Die Juden sind ein lebendiges Bild dafür, wie furchtbar es ist, den Segen Jehovas nicht zu besitzen. Abgeschnitten von der Gunst Gottes, sind sie auch hier ohne Ruhe. Wind säend, ernten sie Sturm! Wie lange noch?'

That this spirit of anti-Semitism continued well after Rutherford's death – at least in the attitude of his successors in Brooklyn – is shown both by quotations from Watch Tower publications as quoted in chapter 2 and an account by Barbara Grizzuti Harrison. She recounts that while at the Brooklyn Bethel headquarters of the Watch Tower in the early 1950s, she witnessed the third Watch Tower president, N.H. Knorr, give a 'trimming' to an elderly Jewish Jehovah's Witness:

> In the Watchtower printery, and at Bethel residence, we worked eight hours and forty minutes a day, five and a half days a week. We filled out time sheets daily at the factory, and there was no time allotted for coffee or rest breaks. An elderly Bethelite on my floor of the factory kept a small supply of chocolates and candies, which he sold to hungry workers at candy-store cost on an honor system; we dropped our nickels and dimes into a box while he was busy at his menial work. I suppose he made a few pennies' profit each day, and I suppose also that he was one of those who received no financial help from outside, so those pennies were important. I can't remember ever having heard him speak.
>
> Knorr heard about the little enterprise and read the old man out, at great length, in public. He tied his attack to the fact that the man was a Jew. The Jews, Knorr asserted, had always been willful, penny-grubbing ingrates. Jehovah had chosen them precisely to show that such unappetizing raw material could be redeemed if they adhered to His laws. The candy seller was, Knorr said, demonstrating all the abysmal qualities that had led the Jews to kill Christ. And so on, for an hour, while I cringed.[55]

How can all of this documented evidence be reconciled with statements that the Witnesses helped the Jews by not observing Nazi boycotts and that they were kind to them in the concentration camps? In the first place, Detlef Garbe's assertion that the Witnesses refused to observe boycotts is really based on a single local study.[56] In any case, there were times when even the German general public refused to support such boycotts, simply because it was not in their interests to do so rather than out of any sympathy for the Jews.[57]

55 Barbara Grizzuti Harrison, *Visions of Glory: A History and a Memory of Jehovah's Witnesses* (New York: Simon and Schuster, 1978), 159.

56 On page 106n80 of *Zwischen Widerstand und Martyrium,* Garbe uses as proof of his contention that Witnesses refused to support boycotts of Jewish stores, material from Walter Struve, 'Die Zeugen Jehovas in Osterode am Harz. Eine Fallstudie über Widerstand und unter drückung in einer kleinen Industriestadt in Dritten Reich,' in *Niedersächsiches Jahrbuch für Landsgeschichte* 62 (1990), 265–95.

However, Watch Tower historian Jolene Chu brings more concrete evidence to support the Society's claims that the Witnesses were helpful to the Jews. She notes that historian Anton Gill credits the Witnesses with 'sheltering and protecting Jewish neighbors during and after Kristalnacht.' She quotes a copy of the Jewish New York Yiddish daily *Der Tog* of July 1939 to the effect that Witnesses in Danzig had protected Jews from Nazi attacks, had shopped in Jewish stores despite Nazi boycotts, and had provided Jewish neighbours with food and milk. She also cites a case where 300 to 400 Witness concentration camp inmates went hungry for four days in 1938 because they had provided food to some 2,250 Jews brought into Buchenwald. Finally she quotes Bruno Bettelheim to the effect that Witnesses never abused other prisoners and were 'exemplary comrades, helpful, correct, dependable.'[58] But Chu neglects to state that Bettelheim also noted their anti-Semitism.

While what Chu says may be true, this does not warrant generalizations such as those made by her, by Garbe, and by the Watch Tower Society. Jehovah's Witnesses – who are perhaps the most active proselytizers in Christendom - have always shown particular kindness to anyone who is a prospective convert. Only after someone has rejected their message do they become cold to that person. So it is quite possible that there were many instances of kindness to Jews by Jehovah's Witnesses both outside and inside the concentration camps based on the assumption that they might become converts. Chu herself points out that the main concern of the Witnesses seems to have been to proselytize:

> The Witnesses were known for sharing their Bible message with other prisoners. 'Though gentile prisoners were forbidden to talk to us,' said a Jewish woman in Lichtenburg, 'these women never observed this regulation. They prayed for us as if we belonged to their family, and begged us to hold out.' BBC reporter Björn Hallstrom said that in Buchenwald, Witnesses were punished for eight days because they 'had not avoided the forbidden paths between the Jewish blocks:' Frustrated by the Witnesses' persistent resistance, the SS regularly announced in Sachsenhausen that prisoners

57 Kershaw, 474, 561–2.

58 Jolene Chu, 'Purple Triangles: A Story of Spiritual Resistance.' Published originally in *Judaism Today* 12 (Spring 1999), 15–19, and republished with the permission of the editors on website www.baycrest.org. The comments cited above appear on page 5 of Chu's website article.

caught talking to Witnesses would receive 25 strokes. Survivor Max Liebster recalls that the SS there isolated the Witnesses and declared their barracks off limits to other prisoners. In Melk, Polish survivor Joseph Kempler says he saw 'a camp within a camp' and was told that the SS kept the 'purple triangles' in it, dangerous prisoners because they taught the Bible.[59]

Perhaps the best analysis of this subject was done in the early 1940s by Hebert Stroup,[60] who carried out his study mainly by associating with ordinary Jehovah's Witnesses and participating in their activities. He carefully dissected the Witnesses' thinking on many subjects, including their attitude toward Jews. He said bluntly: 'The Jews also are hated by the Witnesses. Although this feeling is common among them, it appears strange at first glance, inasmuch as the movement appeals to many Jews. But all who have joined "the Lord's organization" are precious in the sight of Jehovah and are fellow members of a special human group; thus, converted Jews are made welcome, often with the idea that they are "the chosen people." The official literature terms the Jews outside the movement "blind" because they do not accept "the truth."' Regarding those Jews who did not become Witness converts, however, Stroup remarked: 'Prevalent among the Witnesses is the notion that all Jews are rich. Even refugees who have escaped to this country from persecution abroad are believed to have brought "scads of money" with them. One Witness told me fantastic tales about the apparent luxury within some of the homes of Jewish refugees that he had visited. The affluence of the refugees, according to this Witness, is hidden from most people because they do not have the opportunity which he and his fellow workers have of visiting all kinds of homes.' Because the Witnesses' anti-Semitism was based more on religious prejudice than racism, Stroup noted: 'In spite of this generally unfavorable attitude [toward Jews], which is, indeed, sometimes shared by Jewish Witnesses themselves, the movement is able to satisfy its Jewish members, who find in its theology the natural, developed expression of essential Judaism.[61]

59 Ibid.

60 Hebert Hewitt Stroup, *The Jehovah's Witnesses* (New York: Columbia University Press, 1945).

61 Page 154. On page 79 of the same volume, Stroup said: 'The Jehovah's Witnesses also contain a striking number of Jews, recruited from among those who consider themselves spiritual outcasts from formal religious organizations – they cannot maintain the orthodox faith of their fathers; they cannot become members of

There can be no doubt that much of the Watch Tower Society's criticism of the German churches is valid. Few clergy of the major churches spoke out in any way in defence of the Jews or of human rights in general. Some members of the Catholic and Protestant clergy did actively support the Nazi persecution of Jehovah's Witnesses. Furthermore, most churchmen supported the German war effort once it began. The Watch Tower's censuring of Eugenio Pacelli, who became Pope Pius XII on the eve of the war, seems at least partially vindicated by history. Yet even with respect to its denunciations of the German churches in general and Roman Catholicism in particular, the Society's stance deserves criticism.

The Witnesses were heirs to a long tradition of bitter Protestant animosity toward Catholicism. The Watch Tower's first president, C.T. Russell, was the son of Northern Irish Protestant immigrants to the United States, and he regarded Catholicism with a jaundiced eye. For his part, J.F. Rutherford came out of that American populist tradition which was thoroughly antipathetic to the Catholic Church. Rutherford, with some marginal justification, blamed it for much of the widespread North American persecution of his fellow believers during the First World War and for his own brief imprisonment in the Atlanta, Georgia, federal penitentiary on charges that he and seven of his associates had violated the U.S. Espionage Act.[62] As a result, he and his

---

Christian churches. Seeking to preserve the values of their special heritage and yet hoping for a basic spiritual union with all people, they find themselves isolated religiously. To these the Jehovah's Witnesses appears inviting. The word "Jehovah" in the popular title of the organization has an especial appeal. The fact that many of the theological conceptions of the Witness movement are derived from the Old Testament also has some influence. A Jewish leader of a local Company told me that he had been reared by strictly orthodox parents, had been taught Hebrew "until it made my ears stand up," knew the complex ritualistic forms of Jewish orthodoxy, and yet felt that he was not "religious." When he reached the teen age he drifted away from the orthodoxy of his childhood, thereby greatly displeasing his parents. Later, when he heard the message of the Witnesses, he was converted; he believes that it retains all the worth-while emphases of his childhood (although in altered form), along with all that is worth-while "out in the world."'

62 On pages 91 and 92 of *Faith on the March* (Englewood, NJ: Prentice Hall, 1957), A.H. Macmillan tells of how in 1918 he and seven fellow Bible Students at Watch Tower headquarters, including J.F. Rutherford, believed that they were being prosecuted under the American Espionage Act because of the 'anger of one powerful religious organization [obviously the Catholic Church] working against us.' However, he was informed by a number of civil libertarians that there were many organizations anxious to see them convicted. Undoubtedly this was the case, for Protestant clergy

followers became nearly psychotic in their anti-Catholicism. Both Rutherford and Clayton Woodworth heaped the vilest opprobrium on the Catholic Church and published incredibly insulting cartoons of Catholic priests and prelates.

The Catholic hierarchy responded angrily. Its members regarded Jehovah's Witnesses as the most obstreperous of heretics. Unfortunately, because of Catholic clerical influence over many governments in Catholic countries – and even in countries such as the United States, Canada, and Germany, where Protestants were in the majority – harsh laws were often passed (even in democracies) to suppress the door-to-door circulation of their incredibly caustic literature.[63]

The Witnesses might have been able to win the support of Protestants in their quarrel with Catholicism, except that they were only slightly less vitriolic in their denunciations of them than of Catholicism. As a result, a great many Protestants turned a blind eye to their troubles with the Catholic Church, and in some cases Protestant clergy worked alongside public officials to have some of their activities curtailed. So did some members of the business community, who resented Rutherford's diatribes against 'Big Business.' When Rutherford and the Witnesses made pronouncements that seemed more in harmony with socialist or Marxist policies than with those of capitalism, and when they did foolish things such as renting broadcast time over one of their Canadian radio stations to the Ku Klux Klan, they lost a great deal of sympathy among those many who would otherwise have defended their right to publicize their teachings in the name of freedom of speech and religion.[64]

Of course, in the first half of the twentieth century the Catholic Church was hardly a liberal institution. Despite some slight liberalization under Pope Leo XIII (1878–1903), in general it was a thoroughly authoritarian organization. Under Pius X (1903–1914) it had suppressed

---

and various patriotic organizations were just as negative toward the Bible Students as were Catholics.

63 Certainly, Protestants, and various nationalistic and patriotic organizations were also responsible for attempts to outlaw Witness door-to-door preaching, but there can be no doubt that Catholic clergy and lay organizations played a major role in such partially successful attempts.

64 See M. James Penton, *Jehovah's Witnesses in Canada: Champions of Freedom of Speech and Worship* (Toronto: Macmillan of Canada, 1976), chapter 5, 'The Battle of the Airwaves,' 94–110.

Catholic Modernism and Americanism, and under his successors it had moved to strengthen the papacy's control over the church. It lent its support to the most reactionary regimes, from Mussolini's and Franco's fascists in Italy and Spain to various Latin American dictatorships. Even in a democratic country like Canada, it gave its support to the reactionary Union Nationale government of Quebec. And most important, it boosted Hitler's prestige by entering into a concordat with Germany just at the time that he was making himself dictator.[65]

Unfortunately, the Witnesses have never understood that the Catholic community is not monolithic and never has been. As John Cornwell has pointed out so well, the Catholic Center Party in Germany was in many ways committed to democracy and the maintenance of the Weimar Republic.[66] One of its principal leaders, Heinrich Brüning, who served as chancellor during the dying days of the Weimar Republic, fought hard to stop Hitler from establishing a dictatorship.[67] Many members of the German Catholic episcopate were strongly opposed to Nazism, at least until they were undercut by the Vatican.[68] Also, if there were Catholics who were committed to democracy and civil liberties in Germany, there were even more of them in the United States. For example, in 1940, Catholic university legal journals criticized in one voice the U.S. Supreme Court for requiring Jehovah's Witness children to salute the American flag or face expulsion from public schools.[69] And, at least one Catholic prelate, Bishop Francis J. McConnell, joined a number of prominent Protestant and Jewish clergymen in condemning mob violence against the Witnesses.[70]

When Rutherford and the Watch Tower Society tried to blame the Witnesses' persecution in Germany mainly on the Catholic Church, they were misdirecting their fire; their assertion that Hitler and his Nazi thugs were taking their orders from the Vatican was foolish in the extreme. The *Führer* had no desire for a direct confrontation with

65 Cornwell, 130–55.

66 Ibid., 82–3.

67 Ibid., 155–6.

68 Ibid., 134.

69 David R. Manwaring, *Render unto Caesar: The Flag Salute Controversy* (Chicago: University of Chicago Press, 1962), 154–7, 176.

70 These included such outstanding figures as Dr Harry Emerson Fosdick, Rabbi Edward L. Israel, and Dr Reinhold Niebuhr. Their statement in defence of the Witnesses appears in a pamphlet titled 'The Persecution of Jehovah's Witnesses,' published by the American Civil Liberties Union.

Holy Water for Mama and the Babies
(from *The Golden Age*, 8 April 1936, 422)

the Catholic Church and was willing to enter into an arrangement with the Vatican, but he was no practising Christian of any kind. He took actions to please the mainline German churches immediately after coming to power, but this was no more than a political stratagem. Friedrich Zipfel quotes him as saying early on in his dictatorship: 'With respect to the [Christian] confessions, regardless of which ones, everything being equal, they no longer have a future. In any case, not for Germans. Fascism may make its peace with the Church in God's name. I will do that also. Why not? That will not hinder me from eradicating all of the bases of Christianity, root and branch, from Germany. One is either Christian or German. One cannot be both.'[71] In his *Table Talk,* Hitler often damned Christianity and the churches. At one such table talk on 14 October 1941, he expounded at length on his feelings. He rejected the idea that Germans should return to the worship of Wotan, but he also made it thoroughly clear that he regarded Christianity as a 'myth' that would eventually be eliminated by fresh scientific discoveries. In the meantime he was willing to let the churches continue to exist, so long as they did not interfere with affairs of state.[72]

So it is not surprising that Hitler was a great admirer of Friedrich Nietzsche, whose contempt for Christianity was profound. William Shirer writes: 'Hitler often visited the Nietzsche museum in Weimar and publicized his veneration for the philosopher by posing for photographs of himself staring in rapture at the bust of the great man.' In addition, he was enraptured by the mythos of Wagnerian opera and by the Germanic paganism that was so much a part of it. Shirer even suggests that Hitler saw the collapse of the Third Reich as a kind of *Götterdämmerung* (Twilight of the Gods). He writes: 'It is not at all surprising that Hitler tried to emulate Wotan when in 1945 he willed the destruction of Germany so that it might go down in flames with

71 Friedrich Zipfel, *Kirchenkampf in Deutschland: 1933–45* (Berlin Walter de Gruyter, 1965), 9. Hitler's statement reads: 'Mit den Konfessionen, ob nun diese oder jene, das ist alles gleich, das hat keine Zukunft mehr. Für die Deutschen jedenfalls nicht. Der Faschismus mag in Gottes Namen seinen Frieden mit der Kirche machen. Ich werde das auch tun. Warum nicht! Das wird mich nicht abhalten, mit Stumpf und Stiel, mit allen seinen Wurzeln das Christentum aus Deutschland auszurotten. Man ist entweder Christ oder Deutscher. Beides kann man nicht sein.'

72 *Hitler's Table Talk: 1941–1944,* with an introduction and new preface by Hugh Trevor-Roper, translated by Norman Cameron and R.H. Stevens (London: Phoenix, 2000), 58–62.

him.'[73] Thus to state or imply that Hitler was a Catholic in any real sense of that word is to ignore the facts of history. Simply put, it is total nonsense.

What about the attempts by Garbe, Wrobel, and Yonan to clear high Watch Tower officials, especially Erich Frost and Konrad Franke, of the charge that they betrayed their brethren to the Nazis? It well may be that the documents relating to Frost that appeared in *Der Spiegel* were planted by the Communist East German secret police to discredit Jehovah's Witnesses, who had been banned in East Germany. It does not follow, however, that those documents were forgeries. To clear Frost, Franke, and others of having given incriminating evidence to the Gestapo about their brethren, it would be necessary to show that the documents quoted in *Der Spiegel* and photocopied in *Die Zeugen Jehovas* were bogus; and this no one has been able to do.[74] Of course there is the additional argument that the individuals in question divulged information only under physical torture or the threat of it; and the evidence discussed by Garbe and Wrobel points strongly to this being the case. In fact, it seems true not only of them but also of most Jehovah's Witnesses whom the Gestapo arrested.[75] Many men and women are simply unable to withstand torture; they lose control of their mental faculties and will do almost anything to stop the pain. Garbe, Wrobel, and Yonan may be correct concerning this, and if they are, there is no reason to condemn Frost, Franke, and other Witnesses for having broken while in the Gestapo's hands. But if this is so, why did they not say so publicly, and especially in the publications of the Watch Tower Society? If the documents published in *Der Spiegel* and *Die Zeugen Jehovas* about their having given information destructive to their fellow Witnesses are true – and they no doubt are – what is shameful is that Frost and Franke did not simply state that they broke under torture or the threat of it, and move on. Yet, even that fault may

73 William L. Shirer, *The Rise and Fall of the Third Reich: A History of Nazi Germany* (New York: Faucet Crest Books, 1962), 149.

74 Garbe argues that 'Gestapo protocols are not reliable sources that accurately record actual conversations.' Detlef Garbe, 'Social Disinterest, Governmental Disinformation, Renewed Persecution, and Now Manipulation of History?' in Hesse, *Persecution and Resistance*, 265n55. While this may be true, the Gestapo documents mentioned in *Der Spiegel* and reproduced in Gebhard's *Die Zeugen Jehovas* bear Frost's signature. So the claim that the documents are not bona fide will not stand up.

75 See pages 178–80 below.

not have been entirely theirs. In true Jehovah's Witness style, Nathan Knorr seems to have considered it necessary to ignore the facts and act as if Frost, Franke, and others had never compromised. Thus as good Watch Tower servants, always obedient to the Watch Tower president, they ignored what they had evidently done in order to create a false history of always having maintained their 'integrity.' Frost ultimately did write an autobiographical account of his experiences, but it has never appeared or even been quoted in any official Watch Tower publication. In failing to give an accurate public report of what undoubtedly happened, he and other German Watch Tower leaders have left themselves open to charges that they willingly betrayed fellow Witnesses and their God, Jehovah.

What about the strong assertion made by the Watch Tower Society and some historians that Jehovah's Witnesses are forgotten victims of the Holocaust? Concerning this matter, it must be said that all who have asserted it – *except for the Watch Tower Society itself* – have obviously done so with respect to what has been written and done or not done solely in Germany. Even from that standpoint, it is difficult to give it very much credence. Immediately after the Second World War, many individuals testified to the sufferings and conduct of Jehovah's Witnesses in the concentration camps. Many of these testimonies were flattering, and all noted the Witnesses' general unwavering faithfulness to their ideals. Surely statements by Rudolf Höss, Eugen Kogon, and Bruno Bettelheim – who were mentioned earlier – and those by Protestant clergymen Hanns Lilje[76] and Martin Niemöller[77] – which appeared in German – must have been read by educated Germans at least. Then there were the works of Marley Cole,[78] Friedrich Zipfel,

76 Lilje stated in 1947: 'They [Jehovah's Witnesses] can claim to be the only large-scale rejecters of military service in the Third Reich, who did this openly and for the sake of conscience.' Quoted in Wolfram Slupina, 'Persecuted and Almost Forgotten,' in Hesse, *Persecution and Resistance,* 267.

77 Niemöller said: 'We Christians of today stand ashamed before a so-called sect like the Earnest Bible Students, who by the hundreds and thousands went into concentration camps and died because they declined service in war and refused to fire on humans.' Quoted in Slupina, 269.

78 Cole's book appeared in English as *Jehovah's Witnesses: The New World Society.* It was printed by Vantage Press, New York, in 1955. The following year it appeared in German as *Jehovas Zeugen. Die Neue-Welt-Gesellschaft. Geschichte und Organisation einer Religionsbewegung.* The German edition is an expanded version of the English and contains more information on the persecution of the Witnesses in Nazi Germany. It was published at Frankfurt am Main in 1956.

Michael Kater, and John Conway,[79] which appeared in 1956, 1965, and 1969. As David Diephouse has said in reviewing Detlef Garbe's *Zwischen Wiederstand und Martyrium:* 'Detlef's occasional references to Jehovah's Witnesses as "forgotten victims" of the Third Reich (pp. 9, 26) can be taken more as rhetorical flourishes than as sober statements of fact. Garbe's own surveys (pp. 16–40, 508–25) portray an extensive and diverse tradition of scholarship dating back at least to the contributions of Friedrich Zipfel, Michael Kater, and others in the 1960s.'[80]

Since 1945, individual authors writing in English have produced more works discussing the Jehovah's Witnesses under Hitler. Two that deal specifically with the Holocaust are Conway's *The Nazi Persecution of the Churches – 1933–1945* and Christine Elizabeth King's *The Nazi State and the New Religions*. In addition, a number of books written about Jehovah's Witnesses offer much information on what happened to them in Nazi Germany. Besides Cole's *Jehovah's Witnesses: The New World Society,* these include William J. Whalen's *Armageddon around the Corner,*[81] Alan Rogerson's *Millions Now Living Will Never Die,*[82] Timothy White's *A People for His Name: A History of Jehovah's Witnesses and an Evaluation,*[83] Barbara Grizzuti Harrison's *Visions of Glory,* and my own *Jehovah's Witnesses in Canada* and *Apocalypse Delayed: The Story of Jehovah's Witnesses.* So it is simply wrong to hold that Jehovah's Witnesses have been 'forgotten victims.'

It is true that the role of Jehovah's Witnesses in history and society is not one that catches the attention of the general public in Germany – or anywhere else, for that matter. Although they have been calling at homes in North America and Europe for well over a hundred years, few know much about them or care to. Some are aware of their refusal to salute the flag or do military service. Others have heard about their objection to blood transfusions. Beyond that, most people tend to know little about them. The Witnesses may consider themselves the apple of Jehovah's eye, but to most of the world they are at best a nuisance and

79 Conway's book has been published in English in several editions by different publishers under the title *The Nazi Persecution of the Churches – 1933–1945*. It was published in Munich in German in 1969 as *Die Nationalsozialistische Kirkenpolitik 1933–1945. Ihre Ziele, Widersprāche und Fehlschläge.*

80 H-Net Reviews as posted by David J. Diephouse of Calvin College at www2.h-net.msu.edu/reviewsshowrev.cgi?path=10320846443714.

81 New York: John Day, 1962.

82 London: Constable, 1969.

83 New York: Vantage Press, 1968.

at worst an unpatriotic, totalitarian sect or cult. So it is not surprising that, as Wolfram Slupina asserts, they have often been overlooked or, better stated, ignored. But it is difficult to believe, as he argues, that because the history of Jehovah's Witnesses is not well known by most Germans there must be a deep, dark plot – especially among the churches – to persecute them today. Slupina quotes negative comments about them by certain church spokesmen such as Kurt-Helmuth Eimuth, the sect (cult) expert of the Protestant Church in Hesse and Nassau, and gives examples of anti-Witness actions in Germany. But he also shows that there is much sympathy for them there.[84]

Beyond the fact that they are a small movement about which the general public knows little, there are other reasons why the Witnesses have not received a great amount of attention in Germany. Germans, like people of other nations, do not especially want to have their national sins constantly brought to their attention. The Japanese have done little to admit their nation's ill treatment of the Chinese, the Koreans, and other peoples during the 1930s and 1940s. The French do not like to be reminded that many of their people collaborated with the Nazis during the Second World War. The British do their best to forget their crimes in Ireland and India. The United States has been happy to establish Holocaust museums on its soil memorializing Jews and others who died under Hitler, but it has not seen fit to construct similar institutions that tell of American crimes. Nowhere is the genocide that was perpetrated against many North American Native peoples or the viciousness of Indian and African slavery memorialized in the United States in the way that the Holocaust is. So undoubtedly, Germans – who often find the Witnesses tiresome religious pests or worse – do not want to make much of their earlier persecution.

We must also consider the international situation. After the Cold War began, Western nations hoped to entice West Germany into an alliance against the Soviets and their allies. Thus it would not have been useful to emphasize Nazi Germany's sins. The fate of the European Jews was for some years not a matter of significant discourse even among their co-religionists in America.[85] In East Germany, discussions of Nazi persecution usually focused on the sufferings of Communists. After the Witnesses were banned in East Germany in 1950,

84 Slupina, 270–8.

85 See Peter Novick, *The Holocaust in American Life* (Boston and New York: Houghton Mifflin, 1999), ch. 6.

the Communist authorities were not going to give them any positive exposure – they were persecuting them themselves.

The Witnesses did publicize what had happened to their German brethren and other European Witnesses under the Nazis, but they did so largely in their own publications. Wolfram Slupina disagrees with Detlef Garbe's statement that 'only in a very few instances were they interested in informing the public, and thus their memoirs were limited to family and other fellow believers,'[86] but in this case Garbe is quite right. Slupina himself says concerning the Witnesses in 1945:

> Nazi persecution had greatly impeded care for their parishes [German: *Gemeinden* or congregations] and their preaching activities. Besides their concern for their own families, they had the additional task of reorganizing the remaining parishes and Bible-based preaching. *If they had become too immersed in the past they had just survived, it would have hindered or even paralyzed this important work.* Unlike other religious associations, they did not have to go through a so-called rehabilitation process, since they could not be blamed for making concessions to the Nazi system. Their regained freedom literally spurred them on. They looked ahead. With raised heads, they could resume their religious activities. *They felt that they lacked the time for historical documentation*'[87] (italics mine).

Until recently, the Watch Tower Society did everything possible to discourage the work of outside historians and other researchers. Garbe states:

> Although it is correct to attribute widespread silence about the persecution of Jehovah's Witnesses in the Nazi era to many years of disinterest in the West or the ban and disinformation in the East, it must also be stated that the long-standing refusal to deal with this subject is, to a large extent, caused by the structure and peculiarity of the 'Watch Tower Bible and Tract Society.' The exclusive claim of this controversial religious association, whose 'Governing Body' lays claims to the sole truth and its doctrine, which in rational terms is barely understandable particularly for those unacquainted with the Bible, has probably contributed to the neglect of the subject, and also to the

86 Slupina, 268.
87 Ibid., 68–9.

> group's isolation from the outside world. Research efforts, as far as they went, met with reluctance from the Watch Tower Society for a long time. Outsiders could not obtain access to the archives of the Watch Tower Society. Not only anxiety and bad experiences, in particular with journalists concerned with dubious 'exposures,' but also the wish for a monopoly on the interpretation of their own history, had contributed to this uncooperative attitude.[88]

Dietrich Hellmund is even more outspoken about this matter: 'When I was first interested in the history of Jehovah's Witnesses during the Nazi years, I inquired of the Watch Tower Society in New York as well as with the German branch of Jehovah's Witnesses, at that time located in Wiesbaden-Dotzheim. They did everything in their power to prevent me from getting access to the publications of the Watch Tower Society, although at first I was only interested in seeing or borrowing literature that the society itself had published in past decades.'[89]

So if the fate of the Witnesses under the Third Reich has been little publicized in Germany, it does not seem that in most cases they have been forgotten intentionally. It is simply because of historical developments, because of their small numbers and marginal nature, and because of the Watch Tower Society's own policies. Were those policies implemented – in part at least – because the Society felt that there were aspects of its history that were not as pure as it would like others to believe? It may well have been so.

After dealing with the above issues, one still remains. Could Judge J.F. Rutherford really have been ignorant of the nature of Nazism when he wrote the 25 June 1933 *Declaration of Facts?* To answer this question, a more general analysis of the history of the times is necessary.

88 Garbe, 'Social Disintrest,' 257.

89 Dietrich Hellmund, 'Critical Reflection on the Video Documentary "Stand Firm against Nazi Assault": Propaganda or Historical Documentation?' in Hesse, *Persecution and Resistance,* 343.

4

Rutherford's New Nation – 'The Theocracy' in America

For conscientious cussedness on the grand scale, no other aggregation of Americans is a match for Jehovah's Witnesses.

Stanley High, *Saturday Evening Post*

To get a full understanding of the Bible Student-Jehovah's Witnesses' relationship to Nazi Germany, it is necessary to look at their history in the United States.

Originally known simply as Bible Students, they were a direct outgrowth of the Millerite and Adventist movements of the early nineteenth century. As such, they continued in the tradition of setting specific dates for Christ's *parousia* or 'presence,'[1] the rapture of the saints, and the establishment of Christ's millennial reign over the earth. Originally, C.T. Russell adopted a schema which held that Christ Jesus had come invisibly to the earth in 1874, that he had come to his temple for judgment in 1878, that the 'higher calling' or selection of the saints to heavenly life had ended in 1881, and that Christ would fully establish his kingdom on earth in 1914.[2]

1 The Bible Student understanding of *parousia* as 'presence' rather than 'coming,' as it is usually translated from Greek, followed a nineteenth-century practice developed for theological purposes by a number of Protestant translators and Bible exegetes.

2 This schema, which was originally devised by Russell's early associate, Nelson Barbour, is outlined in early copies of *Zion's Watch Tower and Herald of Christ's Presence,* Russell's *The Time Is at Hand* and *Thy Kingdom Come,* the second and third volumes of his *Studies in the Scriptures* as published originally by Zion's Watch Tower and Tract Society in 1889 and 1891. Since then the Watch Tower Society and

It was the First World War rather than Christ's kingdom that came in 1914. Even so, Russell and most of his followers remained undaunted. Russell believed that the war would lead into Armageddon.[3] After his death in the autumn of 1916, his followers predicted, first in 1917 and then in 1918, that the nations would destroy the churches and that Christ would fully establish his millennial reign over the earth by 1925.[4]

This date-setting eschatology led Russell and his Bible Student followers to take a negative attitude toward secular governments, nationalism, and war. Although Russell believed that God had invested the nations with relative authority, he held such authority to be no more than a temporary arrangement. In the tradition of the first Christians, the Anabaptists, and some Adventists, he also held that secular governments, despite having some God-given legitimacy, were basically under the control of Satan. The slaughter of the First World War shocked him, and he took a much stronger stand against military service than he had previously.[5] Canadian immigration officers therefore denied him entry into Canada in 1916,[6] but since the United States was largely against participating in the war until after his death, he experienced no particular problems in his home country.

In January 1917, J.F. Rutherford was elected the second president of the Watch Tower Society and became, to all intents and purposes, the leader of the Bible Student movement. A Missouri lawyer who had

---

International Bible Students Association have produced many editions of *Studies in the Scriptures,* as, more recently, have various independent Bible Student movements. With respect to Russell's ideas concerning 1881, see *Zion's Watch Tower* of October and November 1881, 2–3, or reprints, 288–9.

3 See the 'Author's Foreword' to C.T. Russell, *The Time Is at Hand,* vol. 2, *Studies in the Scriptures* (Brooklyn, NY: IBSA, 1916), i–iv.

4 Originally Clayton J. Woodworth, as co-author of the book *The Finished Mystery,* vol. 7 of *Studies in the Scriptures* (Brooklyn, NY: IBSA, 1917), prophesied on page 268 of that work that the churches would be destroyed in 1917 as a prelude to the battle of Armageddon. When that date passed, he changed this statement and suggested that that event would take place in the spring of 1918. The first 75,000 volumes of *The Finished Mystery* contain the earlier prophecy; later printings contain the revised prophecy. For a discussion of this matter, see the transcript of record of The *United States v. Rutherford et al.* at pages 609 and 610. For Woodworth's teaching on 1925, see *The Finished Mystery,* 128.

5 For a full discussion of Russell's changed views, see M. James Penton, 'Jehovah's Witnesses and the Secular State: A Historical Analysis of Doctrine,' *Journal of Church and State,* 21(1) (1979): 56–61.

6 *Winnipeg Free Press,* 8 July 1916, 1.

served for four days as a substitute judge,[7] he was an impressively tall, dynamic individual who grew unattractively obese in his later years. He was also a thoroughgoing demagogue who manifested a strange charisma based on his powerful oratory and the title 'judge.' It is certain that he was a heavy drinker, especially in his later years. He may well have been an alcoholic.[8]

There is also strong circumstantial evidence that he was somewhat of a womanizer and may have had a mistress in the last years of his life. Regarding Rutherford's possible womanizing, Peter Moyle has written: 'It has also been known, albeit "carefully covered," that Rutherford liked his women and his whiskey.'[9] In support of this allegation, family members of Rutherford's female dietician and nurse are convinced she was his mistress. The woman in question, a Mrs Berta Peale, was a close friend of Bonnie Boyd, Rutherford's stenographer. She accompanied Boyd to a Watch Tower convention in Europe at some point in the mid or late 1930s. At that convention she evidently met Rutherford. Thereafter, in June 1938, she abandoned her non-Jehovah's Witness husband of fifteen years and moved to the Brooklyn Bethel, where, at least outwardly, she became Rutherford's dietician and nurse. In November 1939 her husband, Albert Peale, filed for a divorce from her. It was granted in March 1940. Naturally, these facts raise serious questions. Why did Rutherford accept her at Bethel when she had openly deserted her husband? Such behaviour was in clear violation of biblical teachings as understood by Jehovah's Witnesses. Why did the judge make her his nurse and dietician when he

7 Rutherford was never elected or appointed a regular judge. Fellow lawyers in Missouri named him to the position of substitute judge for four days. Circuit Court Records, Cooper County, Missouri, book 20, 576 (17 February 1897); book 22, 73 (3 June 1899); book 25, 213 (15 March 1905); book 25, 239 (29 March 1905). Evidently there was nothing before the court on two days when Rutherford sat as a 'special' or substitute judge. Although the Watch Tower Society says that he was a 'special judge' for various periods of time, it never indicates how seldom that was. Nevertheless, it must be admitted that he was, in a very restricted sense, a 'judge.' Rutherford obviously liked the title, which he used on the booklet, *Judge Rutherford Uncovers Fifth Column* (Brooklyn, NY: Watch Tower Society, 1940). See also the transcript of record of *Moyle v. Franz et al.*, 841–3, and Gérard Hébert, S.J., *Les Témoins de Jéhovah: Essai critique d'histoire et de doctrine* (Montreal: Les Éditions Bellarmin, 1960), 44–5, 232n7.

8 M. James Penton, *Apocalypse Delayed: The Story of Jehovah's Witnesses*, 2nd ed. (Toronto: University of Toronto Press, 1997), 72–3.

9 Quoted in David Horowitz, *Pastor Charles Taze Russell: An Early American Christian Zionist* (New York: Philosophical Library, 1986), 65.

already had a male nurse and when she had no formal training as either a dietician or a nurse? And why, finally, did he take Mrs Peale, an attractive southern belle, with him wherever he went? That was something he did not do with his male nurse, Matthew Howlett.[10]

Another strong indication that Rutherford may have been sexually adventurous is that his wife obviously felt quite bitter toward him. She had not lived with him for many years. His excuse was that she was an invalid and could not give him his 'marital dues'; however, there was more to the matter than that. He seldom if ever bothered to visit her. So when he was dying of cancer, both she and their son Malcolm practically ignored him even though both were living nearby in southern California.

Despite Peter Moyle's assertion, the facts surrounding Rutherford's highly questionable relationship with Mrs Peale, his alienation from his wife and son, and various rumours that circulated among disillusioned Bible Student-Witnesses that raise questions about his conduct, there is no direct proof that he was sexually immoral. Still, with so much evidence to suggest he was, it is difficult to believe he was not.

More serious to the members of his religious community than either Rutherford's liking for alcohol or his possible womanizing were his extreme delusions of grandeur, as a result of which he came to view his personal ideas as the will of Jehovah. His megalomania made him willing to crush any opposition among his brethren to either his teachings or his actions, with little or no ethical restraint.[11] In many ways he

10 The data presented here are based on information provided by Dr Carl Thoronton, Mrs Peale's grand-nephew, who has taken much time to research her relationship with Rutherford, and from the Transcript of Record of the trial of *Moyle vs. Franz et al.* on pages 1299–1301 and 1381–2. Mrs Peale's name is spelled incorrectly as 'Peal' in the Transcript of Record.

11 There are many such instances where this was true. The document that shows this most clearly is the transcript of record of *Moyle v. Franz et al.* Moyle was the Watch Tower Society's lawyer at its Brooklyn headquarters from 1935 until 1939. He became disgusted with Rutherford's behaviour and wrote a personal letter to him criticizing him for it. In it he said that he was resigning and was going back to Wisconsin. He nonetheless stated that he was willing to continue to represent Jehovah's Witnesses in court. Rutherford would not have it, and brought Moyle before the boards of directors of the Watch Tower Society of Pennsylvania and the Watchtower Society of New York, all of whose members supported Rutherford. When Moyle returned to Wisconsin, Rutherford did everything to have him driven from the Witness movement and shunned by his former brethren, and had him described as a 'Judas' in the pages of *The Watchtower*. Moyle then sued for defamation of character and for the negative effects on his business. He ultimately collected

resembled two contemporary American demagogues, the Louisiana governor and senator Huey Pierce Long and the Witnesses' hated enemy, the Canadian-born, rabble-rousing Catholic priest Father Charles Edward Coughlin.[12] Furthermore, Rutherford often spoke with the pomposity and bombastic belligerence of a Hitler or Mussolini. Although he claimed to be no more than a 'fellow worker' with his Bible Student–Jehovah's Witness brethren, and although his followers have referred to him as 'humble,' no one who looks at these assertions carefully can regard them as valid. In discussing this matter, Raymond Franz wrote:

> Effort is made (on pages 220, 221 of the new history book [*Jehovah's Witnesses: Proclaimers of God's Kingdom*] to deny that the second [Watch Tower] president, Joseph F. Rutherford, sought to gain full and total control of the [Watch Tower] organization. A quotation from Karl Klein is presented to show him as actually an essentially humble man, 'child-like in prayer to God.'
>
> Yet the historical record shows that anyone, including any member of the Board of Directors or of those of the Editorial Committee, who expressed disagreement with him was quickly eliminated from whatever organizational position that person occupied. One has only to talk with others who were at the headquarters during his presidency to know the picture of humility conveyed by Karl Klein does not conform to reality, and that, to all intents and purposes, the 'Judge's' word was law. I was actively associated with the organization during the last five years of his presidency and know the clear effect the man had upon me and the viewpoint that others expressed ... I believe that anyone who simply reads the material found in the *Watch Tower* magazine from the 1920s on through to 1942 can clearly see the spirit, not of humility, but of dogmatism and authoritarianism that the articles breathed. Deprecating, even harsh language is employed against any who dared to question any position, policy or teaching that came forth from the organization of which he was the head.

---

more than $15,000 plus costs from the boards of the two societies. By that time Rutherford was dead.

12 For brief overviews of these two men, see James MacGregor Burns and Susan Dunn, *The Three Roosevelts: Patrician Leaders Who Transformed America* (New York; Grove Press, 2001), 240–1, 293–4, 298–300, 322–3. In many ways Rutherford was in the same populist tradition as Long and Coughlin. All three fulminated against the evils of big business and came to attack President Roosevelt with venom.

> On these same pages, effort is made to demonstrate that Rutherford was not looked upon by the membership as 'their leader,' and his personal denial of such position, made in 1941 just before his death, is quoted in proof. The words are there but the facts are not. While admittedly Watch Tower adherents viewed Christ as their *invisible* leader, the fact is they *did* look upon Rutherford as their *visible* earthly leader, contrary to Christ's injunction at Matthew 23:10: 'Neither be called leaders, for your Leader is one, the Christ.' Rutherford cannot fail to have *known* that the membership viewed him in that light.[13]

Franz went on to reproduce copies of Watch Tower publications from 1931 showing that to Jehovah's Witnesses, Rutherford was in fact 'their visible leader,' 'the Chief' who demanded absolute loyalty.[14]

What displays his personality clearly was the ruthless way in which he seized nearly full control of the Watch Tower Society in July 1917 by staging what amounted to a political putsch[15] and by publishing and widely distributing bitter attacks on the clergy for their support of the First World War.[16] The results of these actions were dramatic. By the spring of 1918, many Bible Students had broken with the Watch Tower Society[17] and American authorities had indicted Rutherford and seven colleagues for violations of the U.S. Espionage Act. Following a lengthy trial, a jury convicted them of having interfered with the American war effort. Thereupon, the judge in the case sentenced them to

13 Raymond V. Franz, *Crisis of Conscience: The Struggle between Loyalty to God and Loyalty to One's Religion,* 2nd. ed., 2nd printing (Atlanta: Commentary Press, 1992), 360.

14 Ibid., 360–3.

15 William Cumberland, 'A History of Jehovah's Witnesses' (doctoral dissertation, University of Iowa, 1958), 118–45. Alan Rogerson, *Millions Now Living Will Never Die: A Study of Jehovah's Witnesses* (London: Constable, 1969), 32–41. James A. Beckford, *The Trumpet of Prophecy: A Sociological Study of Jehovah's Witnesses* (New York: John Wiley and Sons, 1975), 23–4. Penton, *Apocalypse Delayed,* 48–55.

16 This is evident from what was published in *The Finished Mystery,* 248–53, and in particular in the *Bible Students Monthly,* No. 9, which was also presented orally in well-publicized lectures on 30 December 1917. One statement made in *The Finished Mystery,* the *Bible Students Monthly,* and the December 1917 lectures regarding the clergy was especially vitriolic. It reads: 'Ye have preached millions into dreadful death in the trenches, have made them cannon-fodder by the thousands for blood guilty kaisers and czars, kings and generals of your evil order of things.'

17 In the spring of 1918 and for the next several years, many dissident Bible Student movements emerged in the United States, Canada, Great Britain, and many countries of continental Europe. Many of these movements continue to exist.

prison in Atlanta, Georgia. Seven of them, including Rutherford, were sentenced to twenty years each, while an eighth was sentenced to ten years.[18] Despite these events, Rutherford was able to maintain control of the Watch Tower Society. When he was released from prison early in 1919, he set the stage for the rapid growth of the Watch Tower Bible Student movement. This he did by wearing the mantle of a martyr who had been unjustly imprisoned for his faith[19] and by launching a preaching and proselytizing campaign announcing that Christ's kingdom would be established on earth by 1925. Concerning this campaign, he began to emphasize the idea that every Bible Student should be a house-to-house Watch Tower preacher. In 1922, at Cedar Point, Ohio, he proclaimed to his zealous followers: 'Advertise, Advertise the King and the Kingdom.'[20]

Rutherford's program, known as the 'Millions Campaign,'[21] had an amazing effect. In 1919 there were roughly 25,000 Bible Students associated with the Watch Tower organization,[22] but by 1925 there were some 100,000. In that year *The Watch Tower* announced that it had received reports that at least 90,434 had attended the Bible Students' spring annual celebration of the Memorial of the Lord's Supper.[23] When nothing spectacular happened in 1925, many were disillusioned and drifted away. What makes this fact evident is that in 1928 only 17,380

18 *Jehovah's Witnesses in the Divine Purpose* (Brooklyn, NY: Watchtower Society and IBSA, 1959), 80–1. Penton, *Apocalypse Delayed,* 55–6. For years, Watch Tower publications claimed that Rutherford and his confreres were 'sentenced to eighty years.' Undoubtedly, this was done for shock effect; actually, all but one of them were sentenced to four concurrent terms of twenty years. The one was sentenced to ten years.

19 *Divine Purpose,* 85–6. It is undoubtedly true, however, that he and his associates were the victims of wartime hysteria. On appeal, it was recognized that they had not had a fair trial.

20 Ibid., 101–2.

21 *Jehovah's Witnesses: Proclaimers of God's Kingdom* (Brooklyn, NY: Watchtower and IBSA, 1993), 163. This campaign was named after talks given by Rutherford titled 'Millions Now Living Will Never Die.' In 1920 he produced a booklet with the same title.

22 Memorial attendance that year was only 21,411. *Jehovah's Witnesses: Proclaimers of God's Kingdom,* 720. 'Classes' (congregations) with fewer than twenty present were not counted. So there may have been up to 25,000 Bible Students in fellowship with the Watch Tower Society at the time.

23 According to *The Watch Tower* of 1 September 1925, page 263, this count did not include attendance at meetings with fewer than twenty-five people.

people were present at the Memorial.[24] The Watch Tower Society, in evident embarrassment, stopped publishing Memorial attendance statistics for many years.

The failure of Rutherford's prophecy concerning that year was not the only reason for Bible Student defections. By his own admission, he had made 'an ass' of himself over 1925,[25] but that did not deter him from making further prophecies and from gradually taking control of Bible Student congregations that had always been governed democratically by leaders elected by the congregations. Of course, in extending his control over the Bible Student community, he had to move slowly. This he did by debunking several of Russell's teachings, and also by restructuring Russell's date-setting eschatological system, replacing the idea that Russell had played a central prophetic role as the 'faithful and wise servant' and the 'Laodicean' or last great messenger of the Christian church before the full establishment of Christ's kingdom on earth. Having done this, he discredited and replaced democratically elected congregational elders with Watch Tower Society appointees in every congregation that he could; he also imposed Watch Tower–directed weekly study lessons on them.

Rutherford's first major step in changing Russell's chronology came when he published an article in the 1 March 1925 *Watch Tower* titled 'Birth of the Nation.' More than simply changing his predecessor's chronological system in that article, he interpreted Revelation 12 as applying directly to the Bible Students' own experiences during and after the First World War. He argued that Watch Tower directors – by whom he really meant himself – represented the Bible Student community, and he held that the New Nation of Watch Tower Bible Students was at war with Satan and his system. That system, according to the article, included the political, economic, and ecclesiastical organizations of all nations. Significantly, Rutherford published 'Birth of the Nation' over the opposition of an editorial committee that Russell had provided for in his will. Years later, the judge boasted: '*The Watchtower* [*sic*] of March 1, 1925, published the article "Birth of the Nation", meaning the kingdom had begun to function. An editorial committee, humanly provided for, then was supposed to control the publication

24 *Jehovah's Witnesses in the Divine Purpose* (Brooklyn, NY: Watch Tower and IBSA, 1959), 313.

25 WT, 1 October 1984, 24. Penton, *Apocalypse Delayed,* 58.

of *The Watchtower* [*sic*], and the majority of the committee strenuously objected to the article "The Birth of the Nation" [*sic*], but by the Lord's grace, it was published, and that really marked the beginning of the end of the editorial committee, indicating the Lord himself is running the organization.'[26] Quite evidently, what this meant was that Rutherford regarded himself as God's sole spokesman on earth, as Jehovah's channel for revealing 'new light.' As he made clear in his closing comments in 'Birth of the Nation,' those Bible Students who had opposed and broken with him were a part of the 'Judas class.'[27]

'Birth of the Nation' was followed by other *Watch Tower* articles that would eventually change the nature of the Bible Student community. Since according to Rutherford, everything had to be done to promote 'evangelism' – which largely involved the hawking of publications that he wrote – every Watch Tower convention from 1919 on emphasized the importance of advertising the judge's personal messages. This constant barrage of propaganda ultimately convinced many Bible Students that they must 'publish or perish.' By the beginning of the 1920s Rutherford was asserting that all Christians must preach publicly in fulfilment of Matthew 24:14. Yet despite constant pressure, a majority resisted being dragooned by him. Many still maintained the belief from Russell's day that character development or Christian sanctification was more important than proselytizing. Many could not accept the argument that they were required to witness from door to door.[28] Most important, many elected elders resented the Watch Tower's growing authority over and manipulation of local congregations. So, to achieve complete domination over the Bible Student community, Rutherford would have to take several steps. Among them, he would have to destroy the idea of 'character development' or sanctification and the idea that Russell had been the 'faithful and wise servant.'

To erase the idea of personal sanctification among Bible Students, Rutherford published an article titled 'Character or Covenant – Which?' in the 1 May 1926 *Watch Tower*. In this he attempted to discredit character development. When one looks at that article and compares it with Russell's statements on the matter, you will see that Rutherford was attacking a straw man. By discrediting the older Bible Student idea of

26 WT, 1938, 185.
27 J.F. Rutherford, 'Birth of the Nation,' WT, 1 March 1925, 67–74.
28 As an example or Rutherford's bellicose attitude toward such ones, see WT, I929, 119.

character development as 'works righteousness,' he was able, paradoxically, to place greater emphasis on the work of evangelism.

The Watch Tower Society continued to distribute Russell's works for many years, and continued to regard him as the 'faithful and wise servant.' Clearly, then, Bible Students were reluctant to adopt Rutherford's ideas without questioning them. So in the 1 January 1927 *Watch Tower,* Rutherford published an article that was obviously intended to discredit Russell's reputation. Among other things, that article stated: 'The worship of heroes, whether in the church or out of it, is surely of the Devil. It is the enemy's scheme to turn man away from God, by inducing man to reverence some other man; and thereby many fall into the Devil's snare.'[29] Shortly after this, in February of the same year, the Watch Tower Society abandoned the teaching that Russell had been the 'faithful and wise servant.' Henceforth, 'that servant' was to be regarded as the remnant of the elect of God on earth – the Bible Students loyal to the Watch Tower Society, as pictured by the 144,000 saints of Revelation 7:4–8 and 14:1, who had not yet been joined with Christ in heavenly glory.[30]

While Rutherford was discrediting Russell's memory and his teachings, he was strengthening his own control over the Bible Student community. By holding that the 'remnant of the elect,' the 'church class,' or the Bible Student community as a whole was the 'faithful and wise servant' rather than Russell, ordinary Bible Students and (in particular) elected congregational elders could claim that they as much as Rutherford could provide divinely directed teachings or spiritual 'meat in due season.'[31] So Rutherford came up with two new doctrines, which together indicated the ad hoc nature of Watch Tower teachings and which were devised to achieve his program for taking control of the Bible Student movement – control to a degree that even the pope did not enjoy over Roman Catholicism. First, he played a shell game on his brethren by defining the word 'Society' in two dif-

29 WT, 1927, 7.

30 WT, 1927, 56–7. Although Revelation 7:4–8 describes the 144,000 as twelve of the tribes of Israel, Bible Students had always interpreted this passage to apply to 'spiritual Israel' rather than literal, fleshly Israel. Curiously, however, they had always treated the number 144,000 as literal, as do Jehovah's Witnesses today.

31 Most of those who did not agree with Rutherford's new interpretation continued to hold to the idea that Russell had been 'that servant.' Still, they regarded themselves as spirit-begotten members of the church and as free to accept or reject Rutherford's teachings.

ferent ways. To Bible Students 'the Society' had always meant the Watch Tower Bible and Tract Society. In 1919, Paul Johnson, one of Rutherford's harshest critics, had produced an article titled 'The Church Organized in Relation to the Society.' In that article, he argued that the Society should be subservient to the church (the Bible Student Community) rather than the other way around. In evident reply to that article, Rutherford asserted that the term 'Society' meant the entire Bible Student community – the church: 'While the Society is a body corporate with required officers and servants, yet alone these do not constitute the Society. In the broader sense the Society is composed of the body of Christians organized in orderly manner under the Lord's direction for the carrying out of his work.' By this definition, as Timothy White argues, Rutherford was claiming that as the president of the Society, he was actually the president of the church. Although he could not make this claim directly, what he was asserting is clear.[32]

This doctrine did not clarify what the powers of the president were. So Rutherford came up with an even more extreme teaching – one that he had hinted at in 'Birth of the Nation.'[33] What this constituted was the claim that since Christ had come to his temple for judgment in 1918 rather than 1878 – one of the judge's revised eschatological teachings – the Holy Spirit had not been present with Jehovah's people, the Bible Students, since that date. After that year, Jehovah had dealt directly with his faithful and wise servant through angels[34] – angels who communicated directly through Rutherford and the Watch Tower Society as His channel on earth. Ray Mattera writes: 'Although Rutherford disguised his new doctrine as a teaching about the faithful slave, he was in reality claiming that he alone had a direct line to the Deity. He therefore signaled to Watch Tower adherents that there could be

32 Timothy White, *A People for His Name: A History of Jehovah's Witnesses and an Evaluation* (New York: Vantage Press, 1968), 181, 182. WT, 1921, 329.

33 In paragraphs 6, 7, and 9 on page 67 of 'Birth of the Nation,' Rutherford refers to Revelation 11:19, which mentions 'lightnings, and voices, and thunderings,' which he held had occurred when Christ came to his temple in 1918. The lightnings he interpreted as new revelations. For a full discussion of Rutherford's idea of how he personally received 'new light,' see Ken Raines, 'The Holy Spirit Taken Away in 1918,' 'Angelic Channeling,' and 'Light,' *JW Research*, 1, 2 (Spring 1994): 3–5, 6–11, 12–14.

34 Rutherford emphasized this teaching repeatedly. See 'Holy Spirit,' WT, 1930, 259–64. J.F. Rutherford, *Light Book One* (IBSA and Watch Tower Society, 1930), 56, 229. J.F. Rutherford, *Preparation* (Brooklyn, NY: Watch Tower Society and IBSA), 196, 237. J.F. Rutherford, *Jehovah* (Brooklyn, NY: Watch Tower Society and IBSA, 1934), 156, 206–7.

no legitimate authority outside his leadership.'[35] In 1932 he used this doctrine of the absence of the Spirit to abolish the system of elected elders within congregations loyal to the Watch Tower Society and himself.[36]

Just how nonsensical this 'new truth' was is clear. Although Rutherford never abandoned it up to the time of his death, he continued to describe those who made up the 'faithful and wise servant class' as 'spiritually begotten.' He also argued that the Spirit had been poured out on the Bible Students at the 1922 Cedar Point convention, when they were motivated to 'advertise the King and the Kingdom.' Paradoxically, he made this argument in a 1932 *Watch Tower* article in which he proclaimed that Christ was in direct control of the Theocratic organization of Jehovah's Witnesses and was quite evidently not acting through the Holy Spirit.[37] Regarding this matter, Mattera writes:

> How could Rutherford maintain that the Watch Tower community was experiencing a 'second outpouring of the Holy Spirit' and at the same time insist that the Holy Spirit had ceased to function as advocate toward the church? The question either did not occur to him or he did not feel compelled to answer it. Rutherford's argument, therefore, was hopelessly contradictory – indeed it strained the limits of credulity. Nevertheless, it becomes comprehensible when one understands Rutherford's hermeneutics. Rutherford practiced the hermeneutics of expediency. He was determined to banish all opposition to his authority and to stress the indispensability of the preaching work. If persons defected from the movement because they failed to see the cogency of his arguments or refused to yield to his authority – all the better. His attitude toward dissenting members of the movement is the attitude Watch Tower leaders continue to emulate today: either merge or be purged.[38]

35 Ray Mattera, '"This Generation Shall Not Pass Away": Eschatology, Ecclesiology, and Ethics in the Theology of Jehovah's Witnesses with Special Reference to Jesus' Eschatological Discourse' (master's thesis, Northern Baptist Theological Seminary, Lombard, IL, 1999), 32. In referring to the 'faithful slave,' Mattera uses current Watch Tower terminology as found in the New World Translation of the Holy Scriptures. The Greek *doulos* means a slave rather than a free servant, as the Authorized Version now seems to suggest.

36 Penton, *Apocalypse Delayed,* 62–4. Mattera, 32–4.

37 'Jehovah's Organization – Part 2,' WT, 1 September 1932, 259–66. Note, in particular, page 263. See also 'Drama of Vindication – Part Three,' WT, 1 March 1939, 70.

38 Mattera, 33–4.

Rutherford's claims to authority were not unopposed. Many longtime, prominent Bible Students severed their connections with the Watch Tower movement to join some of the groups that had split from it in 1918 or to form new fellowships in association with the Dawn Bible Students Association.[39] At local congregations, bitter schisms often developed between those who followed Rutherford's dicta and those who were determined to remain independent of centralized Watch Tower Society control. It is certain that by far the majority of Bible Students broke with him. In 'Birth of the Nation,' Rutherford estimated that one-third of the 'leaders' of those who had been associated with the Watch Tower in Russell's day had abandoned it.[40] That would probably also have meant one-third of all Bible Students, for the elders would have influenced great numbers of their brethren. By 1929 a far larger number – including many who had joined the movement during the 'Millions Campaign' – had separated from it.[41]

The struggle between Rutherford and the elected elders became extremely bitter. This is shown by a statement he made in his three-volume set, *Vindication*.[42] Therein, he compares elected elders to butting billy goats who have an 'offensive or bad odor.' Curiously, he suggests that those elders faithful to the Society ought to be regarded as a 'wethers' or neutered male sheep. On page 235 of volume 1, he says: 'The Lord makes a difference between "he goats" and the "rams", which according to *Lesser* are called "wethers". A wether is a male sheep that has lost his self importance and arrogance by reason of a surgical operation. A man who is an elder may be like a butting, shoving buck or he-goat, but if he puts away or cuts away his selfishness and then unselfishly serves God's people because of his love for God and his people, he is likened unto a "wether."'[43]

39 The Dawn came into existence in the late 1920s and early 1930s. Unlike most other Bible Student movements of the time, it began an active ministry. For a statement attacking Rutherford's doctrinal and organizational changes, see *When Pastor Russell Died* (East Rutherford, NJ: Dawn Bible Students Association, n.d.).

40 'Birth of the Nation,' WT, 1 March 1925, 68.

41 William Schnell estimates that 'in the decade from 1921 to 1931 almost three-fourths of the Bible Students originally associated with the Society in a loose fashion left the Society's supervision behind.' W.J. Schnell, *Thirty Years a Watch Tower Slave: The Confessions of a Converted Jehovah's Witness* (Grand Rapids, MI: Baker Book House, 1956), 41.

42 Brooklyn, NY: Watch Tower Society, 1932.

43 As further examples of Rutherford's tirades against elected elders, see J.F. Ruther-

Evidence indicates that most elders did not want to be castrated spiritually by the Watch Tower president. *Souvenir Notes from the Reunion Convention of Christian Bible Students*, held at Pittsburgh, Pennsylvania, between 1 and 3 November 1929, indicates that the vast majority of prominent Bible Students who had remained with Rutherford in 1917 and 1918 had finally given up on him and the Society. Among those present at the dissident Reunion Convention were long-time Watch Tower Bible Students such as Scottish pyramidologist Morton Edgar and Dr L.W. Jones of Chicago – people who had supported Rutherford and the Society staunchly for some years during and after the First World War.

Yet Rutherford was undaunted. He was determined to build the 'New Nation' of Jehovah's Witnesses – a name he gave to his loyalist followers in 1931 to differentiate them from other Bible Students – into what he dubbed 'the Theocracy'[44] under his own, unquestioned leadership. He would achieve this by means of Watch Tower–directed preaching work. By 1941, the last full year of his life, there were as many Jehovah's Witnesses as there had been Bible Students in 1925. According to the Society's published statistics, there were nearly 100,000 Watch Tower adherents at the spring, annual Memorial of the Lord's Supper, and there were 106,137 door-to-door Jehovah's Witness 'publishers' or preachers throughout the world.[45]

In building the Theocracy, Rutherford was determined to separate the Witnesses doctrinally in every way possible both from other religions and from secular society. Thus he declared that many popular customs such as Christmas, Easter, birthdays, and even Mother's Day were 'pagan' and to be avoided.[46] Tipping a man's hat to a lady was labelled an act of idolatry.[47]

He condemned worldly governments as of the Devil. Since the first century there had been a significant Christian tradition of regarding the secular state of any nation – and particularly the Roman Empire before the time of Constantine – as of Satan. St John's statement at 1 John 5:19 – 'We know that we are of God, and the whole world is in

---

ford, *Preparation* (Brooklyn, NY: Watch Tower Society and IBSA, 1933), 68, 132, 174, 175, 199, 200, 201, 243, 244, 246, 308, 324, 340, 357, 358, 359.

44 For Rutherford's description of his New Nation, see J.F. Rutherford, *Theocracy* (Brooklyn, NY: Watchtower and IBSA, 1941).

45 *Divine Purpose,* 312.

46 *1975 Yearbook,* 147–9. *The Golden Age,* 1934, 489–90.

47 *The Golden Age,* 1934, 594.

the power of the evil one' – makes that position explicit, and Revelation 13 seems to buttress it in symbolic language. Such open hostility to secular government was tempered, however, both by Jesus and by two significant apostolic passages in the New Testament. Jesus said that Christians should 'render unto Caesar what is Caesar's' (Matthew 22:21; Mark 12:17); and the apostolic passages, found at Romans 13:1–7 and 1 Peter 2:13–17, both call on Christians to honour secular rulers. But Rutherford decided to reinterpret the Romans passage as having reference to human authorities in the church or 'the Society' rather than to the governments of the nations. In an article titled the 'Higher Powers,' which appeared in two parts in the 1 and 15 June 1929 issues of *The Watch Tower,* he claimed that the Apostle Paul's remarks at Romans 13:6, 7 regarding the payment of taxes were nothing more than an aside or parenthetical statement.[48] As for 1 Peter 2:13–17,[49] he took the Apostle Peter's statement regarding submitting to 'every ordinance of man' as applying to ordinances within the church only. As far as references to 'a king' and 'governors' at verses 13 and 14 were concerned, Rutherford simply applied those terms to Christ and to human authorities within the church under him. Since the Apostle Peter had used the Greek word *basileus* or 'king' rather than the Latin *imperator* to designate an emperor, the judge's interpretation did not seem too far-fetched, at least to his followers.[50] Of course, what this all meant was that Rutherford was himself claiming ultimate human authority over Jehovah's Witnesses as a 'governor,' although he was wise enough not to say so openly.

This new 'Higher Powers' doctrine provided Rutherford with free range to rail against secular authorities in the most extreme fashion. He and his subalterns then began to pour out undiluted verbal and printed vitriol on any ruler or government that did something that they considered wrong. They claimed to be 'neutral' in political affairs

48 WT, 15 June 1929, 181–2.

49 According to the King James or Authorized Version, which Rutherford was using, 1 Peter 2:13–17 reads: 'Submit yourselves to every ordinance of man for the Lord's sake: whether it be the king, as supreme; Or unto governors, as unto them that are sent by him for the punishment of evildoers, and for the praise of them that do well. For so is the will of God, that with well doing ye may put to silence the ignorance of foolish men: As free, and not using *your* liberty for a cloak of maliciousness, but as the servants of God. Honour all *men.* Love the brotherhood. Fear God. Honour the king.'

50 For Rutherford's exegesis of 1 Peter 2:13–17, see WT, 1 June 1929, 107–8.

as ambassadors of Christ's kingdom, but their neutrality was of a very strange kind. All it meant was that Jehovah's Witnesses were not to vote, hold public office, or serve in the military of any nation. Unlike ambassadors or diplomatic officials of secular governments, whom the Witnesses claimed to emulate, it allowed them to manifest open hostility to their 'host' governments and to carry on activities with good conscience that were often illegal and sometimes very close to seditious. For example, the Watch Tower president railed constantly against prohibition,[51] and his agents illegally imported liquor from the Canadian branch offices of the International Bible Students Association in Toronto to Watch Tower headquarters in Brooklyn without blinking an eye, even though the U.S. Constitution prohibited the production or possession of alcoholic beverages.[52] As a result, many ordinary Jehovah's Witnesses saw nothing wrong in smuggling dutiable articles across international boundaries or importing items for their own use that were prohibited in certain jurisdictions. Such items could include everything from margarine to liquor to illicit drugs.[53]

Despite his belligerence, Rutherford was mild in his public statements compared to his confidant, longtime supporter, and spokesman, Clayton J. Woodworth. As editor of *The Golden Age* and, later, *Consolation,* Woodworth appealed to the basest instincts of his largely Bible Student–Jehovah's Witness readers. He filled those magazines with bitter diatribes and thoroughly obnoxious cartoons directed against the clergy. He also promoted a campaign against the medical profession by condemning vaccination, aluminum cookware, and the germ theory of disease; at the same time, he gave support to various forms of pseudotherapeutic quackery.[54] Although a spokesman for a

51 Rutherford raised the issue of prohibition in his 'Higher Powers' *Watch Tower* article. In 1930 he even produced a booklet titled *Prohibition; The League of Nations: Of God or the Devil – Which?* In that booklet he made it quite clear that he believed that prohibition was of Satan.

52 Based on a personal interview with Frank Wainright, late Secretary-Treasurer of the International Bible Students Association of Canada, April 1972. According to Wainright only a few senior Witness leaders at the American headquarters of the Watch Tower Society refused to engage in the illegal importation of liquor from Canada.

53 I recall this vividly from personal observation while growing up in a Jehovah's Witness family and from knowing about such behaviour in both Canada and the United States.

54 There are so many such articles on these topics that it would be tiresome to list them.

Christian organization that claimed to be 'neutral,' he also attacked politicians, often by name or through cartoons. For example, he described President Herbert Hoover, a Quaker and a noted humanitarian, as having the 'heart of a tyrant.'[55] He detested President Franklin Roosevelt because he represented a political party that received strong Catholic support. At the end of Roosevelt's first term of office, *The Golden Age* and *Consolation* attacked him and his policies consistently and lampooned him with vicious cartoons. Nonetheless, when it was to their advantage to do so, Rutherford and Woodworth and their associates would use their citizenship to leverage American courts, politicians, and diplomats to the maximum. In effect, Witness 'neutrality' was more than a little bit hypocritical in its application.

Apart from individual politicians, Rutherford in particular had a deep hatred for Great Britain and the United States – a fact that in 1932 led him to become involved in a serious political controversy in Washington, D.C. In the spring and summer of 1932 a 'Bonus Army' of many thousands of unemployed American veterans of the First World War and their families descended on the American capital. In the midst of the Depression that had struck the United States and the world in the fall of 1929, millions were destitute and suffering terribly. Thus the veterans – many of whom were among those millions – demanded that the federal government immediately pay them a bonus of $500, which by law they were supposed to receive in 1945. The U.S. Senate refused to pass the necessary legislation to do this, and many veterans returned home. However, many others stayed and camped on the outskirts of the District of Colombia at the Anacostia Flats; still others occupied various buildings on Pennsylvania Avenue. When on 28 July the District of Columbia police tried to evict them from the buildings on the avenue, a riot broke out and two veterans were shot and killed. Hoover then called out the army under the command of General Douglas MacArthur, who entered the city with six tanks, a column of infantry with fixed bayonets, and a detachment of cavalry with sabres drawn. MacArthur cleared the buildings on Pennsylvania Avenue; however, he then overstepped his orders by directing his forces to the Anacostia Flats. There they drove the veterans and their families from their makeshift camp with tear gas and burned the shacks they had built for themselves. As a result, one baby died from suffocation and a young child was blinded.[56]

55 *The Golden Age,* 20 July 1932, 646.

56 David M. Kennedy, *Freedom from Fear: The American People in Depression and War,* vol. 9, *The Oxford History of the United States* (New York and Oxford: Oxford

A month earlier, J.F. Rutherford had involved himself in the Bonus Army affair. On 26 June he had come to Washington and delivered a lecture – better stated, a jeremiad – to the veterans. This was broadcast over a chain of radio stations in the United States and Canada east of the Rocky Mountains. That speech – 'Can the American Government Endure?' – was vintage Rutherford and was a blistering attack on American society and especially on capitalism. In it he asserted that 'Big Business' controlled practically every economic, political, and religious entity in the United States: 'Every branch of government is contaminated and improperly influenced by Big Business. It controls the two major political parties of America and names and elects at will the public men to office who will best serve its selfish interests. Big Business controls the army and the navy, the guns and the ammunition, and the police power of the nation.'[57] Following these remarks, he stated: 'Big Business either directly or indirectly owns or controls almost all of the newspapers and magazines of America, and which agencies serve as propagandists for Big Business and for their immediate political and religious allies. The same selfish interests own and control the professional clergymen, and these men make merchandise of the Word of God in order to keep the people in ignorance and in subjection to the ruling powers.'[58] Moreover, he held that there was a corporate plot to establish a dictatorship in the United States, which he felt would come about within the year: 'I venture the opinion that before the end of the year the American government will be ruled by a dictator, aided by a company of advisers that are selected and directed by the chiefs of Big Business. Such will be a military rule and one which the people will be compelled to submit to.'[59]

This was incendiary language. In the circumstances, it could have incited to violence many of the veterans, who were bitter over their plight. But Rutherford protected himself from charges of outright sedition by telling them that a revolt would be useless and that they should wait for Jehovah himself, who would soon be acting to destroy the government of the United States and all that it stood for. He proclaimed: 'The American government has been weighed in the balance and found wanting. Together with all other nations, it soon shall fall.'[60]

University Press, 1999), 92, and Howard Zinn, *A People's History of the United States, 1492–Present,* revised and updated (New York: HarperCollins, 1995), 381–2.

57 *The Golden Age,* 1932, 648.

58 Ibid.

59 Ibid., 651.

60 Ibid., 654.

The day before Rutherford delivered his lecture, three hundred Jehovah's Witnesses appeared in Washington to contact members of the Bonus Army and to deliver pamphlets and books throughout the city. The police, the government, and the Electrical Power Company at first tried to stop them, but a number of veterans supported the Witnesses' efforts, and the District of Columbia police chief decided to let them carry on with their activities. Thus they were able to invade public buildings in droves to press their message on government officials and government workers. Some of the workers were terribly frightened, thinking they were being invaded by members of the Bonus Army.[61]

Rutherford's decision to involve himself and the Witnesses with the Bonus Army is not difficult to understand: he wanted to make more converts to his 'New Nation,' and no doubt he did so. Many veterans appreciated his message, and there is anecdotal evidence that some joined the ranks of the judge's Theocracy. There also seems little doubt that his message expressed his deepest feelings. He had never forgotten his nine months in an Atlanta prison, which had seriously affected his health. His hatred of his native land as clearly expressed in 'Can the American Government Endure?' no doubt reflected what was in his heart.

Because of Rutherford's and Woodworth's constant outpourings of last-days prophecies and verbal venom directed at 'the world,' it is small wonder that the Watch Tower Society was able to motivate faithful Jehovah's Witnesses to begin invading quiet communities on Sundays to bring them Rutherford's brand of 'good news' – which householders were told they must accept lest they be destroyed at Armageddon. Many were outraged at these door-to-door campaigns. Householders were often devout members of various churches, and they resented the Witnesses' verbal and printed diatribes against their faiths. Others regarded the Sunday visits to their houses as intrusions on their privacy. Furthermore, municipal governments were eager to control door-to-door peddlers of any kind. So, it was not long before many communities began arresting Witnesses for 'peddling' Watch Tower publications without a licence, for disturbing the peace, and for violating Sabbatarian legislation.

Resistance to the Bible Student–Witnesses' Sunday visitations began in New Jersey, but other states quickly caught up, as well as Canada.

61 Anton Koerber, 'Proclaiming the Kingdom at Washington,' *The Golden Age*, 20 July 1932, 654–5, 669.

Over the next decade many hundreds of Jehovah's Witnesses were arrested in the United States alone.[62] In Quebec they were even charged with seditious conspiracy.[63] In many places they were also subjected to mob violence. Small wonder: instead of being as 'wise as serpents and as harmless as doves,' under the direction of Rutherford's Theocracy they were inviting persecution. When some communities tried to outlaw their door-to-door canvassing, Witnesses organized 'divisional campaigns,' which involved invading those towns and cities in scores and sometimes in hundreds, thus making it impossible for police to arrest them all.[64] They were, as Rutherford told them, like Jehovah's 'locust army' as described by the prophet Joel.

As the 1930s wore on, Rutherford's speeches over radio and at Witness conventions became ever more strident. Rutherford was eventually forced off the air, at which point the Watch Tower Society provided Witness door-to-door 'publishers' with portable phonographs, on which they played records of the judge's caustic sermons – often to unhappy householders.[65] Jehovah's Witnesses, young and old, paraded through cities and towns where the Watch Tower Society held conventions, bearing placards with slogans such as 'Religion Is a Snare and a Racket.'[66] In addition, Watch Tower publications constantly asserted that all governments, as the Devil's tools, would soon be destroyed at Armageddon. For example, *The Watchtower* of 1 December 1939 proclaimed on page 361: 'Every government on earth is now against the Theocracy. The King of the Theocratic government says: "He that is not with me is against me; and he that gathereth not with me scattereth abroad." (Matt. 12:30) The facts now well known fully prove that all the political, commercial and religious organizations are against the kingdom of God. The reason is, because Satan, the invisible "god of this world", and all his power, and the power of his agents, are against the Theocratic government.' Then on the following

62 'At first statistics were not kept, but in 1933 throughout the United States 268 arrests were reported; in 1934, there were 340, in 1935, 478, and in 1936, 11,149.' *Divine Purpose,* 132.

63 *Brodie and Barrett v. the King,* [1936] S.C.R. 118; 65, C.C.C. 289; 3 D.L.R. 81. *Duval et al. v. the King,* (1938) 64 Quebec K.B. 270.

64 *Divine Purpose,* 133–4. For an example of the Society's overt policy of causing ordinary Witnesses to break the law, see Schnell, 143–5. Although Schnell is often extreme in his pronouncements, here he undoubtedly gives a true picture of what was happening.

65 *Divine Purpose,* 137–9. *Jehovah's Witnesses: Proclaimers,* 85, 564–6, 721.

66 *Divine Purpose,* 145.

page the Witness journal proclaimed: 'All the forces of the world under Satan's command are gathered together for the battle of the great day of God Almighty. (Rev. 16:13–16) All of Satan's forces are against The Theocracy and those who stand for The Theocracy. Jehovah's time has come to show his power against all that oppose his government. (Ex. 9:16) It is Jehovah's time when he, by his right hand, Christ Jesus, "should destroy them which destroy the earth."' Yet it was not this general condemnation of everything and everyone outside the Theocracy that brought the most severe persecution down on Jehovah's Witnesses in the United States between 1935 and 1943, or that led to major constitutional battles in the American courts. Rather, it was one of the Watch Tower president's specific teachings – the claim that to salute the American flag, or any national emblem, and to participate in patriotic exercises constituted idolatry.

Three excellent studies outline the history of what became the flag salute controversy: David R. Manwaring's *Render unto Caesar: The Flag Salute Controversy*,[67] Leonard A. Stevens' *Salute! The Case of the Bible vs. the Flag*,[68] and Shawn Francis Peters's *Judging Jehovah's Witnesses: Religious Persecution and the Dawn of the Rights Revolution*.[69] All three works detail, from slightly different perspectives, what happened to Jehovah's Witnesses as a result of this eight-year controversy.

Manwaring provides an excellent history of the development of the flag salute as a patriotic practice in American public schools, and of religious opposition to it. According to him, saluting the flag in schools began in 1892 at the behest of two writers for *Youth's Companion* magazine. Gradually it spread throughout the United States. Between the two world wars, various patriotic organizations encouraged it, and many states passed flag salute legislation. As far as religious opposition to the flag salute was concerned, the first to object to it were certain Mennonites, members of one or more of the many Churches of God, and adherents of the Elijah Voice Society, a schismatic movement of Standfast Bible Students in Washington state. But it was not until Jehovah's Witnesses became openly opposed to the flag salute in 1935 that the matter became one of intense public interest.[70] Manwaring

67 Manwaring, *Render Unto Caesar* (Chicago: University of Chicago Press), 1968.
68 Stevens, *Salute* (New York: Coward, McCann & Geohegan), 1973.
69 Peters, *Judging Jehovah's Witnesses* (Lawrence, KS: University Press of Kansas, 2000).
70 Manwaring, 11–16.

Window dressing. 'Oh, Frankie, it's the same suit Adolf and Benito wore when they started out – and you're so becoming in it. Now where's them nine old men?'
(from *The Golden Age*, 24 March 1937, 393)

writes: 'For the flag-salute controversy to become a major constitutional issue in the courts, there still was lacking a non-saluting sect which had the resources and inclination to sue and sue again and was sufficiently unpopular or truculent to preclude any negotiated settlement. When Jehovah's Witnesses entered the controversy in 1935, they fulfilled amply both requirements. The legal battle over the compulsory flag salute was exclusively a Jehovah's Witness fight.'[71]

It was logical that Jehovah's Witnesses should object to saluting flags. After Rutherford enunciated his 1929 Higher Powers doctrine, the Witnesses regarded the secular state as of the Devil; thus they could hardly be expected to participate willingly in patriotic exercises of any kind. By 1931 the Watch Tower Society was already teaching that patriotic ceremonies confronted Witnesses with the same sort of dilemma that the prophet Daniel's companions, Shadrach, Meshach, and Abednego, had faced when King Nebuchadnezzar of Babylon demanded that they bow down before an image he had constructed.[72] And thus it is not surprising that German Witnesses refused to give the Hitler salute or *Heil Hitler* after the Nazis came to power in 1933.

Jehovah's Witnesses had taken an extreme position on the nature of the secular state; yet it must be admitted that they were dealing with a significant issue. By the 1930s, patriotic exercises had come to be an important means of instilling the values of nationalism in the hearts and minds of the citizens of nation-states, especially among the young. Also, no one can reasonably deny that nationalism has been a great curse of modern times, for it has been responsible for dividing peoples based on language, religion, and ethnic origin. It has also led to terrible wars and some of the worst pogroms in history. So by refusing to participate in patriotic exercises such as the flag salute, the Witnesses were questioning a phenomenon that Friedrich Nietzsche described as 'a scabies of the heart and blood poisoning,'[73] and that Albert Einstein called an 'infantile disease' and the 'measles of mankind.'[74] They were also enunciating the early Christian idea that their loyalty to God must supersede their loyalty to human government. They never tired

71 Ibid., 16.

72 *Jehovah's Witnesses: Proclaimers*, 196.

73 Quoted in Norman Rich, *The Age of Nationalism and Reform, 1850–1890* (New York: Norton, 1977), 47.

74 Written in a 1921 letter to G.S. Viereck.

Sister Jezebel says she's afraid he'll prove a stubborn convert.
(from *The Golden Age*, 24 March 1937, 393)

The 'blessing' of the Hierarchy – Ezekiel 16:33, 34
(from *The Golden Age*, 21 April 1937, 451)

of noting that the first Christians had often been martyred for refusing to burn incense to the Roman emperor's genius.[75]

But Rutherford's approach to the flag salute issue was in one way very wrong. As was characteristic of him, he dealt with the matter in an abrasive fashion and in doing so brought more persecution on his brethren and their children than was necessary. His tactlessness was shown in the approach he took to advertising his and the Witnesses' opposition to the flag salute – an approach that undoubtedly turned what might have stayed a series of scattered, local affairs into a nationwide controversy and, ultimately, an international one. As Leonard Stevens notes, the Founding Fathers of the United States were opposed to compulsory oaths of allegiance. Regarding this matter, George Washington expressed himself forcefully in a letter to General Lafayette.[76] Furthermore, during the 1930s many Americans were openly critical of legally enforced pledges of allegiance to the flag or the nation because of the negative example then being set in Germany. Stevens writes: 'Many people still held the distaste for compulsory oaths expressed by the Father of our country. But most important was the growing awareness of the compulsory flag salute ordered in Germany by Adolf Hitler, who demanded absolute, unswerving loyalty to his swastika flag, hated so much in America. U.S. newspapers often carried pictures of masses of Hitler youth, their stiffened arms raised at an angle with palm and fingers extended toward the Nazi flag. It was unsettling to think that similar photographs could be taken in American classrooms.'[77] So had the Witnesses decided to fight compulsory patriotic exercises and flag salute laws more tactfully and at the state or local levels, the whole matter might not have got out of hand. Unfortunately for many Jehovah's Witnesses, that wasn't Rutherford's way.

On 3 June 1935, at a convention in Washington, D.C., Rutherford held a question-and-answer session on saluting the flag in which he instructed Jehovah's Witness schoolchildren not to salute it.[78] Naturally they obeyed, as they were trained to do. Thus early in September of that year, an eight-year-old Lynn, Massachusetts, schoolboy named Carleton Nichols, Jr, refused to salute the Stars and Stripes and was

75 *Jehovah's Witnesses: Proclaimers,* 196.
76 Stevens, *Salute!* 23.
77 Ibid., 25.
78 *Jehovah's Witnesses: Proclaimers,* 196–7.

expelled from his public school. The Associated Press carried this story all over the United States, and a reporter asked Rutherford why Jehovah's Witnesses would not salute the flag. Instead of giving a subdued answer, he delivered a bellicose nationwide radio talk, 'Saluting the Flag.'[79]

Rutherford's address served to place Jehovah's Witnesses in even worse light publicly; it also placed them in open opposition to the nation in a way that they had not been – at least to the same extent – since the First World War. Speaking specifically of Carleton Nichols, Jr, he proclaimed in his broadcast:

> The refusal to salute the flag, and to stand mute, as this boy did, could injure no one. If one sincerely believes that God's commandment is against the saluting of flags, then to compel that person to salute a flag contrary to the Word of God, and contrary to his conscience, works a great injury to that person. The State has no right by law or otherwise to work injury to the people.
>
> For many centuries Satan the Devil has been the invisible ruler of the nations of the earth. God has suffered or permitted him to so act in order to put a test upon the human race to determine how many will serve God willingly and how many will serve the Devil. For that reason Jehovah God gives this commandment to those who will receive his favor (Exodus 20:3,5): 'Thou shalt have no other gods before me ... Thou shalt not bow down before them or serve them.'[80]

If that statement were not enough to enrage patriotic Americans who regarded their country as under the protection of God, Rutherford went on to pronounce:

> It is written, at Romans 13:1: 'Let every soul be subject unto the higher powers'; and many wrongfully hold that 'the higher powers' are the visible rulers of the nations of earth. This scripture is addressed to the followers of Christ Jesus, and to no others, and 'the higher powers' are Jehovah God and Christ Jesus, and every true follower of Christ Jesus must obey God in preference to man.

79 *The Golden Age*, 23 October 1935, 36–9.
80 Ibid., 36.

The flag of the United States is not the flag of Jehovah God and Christ Jesus. It is the emblem of the power that rules the nation; and no one can truthfully say that God and Christ Jesus rule a government where crime is rampant. Men have organized governments, and Satan the Devil overreaches men and rules them because of their refusal to obey God, and hence the nations of the world are under the control of Satan the Devil, as stated at 1 John 5:19: 'We know that we are children of God, and that the whole world lies in the power of the Evil one.' (*Weymouth*) In proof of this, mark the words of Jesus. That the Devil is the invisible ruler of the world, note this from the Bible: Satan took Jesus up on a high mountain, and, being the god of this world, he showed Him all the kingdoms of the world and offered to give them to Jesus upon condition that Jesus would fall down and worship the Devil. Jesus refused and said (Matthew 4:10): 'Thou shalt worship the Lord thy God, and him only shalt thou serve.'

In further proof, Jesus, at John 12:31, stated that Satan is the prince or invisible ruler of this world. At John 18: 36, He said: 'My kingdom is not of this world.' Jesus directed his followers to pray to God saying (Matthew 6:9–12): 'Thy kingdom come; thy will be done on earth as in heaven.' At 2 Corinthians four it is written that Satan is the god of this world and deceives and blinds the people to the truth.[81]

Near the end of this diatribe, Rutherford launched into an extended attack on the Catholic Church, the U.S. Congress, and Franklin Roosevelt for wanting to send a personal representative to the Vatican.[82]

This language infuriated patriotic organizations. Groups such as the American Legion joined with the many clergy and others who detested Jehovah's Witnesses and who were willing to use every means available to suppress them. By this time the Witnesses were, as Leonard Stevens writes, 'America's most cantankerous religious minority.' Stanley High of *The Saturday Evening Post* wrote:

For conscientious cussedness on the grand scale, no other aggregation of Americans is a match for Jehovah's Witnesses. Defiance of what others cherish and revere is their daily meat. They hate all religions – and say so from the housetops. They hate all governments with an enthusiasm that is equally unconcealed. On phonograph records, sound trucks, the radio and in a Noah's flood of literature, they admit, without conscious blasphemy,

81 Ibid., 37.
82 Ibid., 39.

> that they hold a prior lien on the Almighty. On the rest of us – the Great Unwashed – they look down their spiritual noses. We, they say, have got 'it' coming to us, and 'it' – as they triumphantly prove by Scriptures – is due almost any time now.[83]

Contrary to Rutherford's prediction, the United States did not become a dictatorship, and if Satan was directly in control of the American judicial system, he was ruling as an amazingly committed civil libertarian. For despite their unpopularity, the Witnesses began to win case after case in the American courts and especially in the U.S. Supreme Court. Of these cases, three were perhaps the most important: *Lovell v. City of Griffin*,[84] *Schneider v. New Jersey*,[85] and *Cantwell v. Connecticut*.[86] The first two were fought and won largely based on the argument that neither municipalities nor states had the right to abridge freedom of the press by establishing ordinances that prohibited the door-to-door circulation of tracts and other literature without a police permit. The court's decisions in these cases gave the Witnesses a green light to continue distributing and placing Watch Tower literature throughout the land.[87] As far as *Cantwell* was concerned, it broke new legal ground by declaring unconstitutional a Connecticut statute which held that the solicitation of contributions for charitable or religious reasons was illegal without the approval of the secretary of the public welfare council of a county. Significantly, the Supreme Court held: 'The First Amendment declares that Congress shall make no law respecting the establishment of religion or prohibiting the free exercise thereof. The Fourteenth Amendment has rendered the legislatures of the states as incompetent as Congress to enact such laws.' Interestingly, *Cantwell* involved the playing of a phonograph record titled 'Enemies,' which attacked Catholic doctrine, and the presentation of the inflammatory book of the same name.[88]

Suddenly, however, the Supreme Court rendered a decision that went very much against Jehovah's Witnesses. This was the famous flag salute case of *Minersville School District v. Gobitis*.[89] What had hap-

83 Quoted in Stevens, 32.
84 303 U.S. 444 (1938).
85 308 U.S. 147 (1939).
86 310 U.S. 296 (1940).
87 *Divine Purpose*, 178.
88 Ibid., 178–9.
89 310 U.S. 586 (1940).

pened was this: In November 1935 three young Witness children – Lillian and William Gobitas[90] and Edmund Wasliewski – were expelled from a Minersville, Pennsylvania, public school for refusing to salute the flag. Nearly two years later, Watch Tower lawyers Olin Moyle and Harry M. McCaughey filed papers in a Philadelphia federal court to force the Minersville School Board to allow the Gobitas children back into the school from which they had been expelled without forcing them to salute the flag. Jehovah's Witnesses were overjoyed when the trial judge in the case, Albert Branson Maris, came down solidly on their side, holding that enforced flag salute regulations were contrary to the American Bill of Rights when they infringed on religious freedom. The Witnesses were equally happy when, on appeal by the Minersville School Board, the Federal Circuit Court of Appeals for the Third Circuit upheld Judge Maris's decision and added a stirring ruling on the importance of religious liberty.[91] But things changed at Supreme Court level. There, Rutherford appeared on behalf of the Gobitas family, since Moyle was no longer on the case, having broken with the Watch Tower president. Before the justices of the Court, Rutherford did very badly. Instead of dealing primarily with legal issues, he gave what amounted to a sermon. Leonard Stevens recounts: 'When the impressively tall Judge Rutherford, wearing an unusually colorful suit, stepped to the lectern, it might as well have been a pulpit. He sounded more the evangelical preacher than the lawyer addressing the Supreme Court of the United States. His flamboyant speech favored the Biblical reasons for the Witnesses' opposition to the flag salute and paid hardly any attention to the great constitutional issues at hand. The justices were unmoved and not one asked him any questions.'[92]

George K. Gardner, a Harvard law professor representing the American Civil Liberties Union, made the legal arguments for the Witnesses' side far better than Rutherford. But neither Rutherford's poor performance nor Gardner's more able one seemed to have any impact on the court, except for Justice Harlan Fiske Stone. Justice Felix Frankfurter, who was noted for his super-patriotism and who was deeply concerned about the German invasion of France, which had just begun,

90 As Shawn Francis Peters notes, the correct form of the family name was Gobitas rather than Gobitis, as misspelled consistently in court cases. Peters, 19.

91 For detailed accounts of these events, see Stevens, 46–73, and Peters, 19–45.

92 Stevens, 91–2.

dominated the court. Frankfurter believed strongly that the courts should usually respect the regulations of democratically elected bodies. The Supreme Court thus ruled, in an eight to one decision, that the decisions of the lower federal courts were reversed: Witness children could be expelled from schools for not saluting the flag.[93]

At the time of *Gobitis*, June 1940, there was growing concern throughout the United States over the war in Europe; equally, there was great fear of fifth columnists and pro-Nazis. Thus, when the Witnesses were in effect branded as 'unpatriotic' by the U.S. Supreme Court, they became the targets of terrible persecution. In the circumstances it was easy for many Americans to hate them as both religiously offensive and unpatriotic. There was no way to attack J.F. Rutherford and senior members of the Watch Tower Society directly, but the same was not true of ordinary Jehovah's Witnesses, who as a result suffered as had no religious minority in the United States since the persecution of the Mormons in the 1830s and 1840s.

It is difficult to say just how much actual violence they experienced. Sources differ on this matter. David Manwaring examined U.S. Justice Department files from May 1940 to December 1943 and concluded that there were 843 cases of 'alleged persecution' of Witnesses throughout the nation. Barbara Grizzuti Harrison estimated that there were some 2,500 attacks on them between 1940 and 1944. However, the Watch Tower Society declared – undoubtedly based on its own records – that there were at least 1,500 mobbings. In any case, the ACLU stated specifically that in 1940 alone, 'nearly 1,500 Witnesses endured a total of 335 separate mobbings in 44 states.'[94]

No moral person reviewing what happened to Jehovah's Witnesses during this time can regard it as anything but a shameful chapter in American history. Witnesses' homes, businesses, and kingdom halls or meeting places were defaced, ransacked, and sometimes destroyed. Their automobiles were overturned on several occasions. Their conventions were attacked. Men, women, and children were sometimes hounded ruthlessly from their communities. There were many cases of Witness men being viciously beaten and Witness women being pummelled. In one especially nasty instance, several Witness men were

93 For a full discussion of Frankfurter's thinking and its impact on the Supreme Court, see Peters 'Felix's Fall of France Opinion,' in his *Judging Jehovah's Witnesses*, pp. 46–71.

94 Peters, 302n21.

forced to ingest large quantities of castor oil. One Witness was actually castrated. Many, both men and women, were subjected to false arrest under any number of charges, including sedition, and Witness lawyers attempting to defend their clients were sometimes mobbed and brutalized. Other Witnesses lost their jobs or suffered boycotts of their businesses. The state of Mississippi even tried to outlaw Jehovah's Witnesses as a subversive movement.[95] Perhaps saddest of all, many Witness children experienced tauntings and beatings from classmates and were expelled from school.[96]

All of this occurred as the result of campaigns, led especially by the American Legion and other 'patriotic' organizations. Often various police officers and public officials participated actively in the mobbings, beatings, and acts of vandalism; and in other instances they stood by and watched without lifting a finger while Witnesses were attacked. State and federal officials were slow to try to check this persecution; often they refused to do anything about what was clearly a violation of federal civil rights laws.[97]

It is true that the Witnesses had their public defenders who were shocked at what they regarded as misdirected patriotic zeal of a type that existed in Nazi Germany and other fascist countries. Among those defenders were the First Lady, Eleanor Roosevelt, her son, Elliot, the U.S. Solicitor General, Francis Biddle, and, above all, the ACLU. They all spoke out forcefully, calling on Americans to stop what was happening to the small, besieged religious community. Besides this, the ACLU was active in defending the Witnesses in the courts and in bringing pressure to bear on government officials to intervene on their behalf.[98] As pointed out earlier, a number of Protestant, Catholic, and Jewish clergymen signed a statement calling for a halt to the persecution of the Witnesses despite the continual condemnation that Rutherford and the Witnesses heaped on them and their fellow clergy.[99]

It is interesting that many of the most outspoken critics of what was happening to Jehovah's Witnesses indicated that they believed the Witnesses had a martyr complex and were responsible in part for their

95 Ibid., 187–98.

96 These events are well documented and described in Manwaring, Stevens, Peters, Victor V. Blackwell's *O'er the Ramparts They Watched* (New York: Carleton Press, 1976), and various official Jehovah's Witness histories.

97 Peters gives the best account of these events.

98 Peters, 74, 85, 96–107, 140–1.

99 Ibid., 106–7.

own persecution. Shawn Peters quotes a number of these individuals and notes that Supreme Court Justice Robert Jackson, who ruled in their behalf in the famous *Barnette* case, was highly critical of the way they 'pushed' their religion on others.[100] Furthermore, many rightly felt that they were being altogether too extreme in their attacks on Roman Catholicism.

It is true that the Catholic clergy in Germany wanted to see the Witnesses outlawed and reported them to the Nazis.[101] In Canada, Jean Marie Roderique Cardinal Villeneuve was directly responsible for having them banned from 1940 to nearly the end of 1943.[102] It is also true that certain Catholic priests and lay Catholics in the United States were viciously anti-Jehovah's Witness and sometimes joined in anti-Witness mobs. Still, there is no clear evidence that American Catholics as a whole were more negative to Jehovah's Witnesses than many other groups, and some Catholics, such as Supreme Court Justice Frank Murphy, were among their most outspoken defenders.[103] In effect, then, the Witnesses – and J.F. Rutherford in particular – failed to recognize that the leaders of the American Catholic community, both clerical and lay, were far from united in efforts to suppress them. Consequently, the Watch Tower president continued to pour out contumely of the worst sort on the Catholic hierarchy and thereby made opposition to his brethren even stronger. For example, in the July 1940 Watch Tower booklet *Judge Rutherford Uncovers Fifth Column,* he answered a question from Malcolm Logan of the *New York Post* about why there had been a sudden outburst of violence against Jehovah's Witnesses. He stated: 'Because the Roman Catholic Hierarchy, operating what they call "Catholic Action", are carrying out a well-laid scheme to destroy everything in this world that publishes the truth, and this the Hierarchy are doing in order to camouflage their own wicked action in attempting to grab control of the nations of the earth.'[104] Needless to say, this was not a good way to make friends and influence people; in

100 Ibid., 82, 105–7, 116–19, 238.

101 Guenter Lewy, *The Catholic Church and Nazi Germany* (New York: McGraw-Hill, 1965), 43.

102 M. James Penton, *Jehovah's Witnesses in Canada: Champions of Freedom of Speech and Worship* (Toronto: Macmillan, 1976), 133–4. William Kaplan, *State and Salvation: The Jehovah's Witnesses and Their Fight for Civil Rights* (Toronto: University of Toronto Press, 1989), 63–5.

103 Peters, 199–201, 225–6.

104 Pages 5–6.

fact, it made both Rutherford and the Witnesses seem ridiculous in the eyes of the press and many Americans who might otherwise have supported their civil rights. Rutherford never seemed to realize that both his mouth and his pen were the cause of many of his brethren's most serious trials; or perhaps he did know but failed to care.

While Jehovah's Witnesses suffered mob violence throughout America, while their children experienced harsh treatment from fellow students or were expelled from schools, and while their brethren were facing martyrdom and suppression in Germany and other lands, Rutherford was enjoying life in pleasant and quite opulent circumstances. During the summer months he lived in a penthouse on top of the Watch Tower's Bethel home in Brooklyn, in a retreat on Staten Island, or at the Watch Tower's Kingdom Farm in upstate New York. But he spent his winters in San Diego, California, at a large, Spanish-style house called Beth-Sarim or the 'House of the Princes.' After his release from an Atlanta prison a severe case of pneumonia damaged one of his lungs permanently. Thus he needed to spend his winters in a warm climate. Although it was entirely reasonable for the judge to spend his winters in California, the circumstances surrounding how he did so can only be described as bizarre.

Based on Psalm 45:16 in the King James Bible – 'Instead of thy fathers shall be thy children, whom thou mayest make princes in all the earth' – Rutherford and the Bible Student–Jehovah's Witnesses taught that Jesus' forefathers would be brought back from the dead prior to the battle of Armageddon. So when in the late 1920s he received a private donation to build what became Beth-Sarim, he accepted it with the proviso that the Watch Tower Society would hold it in trust for the 'ancient worthies,' from Abel to John the Baptist. In his book, *Salvation,* published in 1939, he therefore stated:

> At San Diego, California, there is a small piece of land, on which, in the year 1929, there was built a house, which is called and known as Beth-Sarim. The Hebrew words *Beth Sarim* mean 'House of the Princes'; and the purpose of acquiring that property and building the house was that there might be some tangible proof that there are those on earth today who fully believe God and Christ Jesus and in His Kingdom, and who believe that the faithful men of old will soon be resurrected by the Lord, be back on earth, and take charge of the visible affairs of earth. The title of Beth-Sarim is vested in the Watch Tower Bible & Tract Society in trust, to be used by the president of the Society and his assistants for the present, and thereafter to be at the

disposal of the aforementioned princes on the earth ... The house has served as a testimony to many persons throughout the earth, and while unbelievers have mocked concerning it and spoken contemptuously of it, yet it stands there as a testimony to Jehovah's Name; and if and when the princes do return and some of them occupy the property, such will be a confirmation of the faith and hope that induced the building of Beth-Sarim.'[105]

So, along with a small retinue, including his female dietician and his private secretaries, Rutherford used Beth-Sarim as his western retreat and office. While there, he no doubt spent much of his time writing books, booklets, and articles for *The Watchtower*, but there can also be no doubt that while residing at the 'House of the Princes,' as everywhere else, he lived almost like a prince himself. He ate well, drank a lot of alcohol, and drove around in one of two sixteen-cylinder Cadillac cars that a follower, who regarded him as the 'greatest man on earth,' had given him.[106]

Naturally, this behaviour and the entire façade of Beth-Sarim caused many enemies as well as others to laugh at Rutherford and Jehovah's Witnesses. As both Herbert Stroup and Alan Rogerson note, even some Witnesses were taken aback by Beth-Sarim and wished that Rutherford had simply selected it as a western Watch Tower headquarters without trying to fit it into his doctrinal system.[107] Rutherford's followers at Watch Tower headquarters remained undaunted. After the judge's death, they blustered: 'The most recent facts show that the religionists of this doomed world are gnashing their teeth because of the testimony which that "House of the Princes" bears to the new

105 Page 311.

106 These were essentially charges made both by former Canadian Watch Tower branch overseer Walter Salter and by Olin Moyle in personal letters to Rutherford. See Appendix H. Had the 'ancient worthies' been resurrected and come to dwell at Beth-Sarim, as the judge preached, most of them would have had to sleep on the lawn or on the canyonside above which it sits. The entire teaching seems to have been nothing but a foolish scheme to provide Rutherford with a lovely winter home while deceiving the trusting and gullible Jehovah's Witness faithful. For accounts of Beth-Sarim, see *The New World*, 104, and Edmund Charles Gruss and Leonard Chretien, *Jehovah's Witnesses: Their Monuments to False Prophecy* (Clayton: CA: Witness, 1997).

107 Herbert H. Stroup, *The Jehovah's Witnesses* (New York: Columbia University Press, 1945), 42. Alan Rogerson, *Millions Now Living Will Never Die* (London: Constable, 1969), 48.

world.'[108] One must wonder, though, if 'the religionists' were not smirking rather than 'gnashing their teeth.' For probably nothing made Jehovah's Witnesses look so ridiculous as did Beth-Sarim and Rutherford's use of it. One must wonder how even he could have said what he did respecting it and used it as he did with a straight face.

Despite all of Rutherford's rantings and highjinks and the Witnesses' tactless obstreperousness, their tenacious battle to have their rights to freedom of speech, the press, and religion recognized through legal action in the courts eventually won through in the United States. On 3 May 1943 the U.S. Supreme Court ruled in their favour in twelve out of thirteen cases. The following 14 June, Flag Day, the court reversed its ruling in *Gobitis* in *West Virginia Board of Education v. Barnette*.[109] Amazingly, despite their extreme unpopularity, the United States, followed by Canada,[110] ultimately did an outstanding job of protecting them from both mob and legal persecution. Rutherford's dramatic statement that 'the greatest and most oppressive empire on earth is the Anglo-American empire' had proved to be nonsensical – certainly as far as Jehovah's Witnesses were concerned. The same was not true of Hitler's Third Reich.

108 *The New World* (Brooklyn, NY: Watchtower Society and IBSA, 1942), 104.
109 319 U.S.
110 Penton, *Jehovah's Witnesses in Canada*, 202–23.

5

German Bible Student–Jehovah's Witnesses, 1902–1933

> I have gone into the activities of the Society and of its agents, and have read some of the pamphlets which have been distributed by the Society widely in Germany, and I can see that objection could reasonably be raised to them by the German Government. Although acting as a religious society, the pamphlets contain comment of not a purely religious character.
>
> U.S. Consul General George Messersmith,
> U.S. State Department Documents

The history of the Bible Student–Jehovah's Witnesses in Germany before 1933 tended to parallel that of their brethren in the United States. According to an official Watch Tower account, C.T. Russell spent more on the Society's mission to that country than he did on any other, but with poor results.[1] Germany was prosperous before the First World War, and its social welfare programs were superior to those of almost all other nations. So ordinary Germans were not greatly interested in the millenarian message of the Bible Students. Russell's 1911 lecture 'Zionism and Prophecy' did not set especially well with some Germans,[2] as anti-Semitism was already a strong force throughout Germany.[3]

1 *1974 Yearbook*, 67–72, 75.

2 Ibid., 76.

3 For an examination of German attitudes toward Jews before the First World War, see Uriel Tal, *Christians and Jews in Germany: Religion, Politics and Ideology in the Second Reich, 1870–1914,* translated from Hebrew by Noah Jonathan Jacobs (Ithaca, NY: Cornell University Press, 1975).

A change took place following Germany's defeat in November 1918, the flight of Kaiser Wilhelm II, and Germany's agreement to end the First World War. The resulting loss of territories to neighbouring countries, internal fighting with Communist elements, the Allied imposition of extremely heavy war reparations payments, the French occupation of the Ruhr in 1923, and the resulting hyperinflation caused many Germans to re-examine the Watch Tower's message. Many joined the movement and became *Ernsten Bibelforscher* – or, more simply, *Bibelforscher*[4] – and Germany became a hotbed of the Watch Tower Bible Students. Only the United States had more members.

Despite this growth, some of which was related to the 'Millions Campaign' and the showing of Russell's 1913 moving picture 'The Photo-Drama of Creation,'[5] the Watch Tower movement experienced problems. The first, a big one, was when F.L. Alexandre Freytag, Swiss branch overseer of the International Bible Students Association, broke with Rutherford only two years after the latter became Watch Tower president. Beginning in 1919, Freytag developed a movement that taught universal salvation and began to spread it throughout Switzerland, France, Belgium, Austria, Italy, and Germany. That movement, the Church of the Kingdom of God or the Philanthropic Assembly of the Friends of Man,[6] drew some German Bible Students into its fold.[7] In part, this was because of Rutherford's high-handed behaviour in America, which was resented by many Bible Students in many lands.

Despite the Freytag schism, Rutherford succeeded in reorganizing the Bible Student movement in central Europe. In November 1920 he established a Central European Office in Switzerland, which was to oversee Watch Tower activities in France, the Low Countries, Germany, Austria, and Italy as well as Switzerland itself.[8] In Germany he found an able young organizer, whom he selected to direct the work in that country. His name was Paul Balzereit.[9]

4 The German name *Ernsten Bibelforscher* means 'Serious Bible Researchers.' However, since the English term Bible Students is the original one, I have chosen to use it in most other cases.

5 German Bible Students began showing the Photo-Drama in 1914. It was a major factor in spreading their beliefs during and after the First World War. *1974 Yearbook,* 79–80, 83, 87.

6 For a discussion of the Freytag movement, see Jerry Bergman, *Jehovah's Witnesses: A Comprehensive and Selectively Annotated Bibliography* (Westport, CT: Greenwood Press, 1999), 332–3.

7 *1974 Yearbook,* 85.

8 Ibid., 87–8.

9 Ibid.

Rutherford's selection of Balzereit as German branch overseer was made at a time when Bible Students were still not entirely under the direct control of the Watch Tower president. The judge therefore considered it important to appear as if he were respecting the wishes of the Bible Student community, and he deceived some senior German Bible Students into thinking they were electing their director. In an undated letter published under the title 'Converted Jehovah's Witness Expositor,' William Schnell offers the following account:

> One of my boyhood friends, Brother Bucholz, served as a 'pilgrim' [speaker] for Germany for many years until he was incarcerated in a Nazi concentration camp. One time, Bucholz told me that right after World War I, Judge Rutherford came to Germany in order to reorganize the German branch of the Watchtower Society. He called a meeting of seven pilgrim brethren, asking them to nominate and elect a new branch manager. Two brethren, Balzereit and Bucholz, were nominated. It appeared that Brother Balzereit was elected and the results were accepted as the will of the Lord. A few days later, however, five of these pilgrim brethren approached Brother Bucholz and appraised him of the fact that they had all voted for him and that they could not understand how Balzereit was elected by a vote of six to one.
>
> This incident again came to my recollection by a letter received on January 11, 1957 (which I hold amidst many documents) from a man who was once very high in the councils of the Society. Among many other things, this brother [probably Walter Salter, the former Watch Tower branch overseer in Canada] writes: 'You may further be interested to know that the Judge informed me in 1924 how the appointment of Brother Balzereit came about. He said that he (Rutherford) held an election to indicate the choice between Brother Balzereit and another brother for the position, that he took the count of the ballot, and that he himself, being the chairman, did the counting. The outcome was not in favor of Brother Balzereit; the other brother had the majority (I do not recall the other brother's name). However, Judge thought that Brother Balzereit was a much better man, so declared him elected. He felt justified in doing this for the sake of the work. I do not think that many know this, but I was very close to the Judge and traveled with him on numerous occasions over the years, attending conventions in the States, Canada, and in Europe.[10]

10 Reprinted in English in Manfred Gebhard, *Die Zeugen Jehovas: Eine Documentation über die Wachtturmgesellschaft* (Leipzig, Jena, Berlin: Urania-Verlag: 1970), 127. While some may question the validity of this account because at the time of writing

Watch Tower president J.F. Rutherford attempted at first to ingratiate Jehovah's Witnesses with the Nazis. When that failed, he called on German Witnesses to face martyrdom in opposition to Hitler and the Third Reich. (The M. James Penton Collection)

Beth-Sarim, J.F. Rutherford's 'House of the Princes' in San Diego, California, which he used as a winter home. (The M. James Penton Collection)

Group portrait of liberated Jehovah's Witnesses in their prison camp uniforms in the Niederhagen bei Wewelsburg concentration camp. (Wachtturm Gesellschaft History Archive. Courtesy of the United States Holocaust Memorial Museum, USHMM)

A 1962 photo of Erich Frost, who had been a Watch Tower branch overseer for Jehovah's Witnesses during the Third Reich. He spent many years as a Nazi prisoner. After the Second World War he again served as Watch Tower branch overseer. (The Signed Rudolph Collection)

The last photograph of the entire Kusserow family. All members of this Jehovah's Witness family suffered Nazi persecution and almost all were held in concentration camps until the end of the Second World War, except for two brothers who were executed for refusing to serve in the *Wehrmacht*. (Courtesy of USHMM)

Helen Gotthold with her children, Gerd and Gisela. Helen Gotthold, a Jehovah's Witness, was arrested for her anti-Nazi views. She was convicted, condemned to death, and beheaded in the Ploetzesee prison on 8 December 1944. Her children survived. (Courtesy of USHMM)

Adolf Hitler, who proclaimed, regarding Jehovah's Witnesses, *'Diese Brut wir aud Deutschlan audgrottet!'* ('This brood will be exterminated in Germany'), and who boasted at one time that he had had 130 of them executed for refusing to take up arms on behalf of the Third Reich. (From Geoffrey Miles, courtesy of USHMM).

Heinrich Himmler was responsible for the persecution of Jehovah's Witnesses from the early 1930s until the end of the Third Reich and was responsible for the deaths of many. In the later years of the Second World War, he began to take a more benign attitude towards them. (From Geoffrey Miles, courtesy of USHMM)

A striped prison jacket with an inverted purple triangle badge worn by Matthaeus Prival, a Jehovah's Witness, during his imprisonment at Dachau concentration camp. (Courtesy of USHMM)

Two concentration camp badges bearing purple triangles worn by Jehovah's Witnesses. The badge with prisoner number 46436 was issued at Sachsenhausen to Albert Jahndorf; the badge with prisoner number 1989 was issued at Ravensbrueck to Luise Jahndorf. (Courtesy of USHMM)

The mental picture that one gets of Balzereit from the two major sources in both English and German that describe him – the *1974 Yearbook of Jehovah's Witnesses* and William Schnell's *Thirty Years a Watch Tower Slave* – makes it clear that he was a 'company man.' In other words, he was an able manager and someone who wanted to please Rutherford in carrying out his programs. Simultaneously, he adopted certain airs that marked him as an important person within the Bible Student community and at German Watch Tower headquarters. For some years he wore a beard in emulation of C.T. Russell, and he, like Rutherford himself, demanded strict obedience from workers at the German Watch Tower headquarters, which the Society moved to Magdeburg near Berlin from Barmen in western Germany in 1923.[11]

The *1974 Yearbook* admits that Balzereit was 'a good organizer and that the work in Germany made good progress under his direction.' With little evidence to prove its assertion, the yearbook goes on to state: 'His big mistake, however, was in attributing the enormous growth more to his own personal ability than to Jehovah's spirit.' Yet the most that the yearbook can do to support this claim is to cite the fact that he requested, in good German style, to be called 'Mr Director' rather than 'Brother Balzereit' when 'in the presence of worldly people' and that he had a sign placed outside his office with the word 'director' on it.[12]

More substantively, the *1974 Yearbook* accuses him of being 'afraid of persecution.' It asserts that following the distribution of a resolution called 'Ecclesiastics Indicted' throughout Germany in 1924, he was threatened with death and was prosecuted for distributing that extremely condemnatory leaflet. After that episode he tried to soften the Watch Tower message. The yearbook states: 'It is true that he was acquitted [from being responsible for the distribution of the resolution], but when the judge pleaded with him to avoid making such strong statements in our literature in the future, he evidently was determined to follow this advice, for when expressions and statements in *The Watch Tower* or in other publications from Brooklyn seemed to be too strong for him, he would "water them down."'[13] Regarding this

Schnell was a harsh critic of the Watch Tower who was sometimes guilty of exaggeration, his statements here certainly fit with what is known about Rutherford in other situations.

11 *1974 Yearbook,* 97–8. Schnell, 57–8, 67, 74–5.

12 *1974 Yearbook,* 107.

13 Ibid., 100, 107.

matter, it is hard not to have sympathy for Balzereit. 'Ecclesiastics Indicted' was an extremely caustic statement that stirred up a hornet's nest. Although there had long been some opposition to the Bible Students in Germany before 1924, only after that year did the clergy of the major German churches, both Catholic and Protestant, almost in unison try to have the Bible Students outlawed.[14] From that time on, their anger against the Bible Students was white-hot. Knowing this, Balzereit – who had more tact than Rutherford – was anxious to avoid persecution as much as possible. However, he had to carry out many of Rutherford's policies in order to stay in favour with him.

The yearbook also censures Balzereit for 'materialistic desires.' It states as supposed proof: 'Balzereit had enjoyed writing poetry and having it published in the magazine *The Golden Age* under the pseudonym of Paul Gebhard, and now he had written a book and had it published in Leipzig. This book was then added to the list of literature to be distributed by the congregations, who, unaware of the true circumstances, ordered it, thereby bringing Brother Balzereit considerable financial profit. He also had a tennis court built at Bethel [the name given to Watch Tower residences throughout the world] at one time, not so much for the benefit of the whole family as for his own use.'[15]

These criticisms may seem strange to those readers who are unfamiliar with the history of the Watch Tower movement. Taken in the context of the ideology that Rutherford and his successors developed, they become understandable. After Russell's death, Watch Tower leaders at Brooklyn became extremely jealous of any Bible Student or Jehovah's Witness who had the temerity to write a book on a historical or religious topic, even if it was in defence of Witness doctrine or practices. Members of the Witness community were taught to be suspicious of anyone who might write 'independently.' Jerry Bergman relates: 'The Watchtower [Society] has historically manifested very little tolerance toward those who write books, even if they are extremely favorable to the Watchtower point of view and are doctrinally "correct."'[16] A ploy of Watch Tower leaders and many ordinary Jehovah's Witnesses has been to assert that whenever someone within their ranks has written a book, he or she must have done so to make money on it. And after all, only the 'Lord's Organization' is supposed

14 Ibid., 100, 103.
15 Ibid., 107.
16 Bergman, 88.

to have the right to do that. As to whether Balzereit had a tennis court built at the German Watch Tower headquarters, be it for himself or the Magdeburg Bible Student workers, the matter is trivial. It is little more than an attempt to discredit a man whom official Watch Tower history regards as having become an 'apostate' in 1935.

If there is any justification to the charge that Balzereit was materialistic – and there is evidence that he liked to travel and to wear expensive clothes while other workers at the Magdeburg headquarters could not[17] – it seems that he was only mimicking Rutherford. The judge maintained a much more opulent style of life than Balzereit was ever able to enjoy.[18]

Despite the acerbic nature of his autobiography, Schnell's evaluation of Balzereit seems more reasonable. It indicates that Balzereit carried out Rutherford's wishes and was, to a large extent, very much like the Watch Tower president himself. In a chapter called 'Sifting,' Schnell shows how Balzereit turned Watch Tower headquarters at Magdeburg into an ultraloyal Rutherfordite institution from which he excluded all independent-minded individuals. He tells how Balzereit presided over Rutherford's campaign against elected Bible Student elders in Germany – a campaign that like the one taking place in North America at the same time, drove many from the Watch Tower movement.[19] Elsewhere, Schnell relates how Balzereit demanded *'Kadaver Gehorsam'* or (corpselike obedience) from volunteer workers at the Magdeburg Bethel.[20]

While Balzereit was directing the German activities of the Watch Tower Society and the Bible Student-Jehovah's Witnesses, Rutherford was overseeing Balzereit. The judge made several visits to Germany between 1922 and 1933. He was well received by his German brethren and was lauded as Germany's friend, in that he had opposed American participation in the First World War.[21] He once provided each

17 Schnell, 76–7.

18 Balzereit was never guilty of the type of materialism that Rutherford displayed. See the letters to Rutherford written by Walter Salter and Olin Moyle criticizing the former's arrogance, ostentatious style of life, and liking for alcohol, Appendix H.

19 Schnell, 55–9.

20 Ibid., 67.

21 Schnell says: 'Whenever the Judge appeared in post-war Germany, he was billed as that American Friend who had been imprisoned for his opposition to the war; and that really brought out the crowds in Berlin, Munich, Hamburg, Dresden and Leipzig.' Schnell, 25.

person at a convention of nearly starving German Bible Students with two frankfurters, two buns, and a bottle of mineral water – something that made him popular with many.[22] But while visiting Germany, he also succeeded in imposing his will on his German brethren. He made Balzereit and others shave their beards, introduced bright men's clothing to the Bible Student community, and in 1931 forced the removal of pictures of C.T. Russell and himself from the halls of the Magdeburg Bethel.[23]

In the late 1920s, even under the democratic Weimar Republic, Bible Students found themselves in deep trouble with the German authorities for following Rutherford's dictates and distributing his incredibly inflammatory publications. Committed churchgoers resented the Bible Students coming to their doors with such literature, especially on Sundays. The clergy began preaching bitter sermons against them, and as in the United States, Canada, and other countries, the authorities began arresting them for violating antipeddling laws. The *1974 Yearbook* reports that as early as 1922 they began to be charged with illegal peddling and with refusing to pay peddling taxes. The Watch Tower Society states that by 1927, 1,169 Bible Students had been charged and tried under such laws. The following year, 1,660 were arrested on the same charges; in 1929 the number increased to 1,694. These charges were regularly dismissed by the courts; however, by 1929 the authorities, encouraged by the clergy, had found a new and more effective tool for stopping the Bible Students: Sabbath legislation. Thus Bible Students began to be convicted and fined.[24] By the end of 1932, the last year of the Weimar Republic, 2,335 cases were pending against them, largely as a result of clerical action.[25] As the *1974 Yearbook* states: 'Attempts to do this took place all over Germany, but Bavaria held a

22 *1974 Yearbook,* 99. Schnell, 51.

23 Schnell, 50. *1974 Yearbook,* 97–8. All of this was done to discredit C.T. Russell and the practices of the Russell era without saying so directly. Traditionally, Russell had dressed in a long, black frock coat when delivering sermons, and elected Bible Student elders had often copied him. Rutherford decided to break this tradition, and that of wearing beards, to establish a new style representing his own presidency. Curiously, even to this day clothing styles, hair styles, and an antibeard attitude still preoccupy Jehovah's Witnesses. One may be removed as an appointed elder for wearing a beard, and some have even been driven from the Witness community for doing so. Wearing a beard is seen as a sign of 'worldliness and rebellion.'

24 *1974 Yearbook,* 102–3.

25 Ibid., 108.

predominant position, more arrests being made there than any place else. For a time local laws even succeeded in banning the work briefly.'[26]

Another issue that caused the Bible Students grief in Germany was that they were regarded as friendly toward Jews and Zionism. Like Russell, Rutherford was once booed publicly because of this.[27] More seriously, certain ultranationalistic, revolution-minded Germans were beginning to claim that the Bible Students were a front for a worldwide Jewish conspiracy. For example, in 1925 August Fetz published *Weltvernichtung durch 'Bibelforscher' und Juden* (World Destruction by 'Bible Students' and Jews),[28] and various articles began to appear in other books, newspapers, and magazines alleging much the same thing. When Germany was prospering during the late 1920s, this was not such a serious matter. With the coming of the Depression in 1929 and the mass unemployment and suffering that followed, everything changed. The Nazis and Communists both began to receive a greater hearing from the German people, and the Nazis in particular began to express hostility toward the Bible Student–Jehovah's Witnesses.

With the Depression, the Bible Student–Jehovah's Witnesses began to grow spectacularly. William Schnell discusses this period:

> In the Germany of the Weimar Republic everything was going from bad to worse. Democratic processes brought into being by the terms of the Versailles treaty were repugnant to the Germans, because they considered the democratic process and the Weimar Republic as a symbol of their defeat. Unemployment was rampant and hope for better times was fading everywhere. The masses were driven about like lost sheep. Communism on the left claimed millions, the Nazis on the right were growing fast, while the moderate Centrum was shrinking. In the middle, however, were millions who wanted a spiritual and peaceful way of life, and these were the people we were after. We were fishing in the troubled waters of the German population.
>
> Appearing as God's Organization, powerful, unafraid of opposition (actually bearding the lion in his own den, so to speak), we easily became their champions.
>
> If events had not transpired to put the Hitler movement into control, Germany might have become the first Jehovah's Witness state in God's

26 Ibid., 103–5.

27 Ibid., 90–1.

28 Munich: Deutscher Volksverlag, 1925.

Organization. The Nazis and the Communists realized this and began really to oppose us as the third force.[29]

What Schnell says about the Bible Student-Witnesses being so significant is obviously a gross exaggeration, considering how few they were; even so, their growth was spectacular. Between 1932 and the spring of 1933 they grew from 12,484 to 19,268 in the numbers of actual door-to-door preachers or 'publishers.' Their spring Memorial attendance grew from 14,453 to 24,843 over the same period.[30] More important, this small band was distributing Rutherford's pronouncements all over the country and becoming known to almost everyone. Thus what Schnell says about the Nazis and Communists seeing the Bible Students as a 'third force' has more than a grain of truth to it.

During the years leading up to Hitler's appointment as chancellor, the Nazis began to harass Jehovah's Witnesses. Hitler's Brown Shirts (the *Sturmabteilung* or SA) began to disrupt their meetings,[31] and the Nazi Party demanded that its members stop receiving *Das Goldene Zeitalter*,[32] the German edition of *The Golden Age*. Strangely, the Watch Tower Society seemed hardly to respond. True, in answer to a letter from a Frau W.R. published in a 15 October 1929 issue of *Das Goldene Zeitalter* under the title *'Hakenkreuz'* (swastika), the Watch Tower Society did refer to the Nazi Party in strong terms. It attacked the party as of Satan, damned it for the use of the swastika, and criticized it for claiming that Jehovah was the God of the Old Testament and not the New. The article also censured the Nazis for attacking the Jews.[33] It must be remembered that at the time, the Bible Students had not yet changed their stance toward Zionism. In general, though, the Bible Student–Witnesses did little to oppose Nazism overtly until late 1933. English-language Watch Tower publications said practically nothing about its rise or its evils until just before Hitler came to power. Perhaps this was because Rutherford had fixated his hatred on Great Britain and the United States. Perhaps the Watch Tower Society was so preoccupied with its animosity toward the churches that it could not see clearly that there were other, far more dangerous enemies about. Perhaps the Watch Tower president and the Witness commu-

29 Schnell, 71.
30 *1974 Yearbook,* 109–10.
31 Ibid., 108.
32 *1933 Year Book,* 127.
33 See Appendix B.

nity sympathized with the Nazis' antagonism toward the two great English-speaking powers and the League of Nations. Perhaps, as well, it was a factor that two of the Watch Tower's German lawyers were themselves members of the Nazi Party. For whatever reasons, Jehovah's Witnesses were slow to voice much opposition to Hitler.

The question now arises: Could Watch Tower officials have failed to be aware of the nature of Nazism in the early months of 1933, as the Witness magazine *Awake!* has tried to argue? Is it really true that 'in the beginning, the Hitler government worked to conceal its violent and extremist nature'?[34] Can one accept this assertion as at all valid? Looking at the historical record, the answer must be a resounding 'no'. The Watch Tower Society is simply trying to rewrite history.

In a detailed account, Eliot Barculo Wheaton gives a day-to-day synopsis of events in Germany during the first six months of Hitler's chancellorship. In summation, he states:

> Reviewing Hitler's first six months in office, one is primarily struck by the rapidity, violence and scope of the Nazi onslaught. Whatever his ultimate aims, he might have been expected to move with caution for some considerable time and warily feel out the strength of his opponents. Without hesitation, on the contrary, he challenged the whole non-Nazi German world right down the line – not only the millions of Communists but the still more numerous Socialists (from 1912 to 1932 the biggest party in the country), the two Catholic parties, his own Nationalist partners and even, in effect, [President] Hindenburg himself, since Nazi extremism bid fair to outrage the President's conservative nature and he could always call a halt by proclaiming martial law. From the very outset, indeed, Hitler's course bore the mark of fanatical audacity and determination.[35]

Armed with sweeping emergency decrees signed by Hindenburg in February, and with the Enabling Act passed by the Reichstag in March, Hitler steadily accelerated his pace, abolishing established procedures right and left, trampling justice underfoot, and breaking his word whenever it suited to do so. In the process he overthrew and replaced existing *Land* (state) governments, suppressed organs of adverse opinion, commandeered the country's police forces, set up new courts to

34 *Awake!* 8 July 1998, 11.

35 Eliot Barculo Wheaton, *The Nazi Revolution 1933–35: With a Background Survey of the Weimar Era* (Garden City, NY: Doubleday, 1968), 344–5.

serve his ends, destroyed the trade unions, and went far toward co-opting the legal profession. He pronounced Communists and Socialists alike as enemies of the state, and he banned all political parties save his own. At the same time, he came to advantageous terms with the Vatican. He made himself *personna grata* in the eyes of big industry, and he courted the army so skilfully that it never did a thing to impede his progress. As if this were not enough, he recklessly ignored world opinion and launched an open campaign against German Jewry. He set out to cleanse German intellectual and cultural life of ideological 'impurities.' He interfered heavily in church affairs. He threw thousands of people into concentration camps – an infamous step almost without precedent in peacetime, although he himself had foretold it as far back as the summer of 1921 when addressing the rightist National Club in Berlin.[36]

So it is impossible to believe that German Jehovah's Witnesses did not have a clear understanding of the nature of Nazism. No normal, adult German could have failed to do so; everyone in the Reich was being affected by the dramatic and often violent changes taking place. What about in America? Did the public know what was happening in Hitler's Germany? Clearly, yes, they did. The press all over the Western world was shocked when Hitler became chancellor on 30 January 1933, and it exposed what was happening in the Reich from that day forward.

For a good example, as early as 3 February 1933 the *New York Times* was reporting on the steps Hitler was taking to establish a dictatorship. On page 1 it reported that the new right-wing government had banned Communist rallies and that by order of the cabinet, police were searching homes without warrants. On 5 February the *Times* reported in another page 1 article that Hitler had praised Mussolini in a bid for cooperation. The author of that article, Edwin L. James, went on to state: 'But the possibility that Hitler may achieve real power in Germany is a matter of world importance. Should he get power in his hands through the ploy of Parliamentary elections or through a coup, the results would be far reaching not only in the Reich itself but in all Europe. One sees this readily by considering Hitler's idea that a Fascist Germany and Fascist Italy, marching hand in hand, would constitute a great power in the world.' Then, on 7 February – again on page 1 – the *Times* proclaimed that the Reich had gagged the press and

36 Ibid.

suspended the Prussian Diet. On page 1 of the 22 February edition, it reported that the Nazis had attacked a number of Catholic priests.

After the Reichstag fire of 27 February, which the Nazis blamed on the Communists, Hitler obtained from Hindenburg what amounted to legal dictatorial powers. The instrument of this was a decree titled 'For the Protection of the People and the State.' According to William Shirer's translation, it read: 'Restrictions on personal liberty, on the right of free expression of opinion, including freedom of the press; on rights of assembly and association; and violations of the postal, telegraphic and telephonic communications; and warrants for house searchers, orders for confiscations as well as restrictions on property, are also permissible beyond the legal limits otherwise prescribed.'[37] On 1 March the *New York Times* published another series of articles that showed how far Germany had already gone down the path to dictatorship. Those articles stated that the Nazis were suppressing not just the Communists but democratic Socialists as well. One of the articles in question was headlined HITLER'S PRESS CHIEF HINTS BAN MAY LAST and went on to say: 'Intimates Left Papers Will Be Suppressed Permanently – He Warns Foreign Journalists.' The following day the *Times* reported that HITLER INTENSIFIES DRIVE ON THE LEFT and that hundreds had been arrested, and indicated that the British government was profoundly disturbed by these events. On 3 March the *Times* published several alarmist articles on page 1 and on pages 4 and 5. Among them: NAZIS ACT TO CURB THE FOREIGN PRESS and WEIZMANN ASSAILS REICH ANTI-SEMITES. The latter article, datelined London, quoted the noted Zionist and later president of Israel Chaim Weizmann: 'It has only been a few days, he added, since Captain Hermann Wilhelm Goering, Minister without Portfolio, accused the Jews of "organizing the cultural disruption of Germany," and it was a severe shock to civilized people to discover that it was possible for a great people like the Germans to relapse into barbarism in its attitude toward a small, law-abiding minority of its citizens.'

The Watch Tower's own publications indicate clearly that the Witnesses were thoroughly aware of the nature of Nazism and that Hitler's was not just another legitimate government. In 1961, Eric Frost wrote: 'In 1932 the spirit of Nazism began to take over. Often mob action reared its ugly head in connection with the Drama showings. It got so

37 William L. Shirer, *The Rise and Fall of the Third Reich: A History of Nazi Germany* (New York: Balentine Publishing Group, 1960), 271.

bad that it could be presented only under police protection.' In the next paragraph, Frost remarked: 'While visiting the home of one of the Witnesses in Nuremberg in January 1933, we heard the bombastic broadcast from Berlin announcing Hitler's seizure of power [*sic*]. We suspected what this would mean for us.'[38] Anyone who examines the pages of *The Golden Age* can see that Jehovah's Witnesses in America were aware of the nature of the Nazi movement. In its 15 March 1933 issue, on page 369, it reprinted an article from the *Saturday Evening Post* of the previous October on 'German Fascism and the Churches.' In commenting on this article, *Golden Age* editor Clayton Woodworth appended the following note: '(The foregoing is interesting because of the claimed intent of Fascism to spread itself over the world and to take over all government functions. Fascism is anarchy, backed by Big Business and in collusion with the church. It despises constitutions and the laws of the people.)' Shortly after that, in its 12 April 1933 issue, on page 446, *The Golden Age* published a short statement, 'Hitler Makes Germany a Fascist State,' which read: 'Not waiting for the election, March 5 Chancellor Hitler took the bull by the horns and made Germany a Fascist state. The last Socialist police head in Prussia has been removed and any meeting that criticizes the government will be immediately dissolved. State weapons have been issued to Hitlerites.'

It is true that many elements in Germany – including most of the clergy – were euphoric about the legal, National Socialist revolution that was sweeping the country. Many had hated the 'decadence' of the Weimar Republic and longed for a return to the conditions they had known under Wilhelm II. Hitler and the Nazis were playing to that sentiment. As Ernst Christian Helmreich notes in his excellent study, *The German Churches under Hitler,* the 'desecration or defamation' of religious organizations became an illegal offence, the teaching of religion in the schools was increased significantly, and many laws and ordinances were passed to protect the sanctity of Sundays.[39] Hitler was aware of the feelings of pious Germans. He even stated in February 1933: 'Today Christians and no international atheists stand at the head of Germany. I speak not just of Christianity; no, I also pledge that I never will tie myself to parties who want to destroy Christianity ... We want to fill our culture again with the Christian spirit, not just

38 WT, 1961, 244. In speaking of 'the Drama,' Frost is of course referring to the Photo-Drama of Creation.

39 Helmreich, *The German Churches under Hitler,* 129.

40 Quoted in Helmreich from a speech delivered at Stuttgart on 16 February 1933.

theoretically. No, we want to burn out the rotten developments in literature, in the theater, in the press – in short, burn out this poison which has entered into our whole life and culture during these past fourteen years.'[40] Clearly, to some extent the *Führer* and his followers were pandering to the churches; but at the same time they were persecuting certain elements within them and were trying to seize control of them.

All of this should have alarmed the Watch Tower Society, whose members knew quite well that most of the clergy loathed them. They were being harassed constantly by the SA, which ironically was the wing of the Nazi movement with which they had the most in common.[41] Even so, with what amounted to fanatical audacity, Jehovah's Witnesses in Germany – following instructions from Brooklyn – increased their activities as if little had changed since the previous year. Between 8 and 16 April 1932 they participated in a worldwide, door-to-door preaching campaign called 'The Remnant's Thanksgiving Period.' The 19,286 German 'publishers' distributed 2,271,630 pieces of the Society's literature throughout the Reich; the same week, 20,719 of their American brethren managed to distribute only 877,194 pieces of those publications in the United States.[42]

Surprisingly, this brought only a mild immediate reaction from the Reich authorities. They simply demanded that a bloodthirsty cover be removed from the booklet *The Crisis,* which was the primary Watch Tower publication that had been distributed during the 'The Remnant's Thanksgiving Period.' Balzereit, the only senior Watch Tower official who seemed to realize the danger facing the Witnesses, agreed – something that his brethren later condemned as a cowardly compromise.[43] If the central authorities in Berlin were slow to move, two of the *Länder* were not. On 13 April, Bavaria banned the Witnesses, ordered their organization dissolved, and prohibited the distribution of their literature. Five days later, Saxony followed suit. On 26 April the Witnesses attempted to see Hitler himself to express their concerns over what was taking place, but he claimed that he was too busy to see them.[44]

41 After all, the SA, under the leadership of Ernst Röhm, was the left-wing of the National Socialist Party. Like the Witnesses, it detested 'Big Business' and was cool toward the churches.

42 *Jehovah's Witnesses in the Divine Purpose* (Brooklyn, NY: Watchtower Society and IBSA, 1959) 128–9.

43 *1974 Yearbook,* 109.

44 Helmreich, 392.

Two days earlier, on 24 April, the police in Magdeburg had seized the Watch Tower's German headquarters and conducted a thorough search in an attempt to find seditious material. The Nazis must have been wondering whether the Witnesses were promoting Communism at the very time that Hitler's government was suppressing the Communist Party. Much of what Rutherford said in *The Crisis* sounded very much like what the 'Reds' were proclaiming. In page after page the Watch Tower president damned 'Big Business' and blamed it for both the First World War and the Depression. Furthermore, in his closing remarks, he proclaimed something that must have sounded treasonable to the German government: 'The American government has been weighed in the balance and found wanting. It cannot endure. Together with all other nations, it soon shall fall. Such fall will be in spite of everything Big Business, politicians and clergymen, the military and the "strong-arm squad", and the Devil and all his hosts can do to hold together the oppressive rule. It must and will fall because Jehovah God's kingdom is here. Hasten now to take shelter under Jehovah's kingdom.'[45]

The Watch Tower Society in Brooklyn reacted quickly to the Nazi takeover of their Magdeburg properties. Instead of calling on Jehovah alone for help, on 26 April it turned to the U.S. State Department, asking it to intervene with the German government on its behalf. The Watch Tower Society was an American corporation, and under a 1923 friendship treaty between the United States and Germany, American property in the Reich was protected from seizure. The Witnesses were hardly the most loyal Americans, but to its credit on 27 April the State Department instructed the U.S. Embassy in Berlin to investigate what had happened and to lend assistance to the Watch Tower Society if warranted. As a result, the German authorities vacated the Magdeburg Watch Tower headquarters and returned them to the Witnesses. On 2 May the American consulate general was able to report to Washington that through the consulate's good offices, the Witness properties had been freed.[46]

The Witnesses were lulled into believing that they had achieved a significant victory. The Watch Tower branch office in Germany contended that there was no good reason why its offices should be occupied or its work suppressed. But, because Balzereit and others at

45 J.F. Rutherford, *Crisis* (Brooklyn, NY: Watch Tower Society and IBSA, 1933), 28.
46 Helmreich, 392.

Magdeburg realized the danger that the Witnesses still faced, *Das Goldene Zeitalter* published an *Öffentliche Erklärung* or 'Public Declaration' in its 15 May 1933 edition. This was obviously intended to curry favour with the Nazis. The declaration stated that the Witnesses had absolutely nothing to do with Freemasons, or Jews, or political parties; furthermore, it asserted that foreign accusations that Germany was guilty of atrocities were false – something its publishers must have known was a bald-faced lie. Even so, the declaration stated specifically: 'We gladly declare that during the occupation and search of our grounds and buildings, none of our co-workers had any reason for complaints against the officials conducting the search. Despite its absolute thoroughness, the search was carried out without causing any damage. We want to bring this to the attention of our central office in Brooklyn as well as all [Watch Tower] branches in other countries by sending this message. We always have [stressed] and will stress the truth, in order to contradict false ideas about conditions in Germany (known as atrocity propaganda).' In addition, the 'Public Declaration' boasted that two Watch Tower lawyers were Nazi Party members: 'For some years Judicial Counsel Mr. Karl Kohl, a lawyer in Munich and a member of the National Socialist German Workers Party [the Nazis], has been the legal advisor of the "Watch Tower Bible and Tract Society,' as has Judicial Counsel Mr. Horst Kohl – also a member of the National Socialist German Workers Party – for some four years.' Obviously, though, the Society's Magdeburg officers were somewhat embarrassed by the fact that another of their lawyers was a Social Democrat. *Das Goldene Zeitalter* therefore remarked: 'The former Police President of Magdeburg, Judicial Counsel Dr. Bärensprung, a specialist in international governmental and private law, helped us with suspended proceedings, but our absolute apolitical interests prove that we have no connections with the political ideas of the said gentleman; this was purely a matter of his legal qualifications.'[47]

In America, Watch Tower leaders evidently thought that their organization's crisis in Germany was over. Under the title 'Magdeburg Plant Closed and Reopened,' *The Golden Age* of 24 May stated on page 528: 'ON MONDAY, April 24, the German plant of the Watch Tower Bible and Tract Society, at Magdeburg, was closed and thereafter occupied by storm troopers of the Nazis. Protests of the American consul-gen-

47 For the full text of the *Öffentliche Erklärung* or 'Public Declaration' in German and its English translation, see Appendix C.

eral followed, and on the 29th the plant was restored to its owners and reopened. This seems to have marked a turning point in Germany, newspaper accounts reporting that because of this incident orders had been issued forbidding further arbitrary arrests of private citizens by armed Nazis.' In this, the Witnesses were far too optimistic. Ernst Helmreich reports: 'Meanwhile the governments of Bavaria, Saxony, Thuringia, Lippe, Mecklenburg, Hesse, and Württemberg had interdicted the Society's activities and confiscated its property, valued at 750,000 marks. On 18 May the U.S. consul general in Berlin was again asked to lend appropriate assistance. The German minister of the interior, who held the same office in Prussia, thereupon offered to investigate the activities of the state governments, with the surprising result that on 24 June 1933, he banned the Jehovah's Witnesses throughout Germany and ordered their property, valued at about five million marks, confiscated.'[48] Evidently not fully aware that they were already outlawed, the following day the Witnesses met in convention at the Berlin-Wilmersdorf Tennis Hall and adopted Rutherford's *Declaration of Facts*.

As U.S. State Department documents show, American consul Raymond H. Geist then visited the German Ministry of the Interior and obtained a promise that the German government would not confiscate Watch Tower property. He was informed, however, that the ban on the Witnesses and Witness literature would remain.[49] Shortly before the ban of 24 June, J.F. Rutherford had been present in Germany and had sought the help of the American consul. Geist had indicated to him that it would be useless for the American government to try to do more than protect the Watch Tower's physical properties.[50] Following this agreement, in July Consul General George Messersmith wrote to his superiors in Washington:

> I have gone into the activities of the Society and its agents, and have read some of the pamphlets which have been distributed by the Society widely in Germany, and I can see that the objection could reasonably be raised to them by the German Government. Although acting as a religious society, the pamphlets contain comment of not a purely religious character. In view

48 Helmreich, 392.

49 The U.S. Consul General in Berlin (Messersmith) to the Acting Secretary of State, 12 July 1933. U.S. Department of State, *Foreign Relations of the United States, 1933*, 2:409–10.

50 Ibid.

> of the present situation in Germany, I believe it would be entirely useless to endeavor to assist the Society to continue its operations and I doubt very much whether our Government, in view of the nature of the activities, would find it possible to assist it. I believe therefore that the only efforts which we can make on behalf of the Society are in connection with the protection of its physical property.[51]

What Messersmith was saying was that the American government would do its best on behalf of the Watch Tower Society in the limited sphere in which it could legitimately operate because the Society was an American corporation. At the same time, the American consul general emphasized something that Jehovah's Witnesses refused to recognize about themselves and their activities: *they were not as politically neutral as they liked to claim.* Rather, in many ways, they were socially disruptive and stood in the way of what many governments – not just that of Germany – wanted to accomplish. No doubt if Messersmith had read *The Crisis* – as his letter suggests he did – he must have been shocked at its criticism of the United States.

It may seem surprising that the American State Department and its representatives in Germany were willing to help Rutherford and the Watch Tower at all in view of the anti-Americanism spewed forth in Witness literature, especially after the publication of the *Declaration of Facts,* which must have become known to them. Yet they continued to do so.[52] When the police refused to return the Magdeburg properties to the Watch Tower 'as a guarantee that no propaganda will be made by the Society abroad against the German government,' Geist again protested to the German Minister of the Interior, requesting a response 'stating precisely the conditions upon which the property will be released.' He also contacted the State Department to determine whether, under the 1923 Treaty of Friendship, the German government could legitimately seize the property of an American corporation for political reasons.[53]

51 Ibid.

52 In part this was because the United States did not want to see the Nazis set a precedent for seizing American property; however, State Department records indicate as well that American officials did not like the Nazi suppression of religious liberty.

53 The U.S. Consul General in Berlin (Messersmith) to the Acting Secretary of State, 27 July 1933. U.S. Department of State, *Foreign Relations of the United States, 1933,* 2:410–12.

Although Germany still needed to maintain good relations with the United States, the Nazi authorities remained temporarily intransigent. The police continued to occupy the Magdeburg properties in July and August after Geist's recent protest; they even expelled from them Martin Harbeck, the Society's Swiss and Central European overseer and an American citizen.[54] Then they destroyed twenty-five truckloads of Watch Tower publications.[55] However, on 12 September the American Embassy reported that the Society's Magdeburg properties had been returned, although the Witnesses remained banned.

In the meantime the American ambassador, William E. Dodd, had studied the entire matter of the Nazis' actions against the Witnesses and their publishing organizations. On 20 September he submitted a *note verbale* to the German Foreign Office that raised the issue of the ban on the militant American-based sect. On 26 September the *Regierungspräsident* or governor in Magdeburg received orders from Berlin to restore the Society's buildings and to allow Witness personnel to take up residence there again.[56] The Germans' reply to Dodd's note did not come until 13 November. It suggested that the Society could take action under Article 12 of the 1923 treaty, and Harbeck prepared to do so. But before he could act the American Embassy received word from the German authorities that under the presidential decree of 28 February that had followed the Reichstag fire, the German government's actions against the Witnesses could not be contested. Dodd then contacted the State Department, but it evidently decided to take no further action on the Witnesses' behalf.[57]

54 The U.S. Secretary of State (Cordel Hull) to the Ambassador in Germany (Dodd), 9 September 1933. Ibid., 2:412–13.

55 'Despite the energetic attempts of Brother Harbeck, the branch overseer in Switzerland, to prevent it, books, Bibles and pictures weighing a total of 65,189 kilograms were taken from the Society's factory on August 21, 23 and 24, loaded into twenty-five trucks and then publicly burned at the edge of Magdeburg. The printing costs for the material amounted to some 92,719.50 marks.' *1974 Yearbock*, 112.

56 The U.S. Ambassador in Germany (Dodd) to the Acting Secretary of State, December 4, 1933. The German Foreign Office to the American Embassy, Note Verbale, 13 November 1933. The U.S. Ambassador in Germany (Dodd) to the Secretary of State, February 1, 1934. All found in U.S. Department of State, *Foreign Relations of the United States, 1933*, 2: 414–17.

57 The U.S. Ambassador in Germany (Dodd) to the Acting Secretary of State, December 4, 1933. The U.S. Ambassador in Germany (Dodd) to the Secretary of State, February 1, 1934.

On 28 June the Nazis again seized the Watch Tower's Magdeburg properties. Fearing for his life, Paul Balzereit fled to Czechoslovakia. As a result, the administration of Watch Tower's German affairs was placed in Martin Harbeck's hands. But Harbeck was to accomplish little. Over the next year or two the German government still seemed anxious to maintain good relations with the Americans, and in June 1934 the German Ministry of the Interior ordered the governments of the *Länder* to restore Watch Tower and International Bible Student property to Jehovah's Witnesses. Yet the Nazi government maintained its ban on practically all Watch Tower activities and refused to allow the Witnesses the freedom to meet or to proselytize.[58]

On 17 July 1934 the American consul, Geist, wrote to the German Ministry of the Interior to ask about the return of Watch Tower property. On 13 September that department replied to Geist as follows: 'In reply to your kind communication of July 17, 1934, I have the honor to inform you that I have directed all state governments to free the property of the International Bible Researchers organization, including its subsidiary organizations, and no longer to forbid the printing of Bibles and other nonsuspicious writings. Nevertheless, all further activity of the Earnest Bible Researchers, such as teaching and holding of meetings, as well as the preparation and distribution of tracts, flyers, solicitation for members, etc., must remain prohibited.'[59]

The Watch Tower's response to being outlawed in the spring and summer of 1933 was to attempt to have the bans on their work revoked. Both Rutherford and Harbeck decided initially that the best course was to mollify the Nazis by obeying the law and by trying to ingratiate their movement with the Hitler government. Thus Harbeck, as Rutherford's proxy, called on the Witnesses to cease their religious activities completely. In English translation, his letter reads:

Magdeburg, 28 August 1933

My dear friends:

I should like to answer the many inquiries which [we have received] here by means of a circular letter. The Watch Tower Bible and Tract

58 Helmreich, 394.
59 Quoted in ibid., 393–4.

Society is banned. Equally, the activity of the International Bible Students Association.

As authorized by the Watch Tower Bible & Tract Society, and especially as the proxy of the President, Judge Rutherford, I should like to ask you herewith to submit to all current governmental and police authorities' regulations [without] exception. Above all, I would like to entreat you not to disseminate banned publications and not to hold any meetings or lectures without permission issued by the police.

Since the printing of books, pamphlets and magazines is banned, we cannot fill orders for them. Inquiries are therefore temporarily of no use.

We want to be good citizens of the country and give eloquent testimony through our moral conduct and our style of life to the honor of God and the vindication of His Name and Word.

As Judge Rutherford directed me, I convey to you greetings and beg you to persevere in faith and prayer until the Lord gives us an opportunity in His Kingdom to contribute again to the vindication of His Name.

Joined with you in love, I greet you as,

Watch Tower Bible and Tract Society
Brooklyn, New-York, U.S.A.
(By: M.C. Harbeck.)[60]

What is most outstanding about this letter is not just that Rutherford, acting through Harbeck, was calling on German Witnesses not to violate the Nazi bans on them at that time, but that he was indicating that the preaching work would end until the Christ's Kingdom was fully established. As any Jehovah's Witness would have known then, and would recognize today, the Watch Tower Society has long taught that ordinary Witnesses take part in the vindication of Jehovah's name through preaching work. It is therefore hard to believe that Harbeck's letter was anything more than a ploy to keep the Witnesses quiet while he negotiated with the Nazis. There is no doubt that by curbing preaching activities at the time, Rutherford was trying to appease the authorities in Berlin in the hope that they would return Watch Tower properties and lift the ban. After all, he had indicated to an American consular official in Germany that he was hopeful this might be accomplished.[61]

60 For a copy of this letter in German, see Appendix C.

61 In his letter dated 12 July 1933 at Berlin to the U.S. Acting Secretary of State, American Consul General Messersmith outlined the situation involving the

If Harbeck's 28 August letter does not prove that Watch Tower leaders were anxious to compromise with the Nazis, more dramatic evidence demonstrates this. In a petition sent to von Hindenberg, Hitler, and the Minister President of Prussia on 29 September 1933, Harbeck wrote: 'Never have Communists or Marxists been admitted as [Bible Student] fellow believers. Jews are not to be found among Bible Students. So, therefore, all members of the Bible Student fellowship salute the National Socialist government because Hitler and his state acknowledge themselves to be Christians.'[62] Two days later he wrote to Hitler personally, stating that it was incomprehensible that the Nazis had forgotten how the Catholic Church had opposed them and had even prohibited individual Nazis from receiving communion in Catholic churches. Then he went on to say: 'The Bible Students Association itself has never, nor with a single word, attacked the National Socialist state.'[63] If this were not enough, he even wrote to Nazi officialdom 'that since the Jews had never repented for their treason of having crucified Christ, they would have no precedence over other nations.'[64]

Despite Rutherford's 'Fear Them Not' article – or perhaps because of it – Jehovah's Witnesses in Germany remained divided and uncer-

suppression of Jehovah's Witnesses in Germany at the time. Therein he indicated that Rutherford had visited the American Consulate, and he remarked: 'Judge Rutherford was very much concerned as to the status of their affairs in Germany and appeared willing to trust somewhat to possible favorable developments which might come about with the march of affairs.' Quite evidently, however, Witness officials at Magdeburg were not so sanguine. Messersmith noted: 'His representatives in Germany had complained that the pamphlets prepared in New York for this country were not in accordance with the ideas that have come about with the so-called national resurgence. These men being Germans, understood thoroughly the disrepute into which the Watch Tower Bible and Tract Society had fallen in this country.' U.S. Department of State Foreign Relations, 1933, Volume II, 408.

62 'Niemals sind Kommunisten oder Marxisten als Glaubensgenossen aufgenommen worden. Juden befinden sich überhaupt nicht in den Reihen der Bibelforscher. Wohl aber haben alle Glaubensgenossen der B. V. Die nationalsozialistische Regierung um deswillen begrüßt, weil Hitler und sein Staat sich zum Chistentum bekennen.' Detlef Garbe, *Zwischen Widerstand und Martyrium: Die Zeugen Jehovas im 'Dritten Reich."* 4th ed. (Munich: R. Oldenbourg Verlag, 1993), 121–2.

63 'Die Bibelfoscher Vereinigung hat sich niemals auch nur mit einem Wort gegen den nationalsozialistischen Staat gewendet.' Quoted in Gebhard, 275.

64 'Das die Juden das Verbrechen ihres Verrates (dass sie) Jesus Christus kreuzigten, nie bereut haben und das die Juden daher keinen Vorzug über andere Nationen haben werden.' Like Rutherford, Harbeck undoubtedly meant that this would be true with respect to the earthly resurrection during the millennium. Quoted in Gebhard, 275, and noted as found in the Bundesarchiv Koblenz R 43/II 179 Bl. 214.

tain about what to do. A letter from a 'Brother Poddig' shows that some 'brothers' were refusing to accept this article as '[spiritual] food in due season,' and 'some were even trying to prevent the brothers from carrying on any underground preaching.'[65] To this Rutherford responded: 'The article "Fear Them Not" which appeared in the December 1 [German] *Watchtower* was especially for the benefit [*sic*] of our brothers in Germany.'[66] Still, when the Watch Tower Society held a convention at Basel, Switzerland, on 7 to 9 September 1934, German Witnesses remained divided. Rutherford 'was forced to recognize that even the [Society's] traveling overseers present were not of one mind as regards the preaching work.'[67] Small wonder: the bombastic Watch Tower president had at first tried to ingratiate the Witnesses with Hitler, then he had attempted to negotiate with him through the U.S. State Department, and when that failed, he had blamed those of his German brethren who did not want to go ahead with his revised policy of defying the Nazis as lacking in integrity. This must have seemed thoroughly hypocritical to many German Jehovah's Witnesses, who were risking both their freedom and their lives.

Fear of the Nazis and shifts in Watch Tower policy no doubt disheartened many German Witnesses. Various sources suggest that more than half the Witness community stopped meeting and preaching. The Dresden congregation, the largest in Germany, collapsed from a peak of some 1,200 door-to-door 'publishers' to 500.[68] The *1974 Yearbook* claims that there *may* have been 10,000 who were willing to continue such preaching despite the dangers,[69] but this is probably wishful thinking. While it is difficult to say exactly how many continued to do so, evidence suggests that it was no more than two-fifths of the total community, and perhaps fewer.[70] Furthermore, recent evidence

65 1974 Yearbook, 132.
66 Ibid.
67 Ibid., 133.
68 Ibid., 141.
69 Ibid.
70 As pointed out earlier, the *1974 Yearbook* tells that in the spring of 1933, 24,843 people were present at the Witnesses' annual Memorial celebration, in comparison with 14,453 the year before, and the number of 'publishers' or door-to door preachers had risen from 12,484 to 19,268. For a further analysis of German Witness numbers at the time, see Garbe, *Zwischen Widerstand und Martyrium*, 81. On the other hand, according to the *1974 Yearbook of Jehovah's Witnesses*, the number of Witnesses arrested under the Third Reich totalled only 6,019, and from 16 May through 15 June 1936, before a wave of arrests, only 5,930 publishers or 'workers' reported being engaged in preaching. *1974 Yearbook*, 212.

shows that by 1938 more than 500 had renounced their faith while imprisoned.[71] So it is true that those who remained faithful to Watch Tower teachings did so in a way that is quite admirable, in particular if they stood firm until death. But these people represented only a minority of Jehovah's Witnesses in Germany, and even while remaining loyal to what they considered Christian principles, they were often divided among themselves and sometimes treated one another badly.[72]

71 Report No. 20, 30 June 1938 of the *Informationen des geheimen Staatspolizeiamts* (Reports of the Secret State Police Authority) states that 516 Bible Students were released from investigative detention or from serving their prison sentences because of the amnesty of 30 June 1938. Accordingly, 'the released persons have obligated themselves, by written statement, not to become active any more on behalf of the illegal Bible Students Association nor to testify in future any more for the teachings of the same.'

72 *1974 Yearbook*, 174–9.

6

Jehovah's Witnesses in the Crucible of Nazi Persecution

> A few Christians were deliberately provocative of the authorities, but they and those who came forward asking for martyrdom did not represent the thinking of the church at large, which took the position that one should be faithful if brought to trial but should not seek out martyrdom.
>
> Everett Ferguson, *Encyclopedia of Early Christianity*

Because of his concerns about Martin Harbeck's role, Paul Balzereit asked Rutherford if he could return to Germany. Rutherford's harsh reply: 'Return to Magdeburg and stay there and take charge of matters and do what you can but notify Brother Harbeck about everything ... In fact it should not be necessary for you to ask permission to return to Germany, since as far as I am concerned, and this you know, you could have stayed there right from the beginning. You tried to make me believe, however, that your personal safety was dependent on your taking refuge outside the country.'[1] So back in Germany, Balzereit, and with him another high Watch Tower official, solicitor Hans Dollinger, attempted to work out a friendly accord with the Nazis. Despite Rutherford's pronouncements in the article 'Fear Them Not,' and other abrasive challenges to Hitler (see below), they continued to do so until their arrest in the spring of 1935. No doubt they were encouraged in this course by fear as well as by the fact that two of the Society's German lawyers were National Socialists. So as late as 5 January 1935, Dollinger wrote directly to Hitler asking that he re-

1 *1974 Yearbook*, 131.

ceive a report on Jehovah's Witnesses from a proposed deputation that would include Karl Kohl, described as a defender of Hitler in 1924; Dollinger himself; Paul Balzereit; and Nikolaus Freiherr [Baron] von Tornow, an owner of an estate at Kottbus-Saspow and a longtime Bible Student–Jehovah's Witness. In closing this letter, Dollinger flattered the German dictator with these words: 'Thanking you in advance for your kind attention and assuring you of my deepest respect and admiration, I send you a German greeting [an indirect way of saying *Heil Hitler*].' Under his signature appeared this title: 'General Manager of the International Bible Students Association.'[2]

Of course, such pandering to Hitler could go nowhere, because neither the *Führer* nor any of his officials had any use for any church or sect, and because beginning in November 1933 Rutherford took such a strong stand against Nazism that there was no possibility of negotiating anything close to a *modus vivendi* with the Third Reich. In one instance, discussed later, Rutherford's actions had almost driven Hitler to an apoplectic fit. But this did not stop Dollinger from engaging in one of the most shameful acts that a representative of the Watch Tower Society has ever been party to – an attempt to divert governmental wrath from the Witnesses by scapegoating one of their former spiritual brethren and denouncing him to a senior Nazi official.

Briefly stated, what happened was this: A former Bible Student, Ewald Vorsteher, was arrested in the German city of Wuppertal on 31 May 1933 and sent to prison for circulating strongly anti-Nazi statements, attacking their anti-Semitism, and insulting Hitler. In the early 1920s, Vorsteher had been a worker at the Watch Tower's branch offices in Barmen. Then in 1923, while the Watch Tower offices were being moved to Magdeburg, he and some others broke with their former brethren. Evidently, besides having certain doctrinal concerns, he and his associates had taken offence at Balzereit for his expensive and self-aggrandizing actions and at Rutherford for his loose morals. Apparently, the judge's drinking habits shocked them. Thus Vorsteher and those in agreement with him formed a group called the *Wahrheitsfreunde* or Friends of Truth. Consequently, the Watch Tower Bible Student movement disfellowshipped them.[3] Nonetheless, the po-

2 Letter from Hans Dollinger to *Reichskanzler* Adolf Hitler, 5 January 1935. For a copy of this letter and its English translation, see Appendix G.

3 Manfred Gebhard, *Geschichte der Zeugen Jehovas: Mit Schwerpunkt der deutschen Geschichte* (Berlin: Libri Books on Demand, 1999), 183–9.

lice in Wuppertal initially associated Vorsteher with Jehovah's Witnesses and blamed the Witnesses for his actions. Therefore the Witnesses at Magdeburg – and Dollinger in particular – foolishly claimed to believe that this was 'the only specific incident' leading to the ban on the Witnesses in Prussia on 24 June of the same year.[4]

While Martin Harbeck was trying to negotiate the return of the Magdeburg Watch Tower properties, he met with the Wuppertal police chief and pointed out that Vorsteher and the Friends of Truth were in no way associated with Jehovah's Witnesses. The Wuppertal police chief agreed to tell the Prussian Ministry of the Interior in Berlin that a mistake had been made if the Witnesses contacted that ministry.[5] Naturally, they did.

Nothing came of the Witnesses' action, since the Vorsteher incident was not the real reason why the Nazis had banned them. Yet Dollinger kept trying to use it as a basis for having the ban lifted. As late as 29 January 1935 he wrote a letter to a Dr Lang, the government counsel for the German and Prussian Ministry of the Interior, about the Vorsteher affair. In it he condemned Vorsteher in the strongest possible terms for what Jehovah's Witnesses were then doing. In referring to the report of the Wuppertal police chief, he remarked: 'During the copying of this report, I became aware in a very special way of the incredible things this man named VORSTEHER has done. I understand absolutely that the National Socialist government could not put up with it. No government in the world would have tolerated this.' Because he had circulated anti-Nazi publications, Dollinger referred to Vorsteher as having committed 'the fanatical act of a lunatic.' He went on to state that neither Vorsteher nor the Friends of Truth had anything to do with Jehovah's Witnesses. Amazingly, as if the Nazis did not already know what the Watch Tower in Brooklyn and many German Witnesses were then publicizing about the Hitler regime, he wrote: 'In no speech, in no lecture, and not in the general behavior of the Society was there ever, in any fashion, a stand taken against National Socialism.' He asserted that this was true both in Germany and in all other lands.[6] To ingratiate the Witnesses further with Dr Lang, Dollinger then described Vorsteher's disfellowshipment in 1922 or 1923, arguing that it showed that the Watch Tower movement demanded strict obe-

4 Letter from Hans Dollinger to Dr Lang, 29 January 1935. For a copy of this letter and its English translation, see Appendix G.

5 Ibid.

6 Ibid.

dience. No doubt he hoped this would resonate with the Nazi concept of the *Führerprinzip* – the doctrine that there must be absolute obedience to the leader.[7]

In speaking about Jehovah's Witnesses' behaviour toward Nazism, Dollinger was stating an obvious falsehood. He was also playing both the hypocrite and the fool. Along with Balzereit and a few others, he was also refusing to obey Rutherford's 'theocratic' leadership and attempting to undermine it. For when he and Balzereit came to trial in the spring of 1935, they claimed – evidently truthfully – that they had advised their Witness brethren in Germany not to engage in door-to-door preaching and not even to gather for the yearly Memorial of Christ's death.[8] When Rutherford became aware of what they had said in court, he was furious and summarily disfellowshipped them, declaring that the Watch Tower would have nothing to do with them and would not help them out of prison even if it could. Undoubtedly embittered, both Balzereit and Dollinger later repudiated their association with Jehovah's Witnesses. Eventually they were released from concentration camp.[9]

Of course Rutherford cannot be blamed for Dollinger's efforts to scapegoat Vorsteher, nor for his attempts to placate the Nazis after 1933. But he *can* be condemned for driving his German brethren into the fiery furnace of Nazi persecution by demanding that they continue their preaching work and, even more, by making direct attacks on the German government – attacks that were circulated throughout the Reich. It is true that the Witnesses would have suffered some severe persecution for maintaining their principles, and especially for refusing to *Heil Hitler* and to perform military service after Germany introduced universal male conscription in 1935. That said, had they not confronted the Nazis directly, they would certainly have fared much better. But Rutherford seemed not to care about the safety of the Witnesses in Germany, any more than he cared about the safety of his brethren in the United States and other lands.

By the beginning of 1934, Rutherford was furious with Hitler and the Nazis. On 9 February he dispatched a personal letter to the German *Führer* at Brown House, Munich. It began: 'This letter is a kindly

7 German Witnesses spoke of *theokratisches Prinzip* (theocratic principle), which called for obedience to Rutherford and his subordinates in much the same way that the *Führerprinzip* called for total obedience to Hitler.

8 *1974 Yearbook,* 148–50.

9 Ibid., 141.

notice and warning of things that are of vital importance to your welfare.' It then described what was happening to Jehovah's Witnesses in Germany, told of how Jehovah punished persecutors of his people, and stated about German officials: 'They have been warned that those who oppose God and His kingdom shall be destroyed by the Lord at Armageddon. Such notice and warning have been ignored by your government.' To drive the point home, the Watch Tower president wrote: 'The Scriptures plainly declare that what came upon Egypt [in Moses' time] will come in far greater degree upon all the world, and particularly upon those who oppose Jehovah God and His kingdom. You may successfully resist any and all men, but you cannot successfully resist Jehovah God. I demand that you give order to all officials and servants of your government that Jehovah's witnesses [who are of the EARNEST BIBLE STUDENTS AND THE WATCH TOWER BIBLE AND TRACT SOCIETY] in Germany be permitted to peaceably assemble and without hindrance worship God and obey his commandments by teaching to the people the Bible truths concerning God's kingdom under Christ, for which kingdom all Christians have long hoped and prayed.' Finally, Rutherford wrote: 'If by the 24th day of March, 1934, there is no response to this earnest demand and nothing done by your government to grant relief of the aforesaid Jehovah's witnesses in Germany, then God's people in other countries will begin the publication throughout the nations of the earth of the facts concerning Germany's wrongful treatment of Christian people there, and having delivered the testimony, we will submit our case to God.'[10]

When there was no reply to this missive, Rutherford decided to condemn the Nazis openly. On 25 March he delivered a speech on the German situation to a Watch Tower convention at Los Angeles, California, that was broadcast throughout the United States on a nationwide radio network.[11] At the same convention the Witnesses present adopted the following statement of protest:

> For many years Jehovah's witnesses, unitedly working under the WATCH TOWER BIBLE AND TRACT SOCIETY, have engaged in bearing testimony to the name and kingdom of Jehovah God. During the past year the German government without cause or excuse has wrongfully seized, confiscated

10 'The Persecution of Jehovah's Witnesses in Germany,' *The Golden Age*, 25 April 1934, 453.

11 Ibid., 454.

and destroyed the Bibles, song books, furniture and other property of these faithful Christians, prohibited them to meet together and worship God according to His commandments, and has cruelly persecuted and imprisoned many of them, and like Pharaoh of old, that government has wickedly opposed Jehovah and defamed His name.

Therefore, We their brethren as followers of Christ Jesus do earnestly and vigorously protest against such unwarranted treatment of Christians by the German ruling power, and we call upon all true Christians and fair-minded people throughout the earth to join in this vigorous protest and demand that Jehovah's witnesses, without let or hindrance on the part of the German government or others, shall be permitted to go on in their worship and service of Jehovah God in the manner which He commanded, and we register our protest by declaring against Satan and all such oppression and by taking our stand on the side of Jehovah, His kingdom and His people.[12]

In its 25 April 1934 edition, *The Golden Age* reported these events and provided detailed accounts of the persecution of individual Witnesses who had lost their jobs or welfare payments for not voting in Hitler's November 1933 election or for not giving the Hitler salute. In addition, it noted that the police had invaded various Jehovah's Witness homes, had confiscated Bibles and literature, had placed some families under what amounted to house arrest, and had arrested and jailed hundreds.[13] The same issue of the Witness magazine did, however, reprint an article from the *New York Times* which reported that a special German court in Darmstadt had acquitted twenty-nine *Bibelforscher* or Bible Students on the grounds that there was as yet no law under which they could be convicted even though it considered them 'inimical to the state.' The court noted: 'They regard all secular governments as works of Satan.'[14]

Perhaps the Darmstadt decision gave some brief hope to Jehovah's Witnesses both in Germany and elsewhere, but the Nazi persecution continued. Thus in early May, British Witnesses joined their American fellow believers in protesting what was happening in the Reich.[15] In July Judge Rutherford produced an article in *The Golden Age*, 'Beastly

12 Ibid.

13 Ibid., 456–63.

14 Ibid., 463.

15 'British Protest against Injustices to Jehovah's Witnesses in Germany,' *The Golden Age*, 4 July 1934, 636.

Persecution in Germany.'[16] At the end of August *The Golden Age* commented again on the Darmstadt decision and described with horror Hitler's blood purge of the SA and others. But it also noted that it had been the SA that had caused the greatest harm to German Witnesses.[17] So early in October – just a little more than three months after that well-publicized massacre[18] – Rutherford sent a letter to his German followers to meet secretly to pass a resolution against the Hitler regime. Part of that letter reads:

> Every group of Jehovah's witnesses in Germany should gather together at a convenient place in the city where they live, on Sunday morning, October 7, 1934, at 9:00 o'clock. This letter should be read to all present. You should join together in prayer to Jehovah asking him through Christ Jesus, our Head and King, for his guidance, protection, deliverance and blessing. Immediately thereafter send a letter to German government officials which text will have been prepared beforehand and will then be available. A few minutes should be spent discussing Matthew 10:16–24, keeping in mind that by doing as this text says, you are 'standing for your lives.' (Esther 8:11) The meeting should then be closed and you should go out to your neighbors giving them a witness about Jehovah's name, about our God and his Kingdom under Christ Jesus.
>
> Your brothers throughout the world will be thinking of you and will direct a similar prayer to Jehovah at the same time.[19]

This resolution, directed to Nazi officials, stated in part: 'Therefore this is to advise you that at any cost we will obey God's commandments, will meet together for the study of his Word, and will worship and serve him as commanded. If your government or officers do violence to us because we are obeying God, then our blood will be upon you and you will answer to Almighty God.'[20] Simultaneously, Witnesses in other countries dispatched telegrams that read: 'Hitler Gov-

16 *The Golden Age,* 1 August 1934, 680–1.

17 'The Acquittal of Hesse-Darmstadt,' *The Golden Age*, 29 August 1934, 758.

18 For a detailed discussion of the events leading up to the 30 June 1934 blood purge of Ernst Röhm, other members of the SA, and certain Nazi opponents, see Ian Kershaw, *Hitler 1989–1936: Hubris* (New York and London: W.W. Norton, 1999), 505–17.

19 'Jehovah's Witnesses in Germany Standing for Their Lives,' *The Golden Age*, 24 October 1934, 50–1. For the full text of this letter, see Appendix E.

20 Ibid.

ernment, Berlin Germany. Your ill treatment of Jehovah's witnesses shocks all good people of earth and dishonors God's name. Refrain from further persecuting Jehovah's witnesses; otherwise God will destroy you and your national party.'[21]

These actions infuriated Adolf Hitler and made matters far worse for Jehovah's Witnesses in Germany. According to one eyewitness account, Hitler flew into a rage when told of the Witness telegrams from abroad. He 'jumped to his feet and with clenched fists hysterically screamed: "This brood will be exterminated in Germany."' According to Karl R.A. Wittig, who recorded the event, Hitler did attempt to destroy Jehovah's Witnesses: 'Four years after this discussion [at which he, Wilhelm Frick, and Adolf Hitler were present], I was able by my own observations, to convince myself that ... Hitler's outburst of anger was not just an idle threat. No other group of prisoners of the named concentration-camps [Sachsenhausen, Flossenburg, and Mauthaussen] was exposed to the sadism of the SS-soldiery in such a fashion as the Bible Students were.'[22] Christine King, testifying to similar facts, states: 'It is undoubtedly true that they [Jehovah's Witnesses] had enemies in high places, for Hitler himself once [falsely claimed to have] ordered the shooting of some 130 "self-styled Bible students" as an example to other "pacifists."'[23]

Despite this strengthening persecution, the Witnesses in Germany were animated. According to a letter published in *The Golden Age,* many who had once been unwilling to preach to their neighbours decided to do so after the dispatch of the letters and telegrams to Hitler.[24] They organized underground activities and kept them going for the next two years. This angered the Nazis, who responded by

21 Ibid.

22 *Jehovah's Witnesses in the Divine Purpose,* 142. For the original German of this declaration and its English translation, see Appendix E.

23 Christine Elizabeth King, *The Nazi State and the New Religions: Five Case Studies in Non-Conformity* (New York and Toronto: Edwin Mellon Press, 1982), 164. King's remark is based on Hitler's *Table Talk.* There is no evidence that Hitler actually had ordered what he claimed to have done in this instance. Nonetheless, it is evident that he hated the Witnesses.

24 That letter stated in part: 'Our joy was great, and the result was that now many brethren again systematically go from door to door with the Bible in hand and deliver an oral testimony. Even those brethren who have hesitated so far to do this seem to overcome their reluctance and to realize that they have permitted other brethren to restrain them from service.' 'Jehovah's Witnesses in Germany,' *The Golden Age,* 5 December 1934, 146.

intensifying their persecution in various ways, which would continue until their regime collapsed in 1945.

There is no doubt that Jehovah's Witnesses suffered severe persecution in late 1933 and 1934. *The Golden Age* of 25 April 1934 estimated that the Nazi destruction of books and other items in August 1933 cost the Watch Tower Society $750,000.[25] More significantly, many ordinary German Witnesses lost their jobs, pensions, and social assistance cheques because they refused to *Heil Hitler* or to vote in the November 1933 Reichstag elections.[26] In Bavaria, their refusal to vote prompted Reinhard Heydrich to arrest some of them and, in February 1934, to order the confiscation of their mail. The following June, Hans Pfundtner of the German Ministry of the Interior decided that Witnesses working in government jobs (as civil servants, postmen, etc.) should be dismissed because they refused to *Heil Hitler*.[27] *The Golden Age* of 25 April 1934 reported that by the spring of 1934 'in Saxony alone more than 500 brethren were in concentration camps.'[28] The Watch Tower's 'Stand Firm' video has claimed recently that by that time, the police had already visited 4,000 Jehovah's Witness homes and had arrested 1,000 of them. The 'Stand Firm' video and Watch Tower spokesman James Pellechia also say that only four hundred were in concentration camps.[29]

Regarding these claims, it is important to note several things. First, while they do give certain concrete facts that no one can deny, it is difficult to believe that the statistics can be better than rough estimates. How anyone could ascertain how many police house visits there were under the circumstances of the ban is hard to imagine. The statistics for arrests and detentions in concentration camps may be more valid, but there is some room to doubt them as well. This is especially the case since the 'Stand Firm' video and James Pellechia have reduced the number in concentration camps at the time by one hundred. Second, this early persecution was sporadic and much more evident in some parts of Germany than in others. For example, there

25 Page 455.

26 *The Golden Age,* 25 April 1931, 456–61.

27 Ernst Christian Helmreich, *The German Churches under Hitler* (Detroit: Wayne State University Press, 1979), 395.

28 Page 456.

29 James N. Pellechia, 'Teaching Tolerance: A Case Study,' in Hans Hesse, ed., *Persecution and Resistance of Jehovah's Witnesses during the Nazi Regime 1933–1945* (Bremen: Edition Temmen, 2001), 374.

was no ban on the Witnesses in Hesse until 18 October 1933 and in Württemberg until 1 February 1934,[30] many months after other *Länder* had outlawed them in the rest of the country. Also, most of the early persecution took place in two *Länder:* Saxony and Bavaria. Third, according to Friedrich Zipfel there were only a few recorded arrests for illegal activities and there was only one conviction.[31] Fourth, although it is true that many Witnesses were sent to concentration camps in 1933 for distributing the *Declaration of Facts* or banned Watch Tower literature, they were usually released quite soon after. Fifth, most courts either acquitted or released Jehovah's Witnesses when they appeared before them. Specifically, they sometimes held that the Witnesses had done nothing illegal in distributing the declaration.[32] Even after the Nazis had been in power for more than a year, some courts were still dealing leniently with them, as the Darmstadt decision on 27 March 1934 demonstrates. That, however, did not stop local Nazi officials – and especially, the SA – from continuing to harass them. Note, however, that this initial leniency does not put the lie to their later persecution, which would be severe even by the Nazis' standards.

Dramatic changes took place in 1935. On 13 January of that year the Saar region, which had been detached from Germany by the Treaty of Versailles for fifteen years, voted overwhelmingly in a plebiscite to become part of the Reich again. This increased the Nazi government's popularity, and on 17 March, Hitler took the dangerous step of decreeing that Germany would increase its army to thirty-six divisions. He reinstated universal military conscription for all healthy German males of draftable age except clergymen. France, Belgium, Czechoslovakia, Poland, and Italy were shaken by this announcement, but they felt powerless to do anything about it because the British refused to support them. Now nothing stood in the way of German rearmament, and Hitler's popularity soared. To all intents and purposes, the Treaty of Versailles was now irrelevant – a fact made even clearer on 10 March when Hermann Göring announced the creation of a German air force. German generals, who had initially questioned the *Führer*'s wisdom in this matter, hailed him along with the common people.[33]

30 Detlef Garbe, *Zwischen Widerstand und Martyrium: Die Zeugen Jehovas im 'Dritten Reich,'* 4th ed. (Munich: Oldenbourg Verlag, 1999), 98n48.

31 Friedrich Zipfel, *Kirchenkampf in Deutschland 1933–1945* (Berlin: Walter de Gruyter, 1965), 181, 188. Zipfel may be wrong about this.

32 *The Golden Age,* 25 April 1934, 452.

33 Ian Kershaw, *Hitler 1889–1936: Hubris* (New York: W.W. Norton, 1998), 546–54.

On 1 April, less than two weeks after Hitler's sensational announcement concerning the German *Wehrmacht* (armed forces), the Nazi Minister of the Interior ordered the governor in Magdeburg to outlaw the Watch Tower Bible and Tract Society. This he did on 27 April. Then on 21 May the minister rescinded his order of the previous September by which the properties of the Society had been returned. Finally, on 13 July 1935, the minister called on other heads of government in the various *Länder* to take similar steps.[34] In early May, Watch Tower officials in Magdeburg were charged as subversives; the following December they were brought to trial, convicted as charged, and sentenced to prison. The Nazis could take these actions – and increase their harassment of the churches – because they no longer needed the good will of the American or other foreign governments. Hitler was now seen as Germany's saviour. Military conscription had become popular, and nothing stood in the way of the full suppression of the annoying *Bibelforscher*. It is not surprising that the Nazis had now decided to crush them. Germany was a totalitarian state, and its rulers had no intention of tolerating what they regarded as an obnoxious and dangerous 'brood' who were quite prepared to defy them. In June 1935 both the Minister of the Interior and the Minister of Justice decided the Witnesses could be kept in 'protective custody' – concentration camps – after they had served their jail time.[35] There is plenty of evidence that the truculent Witness messages sent to the Hitler government from within Germany and the even more brazen telegrams wired by their brethren from abroad in October 1934 had infuriated Hitler and Nazi Party members throughout the Reich. No doubt these were a major factor in bringing greater governmental persecution down on them. Equally importantly, Jehovah's Witnesses were the most stridently outspoken conscientious objectors in the country, and the Nazis had no intention of putting up with them. The German government now had a new and more potent weapon to use against them. Because the Nazis glorified war and Hitler hated pacifists, the new conscription law provided no exemption for conscientious objectors and could be directed against any antiwar movement in the Reich. A chilling Associated Press article from Berlin dated 19 April 1935 reported: '"The death penalty," it was announced today, "will be invoked in Nazi Germany to exterminate pacifism in time of war or

34 Helmreich, 395–6.
35 Ibid., 396.

national emergency."' Then, in a final paragraph relating to a statement from 'the Board of Jurisdiction and capital punishment,' the article stated: '"One of three articles," the board announced, "is directed against the destructive work of pacifists and anti-military organizations. Persons arranging meetings as well as people attending will be punished. During the time of war or danger of war, life imprisonment will be changed to death penalties for hard cases."'[36]

Despite this increased persecution and the added dangers, the Witnesses continued to meet and proselytize, sometimes in an extremely open manner. *The Golden Age* of 6 June 1935 gives an account on pages 552–4 titled 'The Prisoners for the Lord in Germany.' According to it, when the Witnesses began working in a place simply called H–, there were 'about 31 groups organized' to go from door to door. The article tells what happened next: 'H. v. A was out with the books and was stopped by a policeman, who asked what he had. V. A. did not reply; so the policeman examined him and found that he had books. Later in the evening four policemen came to V. A's flat and there were also some sisters taking part in a study. When the police entered, they said in a rough voice, "What's that? A meeting here?" Then one of the policemen said, "It is you who have sent the statement [of 7 October 1934] to the government." V. A. said, "It is not I who have sent it, but I stand by all that was said in it."' The rest of the article then tells how V.A., the women, and sixty Jehovah's Witnesses in all ended up in concentration camps as a result of this open defiance of the law. At their trial, *the prosecutor attacked Judge Rutherford, not only for agitating in Germany but for his attacks on his own country.*

Today the Watch Tower Society wants ordinary Jehovah's Witnesses and the general public to believe that those who followed Rutherford's instructions were acting with discretion. The book *Jehovah's Witnesses: Proclaimers of God's Kingdom,* published in 1993, states: 'Because they would not abandon their faith and desist from preaching, thousands of Jehovah's Witnesses ... were imprisoned or sent to Nazi concentration camps. There brutal treatment was the order of the day. Those not yet in prison carried on their ministry cautiously. They often worked with just the Bible and offered other literature only when making return visits on interested persons. To avoid arrest, Witnesses would call at one door in an apartment house and then perhaps go to another

36 This article appeared in the *New York Times* of 20 April 1935 and was reprinted in the 8 May 1935 issue of *The Golden Age* on page 498.

building, or after calling at just one house, they would go to another street before approaching another house. But they were by no means timid about giving a witness.'[37] If German Witnesses did carry on their ministry 'cautiously,' it certainly was not in 1935 and 1936.

Although the Nazis censored the mails and attempted to stop Watch Tower literature from entering Germany, it came in from many directions. Copies of *Der Wachtturm* were sent through the mails from Switzerland, France, Czechoslovakia, and Poland in different forms and various sizes. Later, after *Das Goldene Zeitalter* was also banned, it was sent into Germany in the same way, generally from Switzerland. Then, to provide the German Witness community with 'spiritual food,' zealous individual men and women would mimeograph copies of Watch Tower publications and distribute them to their brethren.[38]

Despite this continued activity, the German Witness community was severely crippled in 1936. The Gestapo had established a special unit to investigate their organization, and on 28 August of that year they arrested most of the leading Jehovah's Witnesses throughout the Reich. Those arrested included Fritz Winkler, who had replaced Paul Balzereit as overseer of German Watch Tower activities.[39] Only a week later, on 4 to 7 September, the Witnesses held a convention at Lucerne, Switzerland, at which J.F. Rutherford was present. The *1974 Yearbook of Jehovah's Witnesses* states that 'he was especially interested in how to care for the [German and Austrian] brothers spiritually.'[40] In reality he seems to have been more concerned about having those 'brothers' carry on the Society's preaching work, which entailed attacking the Catholic Church and the Nazi regime. This is shown by the fact that the Lucerne convention adopted an angry, three-and-a-half-page typewritten resolution, which Watch Tower officials sent to Hitler and Pope Pius XI. It read in part, in long, run-on sentences: 'We call on all good people to witness that in Germany, Austria and other places Jehovah's witnesses are cruelly persecuted, imprisoned, fiendishly abused, and many of them killed, and all such wickedness is done against them by a cruel, malicious, wicked power, incited so to do by the religious organization, to wit, the Roman Catholic Hierarchy, which for many years has deceived the people and blasphemed God's holy name. The Hitler

37 Brooklyn, NY: Watchtower Society and IBSA, 1993), 448.
38 *1974 Yearbook,* 113–15.
39 Ibid., 150–1.
40 Ibid., 154.

government, aided and incited by the Jesuits of the Roman Catholic Hierarchy, has inflicted and continues to inflict all manner of cruel punishment upon true Christians even as Christ Jesus and his apostles were persecuted for righteousness.' In a later paragraph, it also stated: 'We raise strong objections to the cruel treatment of Jehovah's witnesses by the Roman Catholic Hierarchy and their allies in Germany as well as in other parts of the world, but we leave the outcome of the matter completely in the hands of the Lord, our God, who according to his Word will recompense in full ... We send heartfelt greetings to our persecuted brethren in Germany and ask them to remain courageous and trust completely in the promises of the almighty God, Jehovah, and Christ.'[41] Shortly thereafter, 200,000 copies of this Lucerne resolution were smuggled into Germany by way of Prague. On 12 December 1936, between 5 and 7 p.m. some 3,450 Witness men and women 'blitzed' the country in a lightning, door-to-door distribution of those imported copies of the resolution and copies of it produced in Germany.[42] This time, instead of calling at people's homes, Witnesses placed this inflammatory tract in mailboxes, under doormats, and in door jambs. Naturally, this rattled the Gestapo, who thought they had brought Witness activities to a halt the previous August by sweeping up the Watch Tower leaders.[43]

The *1974 Yearbook* boasts that between October and December 1936 about 3,600 Witnesses were 'carrying on their preaching commission' and were even distributing Watch Tower publications – something that infuriated the Nazis and brought down further persecution. During that three-month period they placed 300 Bibles, 9,624 books, and 19,304 booklets with members of the German public.[44] Neither Rutherford nor many of his German followers seemed to consider the possibility that by working more quietly – perhaps by preaching by word of mouth alone – they would be less obvious and might avoid arrest more easily. But that was not to be. The Nazis were determined to carry out their agenda whatever the consequences, and so were Jehovah's Witnesses.

The Watch Tower Society admits that distributing the Lucerne resolution caused German Witnesses more problems. The *1974 Yearbook* relates: 'At practically every hearing and trial held after the resolution

41 *1937 Yearbook,* 163. For the full text of the Lucerne resolution, see Appendix E.

42 *1974 Yearbook,* 155.

43 Ibid., 155–6.

44 Ibid.

was distributed on December 12, 1936, mention was made of it. Officials made it even more difficult for many of our brothers because, they claimed, these statements were untrue.'[45] Thus the 'brothers in charge' in Germany and Switzerland suggested to Rutherford that another blitz campaign be held to distribute an 'Open Letter' to the German people. This letter would list some specifics of the persecution that had been aimed at Jehovah's Witnesses. This proved very difficult, however. Erich Frost, who had replaced Fritz Winkler as Watch Tower branch overseer, and other prominent German Witnesses were arrested before they could superintend its clandestine distribution. The Gestapo also seized the rotaprint-mimeograph machine that the Witnesses had planned to use to make copies of the 'Open Letter.' Nonetheless, new stencils of it were made in Switzerland and smuggled into Germany. So on 20 June 1937 the Witnesses – then under the internal German direction of Heinrich Dietschi – carried out their intended blitz.[46]

Among other things, the 'Open Letter' stated:

> As the above-mentioned shows clearly, the fight goes on to rob the German people of the Bible, and to suppress everything that appeals to spiritual freedom and belief in the Bible. Christian patience and shame have kept us back long enough from bringing these outrages to the public in Germany and in foreign lands. We have in our hands an overwhelming amount of documentation that shows the cruel mistreatment of Jehovah's Witnesses. *Among those responsible for such mistreatment especially have been Criminal-Assistant Thiess from Dortmund and Tennhoff and Heimann from the Gestapo in Gelsenkirchen and Bochum.* They did not shrink from mistreating women [by beating them] with bullwhips and rubber truncheons. Criminal-Assistant Thiess from Dortmund and a man from the Gestapo in Ham are especially noted for their sadistic cruelty in the mistreatment of Christian women. *We possess also the names and details of some eighteen cases in which Jehovah's Witnesses were killed violently*. For example, at the beginning of October 1936, *a Jehovah's Witness named Peter Heinen of Neuhüller Street, Gelsenkirchen, Westphalia, was beaten to death by officials of the Gestapo in the city hall of Gelsenkirchen.* This tragic incident was reported to Reich's Chancellor Adolf Hitler. Copies of the report were sent also to Reich's Minister Rudolf Hess and the Chief of the Gestapo, Himmler.[47]

45 Ibid., 157.
46 Ibid., 157–9.
47 For the original German of this portion of the 'Open Letter,' see Appendix E.

Through their activities the Witnesses were becoming a thorn in the Nazis' flesh. As Christine King notes, at first the Nazis regarded them as cranks who could easily be suppressed. Whether they were cranks or not, they could not be suppressed easily. By attacking the German government as Satanic, they were exposing the ruthlessness of the regime and demonstrating that there were Germans who opposed Hitler's totalitarian rule. Thus the Gestapo was forced to devote an inordinate amount of time in trying to curb them, and the government felt that it had to put out two reports in 1936 falsely accusing them of being 'pace-makers for world Bolshevism' and spokespeople for the Jews.[48] In an attempt to show that the Witnesses were anti-German, a similar report the following year contained harsh anti-Nazi quotes from Watch Tower publications.[49]

Jehovah's Witnesses today take great pride in recounting events such as the distribution of letters and broadsides like the 1934 statement of defiance, the Lucerne resolution, and the 'Open Letter.' To them those actions continue to mean that their brethren, and they alone, maintained Christian integrity in carrying on the vaunted 'preaching work.' As shown in Chapter 2, many non-Witness scholars have also admired their courage in standing up to the Nazis in a way that virtually no other group did, with the possible exception of the Communists. Gurtrud Keen, a Communist prisoner in the Morningen concentration camp, stated: 'Time and again, Jehovah's Witnesses were always the most courageous.'[50] Still, it must be asked in retrospect: Was not their courage often an example of fanatical foolhardiness driven by J.F. Rutherford's teachings?

As already mentioned, it is true that even without surrendering certain of their admirable basic principles, Jehovah's Witnesses would inevitably have suffered some severe persecution. Their unwillingness to give the Hitler salute marked them, in the eyes of the Nazis, as enemies of the regime. Many workers lost their jobs as a result of this, and when schoolchildren refused to *Heil Hitler* or to join in other patriotic exercises, both they and their parents suffered. This was not surprising. Even in democratic countries like the United States and

48 Christine Elizabeth King, *The Nazi State and the New Religions: Five Case Studies in Non-Conformity* (New York: Edwin Mellon Press, 1982), 161–2.

49 Ibid., 163.

50 This statement appears on page 12 in Hans Hesse's Foreword to *Persecution and Resistance of Jehovah's Witnesses during the Nazi-Regime 1933–1945.* Keen's original words – *'Am mutigsten waren immer wieder die Jehovas Zeugen'* – were used by Hesse as the title for this book in the original German.

Canada, there were cases where Witness children were taken from their parents, and their parents jailed, because the children would not salute the Stars and Stripes or the Union Jack.[51] Also, as conscientious objectors, men of military age were bound to suffer imprisonment – and some, ultimately, death – for refusing to serve in Hitler's war machine. So on those two counts the Witnesses cannot be faulted.

The situation was far different regarding the circulation of various broadsides that openly attacked the regime and regarding the continuing distribution of inflammatory Watch Tower publications that described the Nazi government and Hitler in particular as of the Devil. While much of what was said about the *Führer* and his henchmen was accurate, it was not wise to broadcast it so openly in Germany at the time. By the spring of 1936, despite earlier disaffection among many segments of the population, Hitler was wildly popular with the German people. He had reintroduced conscription, had rebuilt the *Wehrmacht,* had reoccupied the Rhineland, and had reawakened national pride.[52] His work programs – especially the building of the *Autobahnen* and the armaments industries – also added to his prestige by greatly reducing unemployment. So for distributing what the government considered seditious materials, the Witnesses were making themselves even more unpopular than they long had been among Germans and were making it easier for the Nazis to take harsh measures against them. Today, Jehovah's Witnesses ignore their brethren's reckless behaviour during the dark years of the Third Reich, but the facts are undeniable. There is much evidence from contemporary Watch Tower literature and other sources to show that by openly and brazenly attacking Nazism – and the Catholic Church along with it – the Witnesses were causing themselves and their families more suffering than was necessary.

When Paul Balzereit and his colleagues in Magdeburg were arrested in May 1935, the Watch Tower Society again sent Martin Harbeck to Germany to try to save its properties from confiscation. By this time, however, Germany felt strong enough to ignore its obligations to the

51 Shawn Francis Peters, *Judging Jehovah's Witnesses: Religious Persecution and the Dawn of the Rights Revolution* (Lawrence: University Press of Kansas, 2000), 168–72. M. James Penton, *Jehovah's Witnesses in Canada: Champions of Freedom of Speech and Worship* (Toronto: Macmillan, 1976), 137–43. 159–61. William Kaplan, *State and Salvation: The Jehovah's Witnesses and Their Fight for Civil Rights* (Toronto: University of Toronto Press, 1989), 123–64.

52 Kershaw, 590–1.

United States. The Reich seized the properties and arrested and imprisoned Harbeck. Ten days later, he was released and expelled from the country. The Nazis refused to hear any more from Jehovah's Witnesses or their Swiss-based American representative.[53]

This event and many others like it only strengthened the militancy and outspokenness of J.F. Rutherford and Jehovah's Witnesses. As persecution increased, the Witnesses continued to circulate publications throughout Germany, some of which were stingingly anti-Nazi. The *1937 Yearbook* says that some six thousand German Witnesses had distributed approximately 452,840 books and booklets to the German people during the previous year.[54] The same publication admits, however, that as a result of the circulation of the Lucerne resolution, many more Witnesses were arrested: 'After the Lucerne convention it was reported that the Gestapo had given orders to arrest by the 8th of September all of Jehovah's witnesses who had been active in any way in the witness work. Thus during the past weeks a large number of brethren were again thrown into prison and into concentration camps.'[55] Yet even in 1939, in the face of extreme danger, German Witnesses who were still free were busy circulating caustic Watch Tower publications. Among other books, booklets, and magazines, they even distributed copies of Rutherford's then current booklet, *Fascism or Freedom,* in which he wrote: 'In Germany the common people are peace-loving. The Devil has put his representative Hitler in control, a man who is of unsound mind, cruel, malicious and ruthless, and who acts in utter disregard of the liberties of the people.'[56]

Gestapo officers were most interested in arresting Jehovah's Witness leaders; they believed that by doing so they would put a stop to what the Witnesses were doing. Thus the Gestapo arrested one Watch Tower Reich or branch servant after another despite their having gone underground. Sometimes, when they had difficulty apprehending them, the Gestapo would seize and torture their family members to obtain information to help capture them. For example, after Heinrich Dietschi had avoided capture for many months, the Gestapo arrested his wife and tortured her: 'She was so badly treated that one of her legs was thereafter shorter than the other. Besides that, she had to be com-

53 *1987 Yearbook,* 138. Although the yearbook does not state specifically when Harbeck's arrest took place, it seems quite probable that it was in 1935.

54 Page 152.

55 Ibid., 151–2.

56 Page 11.

pletely wrapped in bandages soaked in alcohol for several weeks after her release.'[57]

It was not only Witness leaders that the Gestapo wanted to arrest. Beginning in 1936, its officers were able to round up large numbers of ordinary, active Jehovah's Witnesses because they were foolishly (and largely ineffectively) distributing anti-Nazi tracts and literature as directed by their leaders in America and Switzerland. In *Nazi Terror: The Gestapo, Jews, and Ordinary Germans,* Eric C. Johnson provides a clear picture of how the Witnesses brought direct persecution on themselves and allowed the Gestapo to apprehend them, imprison them, and often send them to concentration camps. In particular, Johnson discusses the distribution of the 'Open Letter' and its consequences. Witnesses successfully placed some 100,000 copies of it throughout Germany but paid a terrible price for having done so. In the small, largely Catholic, western German community of Krefeld, a fifty-five-year-old worker whom Johnson refers to as Hubert H. was caught 'red handed' handing out the 'Open Letter' by a Nazi *Zellenleiter* or cell leader, Ludwig W. Thereupon, Ludwig W. arrested him and physically dragged him to Gestapo headquarters. There, Gestapo *Kriminalassistent* (criminal assistant officer) Otto Dihr interrogated him over four days. At first Hubert H. refused to give further information than that he had distributed the 'Open Letter' to carry out Jehovah's will, but he eventually broke down – quite probably under torture – and provided information that led directly to the arrest of eight other Witnesses, five men and three women. Johnson notes: 'Clearly Hubert H. had been severely warned about the consequences for himself and his family of further refusal to divulge information. From what is known about Dihr's methods in this and other cases, it is likely that Hubert H. had also suffered immense physical and mental torture over the previous four days. In Dihr's own write-up of the case, filed nearly a month later on July 16, he explained that his interrogation of Hubert H. had, of necessity, been "exhaustive," and that it "had stretched out over several days chiefly because of Hubert H.'s stubborn denials."'

From the information given to Dihr by Hubert H. and the other Witnesses arrested on the basis of the latter's forced testimony, the Gestapo was able to cast its net of Witness arrests throughout much of western Germany. Although all of the eight Witnesses named by

57 *1974 Yearbook,* 161.

Hubert H. tried valiantly to withhold information from Dihr and his henchmen, in the end none was able to withstand the Gestapo's terrible methods. All broke down and gave further information: 'Before Dihr had completed his questioning of the accused sect members in Krefeld, a husband and wife had also implicated one another, and a father provided information that led to the arrest of his son.' One man, Karl H., implicated his own mother, who when 'examined' by the Gestapo explained how the entire 'Open Letter' campaign had functioned. Of all those questioned, the only one who at first seemed able to withstand Dihr's methods was a German veteran of the First World war, Karl W., who had been awarded the Iron Cross for bravery. But when confronted directly by Hubert H., who had admitted he had given copies of the 'Open Letter' to him and that Karl W. had distributed them, the latter finally had to agree it was true.

Dihr was so successful in obtaining information on the Witnesses' latest 'blitz' that he was able to arrest some twenty-five people in Krefeld alone and to bring about the arrest of many others throughout much of the Reich: 'Dihr learned from Johann C. (who had been named originally by Hubert H.) that he had been the leader of the campaign in the entire region of the lower Rhine.' Johann C. confessed that he and Albert W. (Albert Wandres?), who had already fled, had obtained the services of a former truck driver and car owner, Peter L., to pick up and deliver many copies of the 'Open Letter' to various German cities. When arrested, Peter L. proved more cooperative with the Gestapo than most. He showed Dihr where he had driven, and having done so was able to get off with only six months' imprisonment. This particular betrayal 'led to scores of other arrests in the cities to which he had traveled and in other cities where the letters had been handed out.' It also led to his father's seizure and eventual death in a concentration camp.

The conclusions Johnson draws from this extended account are most significant: 'It is important to note that denunciations [by ordinary Germans] played almost no role in the persecution of Jehovah's Witnesses, just as they had played almost no role in the persecution of Catholic and Protestant clergymen who dared to stand up to Hitler's regime or to the destruction of the political left ... Most of the evidence the Gestapo used to bring the Nazi regime's religious adversaries to justice came either from forced confessions or from information the Gestapo received from its own spy network. Very few of these spies came from the ranks of the clergy itself or were members of religious sects like the Jehovah's Witnesses, though some were.'[58] The evidence is clear, then, that had the Witnesses conducted themselves more discreetly, many could have maintained their integrity, gained converts quietly, and avoided much unnecessary suffering. Unlike the Jews and Gypsies, the Nazis had nothing against them from a racial standpoint; all but a few were 'Aryans' whose only 'fault' was their open and often indiscreet opposition to the Third Reich and its totalitarian demands.

It would be wrong to suggest that all of the Witnesses who were imprisoned or sent to concentration camps were picked up by the Gestapo or other police for distributing tracts attacking the National Socialist government or for distributing other Watch Tower literature. It was easy for the police to seize the parents of Witness children who refused to *Heil Hitler* or to accept Nazi indoctrination. It was also quite easy to incarcerate men of military age who refused to be conscripted. It was a simple matter to arrest Witnesses in rural communities, where neighbours and the police had known even before 1933 that they were active Bible Student–Jehovah's Witnesses. In 'Female Jehovah's Witnesses in Morningen Women's Concentration Camp: Women's Resistance in Nazi Germany,' Jürgen Harder and Hans Hesse state the following:

> The places of origin of the imprisoned women reveal an unusual distribution between urban and rural areas, that is typical for this prisoner group. Prior to their imprisonment, only about 12 percent of the Witnesses in Morningen lived in cities such as Berlin, Hamburg or Munich. Except for some local Witness strongholds in Frankfurt am Main, Dresden, and Leipzig, the vast majority of women came from small towns or villages. In particular, the anonymity of big cities made Witness religious activities easier. In smaller towns, it was more difficult to conceal the dissemination of literature in mailboxes and under doormats, missionary activities, and clandestine meetings with fellow believers, from the local population and the authorities. Furthermore, the women and their families were already known as Witnesses before 1933, and especially in provincial and village surroundings, they were closely watched by neighbors and governmental authorities. Thus, many women could easily be arrested during Witness operations, or fell victim to denunciations by their neighbors.

58 Eric C. Johnson, *Nazi Terror: The Gestapo, Jews, and Ordinary Germans* (New York: Basic Books, 1999), 243–50.

It is also significant that many Witnesses in Morningen came from the eastern areas of Germany, mainly from Saxony.[59]

Harder and Hesse have also provided important information regarding why Jehovah's Witness women were placed in Morningen. According to their analysis of the *Schutzhaftbefehle* (warrants for protective custody arrest), most had been arrested either for distributing illegal literature or for participating in illegal meetings. Closely associated with the distribution of illegal literature was the carrying on of missionary work. Interestingly, when unable to obtain printed copies of Watch Tower literature, some Witness women produced their own, evidently as typewritten or handwritten brochures. Another group in Morningen comprised women who had not been active in preaching or proselytizing but who had continued to meet and study with their Witness brethren. Sometimes even meeting with one other Witness on a regular, private basis was regarded as grounds for arrest and confinement in a concentration camp. The Bavarian political police stated: 'Because of the subversive attitude and recklessness of the Earnest Bible Students, it is the duty of the state to remove any opportunity for these elements to sabotage national interests of the German Reich by imprisoning them in protective custody and thus securing public peace and order.' A more important reason for consigning women to Morningen was that some, like Witness men, were reproducing Watch Tower literature by creating carbon copies of it on typewriters and using simple duplicating machines to reproduce it for distribution. As well, some were incarcerated for reorganizing Witness congregations and local groups after the mass arrests of 1937 and 1938. Often, when Witness men were seized by the police, their wives, mothers, sisters, and daughters took over 'the witness work' for them.

By the time of a Watch Tower convention in Paris in the summer of 1937, arrests and interrogations were being carried out with great brutality. Witness George Bär reported that in August 1936, after he was arrested, he experienced the following: 'Every evening at about 10:00 o'clock I would hear prisoners being taken from their various cells. Shortly thereafter I would hear them being beaten downstairs in the basement; I heard their cries and their sobs.' Then, when he was personally brought into Gestapo offices, he was shown how much detailed information on Witness activities the Gestapo had obtained.[60] At

59 Published in Hesse, ed., *Persecution and Resistance,* 43.
60 *1974 Yearbook,* 153.

the Paris convention, which few German Witnesses were able to attend, a 'Brother Riffel' discussed how in the German community of Lorrach and its vicinity alone, 'forty brothers and sisters had been imprisoned, ten of whom had been hanged, gassed or shot, or had starved to death or died due to the results of the concentration camp "medical experiments."'[61]

After the Paris convention, the Gestapo struck again. When Heinrich Dietschi returned to Germany from France, he was arrested.[62] Shortly after that, Albert Wandres, the man who attempted to continue the organized 'witness work' throughout the country was apprehended as well.[63] The *1974 Yearbook* reports: 'With this series of arrests an important era ended for the German brothers. The period of well organized activity was over. Everything now pointed to the start of a new phase in the fighting. The Gestapo's goal was now: Each individual now courageous to hold to Jehovah must be destroyed, thereby destroying the organization.'[64] The same yearbook also states:

> According to a circular released by the Düsseldorfer Gestapo on May 12, 1937, Bible Students were henceforth to be put in concentration camps even in cases where no judicial warrant for arrest existed but simply on the grounds of suspicion. Similar notices were released throughout Germany. Besides, the Bible Students were to be automatically placed in concentration camps after serving their court-appointed terms of imprisonment. This decision was made more severe and extended in April 1939. From now on, only those willing to sign a declaration disassociating themselves from Jehovah and his organization were to be freed. Many brothers were not even given an opportunity to decide whether to sign the declaration.[65]

Former SS *Gruppenführer* Ernst Kaltenbrunner claimed after the war that he had petitioned the Reich Chancellery about the harsh mistreatment of Jehovah's Witnesses. He also recounted the proceedings of a conference held on 5 August 1937 at which the German justice minister noted – on the basis of various expressed concerns – that the Witnesses had not been treated legally from the beginning of the Third Reich. Nonetheless, he was determined to ensure that they were kept

61 Ibid., 161.
62 Ibid., 161–2.
63 Ibid., 162.
64 Ibid., 162–3.
65 Ibid.

'under lock and key.' He made pious statements to the effect that miscarriages of justice should cease; however, local police were to make sure that after Witnesses were released from prison, they were transferred directly to concentration camps.[66]

This eventually led to the Nazi-dictated 'perpetual imprisonment' of many Jehovah's Witnesses in concentration camps and to the execution of hundreds of men for refusing to serve in the military. As pointed out earlier, more than six thousand German Witnesses were imprisoned and an indeterminate but significant number perished.[67] Many survivors lost their children and families, and many came out of the concentration camps suffering from the effects of torture, overwork, and malnutrition.

Not all Witness activity outside prisons and concentration camps stopped. Local groups reorganized, often with women playing important roles.[68] In a subsection headed 'The Stream Continues to Flow,' the *1974 Yearbook* gives an account of how two Witness men, with the help of a number of women, continued to mimeograph and distribute *The Watchtower* in many parts of Germany during much of the war even though this courted execution. What happened was that a loyal Witness, Ludwig Cyranek, wrote letters containing non-controversial information to these women. But written in invisible lemon juice on the same letters were instructions telling them where to take copies of *The Watchtower* and how many. On receiving the letters, the women simply pressed them with a hot iron and the messages became visible. Eventually, Cyranek was arrested on information given to the Gestapo by a Witness traitor named Müller, and on 3 July 1941 he was executed. Some others associated with him were given long prison sentences.[69] But a number of Witnesses still at large continued mimeographing and distributing the *Watchtower*. Julius Engelhardt, like Cyranek, was betrayed by Müller; however, he evaded arrest for some time. The *1974 Yearbook* tells us: 'From the beginning of 1941 to April 1943 he produced 27 issues of the *Watchtower* in an edition of 240 copies and later 360 copies. From the Ruhr territory he arranged for bases in Munich, Mannheim, Speyer, Dresden as well as Freiberg in Saxony and served as treasurer for the entire country.' In 1944, however, after being arrested, Engelhardt and a number of those associ-

66 King, *The Nazi State and the New Religions*, 162–3.

67 For further details, see Appendix I.

68 *1974 Yearbook*, 179–80.

69 Ibid.

ated with him were condemned to death for their activities. Eight of them were beheaded.[70]

When the Nazis marched into Austria in 1938, the Witnesses there were better prepared to maintain their organization. Since they had long experienced persecution in Austria and had been declared illegal in 1935 in that small, overwhelmingly Catholic country, they were more circumspect than their German brethren. At a convention in Prague in 1937, they were prepared for the full weight of Nazi oppression.[71] So they attempted to maintain ongoing contact with the Watch Tower Society in Switzerland. For a time after 1938, they brought copies of Watch Tower literature over the mountains from that country to Vienna. Also, they were to carry on underground printing activities for some time.[72] As Austria was part of the Third Reich until the end of the war, the Witnesses there were able to cooperate with Ludwig Cyranek and his group in the western part of the country.[73] Even so, by 1940 the Gestapo had been able, through arrests, to stop their activity.[74] By the end of the war most Austrian Witnesses had been placed under arrest.[75]

After war broke out in the late summer of 1939, it became almost impossible to get any messages from German Witnesses to Watch Tower headquarters in the United States. The Prague offices of the Watch Tower had been closed even before the outbreak of fighting after the Nazis marched into Czechoslovakia on 15 March 1939.[76] After the German and Soviet occupation of Poland in September of the same year, and the fall of Denmark, Norway, the Netherlands, Belgium, Luxembourg, and France to Hitler's armies between February and June 1940, the Witnesses were outlawed in all of those countries except Denmark.[77] Even in Switzerland, Watch Tower properties were

70 Ibid., 180–2.
71 *1989 Yearbook,* 96–100.
72 Ibid., 101–8.
73 Ibid.
74 Ibid., 108–10.
75 The *1989 Yearbook of Jehovah's Witnesses* reports on page 133: 'Before Hitler's troops entered Austria, there were 549 publishers in this country. Altogether, 445 were thereafter incarcerated for various periods. Between 1938 and 1945, 48 of these, including some of our sisters, were executed. Thirteen were beaten to death, gassed, or made the victims of perverse medical experiments. At least 81 others died in prisons and concentration camps because of disease or exhaustion.'
76 *1972 Yearbook,* 135.
77 The Nazis did not suppress Jehovah's Witnesses in Denmark. Hitler treated Denmark as a model protectorate and allowed it internal self-government.

seized for a time and most of the workers at the Watch Tower's Central European offices were 'driven away.' In late 1940 the Watch Tower Society reported: 'While Switzerland remains nominally a republic, it is in fact now dominated by arbitrary power. Surrounded on every hand by totalitarians, the Swiss government is forced by reason of fear to be submissive to the totalitarians.'[78] Fortunately for Jehovah's Witnesses, however, Swiss restrictions on them were mild. Yet with typical tactless arrogance, they made circumstances difficult for the democratic Swiss government in its relations with the Nazis by distributing Rutherford's inflammatory booklet, *Fascism or Freedom.*[79] There was no comparable freedom in most of the rest of continental Europe, yet the Witnesses failed to show anything like appreciation to the Swiss authorities. To them, Switzerland was just another part of Satan's world.

In the spring of 1941, just before the Nazis invaded the Soviet Union, German armies swept through the Balkans. Thus in practically every country of continental Europe – Denmark, Sweden, and Switzerland excepted – Jehovah's Witnesses became an underground movement and victims of totalitarian persecution of one kind or another. Despite this, copies of *The Watchtower* and other Witness literature continued to enter Germany and other continental countries under German control; these publications were then reprinted and distributed.

The persecution of Jehovah's Witnesses grew worse in 1939. With the outbreak of the war, the first German Witness to die as a conscientious objector, August Dickmann, was shot for refusing to take up arms.[80] Within the next several years many of his brethren were to follow him to similar martyrdom. Some, like Dickmann, were shot; others were beheaded. Nonetheless, most maintained their integrity under the threat of death, and some were even happy to be executed. Perhaps nothing testifies to this fact better than an account by Rudolf Höss, one-time *Kommandant* at Auschwitz. In his memoirs, written just before his execution for war crimes in 1947, he related:

Although relations between the *Führer* and the Danish royal house broke down some time after the German conquest of the kingdom, and Hitler was infuriated by a Danish resistance movement, his representative in Denmark, Dr Werner Best, disobeyed him and refused to impose a harsh policy on the Danes. This gave Jehovah's Witnesses in that democratically minded country a freedom that did not exist anywhere else in German-controlled Europe. See Heinz Höhne, *The Order of the Death's Head: The Story of Hitler's SS,* trans. Richard Barry (London: Penguin Books, 2000), 496–8, and *1993 Yearbook,* 99.

78 *1941 Yearbook,* 168–9.

79 Ibid., 155–6.

80 *1974 Yearbook,* 166–8. Garbe, 420–5.

There were many Jehovah's Witnesses in Sachsenhausen. A large number of them refused to serve in the military and were, therefore, sentenced to death by Himmler as draft dodgers. They were shot to death in the camp in front of the entire assembly of prisoners. The other Jehovah's Witnesses had to stand in the front rank and watch.

Years earlier I had become acquainted with many religious fanatics at the shrines, in the monasteries in Palestine, at the Hejas railway station, in Iraq and in Armenia. They were Roman and Greek orthodox Catholics, and Muslims, both Shiite and Sunni, but the Jehovah's Witnesses in Sachsenhausen, especially two of them, surpassed everything I had experienced.

These two fanatics refused to do anything that was connected to the military in any way. They would not stand at attention, or click their heels together, or lay their hands down at the seam of their trousers, and they refused to remove their caps. They claimed that these displays of respect and honor were for God alone, not men. For them there were no human masters. They would only recognize Jehovah as their lord and master. These two had to be removed from the block of the Jehovah's Witnesses and had to be kept in cells because they constantly challenged the others to behave the same way.

Eicke had sentenced them several times to floggings because of their behavior for not obeying the discipline of the camp rules. They withstood the beatings with such an inner passion that they seemed perverted. They begged the Kommandant for further punishment in order to be better witnesses for their ideas and their God. They refused their army physicals – it was not expected that they would submit – but they even refused to sign any military forms. They were sentenced to death by Himmler.

When they were put into cells and told of the death sentence, they went completely insane with joy and happiness. They couldn't stand the wait until the execution. They wrung their hands over and over, looked up joyously and called out repeatedly, 'Soon we will be with Jehovah. What good luck we have that we have been chosen for this.' A few days earlier they had attended an execution of one of their fellow believers and could hardly be controlled even then. They continuously asked to be shot. This frenzy became a burden to watch. When they were first arrested, they had to be taken by force, but now when their time came, they practically ran double time to their own execution. They did not want to be tied up, so that they would be able to raise their hands to Jehovah. They stood in front of the wooden execution wall with a radiance and ecstasy which was no longer human. This is the way I had always pictured the first Christian martyrs as they waited in the arena to be torn apart by wild beasts.[81]

81 Rudolf Höss, *Death Dealer: The Memoirs of the SS Komandant at Auschwitz,* ed. Steven Paskuly, trans. Andrew Pollinger (New York: De Capo Press, 1996), 102–3.

When other Witness men died for refusing to serve in Hitler's war machine, they did so with the same assurance but usually with more dignity. This is shown by some of the letters written by them just before their executions;[82] some who saw them die bear similar testimony. Most of them had a heavenly hope, since most of them had joined the Witness fold before 1935, when J.F. Rutherford announced that new converts could expect to live eternally on a paradisiac new earth.[83] Those with that heavenly hope therefore expected to be joined with Christ in Jehovah's presence immediately after death.[84] So Höss's comparison of them to early Christian martyrs is understandable: they saw themselves in the same tradition as those martyrs and in most cases proved themselves equally brave.

Shortly after the war, in its 12 September 1945 issue, *Consolation* published an article titled 'Jehovah's Witnesses Triumph over Concentration Camps.'[85] Although it contains the usual Watch Tower rant about the evils of Roman Catholicism, it also provides much useful information on just what happened to the Witnesses in the camps. It details the beatings of Witness women, tells of the bravery of those facing death (often by beheading) for refusing military service, and translates and reprints a copy of the declaration of renunciation of faith that ordinary Witnesses could sign to secure their release. The article also gives a lengthy report on what happened at Buchenwald, the camp in which there were large numbers of Witness men, who there suffered greatly. According to that report, some of which is based on an article by Swedish journalist Björn Hallström, 'the greatest wave of [Witness] arrests began in the spring of 1936,' and a *Strafkommando* (punishment company) was established in Buchenwald in 1937 that

82 For some of these letters, see 'Jehovah's Witnesses Triumph over Concentration Camps, *Consolation,* 12 September 1945, 5–6, and the *1974 Yearbook of Jehovah's Witnesses,* 183–5.

83 As *Jehovah's Witnesses: Proclaimers of God's Kingdom* relates on pages 83 and 84, although Rutherford had asserted as early as 1932 that there would be a class of individuals called 'Jonadabs' who would pass through Armageddon and live on a restored paradise earth, yet 'there was no special effort to gather and organize these individuals with an earthly hope.' But when in 1935 Rutherford identified this class with the 'great multitude' of Revelation 7:9–17, most new Witness converts were slated to be Jonadabs or members of the 'great multitude.'

84 The Watch Tower Society then taught that the saints sleeping in death had been resurrected to heavenly life in 1918 and that those who died thereafter would 'be changed, in a moment, in the twinkling of an eye.' For a discussion of this teaching, see *The Watchtower,* 15 January 1934, 24–5.

85 Pages 3–20.

included practically all Witness men. This meant that they were assigned the heaviest work as a tactic for getting them to abjure their faith and commit themselves to the Third Reich. Hollström reported: 'On the 6th of January 1938, the opportunity offered itself for the Bible students of the Buchenwald concentration camp to purchase their freedom by signing that they would recognize the Nazi state and renounce their belief in the establishment of the kingdom of God. With the exception of but a few who by mistake were given the violet badge (one given to all Bible students) this offer of the camp fuehrer was rejected. Now, because of that, mistreatment and pressure were increased in order to curb this people.'[86] From March to December 1938, Jehovah's Witnesses in Buchenwald were not allowed to receive or send letters or to purchase food. Many came close to starvation and were forced to eat leaves from trees and bushes.[87] Then, on Whitsuntide or Pentecost Sunday 1939, many were forced to engage in a 'drill' that included 'rolling, creeping, hopping, and running' for an hour and fifteen minutes while camp guards kicked and beat them. Witness veterans of the First World War who had lost legs in that struggle were beaten over the head because they could not participate in the drill. Later, when war broke out again in September 1939, the camp commandant assembled the Witnesses and told them that if they refused to fight against England and France, they would have to die. When no one stepped forward to volunteer, the order was given: 'Hands up! Empty your pockets!' Thereupon, the SS guards rushed on them and took what little money they had.[88] All of this was mild, however, in comparison to what the Witnesses in Buchenwald suffered later. In 1940 they were forced to work in the stone quarries and were refused medical attention when sick. The same year, many were forced to stand at the camp gate for hours and days on end for talking to Jewish prisoners – no doubt to preach to them. On one occasion in 1942, for a few 'infractions,' including not listening to a radio broadcast by Hitler, they were robbed of their winter clothing and forced to exercise in the snow until exhausted and steaming.[89]

Buchenwald was only one of the camps in which Witness men were held and in which all suffered terribly and some perished. Eugen Kogon relates: 'When the war broke out the Witnesses at Sachsenhausen

86 Ibid., 8–9.
87 Ibid., 9.
88 Ibid.
89 Ibid., 9–10.

concentration camp were invited to volunteer for military service. Each refusal was followed by the shooting of ten men from their ranks. After forty victims had been killed, the SS desisted.'[90] As terrible as this mass murder was, it does not show just how thoroughly sadistic the SS guards who oversaw the camps were. An account in the *1974 Yearbook of Jehovah's Witnesses* concerning a 'Christmas party' at Dachau gives a clearer picture:

> In Dachau, shortly before 'Christmas,' a large Christmas tree was put up and decorated with electric candles and other forms of decoration. The camp's 45,000 prisoners, including over a hundred Jehovah's witnesses, hoped that they would be able to enjoy a few days of peace. But what happened? At 8:00 o'clock on Christmas Eve when all prisoners were in their barracks, the camp sirens suddenly began to wail; the prisoners were to march out onto the courtyard as fast as possible. One could hear the SS band playing. In marched five companies of fully equipped SS troops. The camp commander, accompanied by SS officers, delivered a short speech telling the prisoners that they wanted to celebrate Christmas with them this evening in their own particular way. He then pulled a list of names from his briefcase and for almost an hour read the names of prisoners who had been recommended for punishment during the last few weeks. The block was brought out and the first prisoner strapped down to it. Afterward two SS men equipped with a steel whip took their places to the right and to the left of the block and began to beat the prisoner while the band played 'Silent Night'; all the prisoners were expected to sing along. At the same time the prisoner being given the twenty-five strokes was forced to count these out in a loud voice. Each time a new prisoner was strapped down to the block two new SS men stepped forward to administer the punishment. Truly a worthy way for a 'Christian nation' to celebrate Christmas.[91]

Concentration camps for women were equally brutal, yet Jehovah's Witness women seem to have been as resolute in maintaining their faith as were Witness men. As indicated above, some were executed, either for carrying on the distribution of Watch Tower literature or, in one notable case – that of Emmi Zehden – for hiding men attempting

90 Eugen Kogon, *The Theory and Practice of Hell: The German Concentration Camps and the System behind Them,* trans. Heinz Norden (New York: Berkley Medallion Books, 1964), 43.

91 Page 170.

to avoid military service.[92] Hundreds more were imprisoned and sent to concentration camps, where some died for their faith and all suffered terribly.

The first camp to which they were sent was Moringen. Jürgen Harder and Hans Hesse have written in some detail concerning this camp. According to them, it served as a concentration camp for women from 1933 to 1939 and as a protective custody concentration camp for juveniles from 1940 to 1944. Harder and Hesse emphasize that conditions in Moringen were very primitive: the dormitories were unheated in winter and the food was terrible. Nearly 45 percent of the women prisoners were Witnesses, who had been brought to the camp in large numbers during 1935, 1936, and, in particular, 1937. 'In June 1937, the proportion of Jehovah's Witnesses to the total inmate population was 17 percent, in July 28 percent, in September 46 percent, in October 80 percent, in November 51 percent, and in December 89 percent.[93]

Of all the camps for Witness women, the most notorious was Ravensbrück. The *1974 Yearbook of Jehovah's Witnesses* reports: 'Another method that was employed to try to break the steadfastness of our sisters was hard physical labor. For this reason a number of sisters were taken to Ravensbrück. It was on 15 May 1939, that the first group arrived, closely followed by others. The camp soon grew to include 950 women, some 400 of them Jehovah's witnesses. All of them were called upon to do the most difficult construction and cleaning up work, jobs normally required only of men. The new camp commander, who was especially noted for his brutality, thought he would be able to wear the sisters down by making them perform hard physical labor.'[94] Ordinarily, Jehovah's Witnesses were not sent to death camps because most of them were ethnic Germans rather than so-called *Untermenschen* or 'subhumans' such as Jews, Gypsies, and Slavs. However, some of their women at Ravensbrück were forced to stand naked before Nazi officers, who would then determine that certain of the older and sickly ones should be sent to Auschwitz to be exterminated.[95] But even in

92 Emmi Zehden's story is told in the 'Stand Firm' video and, also, briefly in Manfred Gebhard, *Geschichte Zeugen Jehovas: Mit Schwerpunkt der deutschen Geschichte* (Berlin: Libri Books on Demand, 1999), 321.

93 Jürgen Harder and Hans Hesse, 'Female Jehovah's Witnesses in Moringen Women's Concentration Camp: Women's Resistance in Nazi Germany,' in Hesse, ed., *Persecution and Resistance*, 42, 43.

94 *1974 Yeabook,* 173.

95 Ibid.

Ravensbrück, many perished simply from overwork and from the terrible conditions. Hundreds were kept there for many years, half starved and often suffering from extreme cold. Often too, they were brutalized. After one visit to that camp, Heinrich Himmler introduced the 'intensified punishment' of women prisoners. This meant that they, like male prisoners, could be given twenty-five strokes with a steel whip on their bare buttocks at the whim of their jailers.[96]

If all of this were not enough, the Nazis also sent juveniles of both sexes to such camps. Martin Guse describes the suffering of Witness youth at Moringen. He notes that a similar camp existed alongside Ravensbrück for Witness girls and young women between thirteen and twenty-five. Eventually, three such camps were established: two in Germany and one in Poland. Guse claims that the idea for these camps came originally from Reinhold Heydrich in 1939 but was supported by Heinrich Himmler himself. Supposedly created in order to incarcerate juvenile delinquents of various sorts who otherwise could not be turned into useful Nazi citizens, the Moringen camp became closely associated with a program directed by Dr Robert Ritter of the Criminal Biological Research Institute or KBI. Ritter had been involved in the genocide of Gypsy communities (the Sinti and Roma) and had carried out pseudoscientific medical experiments on the youth at Moringen, which camp he regarded as 'a treasure trove for the KBI.' Ritter also classified the youth at Moringen and released at least some of them to state hospitals, prisons, and adult concentration camps where, in the last case, they were often slated for sexual sterilization.

Jehovah's Witness youths were not delinquents of the usual sort, but they were regarded as socially dangerous. The Nazis considered them to be fanatics. Because of their refusal to participate in patriotic exercises or to join the Hitler Youth movement – a requirement from 1939 until the end of the Third Reich – they were often sent to Moringen or other juvenile camps, where they suffered as much as adult Witnesses. According to Guse, at least two of them were executed.[97]

As the above accounts, the videos 'Purple Triangles' and 'Jehovah's Witnesses Stand Firm,' and many additional sources[98] show, during

96 Ibid., 174.

97 Martin Guse, 'The Little One ... He Had to Suffer a Lot: Jehovah's Witnesses in the Moringen Concentration Camp for Juveniles,' in Hesse, ed., *Persecution and Resistance,* 96–112.

98 Besides Nazi documentation, perhaps the most important sources are the many personal accounts of former concentration camp prisoners, many of which have

the late 1930s and the early years of the war all incarcerated Jehovah's Witnesses, whether men, women, or juveniles, suffered severe privation in prisons and concentration camps. But by late 1942, conditions began to improve for many of them. There are three reasons why. First, the German government, now embarked on a program of total mobilization and facing possible defeat, decided to use them as workers in sectors necessary to the well-being of the nation. The Witnesses refused to have anything to do with war work, but they were willing to take part in farm labour and in a variety of other activities. Second, the SS found that they were the only reliable prisoners they had who would serve many of their needs. Third, as a result of their conduct and the advocacy of Himmler's personal therapist, Felix Kersten, Himmler himself began to take a more benign attitude toward them.

Regarding the easing of pressure on the Witnesses during the last years of the war, the *1974 Yearbook* states: 'Although the blood of faithful witnesses of Jehovah continued to flow at the Nazi executional centers right up until the regime's complete collapse, yet the weapons of those who had time and again sworn that Jehovah's witnesses would leave the concentration camps only through the crematorium chimneys began to weaken. There were also the problems that the war presented. So especially from 1942/1943 on, there were periods when Jehovah's witnesses were left in comparative peace.' The reason for this was, in part at least, that in 1942 Heinrich Himmler reorganized the administration of the concentration camps by placing Oswald Pohl, head of the *Wirtschafts-und Verwaltungshauptamt* (Economic and Administrative Head Office), in charge of them. Unlike previous camp administrators, Pohl regarded concentration camp prisoners as an asset to the German economy in time of war. Consequently, he wrote to Himmler to declare that the concentration camps should be transformed and that prisoners should be mobilized to serve Germany's economic needs. As a result, Pohl's lieutenant, Richard Glücks, ordered that when prisoners were sent out to work 'it is axiomatic that it is forbidden to strike, kick or even touch a prisoner,' while Heinrich Himmler stated that prisoners should receive more food and better clothing if this would increase their productivity. Pris-

---

been published by the Watch Tower Society and some of which are now being published as autobiographies.

oners were to be encouraged to take interest in their work, and cooperative prisoners were to be praised as examples to less ambitious ones. Some prisoners were even to be trained in the building trade and were to be promised special accommodation or even release from the camps.[99]

The Nazis by now realized that the Witnesses could safely be used in work details outside the concentration camps. Höss wrote about the conditions at Sachenhausen before he became *Kommandant* of Auschwitz: 'In the camp itself the Jehovah's Witnesses were hardworking and dependable; they could have been sent out on work details without guards since they wanted to suffer imprisonment for Jehovah. The problem was that they stubbornly refused to have anything to do with the military or the war.'[100] As the war began to turn against Germany, Nazi officials recognized that Witnesses could serve in important, non-military roles. Thus some Witnesses, such as Erich Frost, were removed from the camps to build a house for an SS officer at Lake Wolfgang in Austria.[101] Later some were sent to work as far away as Alderney in the Channel Islands. Others were sent to Czechoslovakia to work on the estate of Frau Heydrich, widow of the late, notorious Reinhard ('Hangman') Heydrich, a man who had been a harsh enemy of Jehovah's Witnesses.[102] Naturally, these new assignments eased the situation for many.

Something else that helped the Witnesses was SS officers' growing trust in them: they even let themselves be shaved by Witness barbers. Thoroughly war-weary Germans were coming to hate certain elements of the SS, and officers of this elite Nazi organization were often afraid to employ the services of ordinary Germans and most concentration camp prisoners, whom they knew would murder them if they could. They were aware, however, that Jehovah's Witnesses would not harm them. So two Witness barbers, Max Schröer and Paul Wauer, were selected to run straight razors over their faces and necks. SS officers knew they would not try to slit their throats.[103] It was Witness women, however, who became most useful to SS officers and their families, as trustworthy household servants. Höss described the refusal of Wit-

99 Höhne, 389. *1974 Yearbook,* 195.
100 Höss, 103.
101 *1974 Yearbook,* 198.
102 Ibid.
103 *Jehovah's Witnesses: Proclaimers of God's Kingdom,* 663.

ness women at Ravensbrück to roll up first-aid bandages for military field dressings or to respond to roll calls.[104] Even so, he expressed a high degree of respect for them mixed with some contempt:

> A pleasant contrast to this type [mostly prostitutes] were the female Jehovah's Witnesses, called 'Bible Bees' or 'Bible Worms.' Unfortunately, there were too few of them. In spite of their more or less fanatical philosophy, they were very much in demand. They worked as servants for the SS who had large families, in the Waffen SS clubhouse, even in the officer's club, but for the most part they worked on the farms. They needed no guards or supervisors. They worked on the chicken farms at Harmense and on different farm estates. They chose to work hard since this was Jehovah's commandment. They were mostly middle-aged German women but there were also a number of Dutch females represented. I had two older women working for more than three years in our household. My wife often said that she personally, could not take better care of the household than these two women. They were especially touching in the way they cared for our children.
>
> The children hung on them as if they were members of the family. At first we feared that they might try to convert the children to Jehovah. But this never happened. They never spoke about religious subjects, which was truly surprising because of their fanatical attitude. There were also peculiar types among them. One of them worked for an SS officer and was able to anticipate his every wish, but absolutely refused to clean or even to touch his uniforms: not the cap, the boots, or, in fact, anything connected with the military. But as a whole, she was satisfied with her lot. By her suffering imprisonment for Jehovah, she hoped to gain entry into his kingdom, which was expected to come soon. Strangely, all of them were convinced that the Jews were justly suffering and had to die because their ancestors had betrayed Jehovah. I have always believed Jehovah's Witnesses to be poor lunatics who were happy in their own way.[105]

As Höss noted, many Witness women were released to the farms around Ravensbrück. This allowed Felix Kersten, Heinrich Himmler's personal masseur, to ask Himmler to assign several of them to his estate at Harzwalde, which was situated between the Ravensbrück and Buchenwald concentration camps. After learning of the terrible

104 Höss, 103.
105 Ibid., 146.

conditions in the camps, Kersten began to cooperate fully with his Witness employees. Not only did he influence Himmler to take a more benign attitude toward Jehovah's Witnesses, which he did,[106] but he, Kersten, also became involved in importing *The Watchtower* to Harzwalde and through it to Witness prisoners in Ravensbrück and Sachsenhausen. Kersten obtained permission from Himmler to take a young woman prisoner, Anni Gustavsson, from Germany to Sweden, where he had a second home. There she was free to associate with her Witness brethren and to obtain Watch Tower publications. When Kersten travelled back to Germany after visiting Sweden, he would ask her if she wanted to send anything to Harzwalde in his suitcases, which she packed. He knew he would not be searched because of his relationship with Himmler even though there were Nazis who wanted to take action against him.[107] So Kersten became a major conduit for the importation of *Watchtower* magazines to Nazi concentration camps.[108]

Despite the factors described above that made life easier for German and other Jehovah's Witnesses both inside and outside concentration camps during the last several years of the war, it is remarkable that they obtained as much freedom as they did. It is astonishing that they could print *The Watchtower* in the camps and that they could carry on organized preaching campaigns among other prisoners. The following account is given by German refugees in Sweden immediately following the war:

106 In Himmler's letter to his assistants, SS leaders Pohl and Müller, he manifests a growingly benign attitude toward Jehovah's Witnesses based on the influence of Kersten and his wife.

107 *1974 Yearbook,* 196–7, 198–9. Further details are given in the 'Stand Firm' video, but what is not mentioned is that Kersten was taking great personal risks to do what he did. This is shown in a letter written by Walter Schellenberg to him from Berlin on 2 August 1944. According thereto, Schellenberg advised him to approach Himmler and ask him for a safe conduct travel letter (*Schutzbrief*) because some of his Nazi enemies were preparing to take action against him. In addition, Schellenberg indicated that those enemies believed that he was exposing conditions in the concentration camps to the world with the help of *'Bibelforscher'* at Harzwalde.

108 Kersten has given an account of these events in his own memoirs, which were published originally in Swedish under the title *Samtal med Himmler.* Several editions of this work appear in English translation under the title *Kersten Memoirs, 1940–1945.*

> In the concentration camp at Neuengamme, near Hamburg, a great and well-planned offensive was commenced, in the greatest secrecy, in the beginning of 1943. This took the form of fully organized activity for the giving of the witness among the various inhabitants of the camp. Some of the brethren produced literature, and testimony cards were written in the different languages spoken in the camp, while special 'shock troops' were formed for the purpose of bearing the testimony to all the internees in a methodical manner. In this way these were made acquainted with the message, back-calls were made on those who showed interest, book studies were commenced, and even regular lectures were arranged with the aid of an interpreter for Russians and Poles.
>
> This powerful and organized testimony naturally aroused the enemy's wrath, but countermeasures were of no avail. However, towards the end of the year an order came from Berlin that Jehovah's witnesses were to be distributed among all the barracks, and that they were not to be permitted to be in the same barracks together. But instead of this being a hindrance to the work, possibilities for coming into contact with the other prisoners increased. In this way each block was thoroughly worked, and those of good-will who were met received regular instruction. Special Testimony Periods were arranged, with the result that time in the service for The Theocracy and testimonies given were increased. Some of the interested themselves began to take part in witnessing.[109]

Even when the SS became aware of what the Witnesses were doing during these years at Neuengamme and at other camps, they did little to stop them. This meant that the Witnesses could make many converts among other prisoners, both men and women. Many of these were Russians, Ukrainians, Poles, and other eastern Europeans, but there were a few Jews as well. Amazingly, too, they converted a few SS guards.[110] All of this was to be very important later for the spread of the Witness message. At the end of the war, Eastern European converts were to take their newly adopted Witness faith back to their homelands, where it was to spread despite the opposition of Communist governments.

Only at the end of the war were the Jehovah's Witnesses in the Nazi concentration camps again in great danger. As the Allies closed in on the Reich, Himmler ordered the SS to do away with the inmates of the camps, undoubtedly to destroy the evidence of the terrible events that

109 *Jehovah's Witnesses in the Divine Purpose,* 171.
110 Ibid.

had taken place in those places of horror.[111] As a result, the SS organized many 'death marches' to take camp prisoners to the Baltic Sea, load them onto ships, and sink the ships so that there would be no trace of them. Fortunately, most Witnesses and other prisoners escaped this fate. Many SS officers and men were on the run to save themselves from the Soviets and the Western Allies; the Allies were closing in too quickly for the SS to accomplish their terrible mission; and above all, the Witnesses cared for one another on the death marches.[112]

German Witnesses had suffered terribly. On page 212 the *1974 Yearbook* says concerning them:

> During Hitler's rule 1,687 of them had lost their jobs, 284 their businesses, 735 their homes and 457 were not allowed to carry on their trade. In 129 cases their property had been confiscated, 823 pensioners had been refused their pensions and 329 had suffered other personal loss. There were 860 children who had been taken from their parents. In 30 cases marriages had been dissolved due to pressure by political officials, and in 108 cases divorces had been granted when requested by mates opposed to the truth. A total of 6,019 had been arrested, several two, three or even more times, so that altogether, 8,917 arrests were registered. All together they had been sentenced to serve 13, 924 years and two months in prison, two and a quarter times as long as the period since Adam's creation. A total of 2,000 brothers and sisters had been put into concentration camps, where they had spent 8,078 years and six months, an average of four years. A total of 635 died in prison, 253 had been sentenced to death, 203 of these had actually been executed.'

Despite all this, when the war ended on 8 May 1945, they were prepared to reorganize and begin proselytizing among the German people. Disillusioned by defeat and by the collapse of Hitler's 'Thousand Year Reich,' many were willing to listen to the Watch Tower message, and Jehovah's Witnesses grew at an amazing rate until conditions improved in western Germany during the years of the *Wirtschaftswunder* or Economic Miracle of the late 1950s and early 1960s.[113]

111 Writing to camp *Kommandants*, Himmler stated: 'Surrendering is out of the question. The camp is to be evacuated immediately. No prisoner is to fall into enemy hands alive.' *1974 Yearbook*, 205.

112 *1974 Yearbook*, 205–8.

113 Witness growth was particularly rapid in the late 1940s and during the 1950s. By the 1960s it had begun to taper off. In 1965 there were 78,739 active Witness

Understandably, the Watch Tower Society has long emphasized the positive nature of the German Jehovah's Witnesses' resistance to Nazism. It has stressed the bravery of the German and other European Witnesses in the face of terrible persecution. It has claimed that few renounced their faith in order to be released from prisons or concentration camps.[114]

It has also asserted that the Witnesses in the camps were well behaved and gave help to their brethren and other prisoners in ways that no others did. It has pointed out that Witnesses generally faced death with more equanimity than other prisoners, and that many were prepared to risk their lives for the sake of producing and distributing Watch Tower publications. Without doubt, this is all true – something acknowledged by some of those who were their Nazi custodians, such as Himmler and Höss, and by fellow prisoners.

Eugen Kogon spent six years of his life as a prisoner in Buchenwald and knew Jehovah's Witnesses well. In describing them, he wrote: 'At times they had to endure great sufferings, but their patient faith in the end of the world made them loyal and willing workers, for the SS as well as for their fellow prisoners. Apart from a few skilled workers, nurses and calfactors (a kind of houseboy), they were at first assigned to the penal company. On 6 September 1938, the SS offered them the chance to abjure their principles in writing, especially their refusal to swear oaths and render military service, and thus purchase their liberty.' Kogon testified: 'Only a very few failed to withstand this temptation. The others were henceforth subjected to savage pressure in order to break their spirit.' In summation of their role in the camps, Kogon remarked: 'One cannot escape the impression that, psychologically speaking, the SS was never quite equal to the challenge offered them by Jehovah's Witnesses.'[115]

Bruno Bettelheim gave a similar positive account of the Witnesses:

> As conscientious objectors, all Jehovah's Witnesses were sent to the Camps. They were even less affected by imprisonment, and kept their integrity,

---

publishers in West Germany alone and 5,499 in West Berlin. But their bretheren in eastern Germany were under ban, and they had ceased to grow in the previous year in both West Germany and West Berlin. Since then growth has generally been slow, and recent reports show absolute declines in the number of active Witnesses throughout Germany as a whole.

114 To examine this declaration, see Appendix H.

115 Kogon, *The Theory and Practice of Hell,* 42, 43.

> thanks to rigid religious beliefs. Since their only crime in the eyes of the Nazis was a refusal to bear arms, they were frequently offered freedom in return for military service. They steadfastly refused. Members of this group were ... exemplary comrades, helpful, correct, and dependable. They were argumentative ... only when someone questioned their religious beliefs. Because of their conscientious work habits they were often selected as foremen. But once a foreman, and having accepted an order from the S.S., they insisted that prisoners do the work well and in the time allotted. Even though they were the only group of prisoners who never abused or mistreated other prisoners, S.S. officers preferred them as orderlies because of their work habits, skills or unassuming attitudes. Quite in contrast to the continuous warfare among the other prisoners groups, the Jehovah's Witnesses never misused their closeness to the S.S. officers to gain positions of privilege in the camp.[116]

Geneviève de Gaulle also described the Witnesses' fine character in the concentration camps. In an account made shortly after the war and published in *The Watchtower* of 1 September 1955, she stated:

> I am very glad to be able to convey to you my testimony regarding Bible Students whom I met in the Ravensbrück camp. Indeed, I have true admiration for them. They belonged to various nationalities: German, Polish, Russian and Czech, and have endured very great sufferings for their beliefs. The first arrests began ten years ago, and the majority of those who had been brought into camp at that time died from the bad treatment inflicted upon them, or were executed. I know, however, some survivors of that time and other prisoners who had arrived more recently; all of them showed very great courage and their attitude commanded eventually even the respect of the SS. They could have been immediately freed if they had renounced their faith. But, on the contrary, they did not cease resistance, even succeeding in introducing books and tracts into the camp, which writings caused several among them to be hanged.[117]

More recently, she has made similar comments in the 'Stand Firm' video.

A German school teacher, Sally Grubmann, has gone even farther in her praise of the Witnesses: 'The nicest group [in the camp] were the

116 Bruno Bettelheim, *The Informed Heart* (Glencoe, IL: The Free Press of Glencoe, 1960), 172–3.

117 Page 552.

Jehovah's Witnesses. I take my hat off to those people. They helped the sick, they shared their bread, and gave everyone near them spiritual comfort. The Germans hated them and respected them at the same time. They gave them the worst work but they took it with their heads high.'[118]

It is useful to ask: Were the Witnesses always the paragons of virtue as they have been described by foe and friend alike, and if they were, why did they hold up so well compared to other prisoners? As the statements quoted and cited above show, most of those who suffered were outstanding examples of integrity and human decency. Yet there were probably more who denied their faith than has been generally recognized. Rudolf Höss wrote: 'However, there were countless cases of Jehovah's Witnesses voluntarily reporting to the "swearing off." That's how the process was labelled by the Jehovah's Witnesses. They signed a "reverse" in which they renounced their membership in the International Bible Students Association, and in which they pledged to recognize and fulfill the laws and regulations of the state. They also declared that they would not recruit new witnesses for Jehovah.' He added, though, that many of them later chose to withdraw their renunciations of faith: 'The turncoats were put upon quite nastily by their brothers and sisters because of their turning away from Jehovah. Many, especially the women, had retracted their signature because their consciences bothered them. The continuous moral pressure was too strong. It was totally impossible to shake the Jehovah's Witnesses in their belief. Even the turncoats wanted to remain faithful to Jehovah under any circumstances, even though they divorced themselves from their congregation.'[119]

Other data support in general what Höss related. For example, Gestapo files found in Düsseldorf indicate that more than half 'signed off.'[120] This is not surprising; undoubtedly, some Witnesses were recent converts to Watch Tower teachings and were therefore not fully committed to them. Thus they may have signed the declaration to avoid imprisonment. Others no doubt found themselves incapable of withstanding the privation they experienced in jails and concentration camps. It would be wrong to infer, however, that all who signed actu-

118 Silvia Rothchild, *Voices from the Holocaust* (New York: New American Library, 1981), 247.

119 Höss, 104.

120 Garbe, *Zwischen Widerstand und Martyrium*, 305n333.

ally renounced their faith. Discussing this matter, Richard Singelenberg recounts the case of a Dutchman, Wilhelm Hengeveld, who was imprisoned in Germany in 1941 but was released upon signing the declaration. After his release he continued as an active Jehovah's Witness until the Nazis apprehended him again in 1944 and beheaded him.[121] Thus some, with their nearly total contempt for secular authority, may simply have been exercising what the Watch Tower Society was later to call 'theocratic war strategy.' But even if a number did apostatize and remain inactive until 1945, after the war many of them no doubt rejoined the Witness movement. Clearly, they remained loyal to Watch Tower teachings at heart. Höss's perception that 'even the turncoats wanted to remain faithful to Jehovah under any circumstances, even though they divorced themselves from their congregation' seems accurate.

Something that is routinely overlooked concerning the steadfastness of most Witnesses in the concentration camps needs to be mentioned here. There had long been a screening process going on among them which meant that, with some exceptions, only the most zealous reached the camps. If, by taking the 1933 Memorial attendance count, there were nearly 25,000 of them in Germany in the spring of 1933, and if more were added to their numbers by some conversions and through the German acquisition of new territories, it seems that only about one-third of them were imprisoned and that far fewer were sent to the concentration camps. If one uses the more conservative statistic of nearly 20,000 door-to-door 'publishers' or preachers from 1933, that still means that at most only 50 percent of them were incarcerated. Also, as was pointed out earlier, many more of those who were in prisons agreed to 'swear off' and were therefore not sent to the concentration camps. So the Witnesses in the camps were in many ways like the confessors in the early Christian Church, who were a rather elite group prepared to accept martyrdom.

In what amounts to its only fairly objective account of Jehovah's Witnesses under the Third Reich, the Watch Tower history found in the *1974 Yearbook of Jehovah's Witnesses* does admit that there were

121 Based on a review article by Richard Singelenberg of *Persecution and Resistance of Jehovah's Witnesses during the Nazi Regime*, edited by Hans Hesse. Dr Singelenberg's article appeared in the *Journal of Law and Religion* 18(1)(2002–3), 101–19. I am grateful to him for having made me aware of his article, as it appeared on his website, before formal publication.

individuals who renounced their faith.[122] Quite a number of them served in the *Wehrmacht*,[123] and a small group became outright traitors and were responsible for the persecution and deaths of some of their former brethren.[124] It notes too that some refused to participate in the Watch Tower's preaching campaigns and discouraged others from doing so.[125] It also recognizes that divisions sometimes arose among the Witnesses in certain camps. In one instance a charismatic individual arose and became the chief teacher of some four hundred Witness men. Those who did not accept his role and leadership suffered what amounted to excommunication and isolation.[126] Immediately after the war, Swiss Watch Tower branch overseer Franz Zürcher wrote a letter to the German Witness community, recognizing indirectly that Jehovah's Witnesses under Hitler had not been entirely of one mind – as Christine King has claimed – nor had they all 'stood firm.' That letter reads in part:

> To all our beloved fellow servants in Germany
>
> Dear Brethren in Christ,
>
> At last you are free from the Nazi yoke! – Some of you have suffered for years, either in prison or in concentration camps or by other types of persecution ...
>
> No one, however, who was considered worthy of special suffering for the Lord's name will become conceited about this and wear a martyr's halo or exalt himself above others who were not in prison or concentration camps. No one should brag to his fellow humans about his sufferings. Do not forget that many of the brethren who remained at home also had many problems and were under severe pressures. A Christian cannot choose his sufferings. The Lord determines or, rather, permits them.
>
> For this reason, dear brethren, let us not be unfair and take sides nor let us condemn anyone, who, according to our way of thinking, has compromised or was willing to do so. The Lord judges our hearts. Before him we are like an open book.[127]

122 *1974 Yearbook*, 177–8.
123 Ibid.
124 Ibid., 175–6, 178–9.
125 Ibid., 131–2. While the *1974 Yearbook* talks about some unwillingness to preach by some Witnesses in 1933, it says little about this after that. Quite evidently, from the Watch Tower's own statistics, many simply decided not to continue distributing Witness literature or preaching orally to their neighbours.
126 *1974 Yearbook*, 174–5.
127 Ibid., 212–13.

Neither German Witness leaders, fresh out of concentration camps, nor Watch Tower President N.H. Knorr were willing to accept Zürcher's advice. When Paul Balzereit came forward in 1945 to help reorganize the Witness community in Germany, he clashed sharply with those among his former brethren who regarded him as a traitor.[128] Later on the Watch Tower did everything possible to blacken his name, especially after his death, when he could no longer defend himself. This is shown clearly by the *1974 Yearbook*'s attempts to blame him for doctoring the 1933 *Declaration of Facts.* In effect, Knorr took an action against Balzereit, whom he regarded as having apostatized, that was every bit as severe as the one's taken against Christians who had lapsed during persecution by certain extreme North African Christians such as Cyprian and Donatus in the third and fourth centuries of the Christian era.[129]

No one can deny German Witnesses' bravery and fortitude both outside and inside Nazi concentration camps. Yet the question remains: How were they able to manifest those qualities so consistently? There have been several attempts to explain this. The most important of these in English are found in Christine King's *The Nazi State and the New Religions,* written before Dr King became such a naive apologist for the Witnesses, and in an article by Jerry Bergman titled, 'The Jehovah's Witnesses' Experience in the Nazi Concentration Camps: A History of Their Conflict with the Nazi State.'

King's analysis is straightforward. Taking a leaf out of Michael Kater's article, *'Die Ernsten Bibelforscher im Dritten Reich,'* she recognizes the totalitarian nature of Jehovah's Witnesses, whose fanaticism in some ways matched that of the Nazis themselves:

> Of all the sectarians they were, in one sense, the most non-political and therefore the most dangerous. Their concerns were deliberately not with politics, which they considered corrupt, but by this position they placed themselves, in a totalitarian state, in danger of appearing hostile and therefore 'political.' Their teachings on military service could not be tolerated, less for practical danger and more for the ideological attack on National Socialism such a stance represented.

128 Garbe, 135n214. Gebhard, 487.

129 For descriptions of the teachings of Cyprian and Donatus, see W.H.C. Frend, *The Rise of Christianity* (Philadelphia: Fortress Press, 1984), 351–7, 653–7.

By their very survival the Witnesses presented their most serious threat. The Nazi authorities, having identified this ideological enemy, were committed to its destruction; that they were not able to achieve this was a serious criticism of their power. The real reason for the clash between this sect and the Nazi state lies, therefore, not in areas of practical concern, propaganda, refusal to fight, vote or give the salute, but in the clash of two totalitarian systems. Each system, ironically, promised a thousand year Reich and it has been suggested that many of the Nazi rituals came close to those of sectarianism. Whatever the police, lawyers and civil servants believed, and whatever Hitler's personal views on the sect were, there were those in the party who recognized the real basis of this conflict. These were not always those responsible for policies, however, and the fanaticism of a man like Heydrich as well as internal power struggles may help to explain the practicalities of what happened.

In this struggle, two non-democratic, anti-liberal and uncompromising bodies faced each other. In each system, adherents were expected to give themselves up to the movement and obey without question, each believing itself to have a monopoly on the 'truth.'[130] (Italics mine)

Bergman's article surveys most of the important works on the subject in English and some in German, and comes to a basically sociological explanation of why the Witnesses were so firm in their resolve to maintain their principles. He holds, accordingly, that it was their commitment *to community* that was largely responsible. In developing this thesis, he does not seek to understand the psyches of individual Witnesses; rather, he attempts to understand them through their adherence to the group. He argues rightly that their belief system held that all except Jehovah's Witnesses would soon be destroyed at Armageddon. Whether they as individuals survived that battle of the great day of God Almighty or not would depend on their faithfulness, even in concentration camps, to the communal values of the Theocracy. Bergman also recognizes the powerful influence that their desire to proselytize had on them:

It was important for Watchtower followers to impress non-Witness inmates and administrators of the camps because the Watchtower taught that this was one of the most effective ways of selling their faith. They knew that being kind to non-Witnesses might result in a convert. Examples are

130 King, *The Nazi State and the New Religions*, 175–6.

> repeatedly provided in Watchtower literature of persecutors – from husbands who beat their wives for attending Watchtower meetings, to people who threw rocks at the Kingdom Hall – who eventually became Witnesses because of the kindness manifested to enemies while they were persecuting. The Witnesses typically make excellent martyrs, overtly smiling as they are persecuted, confident that their endurance will help the persecutor see the validity of their faith.[131]

It was not just by martyring themselves that Jehovah's Witnesses attempted to influence others. It was also through cleanliness, honesty, good work habits, and kindness, all factors that the Witnesses manifested to the greatest extent possible, and ones that Bergman recognizes. Thus his analysis of the Witnesses in Nazi concentration camps provides a useful overview of what made them behave the way they did. Like Christine King and Michael Kater, Bergman – a former Jehovah's Witness himself – is clearly aware of the Witnesses' totalitarian, absolutist nature. But he does not deal at any length with the role played by J.F. Rutherford and his subordinates in demanding that German Witnesses be willing to seek martyrdom.

Jehovah's Witnesses make additional claims without denying much of what Bergman and others have noted about positive aspects of their conduct. They claim that their behaviour under persecution was based on their obedience to God's spirit-directed organization – despite Rutherford's curious assertion that the Holy Spirit was not present after 1918. They draw parallels between their fortitude under the Third Reich and that of early Christians under Rome. Such comparisons, however, are somewhat misleading. It is true that orthodox Christians in pagan Rome often suffered martyrdom, sometimes of a very terrible kind. Ordinarily, however, early Christians did not seek martyrdom. This is demonstrated by two outstanding cases. The Apostle Paul used his Roman citizenship to escape death at the hands of fellow Jews (Acts 22:22–29; 25:1–12), and Polycarp, the second-century bishop of Smyrna, fled to the countryside to escape death before being apprehended and burned alive.[132] But there was also a heretical Chris-

131 Bergman, 'The Jehovah's Witnesses' Experience in the Nazi Concentration Camps,' *Journal of Church and State* 38 (Winter 1996).

132 'The Martyrdom of St. Polycarp, Bishop of Smyrna,' trans. Kirsopp Lake, *The Apostolic Fathers*, Loeb Classical Library (Cambridge, MA: and London: Harvard University Press and Heinemann, 1970), vol. 2, 312–21.

tian movement in the Roman world whose members behaved much like Jehovah's Witnesses in our own times and who often courted martyrdom. That movement was the Montanists.

Founded in the Roman province of Phrygia in A.D. 156 by a new Christian convert named Montanus, the Montanists spread rapidly and assumed the nature of a sectarian movement within the context of Christianity. Interestingly, like Charles T. Russell and Joseph F. Rutherford, Montanus and two women associates, Prisca and Maximilla, assumed special roles. All 'new prophecy' was to come through them. Only later did the movement develop other minor prophets. Like Jehovah's Witnesses under Rutherford, Montanism was tightly organized and structured. As Hans Lietzmann points out, Montanus had a penchant for organization. He and his followers also emphasized the importance of celibacy. They sometimes taught the value of 'spiritual marriage' or marriage without sexual relations, and they were rigid moralists in ways that Watch Tower Bible Students and Jehovah's Witnesses have generally been despite Rutherford's less than fine example. It was from their eschatology that the Montanists were to develop their primary ideas and, from those ideas, practices that foreshadowed those of the Witnesses by some seventeen hundred years. The Montanists, like twentieth-century Jehovah's Witnesses, pointed to the disastrous conditions of their own age in asserting that they were living in the last days leading up to the millennium. As Lietzmann says: 'The severe distresses, occasioned by the wars of Marcus Aurelius and the dreadful years of epidemic, were really quite fitted to pass as heralds of the final age, and reveal the four apocalyptic horsemen riding over the earth.' Like the Witnesses, the Montanists sometimes delivered false prophecies concerning the destruction of the present world and Christ's second advent. For example, the prophetess Maximilla said: 'After me no other prophet will come, but only the final End.' But what really shows how similar the Witnesses have been and are to the Montanists is their attitude toward both secular government and martyrdom. Lietzmann says: 'It is easy to understand that a Christianity of this kind, which lived in the world of the future, was opposed emphatically to the kingdoms of this world: genuine Christians who belonged to these churches did not avoid persecution by taking to flight, but met them with defiance; and sometimes temperament even drove them to the attack.'[133]

133 Hans Lietzmann, *A History of the Christian Church,* trans. Bertram Lee Woolf (Guildford and London: Lutterworth Press, 1961), vol. 2, 194–203.

Undoubtedly, then, the real motivation behind the Jehovah's Witnesses in Germany and especially in the concentration camps during the years of Hitler's Third Reich was their doctrinal system, which was based primarily on their eschatology. They believed firmly that the Second World War would lead to Armageddon. They had no doubt that they were being attacked by Satan and his human dupes: the churches, the economic systems, and political leaders of all stripes. They felt they knew why Hitler hated them, and they fitted him into their doctrinal scheme by describing him as the ruler of Daniel's 'king of the North.' Unlike almost all the other prisoners in the camps, the Witnesses were convinced that they understood why they were there: they were being persecuted for righteousness' sake as representatives of the Theocracy, Christ's kingdom. Therefore it behooved them to overcome evil with good. Like Christ, they had to expose evil by describing it openly, although they ignored his command to be 'as wise as serpents and as harmless as doves.' Otherwise, they had to act as did he in going like a lamb to the slaughter. In this way they might win new converts to the forces of righteousness. If this meant their suffering and death, what of it? They would have kept their integrity, and they would be rewarded in the resurrection either to heaven or to a paradise earth in which righteousness would dwell.

True, they saw the Watch Tower organization as directed by J.F. Rutherford and his successor, N.H. Knorr, as representative of Jehovah and Christ on earth. They believed firmly that they had to obey that organization in the same way the Montanists felt they must accept direction from the Phrygian prophets. So Rutherford in particular can rightly be held responsible for encouraging German Witnesses to take up the mantle of martyrdom and for 'driving them to the attack.' In doing so, he caused them much terrible anguish and undoubtedly cost some their lives unnecessarily.

7

Riding the Holocaust Bandwagon

Holocaust memory is an ideological construct of vested interests.
Norman G. Finkelstein, *The Holocaust Industry*

Why has the Watch Tower Society made so much of the role of Jehovah's Witnesses under the Third Reich in recent years, when it did not do so to the same extent during the decades immediately following the Second World War? Why have certain scholars been so prepared to defend Watch Tower officials against charges of anti-Semitism and of having tried to ingratiate the Witness movement with the Nazis? The answers are somewhat complex and deserve to be placed in the context of broader historical, political, and sociological developments that have occurred over the last sixty years. Some of these developments have involved the Jewish communities in America and Israel, international politics, and a bitter struggle involving what have come to be labelled 'cults' by their critics (or, conversely, 'new religions' by those who are more sympathetic or at least neutral toward them). In order to understand the Watch Tower's recent fixation on the persecution of Jehovah's Witnesses under Hitler, it is necessary to look at what has happened historically. Let us start, then, by examining American Jewish attitudes toward the persecution of European Jews from 1933 to 1945.

Two Jewish-American scholars, Peter Novick[1] and Norman Finkelstein,[2] assert that the Jewish community in the United States did not

1 Peter Novick, *The Holocaust in American Life* (Boston and New York: Houghton Mifflin, 1999).

2 Norman C. Finkelstein, *The Holocaust Industry: Reflections on the Exploitation of Jewish Suffering* (London and New York: Verso, 2000).

begin to make much ado about the sufferings of European Jews under the Third Reich until the 1967 Six Day War between Israel and its neighbours. They argue that until that time, Jews in the United States did not emphasize the historical importance of the Holocaust, nor did they want to give unreserved support to Israel. After 1967, because the United States committed itself to supporting Israel,[3] and for other reasons discussed below, everything changed. American Jews began to become fervently pro-Israel and began to focus on what had happened to their fellow Jews under Hitler.

Applying the concept of 'collective memory' as developed by the French sociologist Maurice Halbwachs, Peter Novick argues that the collective memory developed by Jews in the United States following a number of events in the 1960s was in many ways 'ahistorical, even anti-historical.' According to Halbwachs, 'present concerns determine what of the past we remember and how we remember it.'[4] Novick thus holds that such events as the capture and trial of Adolf Eichmann, a controversy surrounding the Jewish scholars Hannah Arendt, Bruno Bettelheim, and Raul Hilberg, the release of Rolf Hochhuth's play *The Deputy,* and the Six Day War changed the perceptions of American Jews. These events helped make the Holocaust central to much of Jews' collective thinking, and did so in a way that Novick regards as neither objective nor healthy.[5]

Novick shows that since the Second World War, anti-Semitism in the United States has decreased to the point of insignificance. There are no doors closed to Jews in America today, and they form the most prosperous community in the country.[6] Because the greater acceptance of Jews by gentile Americans continued from the late 1940s through to the 1967 war,[7] during those years American Jewish leaders emphasized how different the United States was from Europe and how it had offered a peaceful haven to Jews. So those leaders held that Jews should seek accommodation with other Americans.[8] The only threat to the continued existence of a healthy and happy Jewish community in the United States was that many Jews had abandoned or were abandoning their faith, were marrying gentiles, and were being

3 Finkelstein, 22. Novick, 146–7.
4 Novick, 3.
5 Ibid., 134–45; 148–51.
6 Ibid., 9.
7 Ibid., 113, 170, 175.
8 Ibid.

assimilated into the larger, mainly Christian society.[9] Despite these facts, most American Jews began to feel paranoid in the late 1960s, contending that scattered incidents of anti-Semitism – usually among black Americans – represented a significant rise in hatred of their community.[10] Some asserted that eventually they would probably be faced with another Holocaust and that it could even happen in America. Only in Israel would they be safe.[11] Consequently, American Jewish leaders began to emphasize the Holocaust and to use it both to buttress support for Israel and to claim that they were still victims or at least potential victims – an important psychological role in modern America and in the Western world as a whole.

The rise and fall of the civil rights movement, the emphasis on 'black history' in the United States, the growth of a new, more radical feminism, the emphasis on gay and lesbian rights, and the development of liberation theology all tended to produce what amounted to the intellectual and social ghettoization of particular groups. Instead of emphasizing what the members of various groups had in common with the larger societies in which they lived, they emphasized their specific ethnic or sexual communities. This was especially true in the United States but was also the case in Canada (where multiculturalism has been enshrined in the Constitution), Great Britain, and to an extent in some Western European nations. Novick states regarding the United States: 'Apart from the Jews, the groups among whom "identities" really took hold – because of the basis of successful mobilization and collective consciousness – were blacks, women, gays, and to a lesser extent, Hispanics.'[12] He adds: 'Their group mobilization and "raised consciousness" was based on their shared experience of collective disadvantage or their individual experience of discrimination, usually both. They organized on the basis of shared grievances against the dominant society, which continued to deny them full and equal participation and gave them less than what they saw as their fair share of rewards. Their shared identity was thus, above all, a victim identity. The hallmark of the fully participating and fully conscious member of the group was belief – however well one was doing personally – in shared victimhood.'[13]

9 Ibid., 178–88.
10 Ibid., 172–6.
11 Ibid., 176.
12 Ibid., 189.
13 Ibid., 189–90.

How did all of this affect the Jews in America? Novick continues: 'It was against this background, and in this cultural climate that virtually celebrated victimhood, that efforts to firm up faltering Jewish identity were mounted.'[14] Although he does not think that Jewish leaders consciously and deliberately used 'victimhood' to strengthen their community, he does think they could now claim it because it had become fashionable. He remarks: 'the heightened status of the victim removed inhibitions that had in previous decades led them to shun that label. The "culture of victimization" didn't *cause* Jews to embrace a victim identity based on the Holocaust; it *allowed* this sort of identity to become dominant, because it was, after all, virtually the only one that could encompass those Jews whose faltering Jewish identity produced so much anxiety about Jewish survival.'[15]

Norman Finkelstein is more outspoken than Novick in condemning what he calls the Holocaust Industry. He asserts that the emphasis on the Holocaust is in part to bolster American support for Israel,[16] but he adds:

> There are also domestic sources of the Holocaust industry. Mainstream interpretations point to the recent emergence of 'identity politics,' on the one hand, and the 'culture of victimization,' on the other. In effect, each identity was grounded in a particular history of oppression; Jews accordingly sought their own ethnic identity in the Holocaust.
>
> Yet, among groups decrying their victimization, including Blacks, Latinos, Native Americans, women, gays and lesbians, Jews alone are not disadvantaged in American society. In fact identity politics and The Holocaust have taken hold among American Jews not because of victim status but because they are *not* victims.[17]

If, as Finkelstein says, 'Holocaust memory *is* an ideological construct of vested interests'[18] within the Jewish community, the same is true to an equally great extent among Jehovah's Witnesses. Although it is true that the Watch Tower Society published some information about the persecution of the Witnesses under Nazism in earlier years, it did not carry on the major, almost tiresome propaganda campaign

14 Ibid.
15 Ibid.
16 Finkelstein, 30–1.
17 Ibid., 32.
18 Ibid., 5.

that it has over the last thirteen years or so. Why? In the first place, as emphasized by Novick and Finkelstein, the Holocaust did not receive much attention until the Jewish community began to make much of it in the late 1960s. There was no ideological bandwagon for a small, unpopular group like the Witnesses to climb onto before that point. Second, only in the late 1960s and the early 1970s did the cult of victimization emerge, which the Witnesses, like many others, could use to their advantage. Third, and most important, not until the 1990s did they begin to find themselves in serious trouble with various governments in Western Europe and the former Soviet Bloc. So until the 1970s or thereabouts, there was no way they could have successfully made much of their sufferings under Hitler, and until the 1990s there was no particular reason for them to claim victim status to protect themselves from discrimination or outright persecution.

During and after the war, Jehovah's Witnesses saw their situation improve in many of the countries in which they lived. In the United States and Canada they won an amazing string of cases before those nations' highest courts. This virtually ensured that they would be safe from persecution and even overt discrimination in those lands. Gradually the severe actions taken against them in many other countries for refusing military or alternative civilian service were softened or ended. In postwar France their young men had been imprisoned for up to ten years for refusing military service. However, after he came to power in 1958, Charles de Gaulle released any who had been incarcerated for more than ten years. Eventually his government passed legislation so that no Witness would serve more than three years in prison.[19] Shortly after that the Witnesses won an important legal victory when the French Watch Tower branch overseer was acquitted of counselling men to avoid serving in the French armed forces.[20] Even more encouraging to them was that in the late 1960s the Swedish government decided their men would be exempted not just from military service but from alternative civilian service as well.[21] With the growth of democracy throughout the world and the fall of dictatorships in Argentina, in the former Communist countries of Eastern Europe, and in the African nation of Malawi, they gained more recognition and more freedom. Even in Turkey – a country not noted for respecting civil liberties – they won

19 *1980 Yearbook*, 133.
20 Ibid., 134–5.
21 *1991 Yearbook*, 161–7.

an important court case.[22] Only the issue of their refusal to accept blood transfusions caused them much trouble in most countries. But conditions began to change for the worse in the 1990s: they began to suffer from the effects of propaganda launched against both them and many other religious movements by what has come to be known as the 'anticult movement.' According to that movement, a variety of unpopular religions dubbed 'cults' were 'brainwashing' people to become converts and holding them in mental bondage.

From what is now known, the Gestapo and the SS were the first to attempt to 'transform worldviews through techniques that create[d] disorientation and hyper-suggestibility followed by intensive indoctrination.' Their techniques included the use of mescaline and barbituates along with intense interrogations and indoctrination.[23] After the war the American OSS – the predecessor of the CIA – decided to follow up on this research by conducting its own. It recovered Nazi documents relating to activities in this area and decided to use them, as well as material from other studies conducted from the 1940s through to the 1970s.[24] 'The primary intent of such research was to develop methods capable of transforming foreign nationals of Communist countries hostile to the US into reliable American "deployable agents", who could then be used to spy upon or otherwise undermine the Communist regimes.'[25] To this end, employees of the CIA carried on covert brainwashing studies in various universities, prisons, and mental hospitals in the United States and Canada on individuals, who without being told were treated as human guinea pigs. To develop hypersuggestible, disoriented states of mind in these individuals, drugs, isolation, sensory deprivation, electric shocks, narcotherapy, and lobotomies and other forms of psychosurgery were administered to them.[26] Sometimes individuals were given drugs such as LSD, with long-lasting, extremely negative results.[27] This was done to destroy previous loyalties before

22 'Turkish Courts Uphold Freedom of Worship for Jehovah's Witnesses,' *Awake!* 8 June 1961, 25–7.

23 Dick Anthony, 'Tactical Ambiguity and Brainwashing Formulations: Science or Pseudo-Science?' in Benjamin Zablocki and Thomas Robbins, eds., *Misunderstanding Cults: Searching for Objectivity in a Controversial Field* (Toronto, Buffalo, and London: University of Toronto Press, 2001), 219–20.

24 Ibid.

25 Ibid.

26 Ibid., 220.

27 A Canadian psychiatrist, Colin Ross, outlined the broad nature of these mind control experiments in Canada in an interview with Wayne Morris aired on station CKLN-FM Toronto on 13 April 1997.

planting new, diametrically opposed ones in their minds. According to psychotherapist Dick Anthony, the macabre programs carried out by the Germans and the Americans failed: 'In spite of the scope and ambitiousness of these German and American mind-control research programs ... in terms of their original goals of improving interrogation and coercive indoctrination tactics beyond that obtainable with physical coercion or other traditional methods, they were complete failures.'[28]

Ignoring these failures, the CIA, acting through Edward Hunter, a propaganda specialist with a cover identity as a journalist, disseminated the idea that brainwashing really worked. Hunter published books which held that individuals – both Chinese anti-Communists and American prisoners of war held during the Korean War – had been converted coercively to communism through brainwashing techniques.[29] Although studies by two American scholars, Robert Lifton and Edgar Shein, raised serious doubts about the effectiveness of brainwashing,[30] proponents of the brainwashing theory claimed that Lifton and Shein actually supported their ideas.[31] They also asserted that certain religious 'cults' that had become active in the 1960s in the United States and other countries were brainwashing people to convert them and to keep them in the flock. Among those academics who

28 Anthony, 220.

29 Ibid., 221.

30 Lifton is blunt about the matter. He states: 'Behind the web of semantic (and more than semantic) confusion lies an image of brainwashing as an all-powerful, irresistible, unfathomable, and magical method of achieving total control over the human mind. It is of course none of these things, and this loose usage makes the word a rallying point for fear, resentment, urges toward submission, justification for failure, irresponsible accusation, and for a wide gamut of emotional extremism.' Robert Jay Lifton, *Thought Reform and the Psychology of Totalism: A Study of 'Brainwashing' in China* (Chapel Hill and London: University of North Carolina Press, 1989), 4. The first edition of this work appeared in 1961.

Shein is no less clear; he states that prisoners of the Chinese Communists were subjected to what he called 'coercive persuasion' and remarks: 'Coercive persuasion involves no more or less of such distortion [of the mind] than other kinds of influence, but our popular image of "brainwashing" suggests that somehow the process consists of extensive self-delusion and excessive distortion. We feel that this image is a false one: it is based on our lack of familiarity with or knowledge about the process and the fact that so much publicity was given to the political influence which resulted in a few cases.' Edgar Shein, *Coercive Persuasion* (New York: Norton, 1961), 4, as quoted in Anthony, 231.

31 See Benjamin Zablocki, 'Towards a Demystified and Disinterested Scientific Theory of Brainwashing,' in Zablocki and Robbins, 166–74.

held that 'cults' brainwashed converts were John Clark and Margaret Singer, both of whom supported the brainwash theory.[32] Flo Conway and Jim Siegelman also contributed much to it in their book which argued that those converts had lost their freedom of will and were under the mind control of the leaders of the religions in question.[33]

During the 1970s and early 1980s the anticult movement took an especially nasty turn. Various members of new religions, and members of religions that were not so new, were being kidnapped and successfully 'deprogrammed.' Many members of the Unification Church (Moonies), the Krishna Consciousness Movement, the Children of God, and a host of other small religious movements were being seized and held until their allegiance to their faith was broken or until they escaped. Sometimes the individuals who were successfully deprogrammed seemed grateful, but others were severely damaged. Often the individuals who carried out these 'deprogrammings' were highly paid deprogrammers with little knowledge of human psychology. Distraught family members, convinced that their child, sibling, or spouse was being held involuntarily by a 'cult,' frequently hired deprogrammers. Police often either turned a blind eye to deprogramming activities or cooperated with the deprogrammers.[34] In other cases, families tried to obtain legal conservatorship over family members who had joined 'cults' or 'new religions,' in order to control their actions and associations and to have them deprogrammed.

Many academics and civil libertarians as well as some clergy of mainstream churches took a strong stand against the brainwashing theory and deprogramming. However, the news media often supported both and, indirectly, the adherents of both. One reason for this was that over the years, certain 'cults,' in the Americas, Europe, and Japan

32 In an address to the Vermont State Legislature in 1976, Clark stated concerning cults: 'The health hazards are extreme. Though I talk primarily about the absolute dangers to mental health and personal development, I must also as a physician draw attention to equally serious, often life-threatening, dangers to physical health.' Quoted in Carol Coulter, *Are Religious Cults Dangerous?* (Dublin and Cork: Mercier Press, 1984), 77.

Margaret Singer is the most important proponent of the psychological model of cult control through brainwashing. Her most important work is *Cults in Our Midst: The Hidden Menace in Our Everyday Lives* (San Francisco: Jossey-Bass, 1995).

33 Flo Conway and Jim Siegelman, *Snapping: America's Epidemic of Sudden Personality Change* (Philadelphia: Lippincott, 1978).

34 I know of several such instances in both the United States and Canada. In fact, some police forces actually established 'cult units' to investigate various new religions.

had become involved in mass suicides, confrontations with governments, and the murder of innocents. The mass suicide of members of the People's Temple at Jonestown, Guyana, in 1978; the tragic immolation of the Branch Davidians near Waco, Texas, in 1993; the suicides of members of the Order of the Solar Temple in Switzerland and Quebec in 1994, 1995, and 1997; the poison gassing of Japanese subway passengers in Tokyo by the Aum Shinrikyo in 1995; and the Heaven's Gate suicides in California in 1997 all led to a general fear of 'cults' and a seeming confirmation of the brainwashing theory. After all, it was often asked, why would individuals behave as had the members of these groups unless they were under some sort of mind control?

Another factor generated fear of cults: many former members of totalitarian groups picked up the jargon being used by the brainwash-theory anticultists and adopted it to attack their former religions. In effect, many of them wanted to use the argument that they or others they knew had been under mind control when they were active members of their former faiths. Therefore, they could not rightly be held responsible for their former allegiance to them. This was especially true of former Moonies, Scientologists, and certain ex-Jehovah's Witnesses after 1975. Many of these 'apostates,' as they came to be called, took up the psychological model of brainwashing either as promoted by Margaret Singer or – after deprogramming began to be looked upon as both illegal and too severe an antidote to 'mind control' – in a modified form as promoted by Steven Hassan.[35]

There is no clear definition of what a cult is or is supposed to be. Experts provide various definitions,[36] and unfortunately the news media and much of the general public tend not to realize that the term is a rather fuzzy ideological construct. Sociologist David Bromley asserts that words such as 'brainwash' and 'conversion' are based on what amounts to 'political' points of view,[37] and the same can rightly be said of such terms as 'cults' and 'new religions.' The word *cult* often has come to mean a religious or political group that some individual or community does not like. The Irish journalist Carol Coulter demonstrates this clearly. She has labelled generally unpopular religions such as the Krishna Consciousness Movement (the Hare Krishnas), the Uni-

35 *Combatting Cult Mind Control* (Rochester, VT.: Park Street Press, 1988).

36 Janja Lalich, 'Pitfalls in the Sociological Study of Cults,' in Zablocki and Robbins, 121–3.

37 David Bromley, 'A Tale of Two Theories: Brainwashing and Conversion as Competing Narratives,' in Zablocki and Robbins, 318–49.

fication Church, the Way International, the Church of Scientology, and Jehovah's Witnesses as cults, and she has even included several para-church organizations under that rubric as well. These para-church organizations include the Catholic lay movement Opus Dei, the Campus Crusade for Christ, Youth with a Mission, and the Wycliffe Bible Translators.[38] All of the above groups, be they organized religions or para-church movements, are strikingly different, one from another, and it would be extremely difficult to show that they have very much in common. However, since Coulter makes the assumption that all are cults, she assumes that they must all be holding their members in some sort of mental thrall. Such a scattergun use of a term that is so amorphous and ambiguous would, of course, be rather laughable were it not taken so seriously both by many people in a number of countries and by certain governments.

The anticult movement has suffered some major defeats in North America as a result of opposition from intellectuals – mainly sociologists and psychologists, who have been able to discredit the idea that cults can brainwash converts. The same is not true in Europe. In Western Europe and in many of the former Communist countries of Eastern Europe, the anticult movement is riding a wave of popularity and has been able to force governments to take action against many so-called cults in those countries, including Jehovah's Witnesses.

A resolution presented to the U.S. House of Representatives on 21 September 2000 demonstrates just how widespread Western European attacks are on groups that have been designated cults. That resolution, presented by Congressmen Salmon, Payne, and Gilman, claimed that a number of European nations were violating the Helsinki Final Act and the Universal Declaration of Human Rights. The resolution listed Germany as a country engaged in discriminatory trade practices by setting up a 'sect filter' requiring foreign firms to state that none of their employees were members of certain religions (specifically, Scientologists). It outlined how the French government had listed some 173 religions as cults[39] and was discriminating against independent Evangelical churches, Scientologists, Jehovah's Witnesses, Unificationists, Southern Baptists, Seventh-day Adventists, the Catholic Charis-

38 See Coulter, chapter 8.

39 The term cult in French has a positive meaning denoting the practice of religion. The word *secte* is therefore used in French as equivalent to the English word cult. Sometimes, as below, English translators render *secte* as sect. Under the circumstances, however, this is incorrect.

matic Renewal movement, Opus Dei, and the Jesuits. Next, it censured Austria for having 'codified a tiered system of government recognition and preferential treatment [of religions], including government funding of religious groups.' It pointed out that the Austrian government had established a 'sect' office to disseminate propaganda on religious groups not recognized by the government. The resolution also criticized Belgium: 'The Parliament of Belgium issued a report in 1967 on "sects" with a widely circulated informal appendix listing 189 groups as suspect, including many Protestant and Catholic groups, Quakers, Hasidic Jews, Buddhists and members of the Young Women's Christian Association (YWCA), based on rumor and speculation found in police files, and implicitly warning the public to avoid such "dangerous" groups.'[40]

Among European countries, France has been most active in attacking groups it regards as cults. An Information Commission on Cults was formed within the French Law Commission in 1981. Following this, in 1982 and 1983, the anticultist Alain Vivien wrote a report at the behest of the prime minister. Published in 1985, it was titled in English translation *Cults in France: Expression of Moral Freedom or Factors of Manipulation*.[41] There was little governmental interest in the subject in the country, however, until the murders and suicides of the Order of the Solar Temple in 1994 and the poison gassing of Tokyo subway passengers by Aum Shinrikyo in 1995. At that point a wave of apprehension swept over the republic, and the National Assembly established a parliamentary commission to examine minority religious groups. The document the commission produced, the Guyard Report, seems to have been the work of individuals largely hostile to religion: 'Input from academics who have specialized in the study of new religious movements was not included; the commission refused to hear them.'[42] As mentioned in the U.S. House of Representatives' resolution described above, the Guyard Report, which was a French National Assembly report, came up with an amazing list of 173 *'sectes'* or cults. Some of the information used by the commission in producing

40 U.S. Congress. H. Res. 588. 110th congress, 2nd sess., 21 September 2000.

41 A.B. Robinson, 'Religious Intolerance in France.' Posted by the Ontario Consultants on Religious Freedom at www.religioustolerance.org/rt_franc.htm [.] See also the '2000 Annual Report on International Religious Freedom: France,' released by the Bureau of Democracy, Human Rights, and Labor of the U.S. Department of State, 5 September 2000.

42 The '2000 Annual Report on International Religious Freedom: France.'

the report came from the *Renseignements Généraux* (the French secret service) and could not be evaluated independently because it was 'classified' and the government refused to release it.[43]

All of the groups labelled cults by French governmental action have been marginalized to an extent. The two that have been attacked most directly have been the Church of Scientology and Jehovah's Witnesses. The Scientologists have been noted for exposing police forces and secret service organizations that resort to various forms of skullduggery, for being strongly critical of psychiatry, and for suing their media critics. As a result they have made themselves highly unpopular with many people and many governments, including that of France. The Witnesses are only slightly less unpopular. Their negativity toward nationalism, their refusal to accept blood transfusions, and their insistent door-to-door preaching work make them disliked by much of the French general public. Evidently, their conservative views with respect to the role of women have alienated the French Socialists.[44] Denis Barthelemy, the secretary general of the Inter-ministerial Mission on Combating Cults, a government task force, has said: 'The practice and comportment of Jehovah's Witnesses are frankly sectarian [read cultic], and can lead to problems that public powers can't allow.'[45] So the French government has taken criminal action against the Scientologists and has tried to tax the Witnesses out of existence.

Even though the Witnesses have been in France since 1900 and their extended community numbers close to a quarter of a million people, the French government has refused to recognize them as a religious association. French fiscal authorities began an audit of that movement in 1996. Two years later, in May 1998, those authorities assessed a 60 percent tax on all donations received by Jehovah's Witnesses from September 1992 through to August 1996. This tax, plus fines for late payment, amounted to more than 300,000,000 francs or more than US$42,000,000. A lien was placed on the National Consistory of

43 Ibid.

44 Elizabeth Bryant, 'France May Limit Religious Practices': A UPI Report dated 23 April 2001 and posted at www.hrwf.net [.] If Bryant is right about the Socialists' attitude toward the Witnesses on the grounds of their teachings on the role of women – and she probably is – this represents a negative attitude toward traditional Catholic and Protestant teachings as well. After all, in many ways Jehovah's Witnesses hold positions on the relations of the sexes that are very close to those of the Vatican, with the exception that Jehovah's Witnesses, like conservative Protestants, do not consider birth control morally wrong.

45 Ibid.

Jehovah's Witnesses' properties in order to force payment. In June 2000, however, the *Conseil d'État,* the highest administrative court in France, held that congregations of Jehovah's Witnesses could be recognized as religious associations and were therefore exempt from taxation.[46] Nonetheless, another court held shortly thereafter that the fine on the National Consistory would have to be paid. The Witnesses appealed this ruling twice, but both appeals failed. If the Witnesses do what they have done in the past, they will undoubtedly take the matter to the highest court in France and perhaps even to the European Court of Human Rights.

While the above events were taking place, the French government brought forward dramatic anticult legislation. On the basis of the concerns expressed in the Guyard Report, on 22 June 2001 the French Chamber of Deputies passed a bill that proclaimed what amounted to all-out war on cults. This bill, which was later passed by the French Senate, was prepared to 'paralyse' cults. It provides for the dissolution of a religious body if one leading member of the group is convicted of a crime. It supports the notion that individuals can be brainwashed by criminalizing the abuse or coercion of anyone 'in a state of psychological or physical dependence caused by the exertion of heavy or repeated pressure or techniques liable to alter the judgment.' It imposes draconian punishments on anyone convicted under the law: individuals can be jailed for up to five years and can lose all their civil rights.[47]

Despite protests from religious organizations great and small, Pope John Paul II, various civil liberties organizations, the American State Department, and several American congressmen,[48] France argues that the law in question does not curb civil liberties but rather enhances them. It takes this position because the people who were responsible for the anticult law seem to believe that cults actually do brainwash people. However, there may be more to the matter. First, there is a strong antireligious spirit in French society that has only grown since the French Revolution. Second, there is an element of anti-Americanism in the French anticult war. As Larry Witham of the *Washington Times* has stated: 'Before the French Senate passed its version of the legislation on May 3, one popular journal called the growing presence

46 Robinson.

47 An English translation of the French Anti-Cult Law, 30 May 2001, has been posted by the Center for Studies on New Religions at www.cesnur.org/2001fr_law_en.htm [.] The official French version is posted at www.cesnur.org/2001/fr_mayo4.htm [.]

48 Robinson.

of groups such as Baptists, Adventists and Jehovah's Witnesses an American "Trojan horse" invading France.'[49] Representatives of the U.S. State Department and Commission on Security and Cooperation in Europe (the Helsinki Commission) 'who have protested the law have been called secret agents of Scientology by the French media.' According to U.S. Congressman Christopher H. Smith, 'overtures to French diplomats over the anti-sect law provoke "resentment."' Smith should know: in Bucharest, Romania, in 2000, when he suggested that the French anticult law would encourage former Communist countries in Eastern Europe to suppress religious freedom, French delegates at the Helsinki Accord hearings actually hissed at him.[50] Yet such behaviour is uncharacteristic: most American protests over the law are shrugged off with Gallic disdain. The French – and for that matter most Europeans – pay no more attention to American complaints about the suppression of religious liberties in Europe than Americans do about European criticisms of capital punishment in the United States.

Although they have not recently experienced the same severe treatment in Germany as they have in France, Jehovah's Witnesses have had problems there as well. In 1993 the *Land* (state) government of Berlin refused to classify them as a 'corporation of public rights' like other religious bodies. In 1997 the Federal Administrative Court in Berlin upheld this decision. The reason given was that Jehovah's Witnesses refused to allow their members to vote in elections and thereby undermined the legitimacy of the state. The Witnesses appealed the matter to the Federal Constitutional Court of Germany, which on 19 December 2000 decided that the Federal Administrative Court's decision was unsatisfactory. But the Witnesses' victory was not complete. A 2001 U.S. Department of State report on religious freedom in Germany makes the following comment:

> Jehovah's Witnesses appealed to the Constitutional Court a 1993 decision of the Berlin State government that had denied the church public law corporation status. In 1997 the Federal Administrative Court in Berlin had upheld the Berlin State Government's decision. The Court concluded that the

49 Larry Witham, 'Probe Urged on French Sect List,' *Washington Times*, 25 May 2001. Posted by the Center for Studies on New Religions at www.cesnur.org2001/fr_may25.htm [.]

50 Ibid.

group did not offer the 'indispensable loyalty' towards the democratic state 'essential for lasting cooperation' because it forbade its members from participating in public elections. The group does enjoy the basic tax-exempt status afforded to most religious organizations. On December 19, 2000, the Constitutional Court found in favor of Jehovah's Witnesses, remanding the case back to the Federal Administrative Court in Berlin. For the first time, the Constitutional Court had examined the conditions for granting the status of a public law corporation and found that for reasons of the separation of church and state, 'loyalty to the state' cannot be a condition imposed on religious communities. The Constitutional Court tempered the victory for Jehovah's Witnesses by instructing the Berlin Administrative Court to examine whether Jehovah's Witnesses use coercive methods to prevent their members from leaving the congregation and whether their child-rearing practices conform to the country's human rights standards. The case had not been resolved by the end of the period covered by this report.

In Eastern Europe the situation is somewhat different, but various North American religions – especially Jehovah's Witnesses – suffer harassment and persecution there as well. After the fall of communism in the nations of Eastern Europe and the former Soviet Union, the peoples of those countries were allowed a great deal of religious freedom. In most countries where Roman Catholicism and Protestantism are dominant, that remains the case today. The same is not always true where Orthodox churches are entrenched, for churches of that faith have little respect for religious toleration or religious freedom.[51] As a result, Jehovah's Witnesses – who in recent years have grown at a much faster rate in the countries of the old Soviet Union than in Western Europe or even the former communist countries of Eastern Europe – have experienced mob violence and other forms of direct persecution in places like Armenia and Georgia.[52] In Moscow, as distinct from

51 This has been the experience of Jehovah's Witnesses in Greece and is becoming evident in other Eastern Orthodox countries. Even Roman Catholicism has suffered discrimination in Russia as a result of Orthodox opposition. See 'Hostile Times,' *Time*, 13 May 2002, 25.

52 The year 2000 U.S. State Department report on religious freedom in Armenia states: 'A religious organization that has been refused registration may not publish newspapers or magazines, rent meeting places, broadcast programs on television or radio, or officially sponsor the visas of visitors. No previously registered religious group seeking reregistration under the 1997 law has been denied. However, the

Russia as a whole, they have recently been banned.[53] Moscow prosecutors have attacked them for public proselytizing and have evidently been successful in having them designated as an antisocial cult.

Following long tradition, the Witnesses wherever possible have used every legal means at their disposal to win the right to practise their religion freely. In France they have acted boldly against the French government's efforts to tax them out of existence. They have appealed to the courts in that country, and they have also denounced vehemently the government's actions against them. For example, on 1 July 1998 they organized a demonstration near the Palais de Chaillot at the Esplanade of Human Rights during which Witnesses from fifteen European Union countries protested the French government's tax on their organization. The late Lyman Swingle, then a member of the Governing Body of Jehovah's Witnesses, said: 'If taxes are owed, the religious organization should pay. However, if our religion is targeted unfairly and illegally for exorbitant taxes, then it has a right to protest ... When the law grants exemption from taxes to religious organizations and that exemption is allowed to the two largest Christian religions in the country but withheld from the third largest Christian religion, then we feel that something is seriously wrong.' In an open letter to French president Jacques Chirac, Swingle also stated: 'The ability to practice religion freely is a basic human right, supported by the United Nations Universal Declaration of Human Rights, the European Convention on Human Rights, and the Constitution of the French Republic. Yet the tax authority believes it has the right to use its power of taxation arbitrarily to restrict some religions but not others.' On 5 July 1998 the Witnesses took out a full-page advertisement on the matter in the *New York Times*; three days later they took out another in the

---

Council still denies registration to Jehovah's Witnesses.' A similar year 2000 State Department report on Georgia states: 'Some nationalist politicians continue to use the views and the institution of the Georgian Orthodox Church as their platform, and criticized some Protestant groups, especially evangelical groups, as subversive. Jehovah's Witnesses in particular are the subject of attacks from such politicians.' Recently, there have been reports of violence against Jehovah's Witnesses in Georgia. For details of events in Georgia, see the *2002 Yearbook of Jehovah's Witnesses*, 14.

53 A recent Associated Press report by Maria Danilova states: 'Reflecting increased pressure on religious minorities in a country dominated by the Russian Orthodox Church, a Moscow court Wednesday [16 June 2004] upheld a ban on activities of Jehovah's Witnesses in the capital.' According to that report, there are some ten thousand Witnesses in the Russian capital.

International Herald Tribune. In these they accused the French government of 'a shocking display of religious discrimination.'[54]

A year later the Witnesses took their case to the European Parliament. CNN News gave the following information on 23 June 1999:

> Strasbourg, France (Reuters) – About 5,000 Jehovah's Witnesses marched in the northern French city of Strasbourg on Friday to protest the French government's attitude toward the Christian sect and its 250,000 members in France.
>
> Church representatives delivered letters to the European Parliament and the Council of Europe urging respect for freedom of religion in Europe and denouncing France's 'campaign of denigration and fiscal discrimination' aimed at the sect.
>
> French authorities have refused to grant the church tax-exempt status, arguing it is a cult rather than a religion. Church officials say the authorities are seeking $48 million in back taxes.
>
> In January 1996, a special commission of the French parliament included the church in a list of religious cults in the country.
>
> The government has since set up a panel to monitor cults, which became a hot issue following the grisly deaths of 16 members of the secretive Order of the Solar Temple in Southeastern France in December 1995.
>
> Jehovah's Witnesses, who are barred by church rules from political activities, military conscription and accepting blood transfusions, insist that they want only to be treated by the authorities in the same way as other Christian religions.
>
> Church members took to the streets in cities and towns across the country in January to distribute 12 million pamphlets accusing the state of trying to dupe the French people by grouping the church with dangerous cults.
>
> The church has operated in France since 1900.

That Jehovah's Witnesses are victims of both antireligious and religious bigotry in Europe and some other parts of the world cannot be denied. It is therefore not surprising that they should attempt to use their sufferings under the Third Reich as a means of arguing that their present-day adversaries are following in the footsteps of Hitler and his Nazi Party. This helps them deflect persecution, especially in Germany. As the *Kölner Stadt-Anzeiger* has stated: 'The Jehovah's Witnesses still have a special something in Germany. By virtue of their

54 Robinson.

fate under National Socialism they have acquired a moral nimbus which makes it difficult on critics today.'[55] But in focusing on their past, they fail to recognize that their 'collective memory' is often as 'ahistorical and antihistorical' as that of members of the Jewish community whom Novick discusses. Furthermore, they refuse to recognize that there are legitimate grievances against them and that their history is not as pure as they like to claim.

Nothing demonstrates more clearly how the Witnesses' view of the past is distorted by the present than Wolfram Slupina's article, 'Persecuted and Almost Forgotten.' Since 1996 Slupina has been in charge of the German Watch Tower Society's public affairs division for schools, education, and memorials for Holocaust victims. He starts his essay with a bold statement that is patently false. He says: 'The National Socialists cruelly persecuted Jehovah's Witnesses without mercy. Using an extremely sophisticated killing machine, they attempted to consign the Witnesses to oblivion by systematically exterminating them. Despite their political neutrality, Jehovah's Witnesses were among the first to be banned and persecuted by the Nazis, who came to power in 1933. Their fate could historically be compared to the Holocaust of the Jews.'[56]

Abundant evidence shows that the Nazis did not want *to exterminate* Jehovah's Witnesses. Rather, they wanted to break their opposition to the values of the Third Reich and turn them into loyal German citizens. Since most Witnesses were ordinary Germans, they were not slated for death in the way that the Jews were. Severe as their plight was – and that plight should not be understated – it was not as bad as that of the Jews and cannot rightly be compared to 'the Holocaust of the Jews.' Regarding this matter, even a fellow Jehovah's Witness, Jolene Chu, disagrees with Slupina: 'Capitulation, not annihilation, seems to have been the Nazi goal for the Witnesses, despite the fact that Hitler had declared about them in 1934, "This brood will be exterminated!" The Gestapo and SS applied the usual torture methods, and in the process hundreds of Witnesses died. But a clue as to the Nazi aim of breaking the Witness resolve is found in a remarkable document offered repeatedly to Witness prisoners – a renunciation of their faith and a pledge of loyalty to the fatherland.'[57]

55 Quoted at www.cisar.org/000921a.htm [.]

56 Wolfram Slupina, 'Persecuted and Almost Forgotten,' in Hesse, 266.

57 Jolene Chu, 'Purple Triangles: A Story of Spiritual Resistance.' Published originally in *Judaism Today* 12 (Spring 1999), 15–19, and posted with the permission of the

After his brief and inaccurate preamble, Slupina goes on for a page and a half bemoaning the fact that the Witnesses have been 'intentionally ignored' since the few years immediately following the Second World War. He uses this problematic thesis to assert that just as the churches brought pressure on *Land* governments and that of the Reich to ban them in the 1920s, they are doing the same thing today. Then he moves into a discussion of Kurt-Hellmuth Eimuth, sect expert of the Protestant Church in Hesse and Nassau, and of the Parliament-appointed Enquete Commission on 'so called Sects and Psychogroups.' From that discussion, he argues that Eimuth and others of his ilk have been working to outlaw Jehovah's Witnesses in the same way that the Nazis ultimately did. In support of that assessment, he quotes Einmuth as saying that Jehovah's Witnesses are an anticonstitutional organization and gives an overview of the court cases that the Witnesses have fought to obtain corporate status.

Slupina is unfair in his analysis. Conditions in Germany are far different today from what they were in the 1920s and during the Third Reich. During those earlier years most clergy truly did want to see the Witnesses outlawed; but today that is not the case. It is true, as he claims, that the activities of anticultists have given the Witnesses somewhat of a bad press, and that there have been scattered acts of violence against individual Witnesses and Witness property; this does not mean they are in great danger in contemporary Germany. Undoubtedly Slupina recognizes that assuming victim status and jumping on the Holocaust bandwagon – even if it requires shading the truth – is a good way to don the halo of martyrdom and to stop adversaries in their tracks.[58]

Commenting on the Witnesses' efforts to improve their social reputation, Detlef Garbe says:

> It is a well known phenomenon, and appropriately frequently deplored, that present disputes are often fought out in interpretations of the past. Reference to the suffering experienced by Jehovah's Witnesses in Hitler's Germany because of their loyalty to their convictions and the boldness with which they confronted the regime, can in today's Germany – sensitized to the subject of Nazi persecution – influence how Jehovah's Witnesses are perceived, despite the existence of negative prejudices. The Watch Tower

---

editors at www.baycrest.org [.] The comment quoted above appears on page 5 of Chu's website article.

58 Slupina, 266–78.

> Society is not unfamiliar with the tendency of other groups to use the history of resistance for self-description, or of the early apologetic writing of the history of the 'church struggle' that was not free from this inclination.[59]

Of course, the Witnesses use other themes besides accounts of their past sufferings to try to protect themselves from real or perceived discrimination and persecution. For example, the 8 January 1999 *Awake!* published a series of articles promoting the idea of religious toleration. In these, the Witness magazine criticized Israel, France, and other countries for religious intolerance and discrimination. In one article, 'Religious Freedom Blessing or Curse?' *Awake!* stated: 'The debate over public and private liberties has been thrust to the fore by the media. Allegations of brainwashing, financial extortion, child abuse, and a host of other serious crimes have been directed against some religious groups, often without any substantial proof. News stories involving minority religious groups have received widespread coverage by the press. Disparaging labels such as "cult" or "sect" have now become a part of everyday usage. Under pressure from public opinion, governments have even produced lists of so-called dangerous cults.' The article then took direct aim at France: 'France is a country proud of its tradition of tolerance and separation of religion and the State. It proudly proclaims itself the land of "Liberty, Equality, Fraternity." Yet, according to the book Freedom of Religion and Belief – A World Report, "an education campaign in schools to foster rejection of new religious movements" has been recommended in that country. Many people think, however, that this type of action poses a threat to religious freedom.'[60]

After making the above fair comment, *Awake!* offered a series of quotes from a number of inadequately documented sources to show how wonderful Jehovah's Witnesses are. According to these quotes, taken from Sergio Albesano of Italy, a Belgian parliamentary deputy, the German newspaper *Sindelfinger Zeitung*, the *San Francisco Examiner*, the *American Ethnologist*, Dr Bryan Wilson, and Professor C.S. Braden, Jehovah's Witnesses are 'model citizens' and paragons of virtue. They pay their taxes on time, are remarkably honest, have stronger marriages than most, contribute to religious liberty, and present no threat to the secular state. Thus the whole article became one of

59 Detlef Garbe, 'Social Disinterest, Government Disinformation, Religious Persecution, and Now Manipulation of History?' in Hesse, 258–9.
60 Page 7.

special pleading rather than a true statement of principles in defence of religious freedom.

In another article, 'Protecting Freedoms, *How?*' the 8 January 1999 *Awake!* gave its definition of religious tolerance and asserted that it is important:

> Tolerance does not mean that everyone should have the same ideas. People might disagree with one another. Some may feel strongly that the beliefs of another person are very wrong. They may even speak publicly of their disagreements. However, as long as they do not spread lies to try to incite prejudice, this is not intolerance. Intolerance is seen when a group is persecuted, targeted by special laws, marginalized, banned, or in some other way hindered from following their beliefs. In the most extreme form of intolerance, some kill and others have to die for their beliefs.[61]

The same article also asserted:

> Jehovah's Witnesses have found that an excellent way to promote tolerance is to talk with others of different beliefs. The Witnesses take seriously Jesus' prophecy that 'this good news of the kingdom will be preached in all the inhabited earth for a witness to all nations,' and they are well-known for their public evangelizing ministry. (Matthew 24:14) In this work, they have the opportunity to hear people of many different religions – as well as atheists – explain their beliefs. In turn the Witnesses are prepared to explain their own beliefs to those who wish to listen. Thus they promote growth in understanding and knowledge. Such knowledge and understanding make it easier for tolerance to flourish.[62]

'Protecting Freedoms, *How?*' invokes UN statements and the Universal Declaration of Human Rights in defence of tolerance and religious freedom – something seemingly strange in view of the Witnesses' long-standing assertion that the UN is the 'image' of the 'wild beast' of the Apocalypse.[63] This may not be as serious, however, as its

61 Page 11.

62 Page 12.

63 Despite the fact that the New York Watchtower Society had been affiliated with the United Nations for some years a Non-governmental Organization (NGO), *The Watchtower* of 15 November 2001 published the following statement about Jehovah's Witnesses: 'Anointed Christians are like alien residents living in tents apart from this system of things. (1 Peter 2:11) "Not even a plague draws near their tent."

self-serving statements about tolerance. Speaking for the Governing Body of Jehovah's Witnesses, *Awake!* demands that Witnesses be extended the right to question and severely criticize other religions' teachings, and complains about the suppression of Jehovah's Witnesses by secular and religious authorities. However, it fails to note that the Watch Tower hierarchy has no qualms about suppressing freedom of speech and association within the Witness community.

Awake! editor James N. Pellechia plays on the theme of tolerance. In an article called 'Teaching Tolerance: A Case Study,' he quotes Detlef Garbe about the Witnesses not regarding 'the Jews as being of less merit simply because of their origin.' He goes on to argue that because the Witnesses were not racists, they were not anti-Semitic: 'Witness doctrine and practice stood in sharp contrast to the strong antisemitic tradition of many churches. The Witnesses' beliefs immunized them against racist indoctrination. Their belief in the brotherhood of man translated into concrete acts of altruism. Historian Christine King cited sources about assistance to Jews.'[64]

In these remarks, Pellechia is no more candid than the magazine he edits. Like Johannes Wrobel and Detlef Garbe, he denies that the Witnesses were ever anti-Semitic. He fails to recognize that Christine King has stated in print that there were times when the Witnesses were less than kind to the Jews in concentration camps and that during their persecution under the Nazis they regarded the Jews as 'Christ killers.'[65]

Watch Tower leaders almost never admit their or their movement's past mistakes, nor do they admit to the harm caused by the totalitarian nature of their organization. Never do Watch Tower publications or Witness spokespeople mention that for an individual Witness to question Watch Tower teachings is regarded as apostasy, no matter how distorted or opaque some of those teachings may be. Never do

---

Whether our hope is heavenly or earthly, we are not part of the world, and we are not infected by such spiritually deadly plagues as its immorality, materialism, false religion, and worship of the "wild beast" and its "image," the United Nations.' See also *Babylon the Great Has Fallen: God's Kingdom Rules* (Brooklyn, NY: Watchtower Society and IBSA, 1963), 580–1.

64 James N. Pellechia, 'Teaching Tolerance : A Case Study,' in Hans Hesse, ed. *Persecution and Resistance during the Nazi Regime 1933–1945* (Bremen: Edition Temen, 2001), 375.

65 Christine King, 'Jehovah's Witnesses under Nazism,' in Michael Bernenbaum, ed., *A Mosaic of Victims: Non-Jews Persecuted and Murdered by the Nazis* (New York and London: New York University Press, 1990, 192.

they state that for a Witness to obtain or read the writings of so-called apostates is an offence that often brings down disfellowshipment. Never do they permit Witnesses in good standing to talk to or even to greet their former brethren who have been disfellowshipped or who have voluntarily 'disassociated' themselves from the Witness community. And never do they pay any attention to the fact that because of these policies, many marriages and families have been broken up, and many individuals have suffered nervous breakdowns, and some people have committed suicide.

The terrible effects of the Watch Tower practice of shunning are detailed in James Kostelniuk's autobiographical account, *Wolves among Sheep*.[66] In that book he relates how his first wife divorced him and attempted to deny him contact with their children because he had left the Witness movement. Then, when she and the children were murdered by her second husband, a Jehovah's Witness, Kostelniuk and his present wife were shunned completely by his former brethren at his own children's funeral. Kostelniuk relates with pain what happened:

> We had looked forward to attending a memorial for Kim [his first wife] and the children that was being held in a large Kingdom Hall in Burnaby [British Columbia]. However, when we arrived at the service with our relatives and some old friends from Vancouver – none of whom was a Jehovah's Witness – we were completely unprepared for the callous and inhumane reception from those present.
>
> Soon after taking our seats at the back of the auditorium, it became clear that the Witness rule against association would not be waived even in a situation such as this. Former friends and relatives – even my father's brother, who had phoned me just the night before to offer his condolences – refused to acknowledge us publicly. Witness after Witness refused to meet my gaze or return my greeting.
>
> The speaker began reading a list of surviving relatives – a list from which my own name was conspicuously absent – and referred to my children throughout the service as Juri and Lindsay Anderson [the name of their stepfather who had murdered them]. A twenty-five-minute eulogy followed, in which Kim and the children were described as 'faithful servants of Jehovah God' and assured of a resurrection. At no point was the manner of their deaths – and at whose hands they died – ever mentioned.[67]

66 Kostelniuk, *Wolves among Sheep* (Toronto: HarperCollins, 2000).
67 Ibid., 108–9.

What happened to Kostelniuk is an extreme case, yet it is because of the cruel practice of shunning – which has been repeated many thousands of times – that it could happen at all. It is because of that practice that many former Witnesses heap bitter criticism on the Witness community and especially its leaders.

Why, then, are certain academics, some of whom are outstanding scholars, so willing to defend Jehovah's Witnesses' historical record and deny their faults, both past and present? One answer is that despite the duplicity of Watch Tower leaders in both Germany and the United States in 1933 and thereafter, the Witnesses did have a better record of opposing Nazism than any significant, organized religion in the Third Reich. Perhaps only some very small groups such as independent Bible Students, Reformed Adventists, and Quakers have as good or better record, but at the time their numbers were minuscule. This is only one factor, however, that has caused and is causing certain historians and other scholars to excuse what Rutherford, Harbeck, and Watch Tower officials at Magdeburg did that was less than noble during the early days of Nazi rule. Another is that like the Jews, the Witnesses have been able to claim past victim status during the Holocaust and in communist Eastern Europe following the Second World War. They proclaim that they were willing martyrs in a way that almost no other victims of the Holocaust or communism were. They can and do honestly claim to be under attack by some within the churches, the anticult movement, and certain governments. They are marginalized; and in the eyes of many academics today that is reason enough to come to their defence and excuse anything they have done or are doing.

Speaking about this tendency in the academic world, Benjamin Beit-Hallahmi shows just how far it has gone. In response to the anticult crusade, scholars of new religious movements (NRMs) have reached the point where they excuse practically anything done by any group that claims to be such a movement. Beit-Hallahmi tells us that four American scholars arrived in Japan to defend Aum Shinrikyo after some of its members released poison gas in a Tokyo subway, killing twelve commuters. He notes that later, despite clear evidence to the contrary, one of them went so far as to state that it was not Aum Shinrikyo but rather North Korean agents who were responsible for this dastardly crime.[68] Elsewhere in the same article, Beit-Hallahmi

68 Benjamin Beit-Hallahmi, '"O Truant Muse": Collaborationism and Research Integrity,' in Zablocki and Robbins, 35–7.

writes: 'NRM researchers give all groups claiming the religion label their imprimatur, and it is quite interesting to note that no group has ever been refused this seal of approval. As far as I know, there never has been a case where a claim to be recognized as an NRM was rejected by scholars. The one axiom uniting all researchers (at least publicly) is that all groups that claim to be NRMs are indeed NRMs.'[69] Earlier, he states: 'In recent years, the NRM research community displayed a general agreement on a hierarchy of credibility ... according to which self-presentation by NRMs was epistemologically and logically superior to all outside accounts and observations. The NRM research community will give more credence to the claims of NRM members and leaders than to claims by former members, outside observers (e.g., the media), government officials (especially law-enforcement officials).'[70]

Beit-Hallahmi is not exaggerating. This is shown by comments on 'apostates' made by three well-known scholars who defend new religions. The first of these, Lonnie Kliever, is chairman of the Department of Religion at Southern Methodist University in Dallas, Texas. Writing at the behest of the Church of Scientology, he asserts that 'neither the quietly appreciative former member nor the vocally aggrieved apostate from a new religious movement can be taken as an objective and authoritative interpreter of the religious movement to which he or she formerly belonged.' He adds that jurists, journalists, and scholars should view the apostate 'as an individual who is predisposed to render a biased account of the religious beliefs and practices of his or her former religious associations and activities.'[71] J. Gordon Melton, author of the *Encyclopedia of American Religions* and one of the four new-religions scholars who went to Japan to defend Aum Shinrikyo, is equally outspoken about apostates: 'To put it bluntly, hostile ex-members invariably shade the truth. They invariably blow out of proportion minor incidents and turn them into major incidents, and over a period of time their testimony almost always changes because each time they tell it they get the feedback of acceptance or rejection from those to whom they tell it, and hence it will be devel-

69 Ibid., 56.
70 Ibid., 39.
71 Kliever's article, 'The Reliability of Apostate Testimony about New Religious Movements,' may be found at www.religiousfreedomwatch.org/experts/apostates/kliever/kliever.html [.]

oped and merged into a different world view that they are adopting.'[72] Bryan Wilson, a world-renowned sociologist and Oxford University Emeritus Fellow, says much the same thing. In a paper titled 'Apostates and New Religious Movements,' he remarks:

> Neither the objective sociological researcher nor the court of law can readily regard the apostate as a creditable or reliable source of evidence. He must always be seen as one whose personal history predisposes him to bias with respect to both his previous religious commitment and affiliations, the suspicion must arise that he acts from a personal motivation to vindicate himself and to regain his self-esteem, by showing himself to have been first a victim but subsequently to have become a redeemed crusader. As various instances have indicated, he is likely to be suggestible and ready to enlarge or embellish his grievances to satisfy that species of journalist who is more interested in sensational copy than in objective statement of the truth.[73]

It may well be true that what Kliever, Melton, and Wilson say is correct about *certain* apostates, but it is difficult if not impossible to believe that their generalizations are true of *all* apostates. Ray Mattera comments on this matter with regard to Kliever's article:

> The sweeping nature of these assertions is extraordinary. Unfortunately, this essay illustrates a recurrent tendency among some sociologists who study non-conventional religions. Many accept the testimony of current members of radical groups uncritically, but treat the testimony of dissident members as fictitious or false. Many of these scholars naively assume that members in good standing of radical movements can, without further ado, be trusted to give an accurate and unbiased account of life in their respective groups. However, that assumption is extremely dubious; it betrays an ignorance of the social dynamics and pressures that undergird life in many radical religious movements.

Mattera goes on to point out that 'in most religious affiliations, open discussion, even debate, regarding matters of belief and practice is common. But in radical religious movements such dialogue rarely, if ever, takes place.'[74]

72 Melton's statement can be found at www.contendingforthefaith.com/summary/experts/melton.htm [.]

73 For the full text of Wilson's article, visit newreligion.on.ca/ENG/Wilson [.]

74 Based on an unpublished article that the author has kindly allowed me to review and quote.

It should also be noted that apostates – individuals who have broken from a great variety of religions – come from many ethnic and social backgrounds, different educational levels, and both sexes. So to lump them together and assert that all lack objectivity and honesty, and that what they say is uniformly doubtful, begs credulity, and common sense. Especially is this so since not one of the three academics just quoted has produced any solid 'scientific data' to back up such sweeping claims about apostates. Furthermore, it must be asked: Can anyone trust the testimony of men who have given themselves so wholeheartedly and unreservedly to the defence of so-called new religions as have Kliever, Melton, and Wilson? Are their assertions that apostates are necessarily biased perhaps not a case of big pots calling little kettles black?

Certainly, what apostates have to say cannot always be trusted to be fair or reasonably objective; that is obvious. But that does not excuse attempts on the part of certain independent scholars – in particular Detlef Garbe, Christine King, and Gabriele Yonan – to deny some of the darker aspects of Witness history and acts that were clearly disreputable. Detlef Garbe does see that the Witnesses were not always heroes in their opposition to Nazism, but he is too willing to excuse certain aspects of their behaviour, especially their anti-Semitism. He also attempts to enhance the specious assertion that Jehovah's Witnesses have been 'forgotten victims,' and he has been less than willing to respond to criticisms of his works by former Witnesses. Very seriously, he has also been less than careful in evaluating what Konrad Franke had said about the 1933 Berlin-Wilmersdorf Watch Tower convention – something that has permitted Johannes Wrobel unjustifiably to attack my article in *The Christian Quest.* In most respects Christine King's published scholarship respecting the Witnesses is sound; however, her remarks in the 'stand Fast' video make her look more than a little foolish. She seems to have been carried away by an almost schoolgirl enthusiasm for the Witnesses by being interviewed for the video. As for Gabriele Yonan, her publications can be discounted almost entirely, at least insofar as they deal with the Witnesses under the Third Reich. Although her *Jehovas Zeugen: Opfer unter zwei deutschen Diktaturen* evidently became a bestseller among German-speaking Jehovah's Witnesses, and it demonstrates how the Witnesses have rather successfully used their Holocaust experience to blunt attacks by anticultists in Germany,[75] it – and her articles on the Witnesses – are

75 See Gabriele Yonan, *Jehovas Zeugen: Opfer unter zwei deutschen Diktaturen: 1933–45;*

extremely naive. To deny that the 1933 Berlin-Wilmersdorf *Declaration of Facts* did not represent an attempt to ingratiate Jehovah's Witnesses with the Nazis and that it was not anti-Semitic shows that Yonan is an apologist rather than an objective historian. Like Kliever, Melton, and Wilson (quoted earlier), Garbe and King sometimes lack critical judgment, and it seems that the lack thereof is Yonan's stock in trade.

John Locke stated: 'Truth, whether in or out of fashion, is the measure of knowledge, and the business of understanding; whatsoever is beside that, however authorized by consent, or recommended by rarity, is nothing but ignorance, or something worse.' That is something that both Jehovah's Witnesses and many of their academic defenders need to learn. For only by absolute honesty can a religious organization, whether it be the Roman Catholic Church, the great Protestant churches, or a sectarian movement like Jehovah's Witnesses, reform itself and reflect the integrity of that gentle Jew, Jesus of Nazareth.

1949–1989 (Berlin: Numinos, 1999), 125–32, and also John Conway's 18 June 1999 review of this book at the Jehovah's Witnesses United website jehovah.to/general/nazi/yonan.htm [.]

Conclusion

There can be no doubt that despite the understandable weakness of some, most German Jehovah's Witnesses stood firm against Nazism during the years 1933 to 1945. That they suffered terribly and with great bravery is beyond question. However, while boasting about their faithfulness and making much of their martyrdom, neither the Watch Tower Society nor Witness apologists provide a complete picture of why they were persecuted or how they behaved under persecution. Jehovah's Witnesses make much of their victimhood under the Third Reich, yet they conveniently ignore a number of facts.

The Witnesses fail to recognize that they themselves were in part responsible for their sufferings. No movement can constantly heap insults on all other religions, the business community, and national governments in the way that the Bible Student–Jehovah's Witnesses did from 1918 onward without provoking a reaction – a reaction had already begun under the democratic Weimar Republic. Long before Hitler came to power, Judge J.F. Rutherford had made them hated by the vast majority of Germans through his and *Das Goldene Zeitalter*'s venom-filled printed diatribes. As Dietrich Hellmund points out, the Witnesses would inevitably have become victims of Nazism, but that persecution might have been delayed and been less severe had it not been for the Witnesses' incredible public militancy.[1]

1 Dietrich Hellmund, 'Critical Reflection on the Video Documentary "Stand Firm against Nazi Assault": Propaganda or Historical Documentation,' in Hans Hesse, ed., *Persecution and Resistance of Jehovah's Witnesses during the Nazi-Regime 1933–1945* (Bremen: Edition Temmen, 2001), 344.

Also, try as the Witnesses and their apologists may to deny it, the record is clear that during the summer of 1933, Watch Tower leaders at all levels attempted to ingratiate their movement with the Nazis by attacking Great Britain, the United States, the League of Nations, the churches, and above all the Jews. The assertion that the Witnesses did not endeavour to scapegoat the Jews and that they were not anti-Semitic – at least from a religious standpoint – simply does not hold up to sober analysis. Furthermore, as Hellmund indicates, it is shocking that the Watch Tower has never apologized for the 1946 statement in the first edition of *'Let God Be True'* that blamed the Jews for their own sufferings.[2]

After the Nazis refused to accept Watch Tower blandishments in 1933, Rutherford began a propaganda war against them that brought terrible persecution on the German Witness community. It would have been reasonable for the Watch Tower Society to publicize what was happening in the Reich in other countries, but to demand that German Witnesses go from door to door with Watch Tower publications and phonographs while under ban was madness. So too was the policy of calling on them to distribute one inflammatory, antiregime broadside leaflet after another. Policies like these led directly to the arrest and imprisonment of many Witnesses who might otherwise have avoided such direct persecution and to the deaths of many of them. Although they felt it necessary to carry on their preaching activities under the ban, they could have done so more quietly, with greater stealth and more common sense. But Rutherford would not have it that way, and he deserves the harshest criticism for driving his German brethren into prisons and concentration camps while he lived like a prince at Beth-Sarim, his California House of the Princes.

From another standpoint, Watch Tower spokespeople place too much emphasis on Witness unity and mutual support as reasons why they survived in greater proportion than other groups in Nazi concentration camps. Unity and mutual support were important factors, but others were more significant. The Nazis did not want to kill all Jehovah's Witnesses; they simply wanted to break their resistance to National Socialism. The Witnesses were not candidates for destruction in the way that Jews, Gypsies, and homosexuals were. Almost none were gassed. More important, during the last three years of the Second World War, they became very useful to the SS. Guards often

2 Ibid., 347.

employed them as workers in their homes and on various projects under greatly improved conditions. Because of this, many survived who otherwise might not have.

Witness historian Jolene Chu writes: 'Some have interpreted the consistent conduct of Jehovah's Witnesses as a response to totalitarian peer pressure from within the religious community. Arguing against this interpretation is the fact that similar conscientious decisions, such as the decision not to sign the declaration [to abjure their faith], were made by Witnesses whether they were in isolation or in a peer group.'[3] But Chu does not document her case, and there is a good deal of evidence to show that peer pressure *was very significant in keeping Witnesses from defecting from their faith.* Rudolf Höss makes this very clear. There is evidence that when isolated in prisons rather than collected in concentration camps, a significant number did defect.

Witness propaganda about other religious groups is also less than objective. The Watch Tower Society has ignored completely the role of independent Bible Students, who also suffered under the Nazis and whose members wore the purple triangle along with Rutherford's loyalists.[4] While it is true that the major churches in Germany did compromise with Nazism to a great extent, the Witnesses fail to give any significant credit to Protestant and Catholic clergy who opposed Hitler on principle and who suffered for their stand. Simone Arnold Liebster tells us: 'Dad often spoke of the many Catholic priests in Dachau; he had many good conversations with them. One had told him, "You *Bibelforscher*, you are in camp because of the first commandment. We priests are here because of the second. We gave bread to prisoners, helped some Jews, or said something against the Party." They had truly acted like the first Christians, choosing to face the lions rather than surrender their loyalty to God.'[5] Sadly, Madame Liebster is one of the few Jehovah's Witnesses to admit that there were Catholic martyrs under the Third Reich. In general, the Witnesses have been unfair not only to Catholic clergy but also to the Catholic Church as a whole in claiming that it was directly responsible for the rise and practices of Nazism. True, the Vatican and many segments of the German Catholic Church may have gone too far in trying to accommodate Hitler, but

3 Jolene Chu, 'From Marginalization to Martyrdom,' in Hesse, 370.

4 Hellmund, 345.

5 Simone Arnold Liebster, *Facing the Lion: Memoirs of a Young Girl in Nazi Europe* (New Orleans: Grammaton Press, 2000), 352.

that did not make them sponsors of the *Führer* and his National Socialist followers. Nazism had its own totally non-Christian philosophy.

In effect, then, Witness historical accounts of their role under the Third Reich are a mixture of fact and fiction. Despite loud protestations to the contrary, their printed publications and 'Stand Fast' video are more self-serving propaganda than anything like objective history. Jehovah's Witnesses are of course not alone in producing such materials or in writing hagiographies for their members, but few Christian communities in the west are as unwilling as the Witnesses to admit their faults. For many years they refused to cooperate in any way with independent researchers. It is true that the Society has recently established archives in Germany to promote Witness history, and in a recent statement, Johannes Wrobel has boasted about its usefulness.[6] Although it is possible to obtain some documents on request from those archives, they are not open to the public. The people who run them are selective about what they will release. Like the Brooklyn headquarters of the Watch Tower Society itself, they do their best to keep documents that are not flattering to the Witness movement or its leaders away from those whom they regard as apostates. As far as the American archives of the Watch Tower Society in Brooklyn are concerned, they remain closed. Unfortunately, they were not catalogued properly for many years and as a result many materials have been misplaced or lost.[7] So it is evident that the Witnesses have little appreciation even for their own history – something they write about in a way that serves their present purposes, with little attention paid to unflattering documentary evidence.

6 Wrobel's statement, 'How the Watchtower History Archive in Germany Benefits Holocaust Research,' is posted at www.jw-russia.org/eng/history/holocaust%20may97wrobel-E.htm [.] In his remarks there, Wrobel tries to connect Witness persecution with that of the Jews and to imply that the Witnesses were always supportive of the Jews.

7 As a Jehovah's Witness in good standing, I did research in the Canadian and British Watch Tower archives in the 1970s and know how poorly kept they were then. I was treated graciously by both Canadian and British Watch Tower officials, but the situation was quite different when I went to Brooklyn. It was evident that the Society's senior officers had no interest in my research, and Nathan Knorr manifested some hostility. In more recent years, Barbara Anderson, a former American Bethel worker who did research for *Jehovah's Witnesses: Proclaimers of God's Kingdom,* has confirmed that little has changed there and that the American Witness archives are still not properly catalogued.

Some scholars, notably in Germany, feel that the Witnesses have become somewhat more open about their history in recent years, but this really does not seem to be the case. Their last major attempt to produce a history of their movement is nothing short of a disgrace that hides more than it reveals. Badly organized and badly written, *Jehovah's Witnesses: Proclaimers of God's Kingdom* is more hagiographa – or, perhaps better stated, hagiolatry – than history. Also, from the continuing efforts of the Watch Tower to hide embarrassing facts about Witness conduct under the Third Reich, it can be said that any supposed openness is purely for tactical reasons, to gain more sympathy from academics. It has nothing to do with a desire to see reasonably objective history written.

Why, then, do Jehovah's Witnesses continue to maintain such a façade concerning their past and many of their present activities? The answer is twofold. First, they regard themselves as Jehovah's chosen people, who have and hold the truth. Thus, anything that seems to question their supposedly unique status is seen as a threat to the very nature of their organizational hierarchy and movement. For this reason they refuse to listen to any internal criticism, and they try to shelter themselves from attacks from without. If they should be forced to admit openly to their many actions that were, clearly, attempts to compromise with the world, they would be seen by many of their members as no better than the churches of Christendom; and that would make them a part of 'Babylon the Great, the world empire of false religion.' Second, because Watch Tower leaders cannot be unaware of many of the historical facts brought out in this work and the weakness of their eschatology – on which their entire supposedly 'theocratic structure' is based – they suffer from extreme paranoia. As a consequence, their approach to history is largely one devoted to stonewalling. Sadly, a movement whose members customarily call it 'the Truth' has for many years adopted the technique of the Big Lie.

APPENDIX A
Background Chronology

DOCUMENT A1

Outstanding Events in the History of Jehovah's Witnesses

1852 Charles Taze Russell is born on 16 February at Allegheny, Pennsylvania.

1868 Russell visits a Second Adventist church and becomes convinced of the doctrine of the soul sleep.

1870 Russell and close associates form a Bible study group.

1876 Russell visits Nelson H. Barbour and adopts his end times chronology.

1878 Barbour's forecast that the church will be raptured in that year fails.

1879 Russell breaks with Barbour and begins publishing *Zion's Watch Tower and Herald of Christ's Presence*. He marries Maria Frances Ackley. Russell's associates and followers begin to call themselves 'Bible Students.'

1881 Russell's forecast that the church will be raptured in that year fails. Based on Barbour's chronology, he looks forward to 1914 and the full establishment of Christ's kingdom on earth. He founds Zion's Watch Tower and Tract Society.

1884 Russell and associates incorporate Zion's Watch Tower Tract Society.

1886 Russell publishes the first volume of his *Millennial Dawn Series: The Plan of the Ages,* known later as *The Divine Plan of the Ages.*

1894 The first 'Harvest Sifting' takes place. Workers at the Zion's Watch Tower 'Bible House' in Allegheny, Pennsylvania, accuse Russell of being dictatorial and mistreating his wife. She defends him publicly and develops the teaching that he is the 'faithful and wise servant' of Matthew 24:45–7.

1897 Maria Russell separates from her husband with great bitterness. A Watch Tower literature depot is opened in Berlin.

1900 The Watch Tower's first branch office is opened in London, England.

1902 A Watch Tower office is opened in Eberfeld (Wuppertal) in western Germany.

1907 Maria Russell divorces her husband from bed and board for 'personal indignities.'

1909 Russell moves the Watch Tower Society headquarters to Brooklyn, New York. The second 'Harvest Sifting' or New Covenant Schism divides the Bible Students. Most remain loyal to Russell.

1914 Russell's prophecy that Christ's kingdom will take full control of the earth by that year fails. Nevertheless, he proclaims that the 'times of the gentiles' have ended. He believes the First World War will end in the Battle of Armageddon.

1916 Charles T. Russell dies on 31 October.

1917 Joseph Franklin Rutherford (best known as 'Judge Rutherford') becomes the Watch Tower's second president. The third 'Harvest Sifting' occurs when Rutherford ousts four members of the Watch Tower's board of directors. Many Bible Student congregations are bitterly divided, and major schisms take place among them, both in America and abroad.

1918 Rutherford and six other Watch Tower leaders are convicted of violating the U.S. Espionage Act. Six are sentenced to twenty years' imprisonment in the federal penitentiary in Atlanta, Georgia. A seventh is sentenced to ten years. The First World War ends without Armageddon having happened.

1919 On appeal, Watch Tower leaders are released from prison, and Rutherford reorganizes the Bible Student movement for a grand preaching work. Declaring that 'millions now living will never die,' Rutherford points to 1925 as the beginning of Christ's millennial rule on earth. Bible Students begin to make many new converts in America and Germany.

1920 A Watch Tower Central European Office is opened in Switzerland. Paul Balzereit is placed in charge of the German branch in Barmen.

1923 German Watch Tower offices are moved from Barmen in western Germany to Magdeburg near Berlin.

1924 The Watch Tower Society releases the resolution 'Ecclesiastics Indicted.' Clergy are inflamed, Rutherford's life is threatened, and Balzereit is taken to court, where he is acquitted of defamation.

1925 Watch Tower prophecy regarding the year 1925 fails. Many abandon the Bible Student movement. Rutherford admits he has made 'an ass' of himself over 1925, and in a *Watch Tower* article, 'Birth of the Nation,' he begins to revise Russell's chronology. Rutherford begins to assume control over Bible Student congregations but is resisted by elected congregational elders. The Watch Tower's escalating attacks on the churches result in growing legal efforts to curb the Bible Students in many parts of the world, including the United States and Germany.

1926 Bible Students begin house-to-house preaching with Watch Tower publications on Sundays. Many arrests follow for violations of Sabbath laws.

1929 Rutherford proclaims in the *Watch Tower* that the 'Higher Powers' of Romans 13:1 are Jehovah God and Christ Jesus. The governments of the nations are held to be demonic.

1931 On 26 July, at Columbus, Ohio, Rutherford calls on Watch Tower Bible Students (as distinct from independent Bible Students) to take the name Jehovah's Witnesses; they do.

1932 *Vindication* Book 2 changes Watch Tower teachings dramatically by stating that natural Jews no longer have any part to play in Jehovah's divine plan. Jehovah's Witnesses are described as 'spiritual Jews.' The system of elective elders is ended in Witness congregations.

1933 Adolf Hitler comes to power in Germany. Jehovah's Witnesses are banned. At first, Witness leaders try to mollify the Nazis. When that fails, Rutherford calls on German Witnesses to defy them even at the cost of their lives.

1935 The Nazis openly defy the Treaty of Versailles by proclaiming the existence of a German air force, by introducing universal conscription for all German men except clergy, and by announcing that conscientious objectors will be executed in time of war. Paul Balzereit and several colleagues are arrested, tried, convicted of crimes against the Nazi state, and eventually sent to concentration camps. Rutherford excommunicates them for failing to uphold Watch Tower policies in court. In America, Rutherford takes a stand against Jehovah's Witnesses saluting any flag.

1936 On 28 August, the Gestapo arrest large numbers of Jehovah's Witnesses, including the latest Watch Tower branch overseer in Germany. The Witnesses hold a convention at Lucerne, Switzerland, and release a declaration attacking Nazism, persecution in Austria, and the Roman Catholic Church. On 12 December, 3,450 Witnesses distribute the 'Lucerne Declaration' throughout Germany. Much Nazi persecution follows.

1937 German Witnesses distribute an 'Open Letter' throughout Germany describing their persecution. Many are arrested, imprisoned, and sent to concentration camps.

1938 Hitler annexes Austria and the Czech Sudetenland. The Nazis extend the persecution of Jehovah's Witnesses to those areas. Rutherford institutes 'theocratic government' among the Witnesses, thus ending any congregational independence from the Watch Tower Society.

1939 The Second World War begins. Jehovah's Witness August Dickmann is the first German conscientious objector to be executed.

1940 Denmark, Norway, the Low Countries, and France fall before German arms. Germany is supreme in continental Europe west of the Soviet Union. Jehovah's Witnesses are outlawed everywhere except in Sweden, Denmark, and Switzerland. In the United States, the Supreme Court holds that Witness children who do not salute the flag may be expelled from public schools. Many Witnesses are mobbed. At the behest of the Catholic cardinal archbishop of Quebec, the Canadian government outlaws Jehovah's Witnesses.

1941 Germany invades the Soviet Union. Japan attacks Pearl Harbor, thus bringing the United States into the Second World War. Rutherford believes that Armageddon is at hand.

1942 Rutherford dies. Nathan H. Knorr becomes the Watch Tower's third president. Nazi persecution of Jehovah's Witnesses eases.

1943 Allies score major victories against Italy, Germany, and Japan. The U.S. Supreme Court reverses its stand on the flag salute. Canada lifts its ban on Jehovah's Witnesses.

1945 The Second World War ends. Jehovah's Witnesses are liberated from prisons and concentration camps in Germany. Their persecution ends except in Spain, Portugal, Greece, the Soviet Union, and Quebec. The Witnesses enter an era of strong growth. The Watch Tower Society takes a public stand against blood transfusions.

1949 Communist East Germany begins the suppression of Jehovah's Witnesses.

1950 Jehovah's Witnesses hold an international convention at New York, where they proclaim themselves to be a 'religion' and release the New World Translation of the Christian Greek Scriptures. Watch Tower's vice-president, Frederick William Franz, announces that the princes of Psalm 45:16 are the overseers among Jehovah's Witnesses rather than Jesus' forefathers. The Watch Tower Society abandons the idea that Jesus' forefathers will be resurrected before Armageddon.

1952 The Watch Tower Society formulates a doctrine which proclaims that those who saw the events of 1914 will survive the Battle of Armageddon.

1958 The Watch Tower 'Divine Will International Assembly' in New York City draws 253,922 Witness delegates and visitors from 123 countries; 7,136 are baptized.

1962 The Watch Tower Society reverts to Charles T. Russell's teaching that the 'Higher Powers' or 'Superior Authorities' of Romans 13:1 are secular governments.

1966 The book *Life Everlasting – In Freedom of the Sons of God* includes a chart which indicates that 6,000 years of human history from Adam and Eve's creation will end in 1975. In line with long-standing Watch Tower interpretations, this implies that the present system of things will end and that the millennium will begin in that year. This chart and further eschatological pronouncements by Witness leaders create a fervour among Jehovah's Witnesses. They begin to experience rapid growth.

1971 A Governing Body of Jehovah's Witnesses is established.

1972 A system of elders is restored in Witness congregations; however, elders are appointed through the Watch Tower Society instead of being elected locally.

1975 Hundreds of thousands of disappointed Jehovah's Witnesses begin leaving the movement when the end of the present age does not come.
1977 Knorr dies, and Frederick William Franz becomes the fourth president of the Watch Tower Society.
1980 Persons desiring doctrinal openness at the world headquarters of Jehovah's Witnesses are purged. These include Raymond Victor Franz, a nephew of Frederick Franz and member of the Governing Body.
1992 Frederick Franz dies, and Milton G. Henschel becomes the fifth president of the Watch Tower Society.
1994 The Watch Tower Society abandons the teaching that Armageddon must come before the generation of 1914 dies off.

DOCUMENT A2

Outstanding Events Relating to the History of Jehovah's Witnesses in Germany, 1933–45

1933

30 January Adolf Hitler named Chancellor of Germany.
27 February The Reichstag Fire.
28 February Reich President Paul von Hindenburg signs a decree 'For the Protection of the People and the State.' This decree takes away the constitutional provisions of the Weimar Constitution guaranteeing civil liberties and lays the basis for a Nazi dictatorship. Immediately after the publication of the decree, many Communists and Social Democrats are arrested, and many newspapers are suppressed.
5 March Germany's last democratic election during Hitler's life is held. With their Nationalist allies, the Nazis gain control of the Reichstag. Jehovah's Witnesses refuse to vote in the election or to join in the Nazi 'revolution.' In March the Witnesses form new legal associations (the *Norddeutsche Bibelforschervereinigung* or North German Bible Students Association and the *Suddeutsch Bibelforscherver-einigung* or South German Bible Students Association). The

	purpose of this is to make the Bible Students (Jehovah's Witnesses) seem less international and less American. This effort fails.
7 April	The Nazis pass a 'Law for the Restoration of Career Civil Service.' This law Nazifies the Civil Service; many Witnesses to lose their jobs as a consequence. The Witnesses refuse to vote or give the Nazi salute.
10 April	Mecklenburg bans the Bible Students Association.
13 April	Bavaria bans the Association.
18 April	Saxony bans the Association.
19 April	Hesse bans the Association.
24 April	In Magdeburg, police and SA occupy the Watch Tower offices and printing plant.
27 April	Watch Tower officials ask the U.S. State Department to intervene with the German government on the society's behalf. It does, and as a result, the police and SA vacate the Magdeburg properties and allow the Witnesses to remain active in Prussia.
15 May	Baden bans the Bible Students Association.
17 May	Oldenburg bans the Association.
19 May	Braunschweig bans the Association.
6 June	Lübeck bans the Association.
24 June	Prussia bans the Association.
25 June	A Watch Tower convention is held at the Berlin Wilmersdorf Tennis Hall. Some 5,000 to 7,000 Witnesses attend. *A Declaration of Facts*, intended to mollify the Nazis, is approved somewhat reluctantly by the delegates present. The Nazis ignore both the declaration and a personal letter sent to Adolf Hitler.
28 June	The Nazis reoccupy the Watch Tower properties at Magdeburg. Bremen and Hamburg ban the Bible Students Association.
Late August	The Nazis remove books, Bibles, and pictures weighing a total of 65,189 kilograms from the society's factory. They load them into twenty-five trucks and burn them at the edge of Magdeburg. The printing costs for the materials amount to some 92,719.50 marks.
12 September	The American Embassy in Berlin is able to report that after strenuous diplomatic efforts, the Society's

Magdeburg properties have been returned. However, the Witnesses remain banned and cannot print literature. On 7 October, Watch Tower workers are again permitted to take up residence in the Magdeburg 'Bethel.'

1 November — J.F. Rutherford publishes 'Fear Them Not' in the *Watch Tower* in English. The article calls on Jehovah's Witnesses to accept martyrdom if necessary in order to continue preaching publicly.

1 December — 'Fear them Not' is published in German.

1934

9 February — Rutherford writes to Hitler saying that if the persecution of Jehovah's Witnesses in Germany is not stopped, he will take action to expose it.

7–9 September — Watch Tower convention at Basel, Switzerland, reorganizes German Witnesses for open resistance to Nazi bans.

7 October — The German government is inundated with domestic letters and foreign telegrams denouncing it and the persecution of Jehovah's Witnesses. Hitler is enraged.

1935

1 April — The persecution of Jehovah's Witnesses is now coordinated under the Reich government rather than those of the states or *Länder*. The Watch Tower Society is dissolved, and its Magdeburg properties are confiscated again. Shortly afterwards, Watch Tower branch overseer Paul Balzereit and several associates are arrested.

1936

Spring — The persecution of Jehovah's Witnesses intensifies. Many Witness children are taken from their parents.

June — The Gestapo forms a special unit to survey and suppress Jehovah's Witnesses.

14 August — The Gestapo begin organizing mass arrests of Jehovah's Witnesses. Despite the killing of some seventeen Witnesses during interrogation and the in-

	carceration of the current Watch Tower branch overseer, the Witnesses are able to reorganize.
4–7 September	A Witness convention at Lucerne, Switzerland, passes a resolution condemning the persecution of German and Austrian Witnesses. It censures the Catholic church as the organization behind the persecution.
12 December	Some 100,000 copies of the Lucerne Resolution are distributed throughout Germany. Witnesses repeat the distribution of this leaflet in February and March 1937.

1937

1937	Witness men and women become major groups within Nazi concentration camps and are subjected to extreme punishments. They are required to wear a purple triangle on their concentration-camp uniforms.
22 April	On release from prison, Witnesses are to be taken into protective custody. Many are in fact sent to concentration camps. In each of the women's camps of Morningen, Lichtenburg, and Ravensbrück, they constitute the largest group of prisoners.
30 June	The Witnesses circulate an 'Open Letter' throughout Germany describing Nazi cruelty.
20 December	The Nazis introduce declaration forms to Jehovah's Witnesses. If they sign these and thereby renounce their faith, they will be released from prison or the concentration camp. Relatively few sign.

1939–45

15 September	Witness August Dickmann is shot for refusing military service. He is the first German conscientious objector to die for his faith. Roughly 250 Witnesses will die later for the same 'offence.'
1939–41	The persecution of Jehovah's Witnesses in concentration camps is especially harsh. Women and children suffer along with men. Many die of maltreatment.
1942	The persecution eases. SS officers use Witness women as domestic help. Witness men are assigned

	to various forms of civilian work outside the concentration camps.
21 July 1944	SS Chief Heinrich Himmler plans to settle Jehovah's Witnesses in eastern Europe after the Second World War to help spread pacifist ideas among Slavic peoples.
8 May 1945	The Second World War ends; Jehovah's Witnesses regain their freedom.

APPENDIX B
A Watch Tower Society 1929 Anti-Nazi Statement

The following statement, which appeared in *Das Goldene Zeitalter*, 15 October 1929, on page 316, is one of the few that the Bible Students published about Nazism before German president Paul von Hindenburg named Adolf Hitler Chancellor of the Reich. It was printed before J.F. Rutherford changed Watch Tower doctrine regarding the Jews, and it therefore shows much more sympathy toward them than did that society's publications after 1931. It is easy to sympathize with the statements made in the letter that prompted the editors of *Das Goldene Zeitalter* to react positively to it and to discuss the evils of Nazism. Even so, neither the letter nor *Das Goldene Zeitalter*'s response can properly be described as apolitical. Certainly what follows would have been regarded by the Nazis and even by their critics as propaganda. Thus the Witnesses' later claims of being 'neutral' must ring hollow.

DOCUMENT B1-A

卐

An die Redaktion des 'G. Z.'

Ich komme heute nochmals auf Nummer 8 des G.Z. zurück, in der wieder einige Worte über den Kommunismus-Artikel von Nr. 2 zu lesen sind. Da Sie die verschiedenen absprechenden Urteile trotzdem als eine Empfehlung ansehen und, wie Sie weiter sagen, sich nicht hindern lassen, das Unrecht bloßzustellen, das manche derer treiben, die auf politischem Gebiet ihren Einfluß mißbrauchen, so denke ich keine Fehlbitte zu tun, im G.Z. auch mal eine Abhandlung über den Nationalsozialismus zu schreiben.

Gelegentlich einer Versammlung vor Jahren wurde uns ein Büchlein ausgehändigt, das aber von Schmähungen über Jehova geradezu strotzte. Auch letzthin sprach ich eine sehr christlichseinwollende Dame, die dieser Partei nahesteht und Jehova als ihren Gott nicht anerkennt. Über Mose las man in Tageszeitungen vor gar nicht langer Zeit einen Aufsaß mit angeführten Bibelstellen und legte diese als eine Art Täuschung gegenüber dem damaligen Volke aus. Noch keine Partei lernte ich kennen, die die Bibel in solchen Mißkredit brachte und das religiöse Empfinden im Menschen dadurch zu töten versucht, wie gerade der Nationalsozialismus, der auf der andern Seite aber jetzt Kraftanstrengungen macht, auch hier große Versammlungen einberuft, um immer neue Mitglieder zu gewinnen, und der, wie jeder ernste Christ erkennt, gegen den wahren Gott Jehova steht. Aus diesem Grunde sind aufklärende Zeilen im G.Z. für jeden Gottesstreiter wohl gewiß auch eine Notwendigkeit, wie ich sie auf allen andern Gebieten mit Freude immer wahrgenommen habe.

Mit freundlichem Gruß Frau W. R.

Unser Antwort:

Der Nationalsozialismus ist eine jener ertremen Erscheinungen der durch die Ereignisse überreizten Volksseele, and denen unsere Zeit so reich ist. Er ist zweifellos – wie auch die verehrte Schreiberin sagt – eine Bewegung, die, ob gewollt oder ungewollt, direkt im Dienste des Feindes der Menschen, des Teufels, und gegen Jehova, den erhabenen Schöpfer von Himmel und Erde, tätig ist.

Wir haben bereits in Nr. 10 des G. Z. (Und zwar in dem Article „Mose als Pulverfabrikant") etwas über die geistige Einstellung solcher Menschen geschreiben, denen das Kreuz von Golgatha zum Haken geworden ist, weil sie nichts weiter kennen als ein Hakenkreuz. Es gibt wohl kaum eine Bewegung, die es wagen kann, ihren Lesern unvernünftigere und widerspruchsvollere Dinge aufzutischen als der fetisch-religiöse Nationalsozialismus, wenn er in belfernden Ausdrücken gegen Jehova (angeblich nur der Gott des Alten Testaments) wettert. Man stellt dabei einfach die dreiste Behauptung auf, daß der Gott des Alten Testaments ein anderer Gott sei als der Gott des Neuen Testaments, wobei diesen Phrasen dreschenden Menschen, bei denen jedes dritte Wort „Judengott" heißt wohl noch niemals in Erinnerung gekommen ist, daß sich Jesus und die Apostel im Neuen Testament ununterbrochen auf der Gott des Alten Testaments beziehen, seine Aussprüche zitieren, seine Gebote wiedergeben usw, usw. Diese ganzen hakenkreuzlerischen Rassenhaß atmenden Tendenzen verfolgen nur das einzige Ziel, nämlich, die Aufmerksamkeit von den wahrhaft Schuldigen abzulenken und einen Sündenbock zu suchen. Das Geschrei „Die Juden haben Schuld" ist eine alte „Haltet-den-Dieb"-List, die nach verlorenen Kriegen unter allen Völkern immer wieder angewandt wurde, um den Unwillen des Volkes von den eigentlichen Schuldigen abzuwenden. Natürlich gibt es auch unter den Juden schlechte Menschen, genau so wie unter den Christen; aber es ist einfach eine unverschämte, nahezu gotteslästerliche Behauptung, daß die Gotteslehren der Bibel oder des Alten Testaments irgendwelchen angeblichen Weltherrschaftsplänen der Juden dienen, oder gar zu diesem Zweck ins Leben gerufen sein sollen. Wenn dies beabsichtigt wäre, enthielte die Bibel nicht so viele Berichte, die angesichts einer solchen Absicht als geradezu unvernünftig angesprochen werden müßten; denn die Bibel – und speziell das Alte Testament – ist voll von Aussprüchen, welche die schärfsten Urteile über das Volk Israel enthalten, in Fällen, wo sie sich von dem wahren Gott Jehova abwandten. Diese Urteile sind so wenig schmeichelhaft, daß es einfach paradox ist, diesem heiligen Buch Judenpropaganda zur Last legen zu wollen. Die Alt- und Neutestamentliche Bibel ist einfach ein Bericht geschichtlicher und prophetischer Tatsachen und Erfahrungen, und ihr Zweck ist der, in Vorbildern und direkten Belehrungen der Menscheit Aufschluß über Gottes Vorhaben mit den Menschen zu geben. Eine jede Bewegung, die darauf ausgeht, das Vertrauen des Volkes in die Bibel zu unterminieren, ist als Gegner Jehovas, des Schöpfers von Himmel und Erde, anzusehen. Letzten Endes kann von gewissen Richtungen des hakenkreuzlerisch orientierten Nationalsozialismus – die Wotan und andere Sagengötzen mehr wieder in ihre Tempel setzen möchten – nur gesagt werden, daß sie ein modernes Heidentum darstellen, das darum für die geistige Verfassung der diesem Heidentum Anhängenden oder Beitretenden um so kennzeichnender ist, weil wir uns heute im 20. Jahrhundert befinden.

Der Nationalsozialismus ist ein Krankheitserscheinung, die zur gegebenen Zeit ihr Ende finden wird. Wir nehmen ihn nicht für ernst, wie breit er sich auch immerhin machen möchte. Nach seiner höchsten Steigerung wird er nur einen um so kläglicheren Untergang finden.

DOCUMENT B1-B
(English Translation)

To the Editorial Office of the G.Z. (*Goldene Zeitalter*)

Today, I want once again to make reference to the article in issue Number 8 of the G.Z., in which some statements are found concerning Communism from issue Number 2. Since you regard your different negative judgments as a recommendation and, as you continue, you do not permit anyone to keep you from exposing the injustice committed by those people who, in the political world, abuse their influence, I do not think it a mistake to have the G.Z. write an article about National Socialism.

During a convention years ago, a little book was handed to us which was filled with degrading statements about Jehovah. A short time ago, I also talked to a lady who pretends to be a good Christian and who is close to this party, but, nevertheless, does not accept Jehovah as her God. Not long ago, we could read an article in the daily newspapers about Moses with passages marked in the Bible as though they were false illusions for the people of an earlier time. I do not know any party like National Socialism that discredits the Bible but, conversely, that convokes great meetings to gain more members and that – as every Christian knows – is against the true God Jehovah. Thus, clear statements in the G.Z. [regarding National Socialism] are really needed by each fighter for God just as I have found them, with great pleasure, concerning every other matter.

With kind regards, Frau W.R.

Our answer:

National Socialism is one of those extreme phenomena brought about by events that have greatly troubled people's souls, of which this time is so rich. National Socialism doubtless is – as our honorable lady writer says – a movement, whether intentionally or unintentionally, that works for the world's enemy, the Devil, against Jehovah, the divine Creator of heaven and earth.

Already, in issue Number 10 of the G.Z. (In the article 'Moses as a Manufacturer of Powder'), we have written something about the mental attitude of these people, to whom the cross of Golgotha has become a hook because they know nothing but a hooked cross [a swastika]. There is hardly a movement in the world that would dare to present its readers with more unreasonable and more contradictory things than 'fetish-religious National Socialism' as it thunders its insulting words against Jehovah (apparently only the God of the Old Testament). The impudent affirmation is made that the God of the Old Testament is another God than the God of the New Testament. These people, who just blather platitudes and whose every other word is always 'the God of the Jews,' apparently fail to remember that Jesus and his apostles in the New Testament refer continually to the God of the Old Testament, they talk about His words, and read His commandments, etc., etc. The tendencies that are full of hooked-cross-like racial hatred only have the object of distracting attention from the really guilty persons and of finding scapegoats. The shouting that 'the Jews are to blame for everything' is an old 'stop the thief' trick that after the last wars has been used by all countries to distract people's hatred from really guilty parties. Obviously, there are bad elements among the Jews as there are also among Christians. But it is an infamous and an almost blasphemous assertion to say that doctrine in the Bible or the Old Testament is used by the Jews as a probable basis for achieving a Jewish World Government or that it [the Old Testament] was created for this purpose. If this were the case, the Bible would not contain so many accounts that – in view of such an intention – would sound so unreasonable. The Bible, and especially the Old Testament, is full of accounts that contain the strongest judgments of the people of Israel in instances when they turned their backs on Jehovah. Such judgments are not flattering to the Jews at all; so it is a total contradiction to blame this Holy Book for making publicity on behalf of the Jews. The Old and New Testament Bible is just a historical and prophetic report of facts and experiences that has as its object the teaching of humankind – based on examples – about God's plan for us. Every movement that has the purpose of discrediting the people's confidence in the Bible has to be considered the adversary of Jehovah, the Creator of heaven and earth. Finally, we can say about certain directions of the bent-cross-like orientation of National Socialism – which wants to put Wotan and other legendary false gods in their temples again – that it represents modern paganism. This is very characteristic of the spiritual condition of those who are already pagans or will become such as we now find ourselves in the twentieth century.

National Socialism is a disease that eventually will be finished. We do not give too much importance to it regardless of how big it may grow. After achieving its highest point [of success], it will come to a very sad end.

APPENDIX C
Documents Relating to the Watch Tower Society's Attempt to Compromise with Nazism

German officials of the Watch Tower Society believed that when the government of Prussia returned the society's Magdeburg properties on 29 April 1933 and allowed both the society and the Bible Students Association to continue functioning, their most serious problems were over. Yet they knew that other *Länder* were still suppressing Jehovah's Witnesses and that they were extremely unpopular with many churches, with elements of the Nazi Party, and with some segments of German society. Their response was to publish a 'Public Declaration' in *Das Goldene Zeitalter* (The Golden Age) on 15 May 1933. Obviously they hoped it would placate Nazi officialdom. They made much of the fact that two of their lawyers were Nazi Party members and that the accounts of Nazi atrocities (*Gruelpropaganda*) being published abroad were false. Of course, when they denied the existence of such atrocities, they had to know they were lying. The country was rapidly becoming a vicious dictatorship. Nazi thugs were roaming the streets; Jews were being beaten, mobbed, and boycotted; and the Communists and Social Democrats were being outlawed and imprisoned. The 'Public Declaration' is provided below both in the original German and in English translation.

Document C1-A
(German Text)

Zitat:
Das Goldene Zeitalter.
Nr. 10 15. Mai 1933
Das Auge der Welt

Öffentliche Erklärung

der „Wachtturm Bibel- und Traktat-Gesellschaft"
und der „Bibelforscher-Vereingung"

I

Die inzwischen wieder beendete Durchsuchung und Besetzung der Grundstücke der Wachtturm Bibel- und Traktat-Gesellschaft ist – wie wir von zuständiger amtlicher Seite erfuhren – erfolgt, weil Anklagen erhoben worden sind, daß die beiden oben genannten Gesellschaften sich kommunistisch betätigten.

Weiterhin erstreckte sich die Durchsuchung in der Richtung auf eventuelle Steuerhinterziehungen, Zollvergehen, usw.

Am Sonnabend, dem 29. April 1933, nachmittags 4 Uhr, aber wurden die Grundstücke, Gebäude und Maschinen bereits wieder an die Vertreter der Gesellschaft zurückgegeben. Das gleiche erfolgte mit den beschlagnahmten Druckschriften. Es wurde ferner amtlich mitgeteilt, daß die zeitchrift „Das Goldene Zeitalter" ebenso wie die Tätigkeit der Bibelforscher-Vereinigung für den Staat Preußen wieder frei seien, weil die sich über eine Woche erstreckende sorgfältige Durchsuchung aller Papiere und Räumlichkeiten der Gesellschaft keinerlei irgendwie belastendes Material hinsichtlich der erhobenen Anschuldigung einer kommunistischen Betätigung ergeben haben.

Wir schließen aus der Räumung des Betriebes und der völligen Freigabe sämtlicher Geschäftsbücher und Unterlagen mit recht, daß auch die Durchsuchung in anderer Richtung – wie wir dies nicht anders erwartet haben – völlig ergebnislos verlaufen ist.

II

Dieser Ausgang der von uns in Ruhe abgewarteten Durchsuchung mußte automatisch aus der Tatsache resultieren, daß wir unsere gesamte Tatigkert auf rein biblischer Grundlage und immer nur in Übereinstimmung mit für diese Tätigkeit geltenden Bestimmungen und Berordnungen der Behörden ausgeübt haben.

Wir erklären gern, daß während der ganzen Dauer dieser einwöchigen Besetzung und Durchsuchung unserer Grundstücke und Gebäude keiner unserer Mitarbeiter irgendwelche Ursache zur Beschwerde gegen die durchsuchennden Beamten gehabt hat. Alles ist trotz der ausgeübten Gründlichkeit in absolut auständiger Form und unter Vermeidung der Verursachung irgendwelcher Schäden vor sich gegangen. Wir geben hiervon sowohl dem Zentralbüro unser

Gesellschaft in Brooklyn, wie auch allen Schwestervereinigungen in andern Ländern durch Übrsendung des Wortlautes dieser Erklärung kenntnis, wie wir stets alles getan haben und auch weiter tun werden, was dazu beiträgt, um falshe Meinungen über Zustande in Deutschland (bekannt als Greuelpropaganda) auf den rechten Weg zurüchzuverweisen.

III

Wie durch diese nun abgeschlossene Durchsuchung unseres Archivs und unserer Grundstücke nun auch amtlicherseits durch Nachprüfung einwandfrei festgestellt wurde, ist die Vereinigung streng christlich und hat keinerlei politische Tätigkeit ausgeübt. Sie unterhält auch keinerlei Beziehungen zu ingendwellcher politichen Partei, noch tat sie dies jemals in der Vergangenheit. Es bestehen nicht und bestanden niemals in irgendwelche direkten oder indirekten politischen Verbindungen, weder zum Kommunismus noch zur Sozialdemokratie oder zu irgendeiner andern atheistischen Richtung. Aus ihrem entschiedenen Eintreten für Gott dokumentiert sich die Bibelforscher – Vereinigung selbst als strengster religiöser Gegner aller gegen Gott gerichteten Strömungen.

Ebenso unwahr ist die immer wiederkehrende und mangels wirklicher Anklagen wiederholte Behauptung, daß Bibelforscher etwas mit Freimaurern oder Juden zu tun hätten. Auf dem Amtsgericht in Magdeburg war jahrelang die Summe von 1000 Mark deponiert für denjenigen, der irgendeinen Beweis dafür vorbringen könnte.

Seit Jahren ist Rechtsbeistand der „Wachtturm Bibel-und Traktat-Gesellschaft" das Mitglied der Deutschnationalen Partei, Herr Justizrat Karl Kohl, Rechtsanwalt in München, seit ca. vier Jahren auch das Mitglied der Nationalsozialistischen Deutschen Arbeiter-Partei, Herr Rechtsanwalt Horst Kohl, München. Daß auch der ehemalige Magdeburger Polizeipräsident, Herr Rechtsanwalt Dr. Bärensprung, als Spezialist für das internationale öffentliche und Privatrecht in einem schwebenden Verfahren mit tätig war, beweist – wegen unserer absoluten politischen Uninteressierheit – keinerlei politische Beziehungen zu den politischen Ansichen dieses Herrn, sondern war nur eine Frage juristischer Qualifikationen.

Die auch von den beiden genannten Münchener Herren mit bearbeitete Devisenangelegenheit bezieht sich übrigens durchaus nicht auf unerlaubte Devisenschiebungen, wie es in der Presse hieß, weil solche niemals stattfanden, sondern stellt lediglich die Klarlegung juristischer Steitfragen des internationalen Privatrechts u. a., die Frage in der Richtig- oder Falschanwendung einer Ausnahmebestimmung in der Devisenschiebungen dar.

IV

Es ist nicht zutreffend, daß Riesengewinne an Literatur gemacht oder ins Ausland verschoben werden, weil alle mit der Gesellschaft oder Bibelforscher-Vereinigung tätigen Personen aus ideelen Beweggründen tätig sind. Niemand hat irgendeinen wirtschaftlichen oder finanziellen Vorteil aus dieser Tätigkeit, im Gegenteil, die ganze missionare Arbeit der Bibelforscher-Bewegung und Wachtturm-Gesellschaft erfolgt unter ständigen Opfern an Zeit, Kraft oder Geld seitens jedes einzelnen Mitarbeiters.

V

Nachstehend geben wir in kurzer Form Kenntnis über die statutengemäß festliegenden Ziele und Zwecke der Wachtturm Bibel- und Traktat-Gesellschaft und der „Bibelforscher-Vereinigung":

§2 der Statuten der im Jahre 1884 in Amerika gegründeten und seither über die ganze Welt in vielen Filialen verbreiteten „Watch Tower Bible and Tract Society" (zu deutsch: „Wachtturm Bibel- und Traktat-Gesellschaft") sagt:

„Der Zweck, zu dem diese Gesellschaft gegründet wurde, ist die Verbreitung biblischer Wahrheit in verschiedenen Sprachen mittels der Veröffentlichung von Traktaten, Büchern, Broschüren und andere religiösen Dokumenten und durch den Gebrauch aller andern gesetzlichen Mittel, die zur Hinausführung dieses Zweckes dienlich sind."

Die Statuten der „Bibelforscher-Vereinigung" sagen über Zweck und Ziel der Tätigkeit der Vereinigung folgendes:

§3 „Der Zweck der Vereinigung ist die Förderung christlicher Erkenntnis mittels Belehrung über den Inhalt der Bibel und Aufklärung der Menschen über alles, was den Lehren der Bibel – dem Worte Gottes – entgegengesetzt ist und mit ihren Forderungen nicht übereinstimmpt, zusammengefaßt:

Den Menschen in ihren Glaubenszweifeln und Gewissenskonflikten beizustehen und ihnen zu helfen, verlorenen Glauben und Gottvertrauen wiederzugewinnen."

§7) Ziffer 1 n. 2: „Die Arbeit der Vereinigung soll ferner dahin wirken:

1.) Menschen, mit denen sie bei ihrer Missionsarbeit in Berührung kommt, zu erziehen, sich so zu verhalten, wie es von Christen erwartet werden muß, damit deren Gesinnung und

Lebenswandel sie zu leuchtenden Vorbildern der menschlichen Gesellschaft macht.

2.) Die Verbreitung alles Schönen, Edlen und Reinen bei sich selbst, in ihrer Umgebung und auch – nach Maßgabe ihrer Fähigkeit – im öffentlichen Leben soll in Verbindung mit dem Gesamtzweck der Vereinigung das eifirige Bemühen aller mit der Vereinigung zusammenarbeitenden Menschen sein."

§8) „Ferner soll die Vereinigung nach Maßgabe der ihr zur Verfügung stehenden Mittel das Recht haben, Unterstützung an arme in Not geratene Menschen zu geben, wo immer – ihrem Ermessen gemäß – eine solche Unterstützung angebracht erscheint."

§ 4) Ziffer 5: „Diese vorgenannten Veranstaltungen dürfen nie zu politischer Agitation benutzt werden."

Was wir glauben:

Wir glauben, daß der allein wahre Schöpfer von Himmel und Erde – wie er selbst in der Bibel sich nennt – Jehova Gott ist. Wir bezeugen seinen Namen und seine Macht (daher der Name „Jehovas Zeugen"). Wir verkünden, daß sein wahrhaftiger Sohn, Christus Jesus, der Erlöser der Menschheit ist, und daß er die Errettung der ganzen Menscheit von Sünde und Tod durch die Auferstehung und Befreiung der Menschen von allen Leiden bringen wird in dem Königreich, um das Jesus uns beten lehrte: „Dein Reich komme, dein Wille geschehe, wie im Himmel also auch auf Erden."

Bibelforscher – Vereinigung (Jehovas Zeugen)
Wachtturm Bibel– und Traktat– Gesellschaft
Magdeburg

DOCUMENT C1-B
(English Translation)

Quotation
Das Goldene Zeitalter
No. 10, May 15, 1933
The Eye of the World

Public Declaration

of the 'Watch Tower Bible and Tract Society'
and of the 'Bible Students Association'

The search and occupation of the grounds belonging to the Watch Tower Bible and Tract Society, which has now been completed, happened because of accusations that the above mentioned societies were involved in Communistic activities.

Furthermore, the search looked into the matter of tax evasions, offenses against customs duties, etc.

By Saturday, 29 April 1933, at 4 P.M., the grounds, buildings, and machinery, as well as confiscated printed materials, were given back to the representatives of the Society. Furthermore, there was an official declaration that the magazine 'The Golden Age' as well as the work of the Bible Students Association for the State of Prussia were free again, since, after a week, a thorough search of all of the Society's documents and properties failed to produce any incriminating material hinting at Communistic activities.

The return of the [Society's] properties and the release of all account books and documents proves to us that even the searches in other directions [such as for tax evasions and custom's violations] did not reveal any wrongdoing.

II

The outcome of these searches, which we looked forward to with confidence, had to reflect automatically the fact that our entire work is based on the Bible and is always done only in accordance with the directives and laws given out by the authorities for those purposes.

We gladly declare that during the occupation and search of our grounds and buildings none of our co-workers had any reason for complaints against the officials conducting the search. Despite its absolute thoroughness, the search was carried out without causing any damage. We want to bring this to the attention of our central office in Brooklyn as well as all [Watch Tower] branches in other countries by sending this message. We always have and will stress the truth, in order to contradict false ideas about conditions in Germany (known as atrocity propaganda).

III

As officially proven through the now terminated search of our archives and grounds, our Society is strictly Christian and does not carry on any political activity. Neither now nor at any time in the past has it had any connection, either direct or indirect, with any political parties. There never were, nor are there now, any political ties with either Communism or Social Democracy, or any other [movement of an] atheistic tendency. The Bible Students Association is proving by its direct stand for God that it is a strictly religious enemy of all ideologies opposed to God.

For lack of real accusations, repeated statements that Bible Students have connections with Freemasons or Jews are also untrue. The sum of I,000 marks was deposited for years at the lower court in Magdeburg for the person who could bring any proof of such statements.

For some years Judicial Counsel Mr Karl Kohl, a lawyer in Munich and a member of the National Socialist German Workers Party [the Nazis], has been the legal advisor of the 'Watch Tower Bible and Tract Society,' as has Judicial Counsel Mr Horst Kohl – also a member of the National Socialist German Workers Party – for some four years. The former Police President of Magdeburg, Judicial Counsel Dr Bärensrpung, a specialist in international governmental and private law, aided us with suspended proceedings, but our absolute apolitical interests prove that we have no connections with the political ideas of the said gentleman; this was purely a matter of his legal qualifications.

The foreign exchange affair in which we were aided by the two lawyers from Munich was not a matter of illegal foreign exchange profiteering as the media made it sound. Nothing of this sort ever took place. Their [the Munich lawyers'] aid was in clarifying legal questions of international private law – such as questions concerning how to properly use an exceptions regulation in the International Foreign Exchange Laws.

IV

It is not true that huge financial gains have been made from literature or been shifted underhandedly to other countries because all those working with the Society or the Bible Students Association are working for idealistic reasons. Nobody gains an economic or financial advantage from this activity; on the contrary, the entire missionary work of the Bible Student movement and of the Watch Tower Society is done with constant sacrifices of time, energy, or money on the part of each of the co-workers.

V

Below, we want to make a brief declaration concerning the objects and purposes [of our movement] as stated in the charters of the 'Watch Tower Bible and Tract Society' and of the 'Bible Students Association':

§2 of the Charter of the 'Watch Tower Bible and Tract Society' (known in German as 'Wachtturm Bibel- und Traktat-Gesellschaft'), which was founded in 1884 in America and now is spread all over the world in many branches, says:

> The reason for which this Society was founded, is the spreading of biblical truth in various languages, accomplished through the media of tracts, books, brochures and other religious documents and through the use of all other lawful means to accomplish this aim.

The Charter of the 'Bible Students Association' says the following about the aim and works of that association:

> §3) The purpose of the Association is the propagation of Christian understanding through teachings about the content of the Bible and the enlightenment of mankind regarding everything that is opposed to the teachings of the Bible – the Word of God – and what therefore does not agree with the Bible's requirements. In short:
>
> To assist people experiencing doubts regarding their faith, in their conflicts of conscience, and to assist them in regaining lost faith and trust in God.
>
> §7) Numbers 1 and 2: The work of the Association should furthermore accomplish [the following]:
>
> 1.) People, with whom they come into contact during their mission work should be educated to behave, as is expected of Christians, so that their convictions and conduct make them good examples for human society.
> 2.) The dissemination of all that is beautiful, noble, and clean in their private lives, in their environment and also – according to their ability – in their public life, should be – in conjunction with the overall purpose of the Society – the main purpose of all who are working with the Association.
>
> §8) Furthermore, the Association shall have the right to give – according to available means – support to the poor at its own independent discretion.
>
> §4) Number 5: These afore-mentioned arrangements must never be used for political agitation.

VI

What we believe:

We believe that the only true Creator of Heaven and Earth, Jehovah – as he calls himself in the Bible – is God. We bear witness to his name and his power (hence our name 'Jehovah's Witnesses'). We proclaim that his true Son, Christ Jesus, is the deliverer of mankind, and that he will bring the deliverance of all mankind from sin and death through his resurrection, and that he will free all mankind from suffering in the kingdom for which Jesus taught us to pray: 'Your kingdom come, Your will be done, on earth as it is in heaven.'

Bible Students Association (Jehovah's Witnesses)
Watch Tower Bible and Tract Society
Magdeburg

The document that appears immediately below, titled *die Erklärung* (the Declaration of Facts), is a word-for-word copy of the original leaflet presented to the 25 June 1933 Watch Tower Berlin-Wilmersdorf Convention and distributed to German officials and the public throughout the Reich over the following several days. The German edition of the *1934 Year Book of Jehovah's Witnesses* reprinted this document but with a number of textual differences. In order to show these differences, I have italicized the words or passages in the 25 June 1933 declaration that are not in the year book edition and have printed the differences found in it in footnotes with English translations. Also, I have printed in bold the one major passage in the original text that is absent from the *1934 Year Book* and have given the translation of it in a footnote as well. The question arises as to why the year book document, as it appears in both English and German, is slightly different from the one that was approved at the 25 June convention. Of course it is impossible to say with absolute certainty at this distance, but it is reasonable to conjecture as follows: Judge Rutherford originally wrote the declaration in English; that is clear. However, in translating it into German for distribution, it is quite probable that Paul Balzereit or some other Watch Tower official at Magdeburg made slight changes in the text and added the one major statement that does not appear in the year book editions. That statement, which falsely claims that Catholics in America, as well as Jews, were trying to boycott Germany because of the Nazis' anti-Semitic policies, sounds very much like what Magdeburg officials of the Watch Tower were saying in the June 1933 Watch Tower letter to Hitler. But when the English edition of the 1934 year book was published in the autumn of 1933 for the following year, it would have presented the original version of the declaration as prepared by Rutherford. Since the German year book was a translation of the English published outside Germany, it would necessarily reflect Rutherford's version as well, rather than the one adopted on 25

June 1933. It should be emphasized, however, that except for the one added false statement mentioned above, the *Erklärung* produced below clearly reflects Rutherford's thinking. The other passages in it that differ from the year book editions are inconsequential.

Document C2-A

(German Translation)

Erklärung

Dieser Kongreß deutscher Männer und Frauen, friedlicher und ordungsliebender Bürger *aus*[1] allen Teilen des Landes, die alle miteinander ernsthaft an dem höchsten Wohl des deutschen Volkes mitarbeiten, hat sich heute, den 25. Juni 1933, offiziell in Berlin versammelt und erklärt freudig seine völlige Ergebenheit gegenüber Jehova Gott, dem Allmächtigen, und seinem Königreich unter Christus Jesus, dessen vergossenes Blut die Menschheit erkauft hat. Wir bekennen, daß die Heilige Schrift, die Bibel, Gottes Wort ist, das den Menschen zur Unterweisung in Gerechtigkeit gegeben wurde, und daß dieses göttliche Wort die Wahrheit ist, die für den Menschen von größter Bedeutung ist, damit er über sein Verhältnis zu Gott Kenntnis erhalte. Wir berufen uns auf das Wort Gottes und möchten nach diesem Maßstabe beurteilt werden.

Christus Jesus ist Jehova Gottes großer Wahrheitszeuge, und als seine treuen und ergebenen Nachfolger sind wir durch seine Gnade Zeugen der Wahrheit. Der Zweck dieser Erklärung ist, den Führern und dem Volk ein wahres und aufrichtiges Zeugnis über den Namen und das Vorhaben Jehovas und über unsere Beziehungen dazu zu überreichen.

Wir sind fälschlicherweise bei den Regierungsbehörden und bei dem deutschen Volke angeschuldigt worden. Damit nun der Name Jehova Gottes in der Auffassung des Volkes erhöht und sein gütiger Ratschluß besser verstanden und unsere Stellung der Regierung gegenüber in rechter Weise dargelegt werden möchte, ersuchen wir hiermit die Führer und das deutsche Volk, die folgende Erkärung des wahren Sachverhalts gerecht und unparteiisch zu prüfen.

1 The German edition of the 1934 year book does not contain the word *aus* and adds the words *die viele andere in*. This slight change indicates that the delegates represented 'many others from' every part of of the country.

Die Schrift erklärt deutlich, das Satan der Teufel, dessen Name auch Schlange und Drache ist, der Hauptgegner Jehova Gottes und der größte Feind der Menscheit ist. Es steht in der Schrift, daß Satan, der seit langem der unsichtbare Herrscher dieser Welt war, die Menschen über die Wahrheit täuscht und verblendet, damit das Licht über Jehova Gott und Christus Jesus nicht in ihre Herzen hineinscheint. (2. Korinther 4:3,4) Satan hat oft durch Betrug, List und Täuschung aufrichtige Menschen veranlaßt, sich gegenseitig zu bekämpfen, damit er sie alle von Gott entfremde und sie vernichte. Vor allen Dingen sollten die Menschen Jehova Gott und seine gütige Vorkehrung zu ihrem allgemeinen Wohlergehen kennenlernen.

Juden

Wenn in unserer Literatur der Ausdruck „Geistlichkeit" gebraucht wird, so bezieht sich dieser Ausdruck auf solche angeblichen Religionslehrer, Priester und Jesuiten, die unrechtmäßige politische Mittel anwenden, um ihre Zwecke zu erreichen, und die sogar ihre Kräfte verbinden mit solchen, die Gott und den Herrn Jesus Christus verleugnen. Das ist dieselbe Klasse, die Jesus als seine Verfolger bezeichnete. Wir üben keine Kritik an aufrichtigen Religionslehrern.

Als Jesus zu den Juden kam, um ihnen die Wahrheit kundzutun, war es die jüdische Geistlichkeit, daß heißt die Pharisäer und Priester, die ihn heftig bekämpfte, ihn verfolgte, und die Ursache war, daß er aller möglichen Verbrechen und Sünden bezichtigt wurde. Sie weigerten sich, die Wahrheit zu hören, und Jesus richtete folgende Worte an sie: „Warum verstehet ihr meine Sprache nicht? Weil ihr mein Wort nicht hören könnt. Ihr seid aus dem Vater, dem Teufel, und die Begierden eures Vaters wollt ihr tun. Jener war ein Menschenmörder von Anfang und ist in der Wahrheit nicht bestanden, weil keine Wahrheit in ihm ist. Wenn er die Lüge redet, so redet er aus seinem Eigenen, denn er ist ein Lügner und der Vater derselben. Weil ich aber die Wahrheit sage, glaubet ihr mir nicht." (Johannes 8:43–45) Obschon die Pharisäer und Priester damals vorgaben Jehova Gott zu dienen, sagte ihnen Jesus, daß sie in Wirklichkeit Vertreter Satans des Teufel seien.

Wir haben keinen Streit mit irgend jemand, auch nicht mit Religionslehrern, jedoch müssen wir darauf aufmerksam machen, daß oft diejenigen, die vorgeben Gott und Christus Jesus zu vertreten, unsere tatsächlichen Verfolger sind, die uns bei den Regierungen der

Länder in falschem Lichte darstellen. Als wahre Nachfolger Christi Jesu haben wir solche Gegnerschaft zu erwarten, und wir erwähnen dies hier zur Erklärung, weshalb wir bei den Führern des Volkes in Verruf gebracht worden sind. Jesus sagte zu seinen treuen Nachfolgern: „Gedenket des Wortes, das ich euch gesagt habe: Ein Knecht ist nicht größer als sein Herr. Wenn sie (die falschen Religionslehrer) mich verfolgt haben, werden sie auch euch verfolgen. Wenn sie (die wahren Lehrer) mein Wort gehalten haben, werden sie auch das eure halten." (Johannes 15:20) Des weiteren erklärte Jesus, daß dieselbe Gruppe von Menschen veranlassen würde, daß seine treuen Jünger bei der Staatsgewalt in falschen Verdacht gebracht werden würden. Seine Worte lauteten: „Ihr aber, sehet auf euch selbst, denn sie (falsche Religionslehrer) werden euch an Synedrien (Polizeigewalt) und an Synagogen überliefern; ihr werdet geschlagen und vor Statthalter und Könige gestellt werden um meinetwillen, ihnen zu einem Zeugnis (andere Übers.: zu einem Zeugnis wider sie)." (Marcus 13:9) Dies erklärt, warum Jehova Gott es jetzt geschehen läßt, daß seine treuen Zeugen in falschen Verdacht kommen und verfolgt werden, nämlich damit solche, die von einem falschen Geist beseelt sind, sich selbst als Feinde Gottes offenbaren und somit wider sich selbst Zeugnis ablegen.[2]

Es ist von unseren Feinden fälschlich behauptet worden, daß wir in unserer Tätigkeit von den Juden finanziell unterstützt werden. Dies ist absolut unwahr, denn bis zur gegenwartigen Stunde ist auch nicht das geringste an Beitragen oder finanzieller Unterstützung für unser Werk von Juden geleistet worden. Wir sind treue Nachfolger Jesu Christi und glauben an ihn als den Heiland der Welt. Die Juden dagegen verwerfen Jesus Christus völlig und leugen absolut, daß er der Welt Heiland ist, der von Gott zum Nutzen des Menschen gesandt wurde. Schon allein diese Tatsache sollte Beweiß dafür sein, daß wir von den Juden nicht unterstützt werden und daß die Anschuldigungen gegen uns in böser Absicht vorgebracht wurden und falsch sind, und nur von Satan, unserem großen Feinde, herrühren können.

Das Anglo-Amerikanische Weltreich is die größte und bedrückendste Herrschaft auf Erden. Hiermit ist das Britische Reich, wovon die

2 The German *1934 Year Book* adds the followng sentence: „Derselbe materialistische Geist, der die Verfolgung Jesu Christi verursachte, besteht auch heute noch und ist verantwortlich dafür, daß wir als seine treuen Nachfolger verfolgt werden." The original, unelegant English reads : 'The same materialistic spirit that caused the persecution of Jesus Christ now exists and is back of the persecution of us, his faithful followers.'

Vereinigten Staaten Amerikas einen Teil bilden, gemeint. Es sind die Handelsjuden des Britisch-Amerikanischen Weltreiches, die das Großgeschäft aufgebaut und benutzt haben als ein Mittel der Ausbeutung und der Bedrückung vieler Völker. Diese Tatsache bezieht sich insonderheit auf die Städte London und New York als Hauptstützpunkte des Großgeschäfts. Dies ist in Amerika so offenbar, das es in Bezug auf die Stadt New York ein Sprichtwort gibt, das heißt: „Den Juden gehört die Stadt, die irischen Katholiken beherrschen sie, und die Amerikaner müssen zahlen." Wir haben mit den erwähnten Gruppen keinen Streit, sondern als Zeugen für Jehova und in Befolgung seiner in der Schrift niedergelegten Gebote müssen wir auf die Wahrheit hierüber aufmerksam machen, damit das Volk über Gott und sein Vorhaben aufgeklärt werden möchte.

Unsere Literatur

Es ist gesagt worden, daß unsere Bücher und Schriften, wenn sie unter dem Volke verbreitet werden, die öffentliche Ordung und Sicherheit des Staates gefährden. Wir sind überzeugt, daß diese Schlußfolge allein der Tatsache zuzuschreiben ist, daß unsere Bücher und Schriften von den Führern nicht sorgfältig geprüft und daher auch nicht richtig verstanden worden sind. Wir machen ergebenst darauf aufmerksam, daß diese Bücher und Schriften im Original in Amerika geschrieben wurden, und daß die Sprache dem offenen und direkten amerikanischen Stil entspricht, so daß sie in der deutschen Übertragung hart erscheint. Wir geben zu, daß dieselben Wahrheiten nicht so derb gesagt und in eine mildere Form gekleidet werden könnten. Die Sprache dieser Bücher entspricht jedoch genau der Redeweise der Bibel.

Man sollte daran denken, daß in dem Britischen Weltreich und in Amerika das allgemeine Volk gelitten hat und jetzt noch sehr leidet durch die Mißherrschaft des Großgeschäfts und der gewissenlosen Politiker; diese Mitßherrschaft wurde und wird von politischen Religionsvertretern unterstützt, und darum waren die Schreiber unserer Bücher und unserer Literatur bemüht, eine offene Sprache zu führen, um dem Volke den rechten Gedanken und das rechte Verständnis zu vermitteln. Die angewandte Redeweise ist jedoch nicht so kräftig und deutlich wie diejenige, die Jesus Christus gebrauchte, als er die Bedrücker und falschen Lehrer seiner Zeit anklagte.

Die nationale Regierung hat sich nun deutlich ausgesprochen gegen die Bedrückung durch das Großgeschäft und gegen verkehrte religiöse

Einflüsse in den politischen Angelegenheiten des Staates. Genau dies ist auch unsere Stellungnahme, und wir erklären ferner in unserer Literatur, warum das bedrückende Großgeschäft besteht, und warum der verkehrte politisch-religiöse Einfluß vorhanden ist; denn die Heilige Schrift erklärt deutlich, daß diese bedrückenden Werkzeuge vom Teufel herkommen, und daß die gänzliche Errettung davon in Gottes Königreich unter der Herrschaft Christi kommen wird. Es ist darum unmöglich, daß unsere Literatur oder unsere Tätigkeit in irgendeiner Weise die öffentliche Ordnung und Sicherheit des Staates bedrohen oder gefährden kann.

Unsere Organisation ist keineswegs politisch; wir bestehen nur darauf, das Wort Jehova Gottes dem Volke zu lehren und dies ohne Behinderung tun zu können. Wir haben nichts dagegen und suchen auch niemand zu hindern, zu lehren oder zu glauben was ihm beliebt. Wir erbitten jedoch die Freiheit, zu glauben oder zu lehren was wir für biblische Lehre halten, und dann mag das Volk entscheiden, was es zu glauben wünscht. Es ist für jedermann von größter Wichtigkeit, Jehova Gott und seine gütige Vorkehrung für die Menschheit kennenzulernen, weil Gott in seinem Worte erklärt hat, daß, wo kein Gesicht oder kein Verständnis seines Wortes ist, ein Volk zügellos wird (and. Übersetzung: umkommt). (Sprüche 29:18) Wir haben alles, was wir sind und haben, unserer Aufgabe gewidmet, damit das Volk ein Gesicht oder Verständnis des göttlichen Wortes erhalten möchte. Es ist daher unmöglich, daß unsere Literatur und unsere Wirksamkeit die öffentliche Ordung und Sicherheit des Landes bedrohen könnte. Anstatt gegen die von der deutschen Regierung vertretenen Grundsätze eingestellt zu sein, treten wir volkommen ein für diese Leitsätze, und weisen darauf hin, daß Jehova Gott durch Christus Jesus die gänzliche Verwirklichung dieser Grundsätze bringen, dem Volke Frieden und Wohlstand schenken und die höchsten Wünsche aller aufrichtigen Herzen erfüllen wird.

Unsere Organisation sucht weder finanziellen Gewinn noch Mitglieder, sondern sie ist eine organisierte Körperschaft christlicher Männer und Frauen, die lediglich in gemeinnütziger Weise damit beschäftigt sind, möglichst unentgeltlich dem Volke das Wort Gottes zu lehren. Unsere Gesellschaft wurde ursprünglich in den Vereinigten Staaten von Amerika im Jahre 1884 unter dem Namen „Watch Tower Bible and Tract Society" gegründet, und 1914 wurde die Gesellschaft nach englischem Gesetz unter dem Namen „International Bible Students Association"" eingetragen. Diese Korporationsbennungen dienen unserer Gesellschaft als gesetzliche Grundlage zur Hinausführung ihres Werkes. Der schriftgemäße Name aber ist: Jehovas Zeugen. Wir betreiben ein absolut gemeinnütziges Werk; denn der Zweck unserer Bewegung besteht darin, dem Volke zu einem Verständnis der Bibel zu verhelfen, wodurch der einzig mögliche Weg zur Segnung und völligen Errettung der Menschheit klargelegt wird. Die Tätigkeit unserer Organisation hat sich über die ganze Erde erstreckt. Bildung, Kultur, und Aufbau des Volkes muß und wird kommen, durch Gottes Königreich, worüber wir das lehren, was in der Bibel niedergelegt ist. Das Heil der Menschen hängt ab von ihrer richtigen Erkenntnis und ihrem Gehorsam Jehova Gott und seinen gerechten Wegen gegenüber.

Die Menschen befinden sich in großer Bedrängnis und benötigen eine Anleitung, den Grund ihrer unglücklichen Lage und den Weg zu ihrer Errettung zu erkennen. Ein Verständnis der Schrift erhellt diese Sache. Anstatt bei den Leuten Geld zu sammeln und dieses zu verwenden, große Bauten zu errichten, oder einzelnen hohe Gehälter zu zahlen,[3] verwenden wir die Mittel zum Druck der frohen Botschaft von Gottes Königreich und bringen diese den Menschen ins Haus, damit sie ohne Mühe über Gottes Vorhaben mit ihnen unterrichtet werden.

Eine sorgfältige Prüfung unserer Bücher und Schriften wird deutlich zeigen, daß die hohen Ideale, die sich die nationale Regierung zum Ziel gesetzt hat und die sie propagiert, auch in unseren Veröffentlichungen dargelegt, gutgeheißen und besonders hervorgehoben werden. Unsere Literatur beweißt ferner, daß Jehova Gott dafür sorgen wird, daß alle, die Gerechtigkeit lieben und dem Allerhöchsten gehorchen, zur bestimmten Zeit diese hohen Ziele erreichen werden. Anstatt daß unsere Schriften und unsere Tätigkeit die Grundsätze der nationalen Regierung gefährden, werden in ihnen diese hohen Ideale sehr unterstützt. Darum hat auch Satan, der Feind aller, die Gerechtigkeit lieben, versucht, unsere Tätigkeit in Verrufung zu bringen und sie in diesem Lande zu verhindern.

Seit vielen Jahren war unsere Bewegung unablässig bestrebt, in uneigennütziger Weise dem Volke Gutes zu tun. Unsere Amerikanischen Brüder haben das Werk in Deutschland auch mit Geldmitteln fleißig unterstützt, und zwar zur einer Zeit, wo sich ganz Deutschland in großer Not befand. Nun, wo es scheint, Deutschland bald von Be-

3 The *1934 Year Book* replaces the words *einzelnen hohe Gehälter zu zahlen* with the words *für das luxuriöse Leben Einzelner aufzukommen*. The English reads; 'to support men in luxury.'

drückung befreit und das Volk in eine bessere Lage gebracht sein wird, bemüht sich Satan, der größte Feind, dieses gemeinnützige Unternehmen hierzulande zu vernichten. **Man möchte uns gestatten, hier darauf aufmerksam zu machen, daß in Amerika, wo unsere Bücher geschrieben wurden, Katholiken als auch Juden sich miteinander verbunden haben in der Beschimpfung der nationalen Regierung in Deutschland und in dem Versuch, Deutschland zu boykottieren wegen der von der nationalsozialistischen Partei verkündigten Grundsätze.**[4]

Völkerbund

Man hat das, was in unseren Büchern oder Schriften über den Völkerbund gesagt wurde, als Grund angenommen, unsere Tätigkeit und die Verbreitung unserer Bücher zu verbieten. Wir möchten die Regierung und das Deutsche Volk daran erinnern, daß es der Völkerbund war, wodurch dem deutschen Volke große, ungerechte und unerträgliche Lasten *aufgelegt*[5] wurden. Jener Völkerbund ist nicht von den Freunden Deutschlands gemacht worden. Die Presse kündigte seinerzeit an, daß in Amerika 140 000 Geistliche eine bestimmte Zeit festgelegt hatten, während der gemeinsame Anstrengungen gemacht werden sollten und auch gemacht wurden, um das Amerikanische Volk zu bewegen, dem Völkerbund beizutreten. Der Kirchenbund in Amerika gab ein Manifest heraus, worin erkärt wurde, daß der Völkerbund „der Politische Ausdruck des Reiches Gottes auf Erden" sei und so wurde dieser von ihnen an die Stelle des Königreich Gottes unter Christi Herrschaft gesetzt. Damals zeigte unsere Organisation unter der sichtbaren Leitung ihres Präsidenten klar und deutlich, daß dieser Völkerbund keine Einrichtung Jehova Gottes ist, weil er bedrückend und unfair ist. Was aber von Jehova kommt kann nicht bedrückend und unfair sein. Die damals vorhandenen Umstände gaben den Anlaß, in unseren Büchern offen über den Völkerbund zu reden und darauf aufmerksam zu machen, daß ein solcher Völkerbund niemals Befreiung und Segnung der Völker bringen kann, weil die

4 This passage does not appear in the *1934 Year Book* copy of the declaration. It reads in English translation: 'We would like to be permitted to stress here that in America, where our books were written, Catholics as well as Jews have joined with one another in insulting the national government in Germany and in the attempt to boycott Germany because of the National Socialist Party's announced principle.'

5 The 1934 year book reads *auferlegt* rather than *aufgelegt*.

Errettung und Segnung nur kommen kann, wenn die Grundsätze, die in Gottes Wort niedergelegt sind, befolgt werden, und nur auf die Weise, wie Jehova sie bestimmt hat.

Seit beinahe einem halben Jahrhundert hat unsere christliche Organisation ihre Tätigkeit in verschiedenen Teilen der Erde ausgeübt. Unsere Bücher sind in mehr als 50 Sprachen erschienen, und mehr als 140 Millionen dieser Bücher sind in den Händen der Menschen. Seit mehr als 30 Jahren sind unsere Bücher und Schriften in ganz Deutschland verbreitet worden, und Millionen dieser Bücher befinden sich in den Händen des deutschen Volkes und werden gelesen. Alle, die diese Bücher gelesen haben, werden bezeugen, daß diese sich gänzlich auf der Bibel stützen, und daß sie ihnen geholfen, sie auferbaut und ihnen die Hoffnung auf die Segnungen gegeben haben, die Jehova Gott seit langem verheißen hat. Aus all diesen Jahren unserer Tätigkeit und bei der weiten Verbreitung unserer Bücher und Schriften kann wahrheitsgemäß kein einziges Beispiel angeführt werden dafür, daß unsere Tätigkeit oder unsere Literatur jemals in irgendeiner Weise die Regierung oder die öffentliche Ordnung und Sicherheit des Landes bedroht hätte.

Das Bestreben unserer Organisation is ausschließlich darauf beschränkt, für den Namen und das Wort Jehova Gottes Zeugnis abzulegen. Es wäre daher von uns ganz unkonsequent, wenn wir versuchen wollten, irgendwelchen Einfluß auf die Regierungen dieser Welt auszuüben oder irgendetwas zu tun, was die öffentliche Ruhe und Sicherheit des Landes gefährden würde. Wir haben weder den Wunsch noch den Gedanken, irgend etwas anderes zu tun, als nur den uns von Gott gegebenen Auftrag, das Wort Jehova Gottes zu verkündigen, auszuführen.

In Amerika, Kanada und in anderen Teilen des Britischen Weltreiches haben die politischen Geistlichen, Priester und Jesuiten die Glieder unserer Organisation ohne guten Grund oder eine Entschuldigung fortgesetzt verfolgt und fahren fort, dies zu tun, und *haben wir Grund*[6] zu glauben, daß ein ähnlicher Einfluß in listiger Weise von dem großen Feind Satan angewandt wurde, um uns und unsere Tätigkeit in Deutschland in Verruf zu bringen. Wir möchten Sie daran erinnern, daß in den letzten Jahren politische Geistliche dem deutschen Volke mehr Sorgen bereitet haben als irgendeine andere Gruppe. Wir wollen uns nicht mit den katholischen Geistlichen streiten, doch wir ersuchen

6 The *1934 Year Book* reads: *wir haben jeden Grund.*

die Reichsregierung, uns nicht nach der falschen Darstellung dieser Männer zu beurteilen, sondern nach dem Maßstab des Wortes Gottes und nach der Tätigkeit, die wir im Einklang damit ausüben. Jehova Gott verfolgt niemand, sonder überläßt es jedem einzelnen, seinen eigenen Weg zu wählen, aber er hält jeden nach seiner Erkenntnis verantwortlich für sein Tun. Jehova Gott hat deutlich seinen Zorn zum Ausdruck gebracht gegen alle, die seine Diener verfolgen. Dies beweist, daß, wer uns verfolgt, nicht Gott dient, sondern von dem Feinde Gottes und des Menschen dazu veranlasst wird. – Psalm 72:4.

Bedeutungsvolle Wahrheiten

Die Heilige Schrift, betrachtet im Lichte heutiger Ereignisse, wodurch göttliche Prophetie erfüllt wird, offenbart: der Zeitpunkt ist gekommen, wo Jehova seinen Namen der ganzen Schöpfung bekanntgeben, rechtfertigen und von der Schändung die Satan auf Gottes heiligen Namen gebracht hat, reinigen wird. (Psalm 83:18) Als Jesus Christus, der große Rechtfertiger, in den Himmel aufgestiegen war, befahl Jehova ihm, bis zu dem bestimmten Zeitpunkt zu warten, wo der Feind niedergeworfen werden sollte. Diese Wartezeit ist jetzt zu Ende, und Gott hat seinen geliebten Sohn gesandt, den Feind aufzutreiben und dann in Gerechtigkeit zu herrschen. (Psalm 110:1–4; Hebräer 10:12,13) Die Welt oder die ununterbrochene Herrschaft Satans ist zu Ende, was durch den Weltkrieg 1914 in Erscheinung trat. Seitdem ist die Zeit, wo das Evangelium vom Königreich den Nationen kundgemacht werden muß. (Mattäus 24:3, 14) Satan ist nun aus dem Himmel hinaus und auf Erden hinabgeworfen worden, und seine Wirksamkeit ist jetzt auf die Erde beschränkt. Es ist sein Bestreben, die Menschen gegen die Wahrheit blind zu machen und sie zugrunde zu richten, und dies ist die Ursache für die gegenwärtigen Leiden der Menschheit. Jetzt haben die prophetischen Worte Jesu Anwendung: „Wehe denen, die auf Erden [die Führer] wohnen, und auf dem Meer [das allgemeine Volk]! denn der Teufel ist zu euch hinabgekommen und hat große Wut, da er weiß, daß er wenig Zeit hat." Offenbarung 12:12.

Das deutsche Volk hat seit 1914 große Not gelitten und hat viele Unger-echtigkeiten durch andere erdulden mussen. Die National-sozialisten haben erklärt, daß sie gegen jede solche Ungerechtigkeit Stellung nehmen, und haben als Leitsatz kundgetan: „Unser Verhältnis Gott gegenüber ist hoch und heilig." Da unsere Organisation diese gerechten Grundsätze durchaus gutheißt und einzig damit beschäftigt ist, die Menschen über das Wort Jehova Gottes aufzuklären, ist Satan in listiger Weise bestrebt, die Regierung gegen unser Werk zu wenden und es zu zerstören, weil wir die Notwendigkeit, Gott zu erkennen und ihm zu dienen hervorheben. Unsere Organisation gefährdet keineswegs die öffentliche Ordnung und Sicherkeit des Staates, sondern sie ist die Bewegung, die für die öffentliche Ordnung, Ruhe und Sicherheit des Landes eintritt. Wir möchten allen vor Augen führen, daß die goße Krise über die Welt gekommen ist, weil dies die Übergangszeit vom Schlechten zum Guten ist. Die Hoffnung der Welt ist Gottes Königreich unter der Herrschaft Christi, wofür Jesus seine Jünger lehrte, ständig zu beten: „Dein Reich komme, dein Wille geschehe, wie im Himmel so auch auf Erden."

Jehova Gottes Macht ist über alles erhaben, und es gibt keine Macht, die ihm erfolgreich widerstehen kann. Sein Zeitpunkt, seine Macht zum Nutzen der Menschheit und zur Rechtfertigung seines hohen Namens auszuüben ist herbeigekommen. In diesem Zusammenhang gestatten wir uns ergebenst, auf die Ermahnung und Warnung Jehovas sowohl an die Führer als auch an das Volk hinzuweisen. Diese Schriftstelle hat auf die gegenwärtige Stunde Anwendung und lautet: „Habe doch ich meinen König gesalbt auf Zion, meinem heiligen Berge ... Und nun, ihr Könige, seit verständig; lasset euch zurechtweisen, ihr Richter der Erde! Dienet Jehova mit Furcht, und freuet euch mit Zittern! Küsset den Sohn, daß er nicht zürne, und ihr umkommet auf dem Wege, wenn nur ein wenig entbrennt sein Zorn. Glückselig alle, die auf ihn trauen!" Psalm 2:6, 10–12

Nachdem sich die nationale Regierung zu den oben erwähnten hohen Idealen bekannt hat, sind wir überzeugt daß die Führer nicht wissentlich das fortschrittliche Zeugniswerk für den Namen Jehovas und seines Königsreiches, das wir jetzt hinausführen, bekämpfen wollen. Wenn unser Werk nur Menschenwerk wäre, so würde es von selbst untergehen. Wenn es jedoch Gottes Werk ist und auf seinem Befehl getan wird, so bedeutet die Bekämpfung dieses Werkes einen Kampf gegen Gott. – Apostelgeschichte 5:39.

Wir appelieren daher an den Gerechtigkeitssinn der Landesführer und ersuchen ergebenst, daß das Verbot unserer Tätigkeit und unserer Literatur aufgehoben werden möchte, und daß man uns eine Gelegenheit gebe, in unparteiischer Weise angehört zu werden, ehe man uns verurteilt. Wir bitten ergebenst darum, daß die Regierung ein Komitee [*sic*] unparteiischer Männer bestimme, um mit einem Komitee [*sic*] aus unserer Organisation zu verhandeln, und daß unsere

Literatur und unsere Tätigkeit in fairer und unparteiischer Weise untersucht werde, damit jedes Mißverständnis behoben werde und wir uns gegenseitig behilflich sein möchten, und damit wir ohne Behinderung dem Gebote Gottes, daß jetzt auf uns Anwendung hat, nachkommen können, nämlich: „Ziehet durch die Tore, bereitet den Weg des Volkes; bahnet die Strasse, reiniget sie von Steinen, erhebet ein Panier über die Völker." – Jesaja 62 Vers 10.

Das deutsche Volk ist ein gottesfürchtiges Volk, und ihm sollte nicht die Möglichkeit genommen werden über Jehova Gott und über seine gütige Vorkehrung, allen die ihn kennen und ihm gehorchen, ewigen Frieden, Wohlfahrt, Freiheit und ewiges Leben auf Erden zu geben, unterrichtet zu werden. Möchten doch alle, die Gott lieben, zusammen arbeiten zur Ehrung und Rechtfertigung seines Namens. Alle, die einen entgegengesetzten Weg verfolgen, müssen selber vor Gott die Verantwortung auf sich nehmen; was aber uns betrifft, so werden wir auf ewig Jehova dienen.

Es wird hierdurch beschlossen, je ein Exemplar dieser Erklärung den hohen Regierungsbeamten ergebenst zu überreichen und sie allgemein zu verbreiten, damit der Name Jehovas immer mehr bekannt gemacht werde.

WATCH TOWER BIBLE AND TRACT SOCIETY, MAGDEBURG
Duck u. Verlag: Watch Tower Bible and Tract Society, Magdeburg

---

A version of the *Erklärung* – or *Declaration of Facts,* as it was styled in English – was published in the English edition of the *1934 Year Book of Jehovah's Witnesses.* The translation of this document that appears in the German year book of the same year is practically identical to the English. It therefore differs slightly from the Erklärung that was distributed throughout Germany immediately following the 25 June 1933 Berlin-Wilmersdorf Witness convention.

DOCUMENT C2-B

(English Text)

Declaration of Facts

This company of German people, who are peaceable and law-abiding citizens representing many others from every part of Germany, all of whom are earnestly laboring for the highest welfare of the people of this land, being now duely assembled at Berlin this 25th day of June, A.D. 1933, do joyfully declare our complete devotion to Jehovah, the Almighty God, and to his kingdom under Christ Jesus, whose shed blood bought the human race. We declare that the Holy Scriptures set forth in the Bible constitute the Word of Jehovah God given to men for their guidance in righteousness, and that the Word of God is the truth, and that it is of greatest importance that man have a knowledge of his relationship to God. We ask to be judged by the standard of the Word of God.

Christ Jesus is Jehovah God's great Witness to the truth, and as his faithful and devoted followers we are, by His grace, witnesses to the truth. The purpose of this Declaration is that we may present a true and faithful witness before rulers and the people as to the name and purpose of Jehovah God and our relation thereto.

We are wrongfully charged before the ruling powers of this government and before the people of this nation; and in order that the name of Jehovah God may be exalted in the minds of the people, and that his benevolent purposes be better understood and our position fairly placed before the government, we do respectfully ask the rulers of the nation and the people to give a fair and impartial consideration to the statement of facts here made.

The Scriptures plainly state that the chief opposer of Jehovah God and the greatest enemy of mankind is Satan the Devil, whose name is also that of Serpent and Dragon. It is written in the Scriptures that Satan, who has long been the invisible ruler of this world, deceives and blinds the people to the truth in order that the light of and concerning Jehovah God and Christ Jesus may not shine into the minds of men. (2 Corinthians 4:3,4) Frequently by fraud, subtility [*sic*] and deception Satan has induced honest persons to war with each other, in order that he might turn them all away from God and destroy them. Above all things, the people need to know Jehovah God and his gracious provision for their general welfare.

Jews

By the term 'clergy,' as used in our literature, reference is made to the class of professed religious teachers, priests and Jesuits who employ improper political means to accomplish their ends and join forces even with those who deny God and the Lord Jesus Christ. That is the same class to whom Jesus referred as his persecutors. We have no criticism of any honest religious teacher.

When Jesus went to the Jews to tell them of the truth, it was the Jewish clergy, that is to say, the Pharisees and priests, that violently opposed him and persecuted him and caused him to be charged with all manner of crimes and offenses. They refused to hear the truth, and addressing them Jesus said: 'Why do ye not understand my speech? even because ye cannot hear my word. Ye are of your father the devil, and the lusts of your father ye will do. He was a murderer from the beginning, and abode not in truth, because there is no truth in him. When he speaketh a lie, he speaketh of his own: for he is a liar, and the father of it. And because I tell you the truth, ye believe me not.' (John 8:43–45) Although the Pharisees and priests then claimed to represent Jehovah God Jesus told them that they were in fact the representatives of Satan the Devil.

We have no fight with any persons or religious teachers, but we must call attention to the fact that it is generally those who claim to represent God and Christ Jesus who are in fact our persecutors and who misrepresent us before the governments and nations. As true followers of Christ Jesus we are to expect such opposition, and we mention it here in explanation of why we have been misrepresented before the rulers of this nation. To his faithful followers Jesus said: 'Remember the word I said unto you, The servant is not greater than his lord. If they [the false religious teachers] have persecuted me, they will also persecute you; if they have kept my saying, they will keep yours also.' (John 15:20) Furthermore, Jesus said that this same class of men would cause his true followers to be wrongfully charged before the ruling powers, his language being: 'But take heed to yourselves: for they [false religious teachers] shall deliver you up to councils [police power]; and in the synagogues ye shall be beaten; and ye shall be brought before rulers and kings for my sake, for a testimony against them.' (Mark 13:9) This explains why Jehovah God now permits his faithful witnesses to be misrepresented and persecuted, namely, that those of a wrong spirit may identify themselves as opponents of God and thus bear witness against themselves. The same materialistic spirit that caused the persecution of Jesus Christ now exists and is back of the persecution of us his faithful followers.

It is falsely charged by our enemies that we have received financial support for our work from the Jews. Nothing is farther from the truth. Up to this hour there never has been the slightest bit of money contributed to our work by Jews. We are the faithful followers of Christ Jesus and believe upon Him as the Savior of the world, whereas the Jews entirely reject Jesus Christ and emphatically deny that he is the Savior of the world sent of God for man's good. This of itself should be sufficient proof to show that we receive no support from Jews and that therefore the charges against us are maliciously false and could proceed only from Satan, our great enemy.

The greatest and most oppressive empire on earth is the Anglo-American empire. By that is meant the British Empire, of which the United States of America forms a part. It has been the commercial Jews of the British-American empire that have built up and carried on Big Business as a means of exploiting and oppressing the peoples of many nations. This fact particularly applies to the cities of London and New York, the stronghold of Big Business. This fact is so manifest in America that there is a proverb concerning the city of New York which says: 'The Jews own it, the Irish Catholics rule it, and the Americans pay the bills.' We have no fight with any of these persons mentioned, but, as the witnesses for Jehovah and in obedience to his commandment set forth in the Scriptures, we are compelled to call attention to the truth concerning the same in order that the people may be enlightened concerning God and his purpose.

Our Literature

It is said that our books and like literature, when circulated amongst the people, constitute a danger to the peace and safety of the nation. We are certain that his conclusion is due to the fact that our books and other literature have not been carefully examined by the rulers and hence are not properly understood. We respectfully call attention to the fact that these books and other literature were written originally in America and the language therein used has been adapted to the American style of plainness of speech and, when translated into German, the same appears to be harsh. We admit that the same truths might be stated in a less blunt and more pleasing phrase, and yet the language of these books follows closely the language of the Bible.

It should be borne in mind that in the British Empire and in America the common people have suffered and are now suffering greatly because of the misrule of Big Business and conscienceless politicians, which misrule has been and is supported by political religionists, and hence the writers of our books or literature have endeavored to employ plain language to convey to the people the proper thought or understanding. The language used, however, is not as strong or emphatic as that used by Jesus Christ in denouncing the oppressors and false teachers of his time.

The present government of Germany has declared emphatically against Big Business oppressors and in opposition to the wrongful religious influence in the political affairs of the nation. Such is exactly our position; and we further state in our literature the reason for the existence of oppressive Big Business and the wrongful political religious influence, because the Holy Scriptures plainly declare that these oppressive instruments proceed from the Devil, and that the complete relief therefrom is God's kingdom under Christ. It is therefore impossible for our literature or our work to in any wise be a danger or a menace to the peace and safety of the state.

Our organization is not political in any sense. We only insist on teaching the Word of Jehovah God to the people, and that without hindrance. We do not object or try to hinder anyone's teaching or believing what he desires, but we only ask the freedom to believe and teach what we conceive the bible to teach, and then let the people decide which they wish to believe.

To know Jehovah God and his gracious provision for mankind is of most vital importance to all persons, because God has declared in His Word that where there is no vision or understanding of his Word the people perish. (Proverbs 29:18) We have devoted our lives and our material substance to the work of enabling the people to gain a vision or understanding of God's Word, and therefore it is impossible for our literature and our work to be a menace to the peace and safety of the nation. Instead of being against the principles advocated by the government of Germany, we stand squarely for such principles, and point out that Jehovah God through Christ Jesus will bring about the full realization of these principles and will give to the people peace and prosperity and the greatest desire of every honest heart.

Our organization seeks neither money nor members, but we are a company or organized body of Christian people engaged solely in the benevolent work of teaching the Word of God to the people at the least possible cost to them. Our organization was originally incorporated in the United States of America in 1884 under the name of the WATCH TOWER BIBLE & TRACT SOCIETY, and in 1914 incorporated under the laws of Great Britain by the name of the INTERNATIONAL BIBLE STUDENTS ASSOCIATION. These are merely the corporate names of our organization for legally carrying forward its work. The Scriptural name by which we are known is 'Jehovah's witnesses'. We are engaged solely in a benevolent work. The purpose of our organization is to aid the people to understand the Bible, which discloses the only possible way for the complete relief and blessing for mankind. Our organization has extended its work throughout the earth. The education, culture and upbuilding of the people must and will come through the agency of God's kingdom concerning which we teach as set forth in the Bible. The salvation of the people depends upon the true knowledge of and obedience to Jehovah God and his righteous ways.

The people are in great distress and in need of help to understand the reason for their unhappy condition and what is the means of relief. The Scriptures, when understood, make this matter clear. Instead of collecting money from the people and using the same to erect great buildings and to support men in luxury, we print the gospel message of God's kingdom and carry it to the homes of the people that they may, at the least inconvenience to themselves, gain a knowledge of God's purposes concerning them.

A careful examination of our books and literature will disclose the fact that the very high ideals held and promulgated by the present national government are set forth in and endorsed and strongly emphasized in our publications, and show that Jehovah God will see to it that these high ideals in due time will be attained by all persons who love righteousness and who obey the Most High. Instead, therefore, of our literature and our work's being a menace to the principles of the present government we are the strongest supporters of such high ideals. For this reason Satan, the enemy of all men who desire righteousness, has sought to misrepresent our work and prevent us from carrying it on in this land.

For many years our organization has put forth an unselfish and persistent effort to do good to the people. Our American brethren have greatly assisted in the work in Germany, and with money freely contributed, and that at a time when all Germany was in dire distress. Now because it appears that Germany may soon be free from oppression and that the people may be lifted up, Satan, the great enemy, puts forth his endeavors to destroy that benevolent work in this land.

League of Nations

The language in our books or literature concerning the League of Nations has been seized upon as a reason for prohibiting our work and the distribution of our books. Let us remind the government and the people of Germany that it was the League of Nations compact that laid upon the shoulders of the German people the great unjust and unbearable burdens. That League of Nations compact was not brought forth by the friends of Germany. In America at one time the public press announced that 140,000 clergymen had set aside a certain period of time in which a concerted movement was to be made, and which was made, to induce the American people to fully endorse the League of Nations. It was the Federation of Churches in America that issued a manifesto stating that the 'League of Nations is the political expression of God's kingdom on earth', and which by them was substituted in the place and stead of God's kingdom under Christ. It was in America that our organization under the visible leadership of its president pointed out emphatically that the League of Nations is not an institution of Jehovah God, because it is oppressive and unfair. It was that condition, existing at the time, which called forth language that appears in our books concerning the League of Nations and also calling attention to the fact that such League of Nations compact can never bring about the relief and blessing of the people, because such relief and blessing can come by adhering strictly to the principles laid down in God's Word and in the manner which Jehovah has pointed out.

For almost half a century our strictly Christian organization has carried on its work in various parts of the earth. Its books are published in more than 50 languages, and upward of 140 million of these books are in the hands of the people. For more than thirty years our books and literature have been distributed throughout Germany, and millions of these are now in the hands of the German people and are read by the people, all of whom will bear testimony to the fact that these books, based strictly on the Bible, are of great help to them and upbuild them and give them hope for a realization of the blessings which Jehovah God long ago promised. In all these years of our work, and in the wide distribution of our books and literature, not one instance can be truthfully cited wherein our work or literature has been a menace to the government or has in any wise endangered the peace and safety of the nations.

The endeavors of our organization being exclusively confined to bearing testimony to the name and Word of Jehovah God, it would be entirely inconsistent for us to attempt to exert any political influence in the governments of this world or to do anything that would endanger the peace and safety of the nation. We have no desire nor inclination to do anything except to carry out our divinely given commission to proclaim the Word of Jehovah God.

In America, Canada and other parts of the British Empire the political clergy, priests and Jesuits have persistently persecuted and continue to persecute those of our organization, and without just cause or excuse; and we have every reason to believe that a like influence has been subtilly [*sic*] employed by the great enemy Satan to misrepresent us and our work in Germany. We remind you that in the years past the political clergymen have brought more sorrow upon the German people than probably any other class of men. We have no desire to fight with the clergymen, but we do ask that the ruling powers of the nation judge us not by the misrepresentation of such men, but that we be judged according to the Word of God and the work we are doing consistent therewith. Jehovah God persecutes no one, but permits each one to chose his own course, holding him responsible for his acts according to knowledge. Jehovah God has emphatically expressed his anger against those who do persecute others who are trying to serve him; and this proves that those who persecute us do not represent God, but that they are incited so to do by the enemy of God and man. – Psalm 72:4

Great Truths

The Holy Scriptures, viewed in the light of present-day events which are in fulfilment of divine prophecy, disclose that: The time has arrived when Jehovah will make his name known to all creation and vindicate his name and clear it from the defamation which Satan has placed against that holy name. (Psalm 83:18) When Jesus Christ, the Vindicator, ascended into heaven Jehovah commanded him to wait until his due time to put the enemy down. That period of waiting has now come to an end and God has sent forth his beloved Son to oust the enemy and rule in righteousness. (Psalm 110:1–4; Hebrews 10:12, 13) The world, or uninterrupted rule, of Satan has ended, and this began to be evidenced by the World War in 1914, and since then until now is the time when the gospel of the Kingdom must be told to the people. (Matthew 24:3, 4) Satan has now been cast out of heaven and down to the earth and now confines his operations to the earth in an endeavor to blind the people to the truth and destroy them, and that is the reason for the presentday sufferings of humanity. The prophetic words of Jesus now apply: 'Woe to the inhabiters [the rulers] of the earth, and of the sea [the people in general]! for the devil is come down unto you, having great wrath, because he knoweth that he hath but a short time.' – Revelation 12:12.

The people of Germany have suffered great misery since 1914 and have been the victims of much injustice practiced upon them by others. The nationalists have declared themselves against all such unrighteousness and announced that 'Our relationship to God is high and holy'. Since our organization fully endorses these righteous principles and is engaged solely in carrying forth the work of enlightening the people concerning the Word of Jehovah God, Satan by subtilty [*sic*] endeavors to set the government against our work and destroy it because we magnify the importance of knowing and serving God. Instead of our organization's being a menace to the peace and safety of the government, it is the one organization standing for the peace and safety of this land.

We beg to remind all that the great crisis is upon the world because the transition period from bad to good is at hand, and the hope of the world is God's kingdom under Christ, for which Jesus taught his followers to constantly pray: 'Thy kingdom come. Thy will be done on earth, as it is done in heaven.'

The power of Jehovah God is supreme and there is no power that can successfully resist him. His time to exercise his power in the interest of humanity and to the vindication of his great name is here. In this connection we respectfully call attention to the admonition and warning of Jehovah God, both to the rulers and to the people, which applies to this very hour, wherein he says: 'Yet have I set my king upon my holy hill of Zion ... Be wise now, therefor, O ye kings; be instructed, ye judges of the earth. Serve the LORD with fear, and rejoice with trembling. Kiss the Son, lest he be angry, and ye perish from the way, when his wrath is kindled but a little. Blessed are all they that put their trust in him.' – Psalm 2:6, 10–12.

The present government having declared adherence to the aforementioned high ideals, we are persuaded that the rulers do not desire to knowingly resist the progressive witness work to the name of Jehovah God and his kingdom which we are now carrying forward. If our work is merely that of men, it will fall of its own weight. If it is of Jehovah God and being carried forward in obedience to his commandment, then to resist it means to fight against God. – Acts 5: 39.

We therefore appeal to the high sense of justice of the government and nation and respectfully ask that the order of prohibition against our work and our literature be set aside, and the opportunity be given us to have a fair hearing before we are judged. We respectfully ask that the government appoint a committee of impartial men to hold conference with a committee of our organization and that a fair and impartial examination of our literature and our work be made, to the end that all misunderstanding may be removed and that we may without hindrance obey Jehovah God's commandment now applying to us, to wit: 'Go through, go through the gates; prepare ye the way of the people; cast up the highway; gather out the stones; lift up a standard for the people.' – Isaiah 62:10.

The peoples of Germany are a Godfearing people and should not be deprived of an opportunity to learn of Jehovah God and of his gracious provision to bring lasting peace, prosperity, liberty and everlasting life on earth to all those who know and obey him. Let all who love God work together to the honor and vindication of his name. All who take a contrary course must take responsibility before God; but as for us we will serve Jehovah forever.

RESOLVED, That copies of this Declaration be respectfully delivered to high officials of the government and that the same be given wide publication to the people, that the name of Jehovah may be further known.

Besides producing the *Erklärung* (or *Declaration of Facts*), the Watch Tower Society, through its German branch offices, sent a letter directly to Adolf Hitler. This letter was probably written by the Watch Tower's German branch overseer, Paul Balzereit, or by someone directly under his supervison. Whether it was approved by Watch Tower president J.F. Rutherford is impossible to say. However, it reflects what appears in the *Erklärung* and was certainly in harmony with the general thrust of Rutherford's policies at the time.

So that there can be no question as to the validity of this document, I present the original of the Watch Tower letter to Hitler before providing the English translation that follows as document C3–B.

Document C3-A

(German Text)

WATCH TOWER
BIBLE AND TRACT SOCIETY
PUBLISHERS OF THE BIBLE STUDENTS ASSOCIATION

GENERAL OFFICES:	GERMAN BRANCH:
117 ADAMS STREET	WACHTTURMSTR. 1–19
BROOKLYN	MAGDEBURG
NEW YORK, U.S.A	POSTSCH.–K.: MAGDEBURG 4042

TELEPHONE, MAGDEBURG 405 56, 405 57, 405, 58
RADIO AND CABLE ADDRESS: WATCHTOWER MAGDEBURG

Sehr verehrter Herr Reichskanzler!

Am 25. Juni 1933 tagte in Berlin in der Sporthalle Wilmersdorf eine ca. 5000 Personen umfassende und mehrere Millionen Deutscher repräsentierende Vertreterkonferenz der Bibelforscher Deutschlands (Zeugen Jehovas), welche bereits seit vielen Jahren Freunde und Anhänger dieser Bewegung sind. Der Zweck dieser, von den Abgeordneten der einzelnen Bibelforschergemeinden Deutschlands besuchten Tagung war, Mittel und Wege zufinden, um dem Herrn Reichskanzler und den übrigen hohen Regierungsbeamten des Deutschen Reiches sowohl als allen Länderregierungen Kenntnis zu geben von folgendem:

Gegen eine auf dem Boden positiven Christentums stehende Vereinigung ernster, christlicher Männer und Frauen wurden und werden in einzelnen Landesteilen Massnahmen ergriffen, die in ihrem Ursprung lediglich als die Verfolgung von Christen durch andere Christen anzusprechen sind, weil die – diese Massnahmen auslösenden – gegen uns erhobenen Anschuldigungen meistens von klerikaler, besonders katholischer Seite aus erhoben wurden und unwahr sind.

Absolut überzeugt von der völligen Objektivität der die Angelegenheit bearbeitenden Regierungsstellen und Beamten, ersehen wir trotz allem, dass – einerseits wohl wegen des Umfanges unserer Literatur und andererseits wegen starker Inanspruchnahme der betreffenden Sachbearbeiter – der Inhalt unserer Literatur und der Sinn unserer Bewegung größtenteils falsch beurteilt wird, und zwar nach dem, was unsere religiösen Gegner – Vorurteil bewirkend – gegen uns vorbringen.

Darum ist das auf dieser Konferenz Besprochene in beigefügter Erklärung der Watch Tower Bible and Tract Society niedergelegt, um es ihnen, Herr Reichskanzler, sowie den hohen Regierungsstellen des Deutschen Reiches und der Länder zu überreichen als Dokumentierung der Tatsache, dass die Bibelforscher Deutschlands als einziges Ziel ihrer Arbeit nur beabsichtigen, die Menchen zu Gott zurückzuführen und den Namen Jehovas, des Allerhöchsten, des Vaters unseres Herrn und Erlösers Jesus Christus, auf Erden zu bezeugen und zu ehren. Wir wissen bestimmt, dass Sie, Herr Reichskanzler, solche Tätigkeit nicht stören lassen werden.

Die Bibelforschergemeinden Deutschlands und ihre Glieder sind allgemein bekannt als Hort wahrhafter Ehrfurcht vor dem Allerhöchsten und als eifrige Pfleger sorgsamer Bibelforschung. Örtliche Polizeibehörden werden immer bestätigen müssen, dass Bibelforscher absolut zu den ordnungliebenden und -erhaltenden Elementen des Landes und Volkes zu zählen sind. Ihre einzige Mission ist Werbung der Menschenherzen für Gott.

Die Watch Tower Bible and Tract Society ist die organisierende Missionszentrale der Bibelforscher (für Deutschland: Sitz Magdeburg).

Das Brooklyner Präsidium der Watch Tower-Gesellschaft ist und war seit jeher in hervorragender Masse deutschfreundlich. Aus diesem Grunde wurden im Jahre 1918 der Präsident der Gesellschaft und die sieben Glieder des Direktoriums in Amerika zu 80 Jahren Zuchthaus verurteilt, weil der Präsident sich weigerte, zwei von ihm in Amerika geleitete Zeitschriften zur Kriegspropaganda gegen Deutschland zu gebrauchen. Diese zwei Zeitschriften „The Watch Tower" und „Bible Student" waren die beiden einzigen Zeitschriften Amerikas, die eine Kriegspropaganda gegen Deutschland verweigerten und darum während des Krieges in Amerika auch verboten und unterdrückt wurden.

In gleicher Weise hat sich das Präsidium unserer Gesellschaft in den letzten Monaten nicht nur geweigert, an der Greuelpropaganda gegen Deutschland teilzunehmen, sondern hat sogar dagegen Stellung genommen, wie dies auch in der beigefügten Erklärung unterstrichen wird durch den Hinweis, daß die Kreise, welche diese Greuelpropaganda in Amerika leiteten (Geschäftsjuden und Katholiken), dort auch die rigorosesten Verfolger der Arbeit unserer Gesellschaft und ihres Präsidiums sind. Durch diese und andere in der Erklärung enthaltenden Feststellungen soll die Zurückweisung der Verleumdung, Bibelforscher würden durch die Juden unterstützt, erfolgen.

Die Vertreterkonferenz dieser fünftausend Delegierten nahm mit grosser Befriedigung Kenntnis von der durch Herrn Regierungspräsidenten zu Magdeburg erfolgten Feststellung, dass die von unseren kirchlichen Gegnern behauptete Beziehung zwischen Bibelforschern und Kommunisten oder Marxisten nicht erweisbar sei (also auch eine

Verleumdung ist). Ein diesbezüglicher Pressebericht, enthalten in der Magdeburger Tageszeitung Nr. 104 vom 5. Mai 1933, lautet:

> **Eine Erklärung der Regierung zur Besetzung des Bibelforscher-Hauses. – Die Pressestelle der Regierung teilt mit: „Die polizeiliche Besetzung des Grundstückes der „Vereinigung der ernsten Bibelforscher" in Magdeburg ist am 29. April aufgehoben worden, weil kein belastendes Material hinsichtlich der behaupteten kommunistischen Betätigung gefunden worden ist."**

Ferner: Magdeburger Tagszeitung Nr. 102 vom 3. Mai 1933

> **„Vom Büro der Bibelforschervereinigung wird uns mitgeteilt, dass die Aktion, die von der Polizei gegen die Wachtturmgesellschaft und Bibelforschervereinigung eingeleitet wurde, inzwichen** ***gänzlich aufgehoben*** **worden ist. Ferner wurde alles freigegeben, da die sorgfältig durchgeführte Durchsuchung ergab, dass sich die Gesellschaften weder in politischer noch in krimineller Hinsicht irgend etwas zuschulden kommen liessen, und weil weiter festgestellt wurde, dass die beiden Gesellschaften absolut unpolitisch und streng religiös sind. – Von der Regierung wurde uns auf Anfrage die Richtigkeit dieser Angaben** ***bestätigt."***

Die Vertreterkonferenz dieser fünftausend Delegierten betonte, dass sie es nach dieser Sachlage unter ihrer Würde halte, sich fernerhin überhaupt noch gegen die verächtliche Verdächtigung marxistischer oder gar kommunistischer Betätigung verteidigen zu müssen. Diese widerlegten Verleumdungen unserer religiösen Gegner tragen eindeutig das Signum religiöser Konkurrenz, die einen ehrlichen Mahner statt mit Gottes Wort, mit dem wenig schönen Mittel der Verleumdung erdrosseln möchte.

Weiter wurde auf dieser Konferenz der fünftausend Delegierten – wie in der Erklärung ausgedrückt – festgestellt, dass die Bibelforscher Deutschlands für dieselben hohen ethischen Ziele und Ideale kämpfen, welche die nationale Regierung des Deutschen Reiches bezüglich des Verhältnisses des Menschen zu Gott proklamierte, nämlich: Ehrlichkeit des Geschöpfes gegenüber dem Schöpfer!

Auf der Konferenz wurde festgestellt, dass in dem Verhältnis der Bibelforscher Deutschlands zur nationalen Regierung des Deutschen Reiches keinerlei Gegensätze vorliegen, sondern dass im Gegenteil –

bezüglich der rein religiösen, unpolitischen Ziele und Bestrebungen der Bibelforscher – zu sagen ist, dass diese in völliger Übereinstimmung mit den gleichlaufenden Zielen der nationalen Regierung des Deutschen Reiches sind.

Unter Berufung auf die angeblich harte Sprache unserer Literature erfolgten einige Verbote unserer Bücher. Die Konferenz der fünftausend Delegierten verwies dazu auf den Umstand, dass der beanstandete Inhalt der Bücher doch nur Bezug nimmt auf Zustände und Handlungen im Anglo-Amerikanischen Weltreich, und dass dieses – speziell England – doch für den Völkerbund und die auf Deutschland gelegten ungerechten Verträge und Lasten verantwortlich zu machen ist. Das im obigen Sinne unserer Literatur Gesagte richtet sich also doch – einerlei, ob in finanzieller, politischer oder ultramontaner Beziehung – gegen die Bedrücker des deutschen Volkes und Landes, aber doch nicht gegen das sich gegen diese Lasten sträubende Deutschland, so daß die erfolgten Verbote absolut unverständlich sind.

Für diejenigen deutschen Ländergruppen, in denen sogar Verbote der Bibelforscher-Gottesdienste, Verbote ihrer Gebetsversammlungen usw. vorliegen, und die seit vielen Wochen auf eine gerechte Lösung dieses, ihr religiöses Leben knebelnden Zustandes warten, wurde folgendes ausgedrückt:

Wir wollen auch weiterhin den erlassenen Verbotsanordnungen Folge leisten; denn wir sind gewiss, dass der Herr Reichskanzler bzw. die einzelnen hohen Landesregierungen diese Massnahmen – durch welche zehntausende christliche Männer und Frauen schliesslich einem dem Urchristen-Leiden vergleichbaren Märtyrertum verfallen müßten – nach Kenntniss der wirklichen Sachlage aufheben werden.

Endlich bekundete diese Konferenz der fünftausend Delegierten, dass die Bibelforscher- bzw. die Watchtower-Organisation eintritt für die Aufrechterhaltung von Ordnung und Sicherheit des Staates, sowie für die Förderung der vorerwähnten, auf religiösem Gebiet liegenden hohen Ideale der nationalen Regierung. Um hiervon vor allen Dingen dem Herrn Reichskanzler, als dem Führer des Volkes, und den übrigen hohen Regierungsbeamten des Deutschen Reiches und der Länder Kenntnis zu geben, wurde das vorstehend kurz gesagte in anliegender Erklärung ausführlich niedergelegt.

Diese beigefügte Erklärung wurde vom Sekretär der fünftausend Delegierten der Bibelforscher Konferenz vorgelesen und von dieser einstimmig gebilligt und angenommen mit dem Auftrag, je ein Exemplar dieser Erklärung zusammen mit diesem Versammlungsbericht dem Herrn Reichskanzler und den übrigen hohen Regierungsbeamten des Reiches und der Länder zu überreichen.

Dies geschieht hierdurch nit der ergebenen Bitte, dem in der Erklärung zum Ausdruck gebrachten Ansuchen geneigtest entsprechen zu wollen:

Nämlich, einer Kommission aus unserer Mitte Gelegenheit zu geben zur verantwortlichen Darlegung des wahren Sachverhalts vor dem Herrn Reichskanzler oder dem Herrn Reichsminister des Innern persönlich. Anderfalls wollte der Herr Reichskanzler eine Kommission von Männern bestimmen, die nicht nur durch religiöse Vorurteile gegen uns eingenommen sind, also von Männern, die selbst nicht beruflich religiös interessieret sind, sondern die wirklich nur – den für solche Fälle geltenden gerechten und vom Herrn Reichskanzler selbst aufgestellten Grundsätzen entsprechend – unsere Angelegenheit vorurteilslos prüfen würden. Mit diesen Grundsätzen meinen wir das in Punkt 24 des Programms der Nationalsozialistischen Deutschen Arbeiterpartei Gesagte:

„Wir fördern die Freiheit aller religiösen Bekenntnisse im Staat, soweit sie nicht dessen Bestand gefährden oder gegen das Sittlichkeits- und Moralgefühl der germanischen Rasse verstossen.

Die Partei als solche vertritt den Standpunkt eines positiven Christentums, ohne sich konfessionell an ein bestimmtes Bekenntnis zu binden. Sie bekämpft den jüdisch-materialistischen Geist in und ausser uns und ist überzeugt, dass eine dauernde Genesung unseres Volkes nur erfolgen kann von innen heraus..."

Wir sind fest überzeugt, daß – wenn man uns religiös vorurteilslos erstens nur nach Gottes Wort and zweitens diesen angeführten Programmpunkten nach beurteilt – die nationale Regierung Deutschlands keinerlei Ursache finden wird, unsere Gottesdienste oder unsere Missionstätigkeit zu hindern.

In Erwartung einer baldigen gütigen Zusage, und mit der Versicherung unserer allergrößten Hochachtung, sind wir, sehr verehrter Herr Reichskanzler

ergebenst

Watch Tower Bible and Tract Society
Magdeburg

DOCUMENT C3-B
(English Translation)

WATCH TOWER
BIBLE AND TRACT SOCIETY
PUBLISHERS OF THE BIBLE STUDENTS ASSOCIATION

GENERAL OFFICES:	GERMAN BRANCH:
117 ADAMS STREET	WACHTTURMSTR. 1 – 19
BROOKLYN	M A G D E B U R G
NEW YORK, U.S.A.	POSTSCH.–K.: MAGDEBURG 4042

TELEPHONE, MAGDEBURG 405 56, 405 57, 405, 58
RADIO AND CABLE ADDRESS: WATCHTOWER MAGDEBURG

Most Honored Mr. Chancellor:

On 25 June 1933, a 5,000-delegate convention of German Bible Students (Jehovah's Witnesses), representing several million Germans who have been friends and followers of this movement for many years, was held in the Sporthalle Wilmersdorf in Berlin. The purpose of this meeting was to find ways and means of making known to you, Mr. Chancellor, and to other high government officials of the German Reich, as well as *Länder* [state] governments, the following:

In some parts of the country measures are being taken against an association of earnest Christian men and women that has positive Christianity as its foundation. Because of their origin, these measures can be regarded as nothing less than the persecution of one group of Christians by another, since the accusations which trigger them [the measures] are leveled from clerical, especially Catholic, quarters and are untrue.

Absolutely convinced of the full objectivity of the government departments and officials dealing with these matters, we nevertheless recognize that because of the volume of our literature on one hand and because of the heavy workload of the relevant case workers on the other, the content of our literature and the purpose of our movement are judged in large part incorrectly, specifically in accord with the views – which cause prejudice – that our religious opponents bring against us.

For this reason the matters discussed at the convention have been set down in the attached declaration of the Watch Tower Bible and

Tract Society in order to convey to you, Mr. Chancellor, and to the senior departments of the governments of the German Reich and the *Länder* as documentation of the fact that German Bible Students intend only, as the sole objective of their work, to lead mankind back to God and to witness to and give honor to the name of Jehovah, the Almighty, the Father of our Lord and Redeemer, Jesus Christ, here on the earth. We are secure in the knowledge that you, Mr. Chancellor, will not let such activity be disturbed.

German Bible Student congregations are generally known as havens of true reverence for the Almighty and as ardent custodians of careful biblical research. Local police authorities must always affirm that Bible Students definitely have to be counted as among those elements of the country and people that love and support order. Their only mission is the recruitment of human hearts that love God.

The Watch Tower Bible and Tract Society is the Bible Students' organizational mission center (for Germany: with head offices in Magdeburg).

The Brooklyn administration of the Watch Tower Society is and in the past has been outstandingly friendly to Germany. For this reason, the president of the Society and seven members of its Board of Directors in the United States were sentenced to 80 years imprisonment because the president refused to use two magazines published by him in the United States for war propaganda against Germany. These two magazines, 'The Watch Tower' and 'Bible Student' [*The Bible Students Monthly*] were the only magazines in the United States that refused [to publish] war propaganda against Germany and were, for this reason, outlawed and suppressed in the United States during the war.

In a similar manner, the administration of our Society not only refused to participate in the atrocity propaganda against Germany, but it took a position against it. This is emphasized by the attached declaration that refers to the fact that the circles that led [in promoting] atrocity propaganda in the United States (commercialistic Jews and Catholics) are also the most eager persecutors of our Society's work and its administration. These and other statements in our declaration are meant to serve as a rejection of the slanderous claim that the Bible Students are supported by Jews.

The representative convention of these five thousand delegates took notice with great satisfaction of the statement by the governing president of Magdeburg that the connection between Bible Students and Communists or Marxists, claimed by our clerical opponents, cannot be substantiated (and thus is slanderous as well). A relevant press report in the *Magdeburg Daily News* No. 104 of May 5, 1933 says:

A government declaration regarding the occupation of Bible Student House. – The government press center announces: 'Police occupation of property owned by the Earnest Bible Students Association has been ended since no incriminating material regarding a claimed Communist activity was found.'

Further: the *Magdeburg Daily News* No. 102 of May 3, 1933 [states]:

From the office of the Bible Students' Association we have received word that the actions initiated by the police against the Watch Tower Society and the Bible Students' Association have been completely ended. All material was released because a careful search revealed that those societies are not guilty either in a political or criminal way, and because it was further determined that both societies are absolutely apolitical and strictly religious [in nature]. Upon our questioning, the government confirmed the correctness of our report.

The representative convention of these five thousand delegates stressed that, following these circumstances, it would find it beneath its dignity to defend itself in future against the contemptible accusation of Marxist or Communist activity. The delegates refuted the accusations of our religious opponents, which are clearly a sign of religious competition. They [the religious opponents] would prefer to throttle a truthful herald of warning with slander rather than [use] the Word of God.

Further, it was stated at the five-thousand-delegate convention – as expressed in the declaration – that Bible Students are fighting for the same high, ethical goals and ideals that the National Government of the German Reich proclaimed regarding the relationship of man to God, namely: honesty of the created towards the Creator!

At the convention, it was stated that there are no opposing views in the relationship between German Bible Students and the National Government of the German Reich, but that, to the contrary, respecting the purely religious and apolitical goals and objectives of the Bible Students, it can be said that these are in complete harmony with the similar goals of the National Government of the German Reich.

Because of the supposedly harsh language of our literature, some of our books were banned. The five-thousand-delegate convention pointed out in this connection that the contents of our books that were objected to referred only to circumstances in the Anglo-American World Empire and that it – especially England – is to be held responsible for the League of Nations and the unjustified treaties and burdens placed on Germany. The things said in the above-mentioned spirit are therefore directed – whether in a financial, political, or Roman Catholic (ultramontane) sense – against the oppressors of the German people and country, not against the Germany struggling against these burdens. Thus the bans [on Bible Student literature] are made absolutely incomprehensible.

To those various German *Länder,* in which there occurred bans on Bible Student religious services, prohibitions of prayer meetings, etc., those [Bible Students], who have waited for weeks for a just resolution of the situation that is stifling to their religious life, expressed the following:

We will continue to conform to the regulations of prohibition issued [against us] because we are confident that you, Mr. Chancellor, or the governments of the *Länder,* will lift these measures – by which tens of thousands of Christian men and women would fall victim to a martyrdom reminiscent of that of the original Christians – once the true state of affairs is known.

Finally, this five-thousand-delegate convention stated that the Bible Student-Watch Tower organization stands for the maintenance of order and the security of the state as well as for the enhancement of the above mentioned, religiously related high ideals of the National Government. In order to make this known above all to you, Mr. Chancellor, as the Leader of the German people, and to other high government officials of the Reich and the *Länder,* the sentiments expressed briefly above were set down in detail in the attached declaration.

The attached declaration was read [publicly] by the secretary of the five-thousand-delegate Bible Student Convention, was approved unanimously [by Convention delegates], and was adopted with the instruction that a single copy of it and of the Convention Report be conveyed to the Chancellor of the Reich and to other high officials of the Reich and the *Länder.*

This is done with the most respectful plea that the request expressed in the declaration be granted in a most positive manner:

Namely, to give a commission [drawn] from within our midst the opportunity of making a responsible exposition regarding the facts to you, Mr. Chancellor, or the Minister of the Interior, personally. Failing that, [we request] that a commission of men be appointed by you, Mr. Chancellor, who are not religiously prejudiced against us – that is of men who are themselves not by profession interested in religious matters but who would alone truly examine our concerns without prejudice and according to the just principles enunciated by the Chancellor of the Reich himself. By these principles we mean the statements in Section 24 of the Platform of the National Socialist German Workers Party:

'We demand the freedom of all religious confessions in the state so long as they do not endanger its existence or conflict with the ethical and moral beliefs of the German race.

'The Party, as such, represents the viewpoint of positive Christianity without associating itself with a specific confession. It opposes the Jewish-materialist spirit domestically and abroad and is convinced that a lasting recuperation of our people can only happen from the inside out ...'

We are firmly convinced that the National Government of Germany will find no reason to hinder our services or missionary activities if we are judged, first, without religious prejudice and, second, according to the Platform points quoted above.

With anticipation of an early, positive assent [to our requests] and with the assurance of our highest esteem, most honored Mr. Chancellor, we remain,

Most respectfully,

Watch Tower Bible and Tract Society
Magdeburg

One of the clearest evidences that Watch Tower officials, including Watch Tower president J.F. Rutherford, were attempting to work out an accord with the Nazis during the summer of 1933 is the following letter, sent by the society's Central European branch overseer, Martin Harbeck, to German Jehovah's Witnesses. In light of Witness doctrine, it is especially shocking because it suggests that the Witnesses' preaching work would be terminated in response to the German government's ban until the millennium. To my knowledge, this letter has never been reprinted in Watch Tower literature, although it is mentioned as an aside in the *1974 Yearbook of Jehovah's Witnesses.* The reason it has never been published is obvious: it shows just how far Watch Tower leaders were initially willing to go in seeking an accord with the Nazis. It is reproduced here with specific thanks to the Hamburg State

Archive, where it is catalogued as from Staatsarchiv Hamburg, Staatsanwaltschaft – Landgericht – Strafrsachen, L 26/ 38 Band 1 36a.

Document C4-A
(German Text)

Watch Tower Bible and Tract Society Brooklyn, New-York, U.S.A.	Abschrift! für die deutschen Freunde bestimmt! Magdeburg, den 28. August 1933

Meine lieben Freunde !

Die vielen Anfragen, die hier eingegangen sind, möchte ich hiermit durch ein Zirkularschreiben beantworten:

Die Watch Tower Bible and Tract Society ist verboten. Ebenso die Tätigkeit der „Internationalen Bibelforscher-Vereinigung".

Als Bevollmächtigter der Watch Tower Bible and Tract Society, und Watch Tower Bible and Tract speziell als Beauftragter des Präsidenten, Richter Rutherford, möchte ich Euch hiermit bitten, Euch den gegenwärtigen Vorschriften und Massnahmen der Regierungs- und Polizeibehörden zu unterziehen. Vor allen Dingen möchte ich Euch ersuchen, keine verbotenen Schriften zu verbreiten und ohne polizeiliche Bewilligung keinerlei Versammlungen oder Vorlesungen abzuhalten.

Da uns der Druck von Büchern, Broschüren und Zeitschriften verboten ist, konnten und können die laufenden Bestellungen nicht mehr aus geführt werden. Anfragen sind daher völlig vorläufig zwecklos.

Wir wollen gute Bürger des Landes sein und auch durch unser Verhalten und unseren Lebenswandel ein beredtes Zeugnis für die Ehre Gottes und die Rechtfertigung seinen Namens und Wortes ablegen.

Ich übermittle Euch die Grüsse, die mir Richter Rutherford aufgetragen hat und bitte Euch, in Glauben und Gebet ausharren, bis der Herr uns in seinem Königreich wiederum Gelegenheit gibt, zur Rechtfertigung seines Namens beizutragen.

In Liebe mit Euch verbunden, begrüsse ich Euch als

Watch Tower Bible and Tract Society
Brooklyn, New-York, U.S.A.
(gez.: M. C. Harbeck.)

Weitergeben und bitte zurückgeben!

Document C4-B
(English Translation)

Watch Tower Bible and
Tract Society
Brooklyn, New-York, U.S.A. Copy!

Intended for German friends!
Magdeburg, 28 August 1933

My dear friends:

I should like to answer the many inquiries that [we have received] here by means of a circular letter. The Watch Tower Bible and Tract Society is banned. Equally, the activity of the International Bible Students Association.

As authorized by the Watch Tower Bible & Tract Society, and especially as the proxy of the President, Judge Rutherford, I should like to ask you herewith to submit to all current governmental and police authorities' regulations [without] exception. Above all, I would like to entreat you not to disseminate banned publications and not to hold any meetings or lectures without permission issued by the police.

Since the printing of books, pamphlets and magazines is banned, we cannot fill orders for them. Inquiries are therefore temporarily of no use.

We want to be good citizens of the country and give eloquent testimony through our moral conduct and our style of life to the honor of God and the vindication of His Name and Word.

As Judge Rutherford directed me, I convey to you greetings and beg you to persevere in faith and prayer until the Lord gives us an opportunity in His Kingdom to contribute again to the vindication of His Name.

Joined with you in love, I greet you as

Watch Tower Bible and Tract Society
Brooklyn, New-York, U.S.A.
(Signed: M. C. Harbeck.)

Circulate and please return.

APPENDIX D
U.S. State Department Documents Relating to Jehovah's Witnesses in Germany in 1933

U.S. State Department documents of the time provide an interesting overview both of the situation in Germany in 1933 and of the response of Jehovah's Witnesses to it. It is clear from those documents that Judge Rutherford was much more sanguine about reaching a favourable accord with the Nazis than were German Watch Tower officials. That said, it is clear that both Rutherford and those officials wanted to do everything possible to satisfy the Nazis that they were not opposed to the Hitler regime. The documents also indicate the sincere desire of the State Department – and especially the Secretary of State, Cordell Hull – to help the Witnesses in Germany even though Rutherford was openly attacking his native land in the most virulent fashion. Clearly, the State Department did not want the Hitler government to seize American property and set a bad precedent; yet just as clearly, the department was concerned about religious liberty. The documents printed below are titled: 'Efforts to Protect Rights of the Watch Tower Bible and Tract Society, an American Religious Organization Operating in Germany.'

DOCUMENT D1

362.1163 Watch Tower/6: Telegram

The Secretary of State to the Chargé in Germany (Gordon)

WASHINGTON, April 27, 1933 – 6 p.m.

46. The Watch Tower Bible and Tract Society, an American corporation, states that it has been informed that the German Government has

forcibly taken possession of the Society's property at Magdeburg, consisting of a printing and bookbinding establishment and real estate valued at $600,000, and that the German authorities have confiscated its books and other personal property.

Please investigate with a view to lending appropriate assistance, and submit a telegraphic report on the situation. The Society's representative in Germany is Paul Balzereit, Magdeburg.

HULL

DOCUMENT D2

362.1163 Watch Tower/8: Telegram

The Consul General at Berlin (Messersmith) to the Secretary of State

BERLIN, May 2, 1933–4 p.m.
[Received May 2–11:45 a.m.]

Referring to the Department's telegram No. 46, April 27, 6 p.m., to the Embassy, I am able to report Watch Tower Society premises again free and Society functioning through the good offices of the Consulate General.

Full report by mail my despatch No. 1269.[1]

MESSERSMITH

DOCUMENT D3

362.1103 Watch Tower/15: Telegram

The Secretary of State to the Consul General at Berlin (Messersmith)

WASHINGTON, May 18, 1933–5 p.m.

Your May 2, 4 p.m. The Watch Tower Bible and Tract Society greatly appreciated your earlier and successful efforts but now reports that the Governments of Bavaria, Saxony, Thuringia, Lippe, Mecklenburg, Hesse and Wurttemberg, have officially interdicted its activities and confiscated its property valued at about 750,000 Reichsmarks.

1 Not printed.

Please investigate, extend appropriate assistance, and telegraph results.

HULL

DOCUMENT D4

362:1163 Watch Tower/16: Telegram
The Consul at Berlin (Geist) to the Secretary of State

BERLIN, May 27, 1933–11 a.m.
[Received May 27–6:38 a.m.]

Referring to Department's telegram of May 15 [18], 5 p.m., I made representations last week to the Ministry Interior on behalf of the Watch Tower Bible Society. Matter being investigated through authorities German states where activities have been forbidden. No decision reached yet. See my despatch sent confidential May 22nd.[2]

GEIST

DOCUMENT D5

362.1163 Watch Tower/23
The Consul General at Berlin (Messersmith) to the Acting Secretary of State
No. 1428

BERLIN, July 12, 1933.
[Received July 28.]

SIR: I have the honor to refer to my despatch No. 1324 of May 22, 1933,[3] making a report to the Department with regard to the seizure by the police throughout Germany of the property of the Watch Tower Bible and Tract Society. The Consulate General has been in close contact with Mr. Hans Dollinger, the Magdeburg representative of the Watch Tower Bible and Tract Society and also with Mr. Paul Balzereit, representative for central Europe, as well as with Judge J. F. Rutherford of Brooklyn, New York. As was reported in the previous despatch, the property at Magdeburg was seized soon after the National Socialist Government came into power and after ten days, through the

2 Not printed.
3 Not printed.

intervention of the Consulate General, the property was again released. In the meantime a general action on the part of members of the National Socialist Party began against the activities of the Society throughout Germany, so that one decree after another was promulgated by the various states of Germany, excluding Prussia, which eventually was the last to forbid the activities of this Society. Judge Rutherford, the President of the Society in Brooklyn, New York, has been in Europe for a number of months and took the opportunity to come to Germany a number of weeks ago and called at the Consulate General where he had a long interview with Consul Geist with regard to the status of the affairs of the Watch Tower Bible and Tract Society in Germany. It was then explained to Judge Rutherford that the German authorities throughout the country had taken the view that not only the pamphlets but the teachings and the activities of the bible instructors who are attached to their organization throughout the country are inimical to organized Government, the established church and society. Judge Rutherford was very much concerned as to the status of their affairs in Germany and appeared willing to trust somewhat to possible favorable developments which might come about with the march of affairs. His representatives in Germany had complained that the pamphlets prepared in New York for this country were not in accordance with the ideas that have come about with the so-called national resurgence. These men being Germans, understood thoroughly the disrepute into which the Watch Tower Bible and Tract Society had fallen in this country. It was pointed out to Judge Rutherford that the Consulate General would be unable to make any representations to the German Government regarding the ban that had been put upon their activities and that it could use its good offices only to protect the physical property of the organization excluding pamphlets, booklets and brochures which the police had condemned as being anti-revolutionary and communistic in tendency.

The work of the Society has been at an utter standstill in all the states of Germany except Prussia; but on June 24 a decree was issued by the Prussian Ministry of the Interior and signed by Dr. Grauert, the Under Secretary of State in that Ministry. A copy of this decree is enclosed herewith,[4] and it will be noted from the translation herewith enclosed that in the decree the property of the organization was ordered confiscated by the Government. As this is the first instance of

4 Not printed.

this sort which has come to the attention of the Consulate General, the legal phases of it have presented certain complexities. The decree of February 28, 1933 of the Reich President, referred to, confers as the Department knows, very large powers upon the state in confiscating the property and providing for the arrest of persons without trial whose activities are considered dangerous to the state. In the decree of June 24 forbidding the activities of the Society throughout Germany, it was also provided that the property be confiscated. This is identical to the action taken against the Communistic Party and against the Social Democratic Party, in which cases the property including real estate, moneys in the bank, and equipment of all sorts including automobiles and motorcycles, have been confiscated. In view of the seriousness of this situation, Consul Geist visited the Ministry of the Interior and had a conversation in the premises with Staatssekretaer Grauert who is the Under Secretary in that Ministry. A copy of Mr. Geist's memorandum of this conversation is enclosed herewith.[5] It will be seen from the contents of this memorandum that Consul Geist was able to secure a reversal of the decision as to the confiscation of the property of this Society, which it is understood is valued at about 5,000,000 marks. The German authorities insist upon the Society liquidating its holdings in Germany, but it is believed that the Consulate General will be able to obtain sufficient delay with regard to the disposition of their property so that a minimum loss may be sustained.

There is, however, little doubt but that the Watch Tower Bible and Tract Society will be unable either to do any kind of printing in this country even for use abroad, or to continue any kind of activities, and that it is destined to lose considerable money in the liquidation of its affairs. The ban against the Society has been published in numerous newspapers throughout Germany and definite action has been taken by all of the states. At the present time the big plant at Magdeburg is closed and in the hands of National Socialist Storm Troops and a National Socialist flag is flying on the premises. It is expected, however, that the decision of the Ministry of the Interior will presently be made known to the local managers of the Society so that preparations can be commenced to liquidate their affairs. The Department undoubtedly will receive strong protests when it is definitely realized by the American organization that the Society must leave Germany; but it is believed that nothing further can be done in their behalf than to se-

5 Not printed.

cure a delay so that the liquidation of the interests can be accomplished without too great a loss and so that they will have facilities for transferring abroad, presumably to Prague, the necessary equipment to fit up a new plant, as well as any funds which will accrue if the property can be disposed of. The Consulate General anticipates considerable difficulties in these transactions and will afford the Society in every case whatever aid is proper and feasible.

In this connection I should inform the Department that in the action which it has taken on behalf of this society, it has proceeded constantly only after close consultation with the Embassy. The Chargé d'Affaires, Mr. Gordon, and I, after very careful examination of all the circumstances, are of the opinion that in protecting the interests of the Society, such efforts could not go beyond saving the physical property which it has in Germany, this not to include the actual printed pamphlets which are in the country. I have gone into the activities of the Society and of its agents, and have read some of the pamphlets which have been distributed by the Society widely in Germany, and I can see that objection could reasonably be raised to them by the German Government. Although acting as a religious society, the pamphlets contain comment of not a purely religious character. In view of the present situation which exists in Germany, I believe that it would be entirely useless to endeavor to assist this Society to continue its operations and I doubt very much whether our Government, in view of the nature of the activities, would find it possible to assist it. I believe therefore that the only efforts which we can make on behalf of the Society are in connection with the protection of its physical property, the release of which, as the Department will note from this despatch, we have been able to secure.

Respectfully yours, GEORGE S. MESSERSMITH

DOCUMENT D6

362.1163 Watch Tower/19: Telegram

The Consul General at Berlin (Messersmith) to the Acting Secretary of State

BERLIN, July 15,1933 noon
[Received July 15–9:1O a.m.]

We have had several conversations recently with representatives Watch Tower Society. Lately government again seized property and interdicted all activities throughout Germany. We succeeded several days ago obtaining assurances Ministry Interior that physical property including plant Magdeburg will not be confiscated and eventually released. Ban on all activities continues and in view of nature pamphlets, activities and general situation in Germany Embassy and Consulate General have considered it impossible to object to ban on activities and I believe Department will take same attitude. Local representatives society understand our position. Full report forwarded despatch No. 1428, July 12. Suggest Department defer further consideration pending receipt foregoing in answer to Department's telegram.

MESSERSMITH

DOCUMENT D7

362.1163 Watch Tower/31

The Consul General at Berlin (Messersmith) to the Acting Secretary of State

[Extract]

No. 1461 BERLIN, July 27, 1933.

[Received August 11.]

SIR:

Consul Geist called again on Ministerialdirigent Fischer in the Prussian Ministry of the Interior and explained that the measures taken by the German authorities are utterly defeating the demands which they have made on the Watch Tower Bible and Tract Society. A demand was made that the property be released under conditions which would make it possible for this society to afford a reasonable protection to its property and financial interests. Consul Geist pointed out that it appears reasonable that every facility should be granted an American firm to save its property from ruin, and it should be given facilities to avoid unusual and extensive losses; that the purpose of the German Government is wholly served, if their operations do not continue, as the Consulate General has not gone into any discussion of the reasons for which the activities of this society have been forbidden. Consul Geist protested against levying rent for the property belonging to an American firm and pointed out that this was an extraordinary procedure, and a violation of property rights. A protest was made against the position of the German Government in requiring that the property of the Watch Tower Bible and Tract Society remain in the Government's possession as a guarantee that no propaganda will be made by this society abroad against the German Government. This is tantamount to confiscation, and if such confiscation is made without due process of law in the courts, it certainly renders insecure the existence of all American property in Germany. Consul Geist demanded that the property be freely and wholly turned over to the owners to make such disposition as they saw fit, so long as they violated no injunction placed on them regarding their activities. Consul Geist also pointed out that the Consulate General believed that the German authorities were sincere in this action and desired nothing more than to assure themselves that the alleged subversive activities of this society be stopped, and that the German Government had no ulterior intention of obtaining this society's property. Dr. Fischer stated that this assumption was true, and that the purpose back of this action was not to seize the property.

It may be pointed out in this respect that the representatives of the society have the impression that there is no real basic evidence against the Magdeburg organization. There is no doubt that some of the tracts do not coincide with National Socialist ideas, but it is not believed that these are either genuinely subversive or revolutionary, as we understand the terms 'subversive' or 'revolutionary'.

It would be easy enough for the police to see that no printing was done in the establishment, or other activities carried on, to which they could take objection. The Consulate General is of the opinion that the procedure in the confiscation of this property has been an extraordinary action wholly unjustified by the facts. The Consulate General has requested a statement from the Prussian Ministry of the Interior stating precisely the conditions upon which the property will be released, and as soon as this letter is received, the Consulate General will communicate further with the Department. In the meantime it would be appreciated if the Department would study the facts in connection with this case as they have heretofore been reported, and advise the Consulate General whether or not, under the Treaty,[6] the property of an American firm for certain alleged political reasons, can in this way be seized and confiscated.

Respectfully yours, GEORGE S. MESSERSMITH

6 Treaty of Friendship, Commerce and Consular Rights, between the United States and Germany, signed at Washington, 8 December 1923; *Foreign Relations,* 1923, vol. 2, p. 29.

DOCUMENT D8

362.1163 Watch Tower/34: Telegram
The Secretary of State to the Consul General at Berlin (Messersmith)
WASHINGTON, September 7, 1933–5 p.m.

Representative of the Watch Tower Bible Tract Society informs Department that an order has been issued by the German authorities requiring the vacating of the Home at Magdeburg owned by the Society and now occupied by Harbeck, an American citizen and the Society's resident manager, and that a portion of the Society's property including books is being burned today by soldiers or police acting as custodians of the Society's factory. You are requested to lend appropriate assistance and report by cable.

HULL

DOCUMENT D9

362.1163 Watch Tower/34: Telegram
The Secretary of State to the Ambassador in Germany (Dodd)
WASHINGTON, September 9, 1933–2 p.m.

111. The complaint of the Watch Tower Bible and Tract Society in regard to the seizure of its property and the suppression of its activities in Germany has been before the American Consulate General at Berlin and has been the subject of reports by the Consulate General to the Department. You may communicate the substance of this instruction to the Consulate General.

The Society was organized under the laws of Pennsylvania. It established a branch office at Barmen, Germany, in 1909. In 1921, the office was moved to Magdeburg, Germany, where headquarters in Germany were established. The Society owns valuable real estate and personal property at Magdeburg.

Since establishing the branch office in Germany, the Society has been engaged in the publication and distribution of books and tracts on religious subjects. The Society was not molested until on or about April 24, 1933, when German authorities, without explanation, (1) took possession of the real estate belonging to the Society and seized equipment and other personal property and (2) suppressed the Society's activities which were similar in 1933 to activities continuously conducted by the Society from the time it established a branch in Germany.

In connection with (1) the Department is also informed that recently the German authorities burned some of the Society's publications and required the Society's resident manager, an American citizen, to vacate the home occupied by him and owned by the Society.

The Department understands that while general allegations have been made by German authorities about the Society's teachings and practices, the German authorities have not instituted proceedings in which they are required to specify and prove charges and in which representatives of the Society would be given opportunity to answer and defend.

It is unfortunate that purely administrative action entailing such drastic consequences without other than ex parte proceedings should be taken and maintained in Germany, and that apparently the obligation to administer justice by orderly processes of law has been disregarded. Under Article 12 of the Treaty of 1923, between the United States and Germany, the Society is entitled to an opportunity to defend its rights in the courts.

In view of the right of the Society declared by treaty to an opportunity to defend and inasmuch as the Society's property was seized and its activities suppressed by administrative action without judicial process, it is desired that you communicate with the German Foreign Office in the sense of the foregoing.

You should request that prompt steps be taken to restore the property to the possession and control of the Society. You are authorized in your discretion to subordinate as a matter of expediency the question of the resumption of the Society's activities, keeping in mind, however, that the principle upon which a complaint rests regarding this ban on the activities is the same as in the case of the confiscation or destruction of property, namely, the absence of a proper judicial hearing as provided for under Article 12 of the Treaty of 1923.

HULL

DOCUMENT D10

363.1163 Watch Tower/35: Telegram

The Ambassador in Germany (Dodd) to the Secretary of State

BERLIN, September 12,1933–noon.
[Received September 12–8:55 a.m.]

142. Department's 111, September 9, 2 p.m. Consulate General states Society's real and personal property has been released although activities of Society still remain prohibited. Embassy making careful study of actual present status of the facts in the case and until this is completed, I do not consider it advisable to make representations to the Foreign Office.

DODD

DOCUMENT D11

362.1163 Watch Tower/56

The Ambassador in Germany (Dodd) to the Acting Secretary of State

No. 309 BERLIN, December 4, 1933
[Received December 14]

SIR: With reference to my despatch No. 158 [*156*] of September 20,[7] on the subject of the Watch Tower Bible and Tract Society, I have the honor to enclose copies and translation of a note verbale dated November 13, from the Foreign Office, and of its enclosure, the decree of June 24[8] issued by the Prussian Ministry of the Interior suppressing the activities of the Society in Prussia and confiscating its property. The Ministry's decree is based on the Presidential decree of February 28, suspending, on the ground of the existing danger of a communist uprising, certain articles (114, 115, 117, 118, 193, 124, and 154 [*153?*] of the German Constitution relating to personal guarantees. This decree is still in force.

The Departments's attention is invited to the first sentence in paragraph 3 of the note verbale, wherein allusion is made to the legal remedies alleged to be available to the Society, although in the following sentence the Foreign Office appears to express the belief that the Treaty of 1923 gives the Prussian authorities the right to withdraw their approval of the Society, in accordance with the laws of Prussia and the Reich.

On December 1, however, the Embassy gave a copy of the pertinent excerpt from the *note verbale* to Mr. Harbeck, the Society's superintendent for Central Europe, who had just arrived from Switzerland. He expressed grave doubt whether the remedy suggested by the German Government would afford any relief but added that he would consult

7 Not printed.

8 Decree of June 24 not printed.

the Society's attorney. The Embassy has learned subsequently from the Consul in charge, Mr. Geist, who is thoroughly familiar with this matter, that he had been informed by Mr. Harbeck of the latter's intention to press the case in the courts.

During the conversation on December 1, Mr. Harbeck stated that the Society's property in Magdeburg had been restored to it, as set forth in paragraph 4 of the German Government's note, but that all religious activities are forbidden.

Respectfully yours,

For the Ambassador:
J.C. WHITE

[Enclosure–Translation]

The German Foreign Office to the American Embassy
No. III A 3495

NOTE VERBALE

In reply to note verbale No. 61 submitted here on September 20, 1933, by Mr. O'Donoghue, Secretary of Embassy, relative to the branch of the American Watch Tower Bible and Tract Society in Magdeburg, which was forbidden by order of the Prussian Ministry of the Interior, the Foreign office has the honor to inform the Embassy of the United States of America as follows:

The grounds on which the Prussian Government, within the scope of an action directed against the International Association of Bible Students together with all its subsidiary organizations, dissolved and prohibited the branch of the above-mentioned American society known in Germany as the Watch Tower Bible and Tract Society, are shown in the text or the Ministerial Decree of June 24, 1933, of which a copy is enclosed and to which reference is made. The procedure adopted in the action against the Society conforms with the pertinent legal provisions of the Reich or States.

The claim to free admission to the courts provided for in Article XII of the German-American Treaty of Friendship, Commerce and Consular Rights of December 8, 1923, has been complied with in that the legal recourses provided for in the Prussian Police Administrative Law include also suits in the administrative court. The principle contained in the second paragraph of the same Article might, however, be looked upon as decisive in the present case, namely, that the right of the forbidden society to carry out its activity in the Free State of Prussia was contingent upon the approval of the Prussian Government given in conformity with the Reich and State laws, but that it ceased automatically at the moment that the previously granted approval was revoked in accordance with the Reich and State laws.

As the Prussian Ministry of the Interior informs the Foreign Office, it was at the time suggested to the Watch Tower Bible and Tract Society to remove its organization to some other country, and it was expressly permitted to move its machines and other equipment from here to such place for that purpose. Besides, out of consideration for the representations made by the Consul General of the United States, the Regierungspräsident in Magdeburg was instructed on September 26, 1933, to rescind the confiscation of the property of the prohibited Society. Furthermore, the former personnel of the Society was permitted to live in its buildings again.

On the other hand the preparation of pamphlets and broadsheets, carried on by the Watch Tower Bible and Tract Society in the past, as well as its activity with regard to teaching and holding meetings, must remain forbidden. Consequently the regulation will also remain in force, in accordance with which a guarantee must be insured, by means of supervision of the pertinent buildings of the forbidden Society, that neither printed matter of any kind is prepared there, nor political or religious meetings held, nor any teaching done.

BERLIN, November 13, 1933.

DOCUMENT D12

362.1163 Watch Tower/60

The Ambassador in Germany (Dodd) to the Secretary of State

No. 497 BERLIN, February 1, 1934.
[Received February 17.]

SIR: I have the honor to refer the Department to my despatch No. 309 of December 4, 1933, forwarding a copy and translation of a note verbale on this subject from the German Foreign Office, in paragraph two of which is set forth the legal remedy available to the Society under Article XII of the German-American Treaty of 1923, should it desire to seek a judgment of the courts on the action of the Prussian Government forbidding the Society to continue its religious activities in Prussia. The Department was informed that Mr. Harbeck, the Society's superintendent for Central Europe, intended to follow the advice of the Reich authorities.

On January 9, however, the Embassy learned from the Consulate General that the Society in July 1933 had attempted to obtain relief in the manner described by the Foreign Office four months later. The court, however, curtly refused to consider the appeal of the Society, stating that orders issued by the executive on the basis of paragraph 1 of the Presidential Decree of February 28, 1933, cannot be legally contested.

There are transmitted herewith a copy of Mr. Geist's letter and copies and translations of a letter addressed to him by Mr. Balzereit, the German superintendent of the Watch Tower and Bible Society, and of its enclosures.[9] The first of these is a copy of the court's decision, and the second, a statement prepared by the Society setting forth the alleged monetary damages occasioned to it by the acts of the Prussian officials. A copy of the former, certified by the Consulate General, is in the possession of the Embassy.

The Presidential Decree mentioned by the court in the foregoing decision suspends various Articles of the German Constitution containing personal guarantees. The pertinent portion of this decree reads, in translation, as follows:

GERMANY
417

'Articles 114, 115, 117, IIS, 123, 124, and 153 of the Constitution of the German Reich will be suspended until further notice. Therefore restrictions are permissible of personal liberty, of the right of free expression of opinion, including freedom of the press, and the right of association and assembly; together with the invasion of postal and telegraphic and telephone secrecy and orders for house searchings, and confiscations as well as restrictions, of property beyond the legal limitations otherwise applicable in such cases.'

It seems evident that regardless of the contention of the judicial authorities that in virtue of the President's Decree of February 28, 1933, they were unable to consider the Society's plea, the situation indicated by the Department in its telegram of September 10, 1933, still exists, and that Article XII of the Treaty of 1923 has apparently

9 None printed.

proved of no avail. The Society has been unable to defend its rights in the courts.

The question arises therefore, whether since local remedies have apparently been exhausted, grounds exist for interposition by the Government of the United States. According to Hyde's text book on International Law, Volume I, page 491,

'A denial of justice, in a broad sense, occurs whenever a State, through any department or agency, fails to observe, with respect to an alien, any duty imposed by international law or by treaty with his country. Such delinquency may, for example, be manifest in arbitrary or capricious action on the part of the courts, or in legislative enactments destroying the exercise of a privilege conferred by treaty, or in the action of the executive department in ordering the seizure of property without due process of law.'

In the case under consideration the foregoing quotation appears pertinent. It is true that the property at Magdeburg has been restored to the Society, but it seems equally true that the latter may be suffering monetary loss through inability to use its property, and that no legal relief is available. Not only has Article XII been nullified, but also, it would seem, paragraph 3 of Article I.

I desire also to call the Department's attention to the following excerpts from Hyde which relate to the same subject: Volume I, Section 282, page 494, Section 283, pages 496 and 497.

In making these suggestions I am not, of course, attempting to pass upon the merits of the views expounded by the Prussian authorities concerning the alleged objectionable teachings and doctrines of the Society. This aspect of the question, however, would seem in no wise to limit its right to defend its case. That right has been denied. Accordingly I venture to lay the matter before the Department for such additional instructions as may be appropriate.[10]

Respectfully yours, WILLIAM E. DODD

10 Copies of enclosures to this despatch were transmitted to Mr Chandler P. Anderson for the Watch Tower Bible and Tract Society in a letter dated 28 March 1934 (362.1163 Watch Tower/65). Apparently no further action was taken by the department.

APPENDIX E
Documents Relating to the Watch Tower's Attacks on Nazism

The following letter shows Judge J.F. Rutherford's mindset in early 1934 and his willingness to challenge Hitler personally. Another very interesting aspect about it is that in it Rutherford mentions the *Declaration of Facts* adopted at the Berlin-Wilmersdorf convention and states that he is enclosing a copy of it to the Nazi leader. This is further proof of Rutherford's and the Watch Tower's total support for that document as it was distributed throughout Germany in the previous year.

DOCUMENT E1

Rutherford to Hitler, 9 February 1934

Sir:

This letter is a kindly notice and warning of things that are of vital importance to your welfare. You will find it to your interest to read it carefully.

In Germany for many years faithful and good men and women have been teaching the doctrines of God's Word, which people jointly work under organizations bearing the name of EARNEST BIBLE STUDENTS and the WATCH TOWER BIBLE & TRACT SOCIETY, which names merely represent the Society or corporate organization for carrying on their work. These men and women are devoted to Jehovah God and serve Him as His witnesses, telling the people what is the truth of the Bible. They seek to do good to all men and injury to none.

In the early spring of 1933 your government without just cause or excuse forcibly compelled these earnest Christian people, who are Jehovah's witnesses, to cease the worship of Jehovah God in the way in which God has commanded them to worship; seized their Bibles, song books, Bible textbooks, and other Bible literature, and their furniture, drove them out of their places of worship, and forbade them to assemble together to study the Scriptures and to worship God, and to preach the truth to others.

Your government also without just cause or excuse seized a great amount of books, Bibles, paintings, paper and other material, and destroyed the same by fire, which property belonged to the aforesaid Society. Many of these innocent and faithful witnesses of Jehovah God your officers have incarcerated in prison, and illtreated them. Your being a very busy man, probably many of these things have not been brought to your attention; but that is not the fault of those who have been unjustly and cruelly treated.

Enemies of Jehovah's witnesses have maliciously misrepresented them and told vicious lies against them in order to induce your government to do injury to them. In order that the government might be informed as to the real facts more than seven thousand of Jehovah's witnesses assembled in Berlin, Germany, on the 25th day of June, 1933, and there issued a Declaration setting forth the facts concerning their work in Germany, which declaration was furnished to all the high officials of your government, and millions of copies thereof were distributed amongst the people until such distribution was forcibly stopped by officers of your government. That Declaration, a copy of which is hereto attached, called upon your government to see to it that these faithful people, who are Jehovah's witnesses, might 'without hindrance obey Jehovah God's commandments and worship Him as commanded,' and tell the people of His kingdom for the blessing of all 'the families of the earth'.

That request has been ignored by your government, and you have refused to permit these witnesses of Jehovah to serve Him and worship Him as commanded by the Most High.

These faithful followers of Christ Jesus and who are Jehovah's witnesses have waited and suffered long, hoping that you would cause their unjust treatment to cease and permit them to go on with their worship and service to Jehovah God without interference. But you have failed to do so. During the past ten years the rulers and people of Germany have received notice by the wide publication of literature that God's kingdom is here and that His King, Christ Jesus, will establish a righteous government on earth for the blessing of the people. They have been warned that those who oppose God and His kingdom shall be destroyed by the Lord at Armageddon. Such notice and warning have been ignored by your government.

Permit me to remind you that Jehovah God sent His servant Moses to Egypt to give notice and warning to Pharaoh that he must let God's chosen people go and worship Him in the manner that He had commanded. Such notice and warning Pharaoh not only ignored, but he defied Jehovah God, and the result was that Jehovah killed all the firstborn of Egypt and then destroyed the ruling power. (See Exodus 12:29, 30; 14;23–28) The Scriptures plainly declare that what came upon Egypt will come in far greater degree upon all the world, and particularly upon those who oppose Jehovah God and His kingdom. You may successfully resist any and all men, but you cannot successfully resist Jehovah God.

Pharaoh said to Moses: 'Who is the LORD [Jehovah], that I should obey His voice?' (Exodus 5:2) Later he learned to his sorrow who Jehovah is. Jehovah's witnesses have done everything within their power to show your government that they only want to freely worship Jehovah God and serve Him as He has commanded them, but their efforts have been ignored and their maltreatment continues by your officials. Once more in their behalf, as the president of the Society or organization under which they work, and in the name of Jehovah God and his anointed King, Christ Jesus, I demand that you give order to all officials and servants of your government that Jehovah's witnesses [who are the EARNEST BIBLE STUDENTS and the WATCH TOWER BIBLE & TRACT SOCIETY] in Germany be permitted to peaceably assemble and without hindrance worship God and obey His commandments by teaching to the people the Bible truths concerning God's kingdom under Christ, for which kingdom all Christians have long prayed.

If by the 24th day of March, 1934, there is no response to this earnest demand and nothing done by your government to grant relief of the aforesaid Jehovah's witnesses in Germany, then God's people in other countries will begin the publication throughout the nations of the earth of the facts concerning Germany's wrongful treatment of Christian people there; and having delivered the testimony, we will submit our case and leave it to Jehovah God by and through Christ Jesus to administer the punishment of the guilty ones in His own good way. Permit me to remind you that Jehovah warns that no one shall oppress His anointed. (Psalm 105:15) Christ Jesus is now on His throne, and the battle of the great day of God almighty is just ahead, and it will be the greatest tribulation ever known, and there is just one way of escape: 'Be wise now, therefore, O ye kings; be instructed, ye judges of the earth. Serve the Lord with fear, and rejoice with trembling. Kiss the Son, lest he be angry, and ye perish from the way, when his wrath is kindled but a little. Blessed are all they that put their trust in him.'

Respectfully submitted,
Watch Tower Bible & Tract Society
By

(Signed) J. F. Rutherford
President

DOCUMENT E2

Since neither Hitler nor his government bothered to respond to Rutherford, and the persecution of Jehovah's Witnesses continued in Germany, the bellicose Watch Tower president decided to expose the Nazi regime and to challenge it openly. This resulted in German Jehovah's Witnesses sending the letter that appears below to German officials on 7 October 1934. It appears as reprinted here in the *1974 Yearbook of Jehovah's Witnesses*, pp. 136–7. Not surprisingly, it angered the Hitler government and brought increased persecution on the Witnesses.

TO THE OFFICIALS OF THE GERMAN GOVERNMENT

The word of Jehovah God, as set out in the Holy Bible, is the supreme law, and to us it is our sole guide for the reason that we have devoted ourselves to God and are true and sincere followers of Christ Jesus.

During the past year, and contrary to God's law and in violation of our rights, you have forbidden us as Jehovah's witnesses to meet together to study God's Word and worship and serve him. In his Word he commands us that we shall not forsake the assembling of ourselves together. (Hebrews 10:25) To us Jehovah commands: 'Ye are my witnesses that I am God. Go and tell the people my message.' (Isaiah 43:10, 12, Isaiah 6:9; Matthew 24:14) There is a direct conflict between your law and God's law, and, following the lead of the faithful apostles, 'we ought to obey God rather than men,' and this we will do. (Acts

5:29) Therefore, this is to advise you that at any cost we will obey God's commandments, will meet together for the study of his Word, and will worship him and serve him as he has commanded. If your government or officers do violence to us because we are obeying God, then our blood will be upon you and you will answer to Almighty God.

We have no interest in political affairs, but are wholly devoted to God's kingdom under Christ his king. We will do no injury or harm to anyone. We would delight to dwell in peace and do good to all men as we have opportunity, but, since your government and its officers continue in your attempt to force us to disobey the highest law of the universe, we are compelled to now give you notice that we will, by his grace, obey Jehovah God and fully trust Him to deliver us from all oppression and oppressors.

DOCUMENT E3

Jehovah's Witnesses outside Germany sent the following telegram to Hitler personally at the same time that their German brethren were dispatching the above letter.

Telegram to Hitler

Your ill-treatment of Jehovah's witnesses shocks all good people of earth and dishonors God's name. Refrain from further persecuting Jehovah's witnesses, otherwise God will destroy you and your national party.

DOCUMENT E4-1

When Hitler was made aware of the Witness telegrams, he reacted with apoplectic rage. A witness, Karl Wittig, who was present at the time, gives the following description of how the Nazi leader behaved. Wittig's account is reprinted from the original German, with an English translation (Document E4-2). Both documents are taken from the book *Jehovah's Witnesses in the Divine Purpose* in its respective German and English editions.

Declaration of Karl Wittig
(German Text)

ERKLÄRUNG – Am 7. Oktober 1934 suchte ich in meiner Eigenschaft als damaliger Bevollmächtigter General Ludendorffs nach vorausgegangener Aufforderung den damaligen Reichs- und Preußischen Minister des Innern, Dr. Wilhelm Frick, im seinerzeitigen Reichsministerium des Innern in Berlin, Am Königsplatz 6, auf, um von Ietzterem Mitteilungen entgegenzunehmen, die den Versuch enthielten, General Ludendorff zur Aufgabe seines ablehnenden Standpunktes dem nationalsozialistischen Regime gegenüber zu bewegen. Während meiner Unterredung mit Dr. Frick erschien plötzlich Hitler und beteiligte sich an den Verhandlungen. Als unser Gespräch zwangsläufig auch das bisherige Vorgehen des nationalsozialistischen Regimes gegen die Internationale Bibelforscher-Vereinigung [Jehovas Zeugen] in Deutschland streifte, legte Dr. Frick Hitler eine Reihe aus dem Auslande eingelaufener Protesttelegramme gegen die Verfolgung der Bibelforscher im "Dritten Reich" mit folgendem Bemerken vor: „Wenn sich die Bibelforscher nicht gleichschalten, dann werden wir sie mit den schärfsten Mitteln anfassen", worauf Hitler aufsprang, seine Hände zasammenballte, sie erhob und hysterisch schrie: „Diese Brut wird aus Deutschland ausgerottet werden!" Vier Jahre nach dieser Unterredung habe ich mich während meiner sieben Jahre dauernden Schutzhaft, die bis zu meiner Befreiung durch die Alliierten anhielt, in der Hölle der nationalsozialistischen Konzentrationslager Sachsenhausen, Flossenbürg und Mauthausen aus eigener Anschauung davon überzeugen können, daß es sich bei dem Wutausbruch Hitlers um keine leere Drohung gehandelt hat, denn keine Häftlingskategorie ist in den genannten Konzentrationslagern dem Sadismus der SS-Soldaten in einer solchen Weise ausgesetzt gewesen wie die Bibelforscher; ein Sadismus der durch eine derartige nicht abreißende Kette physischer und seelischer Quälereien gekennzeichnet war, die keine Sprache der Welt wiederzugeben imstande ist.

DOCUMENT E4-2
(English Translation)

DECLARATION – On October 7, 1934, having been previously summoned, I visited Dr. Wilhelm Frick, at that time Minister of the Interior of the Reich and Prussia, in his home office of the Reich, located in Berlin, 6 am Königsplatz, since I was a plenipotentiary of General Ludendorff. I was to accept communications, contents of which were an attempt to persuade General Ludendorff to discontinuance of his objection to the Nazi regime. During my discussion with Dr. Frick, Hitler suddenly appeared and began taking part in the conversation. When our discussion obligatorily dealt with the action against the International Bible Students Association [Jehovah's Witnesses] in Germany up until now, Dr. Frick showed Hitler a number of telegrams protesting against the Third Reich's persecution of the Bible Students, saying: 'If the Bible Students do not immediately get in line we will act against them using the strongest means.' After which Hitler jumped to his feet and with clenched fists hysterically screamed: 'This brood will be exterminated in Germany!' Four years after this discussion I was able, by my own observations, to convince myself, during my seven years in protective custody in the hell of the Nazi's concentration-camps at Sachsenhausen, Flossenburg and Mauthausen – I was in prison until released by the Allies – that Hitler's outburst of anger was not just an idle threat. No other group of prisoners of the named concentration-camps was exposed to the sadism of the SS-soldiery in such a fashion as the Bible Students were. It was a sadism marked by an unending chain of physical and mental tortures, the likes of which no language in the world can express.

DOCUMENT E5

The Witnesses held a convention at Lucerne, Switzerland, from 4 to 7 September. 1936. Judge Rutherford was present and discussed the situation in Germany with those leaders of the German Witness organization who had not yet been arrested in the recent Nazi sweeps. Among those already arrested (since 28 August) was Fritz Winkler, the German Watch Tower branch overseer. At the Lucerne meeting, Erich Frost was named to replace Winkler, and the convention released the resolution that appears below. Undoubtedly composed either by Rutherford or under his direction, it demonstrates his continuing misguided belief that the Catholic church was the driving force behind the persecution of the Witnesses in Germany as well as in still-independent Austria.

The Lucerne Resolution is taken from pages 162 to 164 of the *1937 Yearbook of Jehovah's Witnesses.*

Resolution at Lucerne
(Adopted Unanimously)

JEHOVAH'S WITNESSES now assembled in Lucerne, Switzerland, having come from many parts of the earth to worship Jehovah in spirit and in truth, take this occasion to give thanks to the Almighty God, whose name alone is Jehovah, for his manifold blessings.

Knowing full well that Jehovah always faithfully performs his promise, and that long centuries ago he promised that he would establish on earth his kingdom of righteousness with Christ Jesus as the world's rightful Ruler; and now seeing from the fulfillment of prophecy that the day of Jehovah's kingdom is here, we rejoice in the privilege of being his servants and his witnesses and we do declare our unqualified allegiance to the Almighty God and his kingdom, and delight to make known to suffering humankind that the kingdom of God under Christ is the only hope of the people.

We fully appreciate that Satan is the great enemy of all who serve Jehovah God and that Satan has used religionists at all times to oppose and persecute those who worship God in spirit and in truth. For this reason many true followers of Christ Jesus are today prevented from attending this convention, they being held in restraint in Germany and in other places, not for wrongdoing, but because they serve God and Christ Jesus and declare his Word and his kingdom as God has commanded them to do.

The law of Jehovah God is supreme. He is above all; and as Jesus and the apostles served God first, last, and all the time, and as they declared so we declare, we will obey God rather than men.

We call all good people to witness that in Germany, Austria and other places Jehovah's witnesses are cruelly persecuted, imprisoned, fiendishly abused, and many of them killed, and all such wickedness is done against them by a cruel, malicious, wicked power, incited so to do by the religious organization, to wit, the Roman Catholic Hierarchy, which for many years has deceived the people and blasphemed

God's holy name. The Hitler government, aided and incited by the Jesuits of the Roman Catholic Hierarchy, has inflicted and continues to inflict all manner of cruel punishment upon true Christians even as Christ Jesus and his apostles were persecuted for righteousness.

Jehovah God has commanded his servants to now give warning to such wicked ones (Ezekiel 33:8, 9) that full responsibility may rest upon the wicked for their wrongdoing, and for that reason we now sound the warning to the rulers in Germany and to the Roman Catholic Hierarchy, and to all like organizations that cruelly persecute the true and faithful followers of Christ Jesus, that the fate of such God declares is complete destruction. (Psalm 145:20) Jesus Christ, at Matthew 25, pronounces Jehovah's judgment against such wicked persecutors who persecute the true followers and brethren of Christ Jesus, in these words: 'Inasmuch as ye have done it to [cruelly ill-treated] the least of these my brethren, ye have done it unto me. Depart from me, ye cursed, into everlasting fire, prepared for the Devil and his angels. These shall go into everlasting destruction.'

We vigorously protest against the cruel treatment of Jehovah's witnesses by the Roman Catholic Hierarchy and its allies in Germany and in all other parts of the world, but we are delighted to leave the end thereof entirely in the hand of the Lord God, who, according to his Word, will render a full recompense.

We sound the warning to all mankind that if they would live they must refuse to give aid and support to religionists who persecute the true followers of Christ Jesus, and that they must take their stand on the side of righteousness and give heed to the words of Jehovah, to wit: 'Behold my servant, whom I have chosen ... He shall show judgment to the nations ... And in His name shall the nations hope.' – Matthew 12:18–21.

As the followers of Christ Jesus we have no part in and no interest in the political affairs of this world. Our sole purpose and commission is to make known the name and the kingdom of God under Christ, that the people may be informed and intelligently choose whom they will serve.

We send loving greetings to our persecuted brethren in Germany and bid them to be of good courage and to rely solely upon the promises of the Almighty God Jehovah, and Christ, and to remember the words of Jesus: 'Shall not God avenge his elect shortly? He shall avenge them' (Luke 18:7, 8); and, further, the words of the Lord Jesus addressed to his faithful servants: 'Be thou faithful unto death, and I will give thee a crown of life.' (Revelation 2:10) Blessed is your lot that you are permitted to endure all manner of suffering for the sake of the name of Jehovah and his kingdom under Christ.

The everlasting peace, joy and life of the people depend entirely upon the great 'Prince of Peace,' whose government will be administered in peace and righteousness. Isaiah 9: 6, 7; 32:1.

RESOLVED that a copy of this resolution be sent to Mr. Hitler and to the pope at Vatican City as the head of the Roman Catholic Hierarchy,

DOCUMENT E6-1

The Nazis were shocked at the continuing activity of Jehovah's Witnesses after the arrests of their leaders and many members in the late summer of 1936. In particular, they were taken aback by the widespread distribution of the Lucerne Resolution. The distribution of that document simply brought about more Witness arrests and many who were apprehended were treated with great cruelty. Curiously, instead of lying low, Witness leaders in Switzerland – undoubtedly with the support of J.F. Rutherford – decided to expose what the Nazis were doing to them by means of an *Offener Brief* (Open Letter) to be distributed throughout Germany in the same clandestine manner that the Lucerne Resolution had been. Since the Nazis had claimed that much of what had been stated in the Lucerne Resolution concerning the persecution of the Witnesses was false, the Open Letter gave detailed information on what was taking place. Since this letter is a long and detailed statement, only the portion of it describing direct instances of persecution is reprinted here.

By apprehending some of the Witnesses who distributed the letter, the Gestapo were able to make further sweeping arrests of Jehovah's Witnesses and to almost entirely halt any significant organized Witness activities within the Reich. Thus, while the Watch Tower Society continued to point to the distribution of the Lucerne Resolution and the Open Letter as brave Witness acts of faith, from the standpoint of maintaining their organization and community, these distributions were serious mistakes. They were nothing short of acts of suicidal religious fanaticism that often led to unnecessary martyrdom.

The 'Open Letter' was distributed on 30 June 1937.

Offener Brief

An das bibelgläubige und Christus liebende Volk Deutschlands!

. . . .

Märtyrer des christlichen Glaubens

Obiges zeigt deutlich, daß der Kampf darauf ausgeht, dem deutschen Volke die Bibel zu rauben und alle zu unterdrücken, die sich auf die geistige Freiheit und den Glauben der Bibel berufen. In christlicher Geduld und aus Scham haben wir lange genug zurückgehalten, die Öffentlichkeiten in Deutschland und in Auslande auf diese Schandtaten aufmerksam zu machen. Es befindet sich in unseren Händen ein erdrückendes Beweismaterial von oben erwähnten grausamen Mißhandlungen der Zeugen Jehovas. *Bei der Mißhandlung haben sich unter anderen besonders der Kiminal-Assistent Theiss aus Dortmund, Tennhoff und Heimann von der Geheimen Staatspolizei Gelsenkirchen und Bochum hervorgetan.* Man hat sich nicht gescheut, Frauen mit Ochsenziemern und Gummiknüppeln zu mißhandeln. Für sadistische Grausamkeit bei der Mißhandlung von chritlichen Frauen ist, wie erwähnt, besonders Kriminal-Assistant Thiess Dortmund und ein Mann der Staatspolizei in Hamm bekannt. *Wir besitzen auch nähere Angaben und Namen von ca. 18 Fällen, wo Jehovas Zeugen gewaltsam getötet worden sind.* Anfangs Oktober 1936 wurde zum Beispiel der in der Neuhüllerstraße, Gelsenkirchen, Westfalen, wohnhaft gewesene *Zeuge Jehovas, Peter Heinen, von Beamten der Geheimen Staatspolizei im Rathaus zu Gelsenkirchen erschlagen.* Dieser traurige Vorfall wurde dem Herrn Reichskanzler Adolf Hitler berichtet. Abschriften davon erhielten auch der Reichsminister Rudolf Hess und der Chef der Geheimen Staatspolizei, Himmler.

DOCUMENT E6-2
(English Translation)

To the Bible-believing and Christ-loving People of Germany

....

Martyrs of Christian Faith

As the above-mentioned shows clearly, the fight goes on to rob the German people of the Bible, and to suppress everything that appeals to spiritual freedom and belief in the Bible. Christian patience and shame have kept us back long enough from bringing these outrages to the public in Germany and in foreign lands. We have in our hands an overwhelming amount of documentation that shows the cruel mistreatment of Jehovah's Witnesses. *Among those responsible for such mistreatment especially have been Criminal-Assistant Thiess from Dortmund and Tennhoff and Heimann from the Gestapo in Gelsenkirchen and Bochum.* They did not shrink from mistreating women [by beating them] with bullwhips and rubber truncheons. Criminal-Assistant Thiess from Dortmund and a man from the Gestapo in Ham are especially noted for their sadistic cruelty in the mistreatment of Christian women. *We possess also the names and details of some eighteen cases in which Jehovah's Witnesses were killed violently.* For example, at the beginning of October 1936, *a Jehovah's Witness named Peter Heinen of Neuhüller Street, Gelsenkirchen, Westphalia, was beaten to death by officials of the Gestapo in the city hall of Gelsenkirchen.* This tragic incident was reported to Reich's Chancellor Adolf Hitler. Copies of the report were sent also to Reich's Minister Rudolf Hess and the Chief of the Gestapo, Himmler.

APPENDIX F
German Watch Tower Attempts to Escape Nazi Persecution

Two letters written by Watch Tower solicitor Hans Dollinger to Adolf Hitler and to Government Counsellor Dr Lang respectively, as well as a statement trying to blame the banning of Jehovah's Witnesses on one Ewald Vorsteher of the Bible Student *Wahrheitsfreunde* or Friends of Truth, demonstrate the fears of German Watch Tower leaders at Magdeburg in January 1933 and their willingness to scapegoat others. Dollinger's open attack on Vorsteher in his letter to Lang seems quite inexcusable, as does his false claim that Jehovah's Witnesses had not opposed the Nazis up until that time.

How Dollinger could have written what he did with a straight face is difficult to understand. He must have known that the Vorsteher incident *was not the real reason* why the Nazis had banned the Witnesses, and he must also have been well aware of Rutherford's open attack on Hitler and the German authorities in the fall of 1934. Interestingly, Dollinger's actions seem quite reminiscent of J.F. Rutherford's behaviour in the United States in 1918, when the latter was facing possible imprisonment for violating the American Espionage Act.

DOCUMENT F1-A
Hans Dollinger to Adolf Hitler
(German Text)

Hans Dollinger Magdeburg, den 5. Januar 1935
Magdeburg Am Fuchsberg 4/5

An den
Führer und Reichskanzeler!
Herrn Adolf Hitler

Persönlich *Berlin*

Sehr geehrter Herr Reichskanzeler!

Seit fast zwei Jahren ist die "Bibelforschervereinigung" verboten,

Wiederholt, – das letztemal vor einem Jahr, – bitte ich ergebenst eine Deputation empfangen zu wollen, die einen Bericht über diese bedauerlichen Tatsachen vortragen könnte. Diese Deputation würde bestehen aus den Herren:

1) Justisrat Karl Kohl, München (Hitlerverteidiger 1924)
2) Dollinger Hans, Syndikus, Magdeburg,
3) Balzereit Paul, Direktor, Magdeburg
4) Nikolaus Freiherr von Tornow, Gutsbesitzer, Kottbus-Saspow

Mit der ausdrücklichen Versicherung meiner grossen Wertschätzung und Ergebenheit.

Zeichne ich mit herzlichem Dank im Vorraus

Mit Deutschen Gruss!

Hans Dollinger (signed)
Bisher. Generalbevollmächtiger der
Bibelvorschervereinigung

DOCUMENT F1-B
(English Translation)

Hans Dollinger
Magdeburg

Magdeburg, January 5, 1935
Am Fuchsberg 4/5

To the *Führer* and Reich Chancellor
Most Honorable Reich Chancellor:

Confidential

It is almost two years ago that the 'Bible Students Association' was outlawed.

On several occasions – the last time one year ago – I asked you to be kind enough to receive a deputation, which could give you a report concerning these very lamentable happenings. This deputation would consist of the following gentlemen:

1) Legal Counsel Karl Kohl, Munich (Defense of Hitler 1924)
2) Dollinger Hans, Solicitor, Magdeberg,
3) Balzereit Paul, Director, Magdeberg,
4) Nikolaus Baron von Tornow, Proprietor, Kottbus-Saspow

With the explicit assurance of my deepest respect and admiration, I send you my heartfelt thanks in advance

With a German greeting!

(signed) Hans Dollinger
General Manager of the Bible Students Association

DOCUMENT F2-A
Hans Dollinger to Government Counsel Dr Lang
(German Original)

Hans Dollinger
Magdeburg.
Watch Tower Society.

z.Zt.Berlin,den 29.Januar 1935.

III P 3233 / 10 XXXI

Herrn

Regierungsrat Dr.Lang

Berlin.
Reichs-u.preuss.Ministerium des Innern.

Sehr geehrter Herr Regierungsrat!

Versprechensgemäss überreiche ich ergebenst in der Anlage die Abschrift des Berichtes des Herrn Polizeipräsidenten in Wuppertal.

Bei der Abschrift dieses Berichtes ist mir in besonders eindringlicher Weise das Ungeheuerliche des Tuns dieses Mannes namens Vorsteher zum Bewusstsein gekommen. Ich verstehe es durchaus, dass der nationalsozialistische Staat sich Derartiges nicht bieten lässt. Das würde kein Staat der Erde sich bieten lassen.

Schmerzlich empfinde ich es, dass diese Wahnsinnshandlung eines verdrehten Menschen, der seine "Erzeugnisse" wahllos an jede Adresse, der er habhaft werden konnte, versandt zu haben scheint, als Grundlage für das Verbot einer wirklich tiefreligiösen christlichen Religionsgesellschaft, der "Bibelforschervereinigung", dienen musste.

Ich bin davon überzeugt, dass bei den Behörden sicherlich nicht genügend Einblick in die Tatsache, dass die "Wahrheitsfreunde" mit der "Bibelforschervereinigung" in keinerlei Konnex standen, vorhanden war und nur darauf das Bibelforscherverbot zurückzuführen ist.

Die "Bibelforschervereinigung" hat niemals in allen den Jahren, in welchen der Nationalsozialismus im Kampfe um Deutschland stand, versucht, diesen Kampf zu beeinträchtigen.

In keinem Vortrag, in keiner Schrift und auch nicht im Gesamtverhalten der Vereinigung wurde gegen den Nationalsozialismus in irgendeiner Form Stellung genommen. Dies trifft sowohl für Deutschland, auch für die Hunderttausende unserer inländischen Glaubensfreunde, - als auch für das gesamte Ausland zu.

Wir müssen es entschieden ablehnen, für das, was dieser Vorsteher getan hat, die Verantwortung tragen zu müssen.

Vorsteher ist ein Eigenbrötler, der von uns 1922 oder 1923 deshalb ausgeschlossen wurde, weil derselbe die von der Vereinigung beachteten und mit den Gesetzen in Uebereinstimmung befindlichen Richtlinien nicht einhalten wollte.

Es muss doch <u>für</u> die Vereinigung sprechen, dass sie unter keinen Umständen duldete, dass in Fragen des gesetzmässigen Handelns einzelne nach dem eigenen Kopfe marschierten. Diese jederzeit unnachsichtlich gehandhabte Konsequenz gibt doch allein der Behörde die <u>Gewähr</u>, dass keinerlei zweifelhafte Elemente geduldet wurden und nicht einzelne nach eigenen Ideen tätige Menschen die Vereinigung nur als Sprungbrett und Plattform benutzen durften.

Hierauf haben wir alle die Jahre das grösste Gewicht gelegt und <u>es gibt keinen Fall</u>, dass Angehörige der Vereinigung entweder selbst in einen Konflikt mit dem Gesetz kamen oder die Vereinigung in einen solchen hineinzogen.

Es kann daher nur als <u>tragisch</u> bezeichnet werden, dass ein Fall, der den Willen zur streng gesetzmässigen Tätigkeit der Vereinigung <u>beweist</u>, durch Umstände, die wir nicht zu verantworten haben, der Vereinigung zum Verhängnis werden sollte.

Ich hoffe und bitte, dass eines Tages die Dinge nachgeprüft werden und wir eine Gelegenheit erhalten, Rechenschaft abzulegen, - denn dann wird ohne Zweifel die ungeheure seelische Not meiner Glaubensbrüder durch eine völlige Rehabilitierung von Amts wegen zu Ende gebracht werden.

Mit deutschem Gruss!

[signature]

DOCUMENT F2-B
(English Translation)

Hans Dollinger
Magdeberg,
Watch Tower Society

Berlin, January 29, 1935

Government Counsel Dr. Lang
Berlin
Reich and Prussian Ministry of the Interior

Most honorable Government Counsel:

As promised, I am honored to submit the enclosed copy of the report of the Chief of Police in Wuppertal.

From that copy I became painfully aware of the outrageousness of what this man named Vorsteher has done. I can readily understand that the National Socialist state will not put up with such a thing. No state on earth would put up with it.

I feel deep pain that this act of madness by a crazy man, who seems to have arbitrarily sent his 'products' to any address he could obtain, had to serve as the basis of a prohibitive order against a really religiously-minded Christian denomination, the Bible Students Association.

I am convinced that there was no sufficient insight on the part of the authorities regarding the fact that the Friends of Truth have no connection whatsoever with the Bible Students Association, and that this is the only cause that can be traced back to the prohibitive order against the Bible Students Association.

Never during all the years that National Socialism fought for Germany has the Bible Students Association tried to impair that fight.

Neither in any talk given, nor in written form, nor in its overall policies has the Association given any negative statement against National Socialism. This applies to Germany and the many hundred thousands of fellow [Bible Student] believers as well as to [those in] foreign countries in general.

We must definitely refuse to be held responsible for what this Vorsteher has done.

Vorsteher is a loner who was disfellowshipped by us in 1922 or 1923 since he was not willing to keep to the rules that are followed by the Association and that are in accordance with the law.

It should speak for the Association that under no circumstances did it allow persons to go their own way regarding matters of conformity to the law. This position, which has always been strictly enforced, is the sole warranty to the authorities that under no circumstances were any dubious elements tolerated in the Association nor could any independent minded individuals use it for a springboard and platform.

Throughout the years we have attached utmost importance to this factor; and there is no case in which followers of the Association either got into conflict with the law themselves or dragged the Association into such a conflict.

It can only be described as tragic that in a case in which the Association proves its intention to be strictly law-abiding, it should be undone because of circumstances for which we cannot be held responsible.

I hope and ask that some day you will check matters, and that we be given the opportunity to account to you – for in that way the immense spiritual pain of my fellow believers will be brought to an end by their complete rehabilitation by order of the authorities.

With a German greeting,

(Signed) Hans Dollinger

DOCUMENT F3-A
Regarding the Bible Students Association
(German original)

Wichtig.

Betrifft: Bibelforschervereinigung. III P 3233/10

Die Ursache des Verbotserlasses vom 24.6.33 (II 1316 a/23.6.33) und der einzige konkrete Vorfall, den der Erlass anführt, ist der

Bericht des Pol.Präs.v.Wuppertal v.31.5.33 I Ad I 6000ø1

Dieser Bericht ist irrtümlich erfolgt, wie das Pol.Präs.Wuppertal einräumt.

Der Bericht des Pol.Präs. in Wuppertal ist unter der Annahme abgegeben worden, dass der in Frage stehende Vorfall auf die "Bibelforschervereinigung" Anwendung findet. Nachträglich wurde dieser Irrtum eingesehen.

I.

Der Unterfertigte und der amerikanische Staatsbürger M.C.Harbeck, Brooklyn, waren am 2.10.1933 in Wuppertal beim Polizeipräsidium vorstellig, die Besprechung fand unter Herbeiziehung der Akten beim Leiter der politischen Abteilung (Beine) statt.

Hierbei wurde festgestellt:

II.

Der vom Pol.Präs. berichtete Vorfall, der schliesslich zum Verbot der Vereinigung führte, bestand darin, dass ein gewisser Ewald Vorsteher aus Barmen am 31.Mai 33 gehässige Angriffe auf den Reichskanzler gerichtet hatte und hierbei verhaftet wurde. Vorsteher war bis 1923 Bibelforscher, trennte sich 1923 von dieser Vereinigung und gründete eine eigene Bewegung, Gesellschaft der Wahrheitsfreunde genannt, deren Hauptaufgabe darin bestand, die Bibelforschervereinigung zu bekämpfen. Seine 1923 herausgegebene Zeitschrift wurde 1925 oder 1926 mangels Leser eingestellt. Er hat nach 1923 mit der Bibelforschervereinigung keinerlei Beziehung mehr unterhalten, die Vereinigung ihrerseits hatte ihn offiziell ausgeschlossen.(1923)

III.

Vorsteher wurde in Düsseldorf wegen der Beleidigung der Regierung zu längerer Gefängnisstrafe verurteilt. (Aktenzeichen: 16 b KM 45/33 St.A.Düsseldorf.)

Die Gerichtsakten dürften diese unsere Erklärung ergänzen.

IV.

Das Polizeipräsidium in Wuppertal <u>weiss</u>, dass der seinerzeitige Bericht falsch ist. Dieses wurde mir im Polizeipräsidium anlässlich des erwähnten Besuches am 1.10.33 auf meine Frage hin ausdrücklich vom Leiter der politischen Abteilung bestätigt. (Beine)

Letzterer hat uns gesagt, dass er weiss, dass Vorsteher kein "Bibelforscher" sei, sondern ein "Wahrheitsfreund".

Auf meine Frage, ob ihm bekannt ist, dass die "Wahrheitsfreunde" mit der Bibelforschervereinigung weder identisch sind, noch mit derselben Beziehungen unterhalten, wurde bejahend geantwortet.

Auf meine Bitte, den Vorfall dem preuss.Innenministerium zu berichten, legte uns dieser Beamte nahe, das Innenministerium zu bitten, einen Bericht anzufordern, den er dann geben wird. Er sagte wörtlich:" Sie müssen veranlassen, dass das Ministerium einen Bericht in der Sache anfordert, dann werden wir die Angelegenheit nach den inzwischen getroffenen Feststellungen richtigstellen."

V.

Die Angelegenheit wurde am 5.10.33 dem preuss.Innenministerium (Min.Dir.Fischer) vorgetragen und es wurde gebeten, den Bericht von Wuppertal anzufordern.

VI.

Diese Sache ist das <u>einzige</u> konkrete "Material", das zum Verbot Veranlassung gab.

28.I.35. [illegible signature]

DOCUMENT F3-B
(English Translation)

Important

Regarding the Bible Students Association

The *cause* of the imposition of 24 June 1933, and the only specific incident affecting that imposition:

The report given by the Chief of Police in Wuppertal on May 31, 1933, v.31.5.33 I Ad 60001.

This report was given erroneously, as the police headquarters in Wuppertal concedes.

The report of the police headquarters in Wuppertal was given on the assumption that the incident in question applies to the Bible Students Association. This was subsequently recognized as an error.

I.

The signatory and the American citizen M.C. Harbeck, Brooklyn, approached the police headquarters in Wuppertal on 2–10–33; the meeting took place while drawing upon the files of the director of the Political Department (Beine).

It has been stated:

II.

The incident reported by the police headquarters, which subsequently led to the prohibitive order against the association, consisted of spiteful charges against the Chancellor of the Reich made by a certain Ewald Vorsteher from Barmen on May 31, 1933, who straightaway came under arrest. Until 1923, Vorsteher had been a Bible Student; in 1923 he left the association and established a separate movement called Society of the Friends of Truth, the principal task of which was the fight against the Bible Students Association. His magazine, for the first time published in 1923, had ceased publication in 1925 or 1926 owing to lack of readers. After 1923, he no longer kept any contact with the Bible Students Association, the Association on its part having disfellowshipped him officially (1923).

III.

At Dusseldorf, Vorsteher was sent to prison for having libeled the government (Ref.Nr. 16 b KM 45/33 St.A. Dusseldorf).

The court record should add to our explanation.

IV.

The police headquarters in Wuppertal knows that the report given is wrong. On the occasion of the visit on 1-10-33 mentioned above, this was explicitly confirmed by the director of the Political Department (Mr. Beine) to my question. The last-named said to us that he knew that Vorsteher is no Bible Student, but a Friend of Truth.

My question as to whether he knew that the Friends of Truth are neither identical to the Bible Students Association, nor keep up contact to them was answered positively.

At my request as to whether he could report the incident to the Prussian Ministry of the Interior, that official suggested that we ask the Ministry of the Interior to request a report, which he would give them. Literally he said: 'You have to see to it that the Ministry asks for a report in this case; then we'll correct the matter according to the facts stated.'

V.

The case was presented to the Prussian Ministry of the Interior at 5 October 1933 (Fischer, Head of Ministry Department). It was requested [that the Ministry] ask for the report from Wuppertal.

VI.

This incident proves to be the only specific 'matter' leading to the ban.

(Signed) Hans Dollinger

APPENDIX G
Nazi Documents Relating to the Persecution of Jehovah's Witnesses

Official Nazi documents from the late 1930s, some of which were first published in Die Zeugen Jehovas: Eine Dokumentation über die Wachtturmgesellschaft, show how determined the Gestapo and other Nazi organizations were to destroy the Witness movement. For that movement had remained amazingly active in carrying on its banned preaching work with the Bible. It had continued to print Watch Tower literature, and some Witnesses were even carrying portable phonographs and phonograph records to the homes of people interested in their message.

Some – in particular the newsmagazine *Der Spiegel* and the former East German Communist regime – have interpreted these documents as showing that German Witness leaders were actually 'traitors' to their faith. But they need not be understood in that way. Nor is it necessary to deny their accuracy, as some Witness apologists have attempted. Rather, it now seems evident that these undoubtedly bona fide documents indicate how, when arrested and under interrogation, *almost all Jehovah's Witness leaders broke down, confessed their roles, and gave information to the Gestapo concerning their fellow workers or 'servants.'* What should be taken from this fact is not that they were intentional traitors, but rather that they simply could not stand up to what amounted to extreme torture or the threat thereof. Significantly, almost all of them later refused to renounce their faith in order to escape incarceration in concentration camps.

It was not just Witness leaders who were unable to keep from divulging the nature of their activities and organization. Ordinary Witness men and women almost always tried to resist giving the Gestapo information when arrested, but were tortured into doing so.[1] Yet the Watch Tower Society in Brooklyn, in its desire to make the world believe that German Jehovah's Witnesses were almost always able to 'stand firm against Nazi persecution,' has never admitted that German Witnesses were unable to remain silent under Gestapo interrogation. As a result, it has left a number of late, important German Witness officials open to the charge that they willingly cooperated with the Nazis. Quite evidently, the society has been more eager to enhance the reputation of German Jehovah's Witnesses as true martyrs to their faith than it has been to protect the reputations of some of its most loyal servants.

The following documents describe the information given by three major German Jehovah's Witness leaders as a result of interrogation. Two of these men played important roles in the German Witness community as senior Watch Tower officials after the Second World War. These three were Fritz Winkler, Konrad Franke, and Erich Frost. Other Gestapo documents printed here show that even after the arrest of Watch Tower leaders, German Jehovah's Witnesses continued to reorganize and press on with spreading their message publicly under severe persecution. Finally, included in this appendix is a copy of the declaration that Witnesses were asked to sign in order to secure their release from incarceration.

After Paul Balzereit, Hans Dollinger, and several associates at the Watch Tower offices in Magdeburg were arrested in the spring of 1935, Fritz Winkler became the Watch Tower Society director or *Reichsdiener* (reich servant) for Germany. However, he was arrested in a Gestapo sweep on 24 August 1936. A Gestapo letter of 28 August 1936, printed below and translated into English, tells what information was obtained from him and how important that information was.

DOCUMENT G1-A

Prussian Secret State Police (Gestapo) Letter re. International Bible Students Association and Fritz Winkler

(German Original)

1 See Eric A. Johnson, *Nazi Terror: The Gestapo, Jews, and Ordinary Germans* (New York: Basic Books, 1999), 238–50.

Preussische Geheime Staatspolizei
Geheimes Staatspolizeiamt
Der Politische Polizeikommandeur
der Länder
II 1 B 1 - S 1035/36

Berlin, den 28.August 1936.

1483

An
alle Staatspolizeistellen und Politischen Polizeien der Länder
-nachrichtlich den Herren Regierungspräsidenten und Oberpräsidenten in Preussen.

Betr.: Internationale Bibelforschervereinigung.
Anl. : 2 Blattsammlungen und 2 Pausskizzen sowie einige rote und grüne Gutscheine.

In der Anlage übersende ich zur Kenntnisnahme Abschrift der Vernehmungsniederschrift des IBV- Mitgliedes W i n k l e r v.24.8.1936 sowie eine Aufstellung über die von der IBV in Deutschland verteilten Grammaphonapparate nebst Zubehörteilen und Schallplatten und ferner eine Skizze über den Aufbau der illegalen IBV in Deutschland und eine Sonderskizze für das Gebiet Berlin. Weiterhin füge ich einige der roten und grünen, auf Seite 21 der eben genannten Abschrift erwähnten Gutscheine bei.

scheine bei.

Winkler hatte die oberste Leitung der IBV in Deutschland. Aus seinen Aussagen sind im einzelnen der Aufbau, die Hauptfunktionäre, die Arbeitsweise, insbesondere die Art der Nachrichtenübermittlung, des Buchvertriebes, die Verteilung von Grammaphonapparaten u.Schallplatten sowie des Geldverkehrs zu ersehen. Im Zuge einer grösseren Aktion ist bereits die gesamte Zentralleitung der IBV ausgehoben worden.

Ich

- 2 -

Ich ersuche nunmehr, auf Grund der anliegenden für den jeweiligen Bezirk in Betracht kommenden Unterlagen, in den einzelnen Bezirken die weiteren Massnahmen zu treffen. In erster Linie sind die von Winkler angegebenen Bezirkdienstleiter festzunehmen. Durch ihre anschliessende Vernehmung sind die ihnen unterstellten Dienstleiter, Postanlaufstellen Bücherlager, W.T.- Hersteller, Literaturanlaufstellen usw. festzustellen. Die Untergliederung bei den dortigen Bezirkdienstleitern muss in den übrigen Bezirken der aus der zweiten Skizze ersichtlichen Untergliederung des Berliner- und des Brandenburgisch- Schlesischen Bezirks entsprechen. Die süddeutschen BDL haben möglicherweise die Literatur über die schweizer bezw. französische Grenze erhalten.

süddeutschen BDL haben möglicherweise die Literatur über die schweizer bezw. französische Grenze erhalten.

Mit Rücksicht darauf, dass voraussichtlich an der am 4.9. 1936 in Luzern (nicht wie auf Seite 21 der Vernehmung Winklers angegeben) beginnenden Tagung auch deutsche Funktionäre teilnehmen werden, ersuche ich, die Massnahmen einheitlich am 31.8. 1936 einzuleiten. Über das Ergebnis ist fortlaufend und ausführlich unter Beifügung der wesentlichen Vernehmungsniederschriften zu berichten.

In Vertretung:
gez.: D...

Beglaubigt:
Kanzleiangestellte.

DOCUMENT G1-B

(English Translation)

Prussian Secret State Police Berlin, August 28, 1936.
Secret State Police Office
The Political Police Commanders of the *Länder*
II 1 B 1 - S 10 35/36

To
all State Police Offices and Political
Police of the *Länder*
2 copy to the heads of the government districts
and the senior presidents in Prussia.

Re: International Bible Students Association
Enclosure: 2 compilations of sheets and 2 sketches as well as some red and green coupons.

. . . .

Enclosed I send a copy of the interrogation protocol of the IBSA-member Winkler of August 24, 1936, for your attention, as well as a list of the phonographs distributed in Germany by the IBSA together with accessories and records, plus a sketch about the organization of the illegal IBSA in Germany and a special sketch for the Berlin area. In addition to this, I enclose some of the red and green coupons on page 21 of the above- named copy.

Winkler was the chief leader of the IBSA in Germany. From his individual testimony can be gathered the structure of the organization, the main functionaries, the mode of operation, especially the way of transmitting information, the sale of the books, the distribution of phonographs and phonograph records, as well as financial transactions. Following greater [Gestapo] action, the complete central leadership of the IBSA has been broken up.

Therefore, I request that further measures in the respective districts be taken on the basis of the enclosed material for the respective districts. Primarily, the district service leaders, named by Winkler, have to be apprehended. Following their interrogation, their subordinate service leaders, mail places, book storage rooms, Watch Tower producers, literature places, etc., have to be found out. The sub-organization with regard to the district service leaders has to correspond to the sub-organization of the remaining districts of the Berlin and Brandenburg-Silesian district, as can be seen from the second sketch. The South German district leaders may have received their literature via the Swiss or French borders.

Taking into account that German functionaries, too, will attend the meeting in Lucerne on September 4, 1936 (not as stated on page 21 of the interrogation protocol on Winkler), I request that unified measures be taken on August 31, 1 936. The results must be reported an ongoing and detailed manner; the substantial interrogation protocols have to be enclosed.

(Signed and sealed)

Winkler's confession resulted in the arrest of a number of additional Witnesses, including Konrad Franke. Born in 1910 and baptized as a Bible Student at the age of fourteen, Franke became a Watch Tower pioneer or full-time evangelist in 1931. He was present at the 1933 Berlin-Wilmersdorf Watch Tower convention in 1933 and was arrested several times thereafter. In the late summer of 1936 he began a nine-year stint in Nazi prisons and concentration camps. During his last period of incarceration, he was a prisoner in Sachsenhausen. He participated in a prisoners' 'death march' from Sachsenhausen to Schwerin in April 1945. He later served as a senior Watch Tower official, and for some years was a branch overseer in Germany. He died in 1983. The following is Franke's confession made before the Gestapo.

DOCUMENT G2-A
Konrad Franke's Confession, September 9, 1936, at Darmstadt
(German Original)

A b s c h r i f t

5+ Anl. 1

Geheimes Staatspolizeiamt
Darmstadt

Darmstadt, den 9. 9.36

1) A 5 2) B 422 97

Aus der Schutzhaft vorgeführt erklärt
F r a n k e , Konrad
zur Wahrheit ermahnt folgendes:

Ich sehe ein, dass ein weiteres Leugnen keinen Zweck hat. Ich bin bereit, die volle Wahrheit zu sagen, insbesondere nachdem mir Reichlei-Winkler (z.S. in Berlin in Haft) einen Brief hat zugehen lassen, in welchem er mich auffordert, die Wahrheit zu sagen, da die Polizeibehörden über meine Tätigkeit völlig informiert ist.

Ich bin Zeuge Jehovas seit längerer Zeit, wie das in meiner Vernehmung vom 31.8. und 1.9.1936 vor der Staatspolizeistelle Mainz angegeben ist. Auf diese Vernehmungen nehme ich auch hinsichtlich meiner Einstellung dem Staat gegenüber Bezug.

Mit der Organisation meines Bezirkes bin ich noch nicht mehr weit durchgekommen, da ich ausserhalb Mainz und Wiesbaden bei den Geschwistern unbekannt war und mich erst von einem anderen bei ihnen einführen musste. Ich habe bisher in meinem Bezirk mit folgenden Dienstleitern in Verbindung gestanden:

1.) Frankfurt/Main S t e i n b a v h , Valentin, Schwarzburgstr. 26
2.) Mannheim Karl H a a s , Luisenring 54
3.) Karlsruhe M ü h l h ä u s e r , Vorname? Grenzstr. 4
4.) Offenburg Albert K e r n , Lindenplatz 12
5.) Singen Erich A r n o l d , Hauptstr. 12
6.) Speyer S a n d , (Vorname u. Anschrift unbekannt) Mit diesem habe ich mich nur in Mannheim getroffen.
7.) Mainz Diesen Bezirk habeich selbst bearbeitet.

Diese Dienstleiter habe ich etwa monatlich einmal besucht. Die Auslagen für die Bahnfahrten habe ich mit den eingenommenen Geldern verrechnet.

Die Wachtturm-(W.T.) Abschriftenherstellung war zur der Zeit als ich den Bezirk übernahm bereits eingerichtet. Die Original W.T. wurden an den Dienstleiter (D.L.) Mühlhäuser gesandt. Absender war meines Wissens das Bibelhaus Bern/Schweiz. Die Herstellung der Abschriften wurde durch Mühlhäuser besorgt.

Bei dem letzten Treffen mit Winkler am 1.8.1936 erfuhr ich,dass in der Zeit vom 4. bis zum 7-9.36 eine Hauptversammlung in Luzern stattfinden sollte. Für diese Versammlung sollten Sonderberichte über Verhaftungen,Misshandlungen usw. von Zeugen Jehovas gegeben werden. Derartige Fälle sollten in den einzelnen Bezirken gesammelt werden. Die Berichte hierüber sollten an

R u b a u , Danzig

gegeben werden,der eine Woche nach Winkler die einzelnen B.D.L. besuchen wollte. Rubau kam dann auch wie verabredet auf der Durchreise nach Mainz. Hier übergab ich ihm mehrere Zettel mit Meldungen verschiedener Geschwister darüber,dass Geschwister zur Wahl angehalten worden sind.Rubau hatte ich bei einer Zusammenkunft der B.D.L. in Berlin kennengelernt. Er ist etwa 1.65 m gross,hagere Gestalt,schmales Gesicht,bartlos und trägt meines Wissens eine Brille. Er ist meiner Schätzung nach 35 Jahre alt.

Rubau brachte mir bei dieser Gelegenheit auch ein Päckchen von den Gutscheinen zu M 10.- und M 5.- mit,die für die Reise der Geschwister zu der Hauptversammlung nach Luzern dienen sollten. Ich hatte daher auch schon vor dem ersten August Reisegelder von den Geschwistern,die nach Luzern fahren wollten, eingenommen. Es hatten an mich

H a a s , Mannheim
K e r n , Offenburg,

insgesmt gegen M 200.-- aus ihren Bezirken abgeliefert,die ich am 1.8. an Winkler weiterleitete.

Ich habe die volle Wahrheit gesagt und bin auch bereit bei etwaigen Unstimmigkeiten Aufklärung zu geben.

Selbst gelesen, genehmigt und unterschrieben
gez. Konrad F r a n k e

Reg. Assessor Gestapa Berlin
gez. L i s c h k a

DOCUMENT G2-B
(English Translation)

Copy

Office of the State Secret Police
Darmstadt

Darmstadt, September 9, 1936

Brought from preventive detention,
Franke, Konrad
warned to tell the truth, states:

I understand that there is no use in denying further. I am prepared to tell the truth, especially after Reichsleiter [Reich leader] Winkler (presently imprisoned in Berlin) has sent me a letter asking me to tell the truth, since the police authorities are fully informed about my activity.

I have been a Jehovah's Witness for a long time, something stated in my interrogation protocol of August 31, and September 1, 1936, before the State Police at Mainz. I shall refer to those questionings with respect to my view about the state.

I have not yet finished organizing my district, since I was unknown to the brothren outside Mainz and Wiesbaden, and had to be introduced to them by another person at first. Up to now, I have been in connection with the following service leaders in my district:

1.) Frankfurt/Main: Steinbach, Valentin, Schwarzburgstr. 26
2.) Mannheim: Karl Haas, Luisenring 54
3.) Karlsruhe: Muhlhauser, given name?, Grenzstr. 4
4.) Offenburg: Albert Kern, Lindenplatz 12
5.) Singen: Erich Arnold, Hauptstr. 12
6.) Speyer: Sand, (given name and address unknown) I only met him in Mannheim.
7.) Mainz: This was my own district.

I visited these service leaders once in a month. I have debited the cost of the railway tours to the money taken [from the brothren].

The production of copies of the Watchtower magazine was already established when I took over the district. The original Watchtower magazines were sent to the service leader in Muhlhäuser. As far as I know, they were sent from the Bern Bible House in Switzerland. Muhlhäuser cared for copying them.

During the last meeting with Winkler on August 1, 1936, I got to know that a major assembly was to take place at Lucerne from September 4–7, 1936. At this assembly, special reports concerning arrests, abuses, etc. were to be given by Jehovah's Witnesses. Such cases were to be gathered in the respective districts. The reports were to be sent to

Rubau, Danzig,

who intended to visit the respective district servants one week after Winkler. Passing through Mainz, Rubau came as arranged. There I handed several sheets of paper over to him with reports from different brothers about the fact that brothers were forced to vote in elections. I had got to know Rubau at a district servant meeting in Berlin. He is approximately 1.65 meters in height, gaunt, has a small face, no beard, and to my knowledge he wears glasses. I guess he is 35 years old.

On that occasion, Rubau handed a package to me, containing vouchers a RM 10,– and RM 5,– which were to serve for the brothrens' trips to the general convention at Lucerne. I had already collected travelling money from the brothren who wanted to travel to Lucerne, before August, 1.

Haas, Mannheim
Kern, Offenburg

had already handed me RM 200,– from their districts, which I passed on to Winkler on August 1.

I have told the truth and am prepared to explain possible inconsistencies. Read for myself, approved,

Signed Konrad Franke

Reg. Assessor Gestapa Berlin
Signed: Lischka

Following the arrests of August and September 1936, the Gestapo believed for a time that they had destroyed the International Bible Student Association in Germany. But to their shock, the Witnesses distributed the Lucerne Resolution throughout the Reich only three months later. Although they were able to apprehend a number of Witness district servants in the following months, they were frustrated by the continuing illegal activities of Jehovah's Witnesses. Thus they determined to establish a special commando unit under the direction of specialists to destroy the IBSA as a movement.

DOCUMENT G3-A
Urgent Matter
(German Original)

Eilt sehr!

II 1134 - VA.1541 C.
Kp.- Nr. 409/37.

36364
II 113
22 April 1937

Chef der ... polizei
Eing.: - 6. 4. 1937
C vorlegen

Betr.: Aktion gegen die illegale Bibelforschervereinigung.
Vorg.: diess.Schreiben VA.1541 - Nr.410/37 vom 22.3.1937.

Im August 1936 wurde die erste Aktion gegen die illegale I.B.V. vom Geheimen Staatspolizeiamt in Zusammenarbeit mit dem zuständigen Referenten des SD-Hauptamtes durchgeführt. Mit Ausnahme der nach der Schweiz (Luzern) gereisten Bezirksdienstleiter R a b e, D i t s c h i, F r o s t und W a n d r e s konnten sämtliche Hauptfunktionäre festgenommen werden.

Durch die am 12.12.36 veranstaltete Flugblattaktion der I.B.V. wurde offenbar, dass bereits eine zweite illegale Organisation der I.B.V. im Reich bestand. Durch die Festnahme des BDL. R a b e und durch dessen Aussagen konnte mit der zweiten Aktion gegen die I.B.V. begonnen werden. Diese führte zur Festnahme der Bezirksdiener D a u t, S i e b e n e i c h l e r, N a w r o t h und des Reichsdieners F r o s t. Die Bezirksdiener D i t s c h i, W a n d r e s, F e h s t, S t i c h e l und F r i e s e befinden sich noch auf freiem Fuß. Sie leben illegal.

Der Erfolg dieser Aktion ist z.Zt. durch die Personaländerungen im zuständigen Dezernat II B 2 des Gestapa in Frage gestellt Nach hiesiger Ansicht muß auch diese Aktion als gescheitert angesehen werden, wenn sie nicht mit allen Mitteln und mit aller Energie durchgeführt wird. Solange noch ein Hauptfunktionär der illegalen I.B.V. auf freiem Fuß ist, muß mit der sofortigen Neuorganisation der I.B.V. gerechnet werden.

Es wird daher zur erfolgreichen Bekämpfung der I.B.V. vorgeschlagen, aus den einzelnen Stapostellen sachkundige Beamten zu einem Sonderkomando zusammenzustellen und diesen einige mit der Materie vertraute Sachbearbeiter der SD-Oberabschnitte zur Verfügung zu stellen. Die Erfahrung aus den beiden Aktionen hat gezeigt, daß Beamte, die keine Sachkenntnis auf diesem Gebiete haben, für derartige Aktionen ungeeignet sind,

I. an Stbf. mit der Bitte um Kenntnisnahme und Entscheidung über Vorlage bei C.

II. Wiedervorlage bei II 1134 sofort.

Stbf.	I 1	II 1	II 11	II 113	II 1134 2 April 1937.

DOCUMENT G3-B
(English Translation)

Urgent Matter!

II1134-VA. 1541 C. Chapt. No. 409/37.

Re: Action against the illegal Bible Students Association-Dossier: This letter VA.1541 - No. 410/37 of March 22, 1937.

April 2, 1937

In August 1936, the first action against the illegal IBSA was taken by the Gestapo office in cooperation with the concerned consultant of the Security Service headquarters. With the exception of district service leaders Rabe, Ditschi, Frost, and Wandres, who had travelled to Switzerland (Lucerne), all the main functionaries were able to be arrested.

Through the pamphlet campaign of December 12, 1936, it became obvious that there already existed a second illegal organization of the IBSA in the Reich. Through the capture of district service leader Rabe and his testimony, we were able to launch a second action against the IBSA. This led to the arrest of the district servants Daut, Siebeneichler, Nawroth, and of the branch servant Frost. The district servants Ditschi, Wandres, Fehst, Stichel, and Friese are still at large. They live outside the law.

The success of this action is presently in question because of the staff requirement in the relevant Department II B 2 of the Gestapo office. We think that this action, too, must be regarded as failed if it is not performed with the most expeditious means and with energy. As long as a main functionary of the illegal IBSA is at large, we still will have to reckon on the immediate reorganization of the IBSA.

We therefore suggest fighting successfully against the IBSA by creating a special commando unit consisting of competent officials from the respective state police offices, and appointing some competent specialists of the Security Office main bureaus to supply direction. The experience from both [previous] actions has proved that officials who are not competent in this area, are incapable for such actions ...

[As will be noted, I have not included reference statements or the initials that appear at the end of this document – M.J.P.]

It is not surprising that Erich Frost has been regarded as a traitor to his faith and his brethren in view of the extensive information, including his own background and activities, that he gave to the Gestapo in April 1937. However, evidence presented earlier is that he, like other Watch Tower officials, was simply unable to withhold that information.

DOCUMENT G4-A
Erich Frost's Confession, 2 and 26 April, 1937 at Berlin
(German Original)

Ad. II B Berlin, den 2. April 1937.

Verhandelt!

Vorgeführt erscheint Erich Frost, geboren 22.12.00 zu Leipzig, ohne festen Wohnsitz,und erklärt:

Ich stehe jetzt im 36. Lebensjahr und bin seit 1922 Zeuge Jehovas. Die diesbezügliche Taufe habe ich am 4. März 1922 erhalten. Wer mich getauft hat, kann ich heute nicht mehr angeben. Ich will hierbei bemerken, dass auch meine Eltern bereits um diese Zeit Bibelforscher, wie wir uns früher nannten, waren.

Nachdem Balzereit, festgenommen war und an seiner Stelle der Glaubensbruder Winkler das deutsche Werk der Zeugen Jehovas leitete, befand ich mich in der Tschechoslowakei, wo ich das Schöpfungsdrama aufführte. An dem Luzerner Kongress im September 1936 habe ich teilgenommen und wurde vom Richter Rutherford an Stelle des festgenommenen Winkler mit der Leitung des deutschen Werkes unter Anlehnung an das Prager Büro, dem der Bruder Dw e n g e r vorsteht, beauftragt. In Luzern fand daraufhin eine Konferenz statt, die sich lediglich mit der Weiterführung des deutschen Werkes befasste. Es fand eine Neueinteilung der Bezirke in Deutschland statt, die von folgenden Brüdern übernommen wurde.

Georg R a b e, Bezirkdiener für
1. Ostpreussen
2. Westpreussen
3. Pommern
4. Mecklenburg.

Artur N a w r o t h. Bezirkdiener für
1. Ostschlesien
2. Grenzmark.

August F e h s t. Bezirkdiener für
1. Westschlesien
2. Sachsen (östlich der Elbe), nach der Festnahme des Bezirkdieners Wilhelm E n g e l, festgenommen im Dezember 36 oder Januar 37.

Otto D a u t h. Bezirksdiener für
1. Berlin
2. Mark Brandenburg.

Fred M e i e r. Bezirksdiener für
1. Westsachsen bis einschliesslich Anhalt.

Walther F r i e s e. Bezirksdiener für
1. Thüringen
2. Harzgebiet.
3. Hannover

Heinrich D i t s c h i. Bezirksdiener für
1. Schleswig-Holstein
2. Oldenburg
3. Ruhrgebiet, Westfalen.

Albert W a n d r e s. Bezirksdiener für
1. Rheinland
2. Baden
3. Württemberg.

Karl S i e b e n e i c h l e r. Bezirksdiener für
1. Bayern.

Über eine direkte Einteilung der Bezirke in sogenannte Unterbezirke bin ich nicht genau orientiert. Bekannt ist mir lediglich, dass in den grossen Bezirken von D i t s c h i und W a n d r e s Mitarbeiter bezw. sogenannte Unterbezirksdiener tätig waren.

Für D i t s c h i kommen hierfür in Frage:
1. Lü d e n s c h l o ß, Vorname vermutlich Ernst.
2. F e n n h o f e n, die Schreibweise seines Namens und sein Vorname sind mir nicht bekannt; er heißt mit Vornamen vermutlich Erich. Ditschi sprach immer von einem Erich.

Für W a n d r e s kommen hierfür in Frage:
1. S c h l ö m e r, vermutlich Hermann.
2. S t i c k e l, Ludwig.

Soweit in den einzelnen Bezirken keine Unterbezirke eingerichtet waren, wurde diese einzelnen Bezirke organisatorisch in Gruppen und diese wiederum in Zellen eingeteilt.

Den Bezirksdiener August F e h s t kenne ich seit dem Jahre 1931. Ich war früher mit ihm in der Tschechoslowakei als Bibelforscher tätig. Seine Wohnung ist mir nicht bekannt. In Deutschland muss er sich mindestens 1 Jahr lang ohne feste Wohnung aufhalten. Auch er war mit in Luzern, seit dieser Zeit ist er der Bezirksdiener für Westschlesienund Ostsachsen. F e h st lieferten bei den bekannten Treffs in Berlin wenig oder überhaupt kein Geld ab, im Gegenteil, er liess sich von mirnoch grpssere Beträge aushändigen, die er zur Bezahlung der Schmuggler, welche ihm verbotene Literatur der illgalen IBV aus der Tschechoslowakei nach Deutschland brachten, benötigte. Ausserdem benötigte er viel Geld zur Versendung dieses Schriftmaterials an die Deckadressen der einzelnen Bezirksdiener. Nur in einem Falle in Berlin am 6. März 37 übergab mir F e h s t einen Betrag von ca. 500.-RM. Quittungen über alle mir ausgehändigten Gelder wurden nicht ausgestellt. Das trifft in jedem Falle zu. Fehst selbst verschaffte sich die Literatur aus der Tschechoslowakei durch den Glaubensbruder W a g n e r aus Warnsdorf/CSR. Durch Wagner stand Fehst in ständiger Verbindung mit dem Zweigbüro der IBV in Prag wegen Belieferung von IBV-Literatur. Schätzungsweise sind durch Wagner ~~etwa~~ 40 000 Bücher und Broschüren der IBV über die Grenze bei Spindlersmühle im Riesengebirge sowie bei Warnsdorf (Zittauer Gebirge) gebracht worden. F e h s t übernahme diese Sendungen und verschickte sie an die einzelnen Deckadressen der anderen 6 Bezirksdiener. Einen Teil der Literatur hielt Fehst für seinen Bezirk zurück. Insgesamt enthielten die Sendungen folgende Bücher und Broschüren:

1.) Das Buch "Reichtum", etwa 900 Exemplare,
2.) Die Broschüre "Entscheidung", etwa 35 000 Exemplare,
3.) Die Broschüre "Oberherrschaft", etwa 2000 Exemplare,
4.) Die Broschüren "Gesundheit und Leben", "Schlusskampf", "Frohe Botschafr" ua. mehr, etwa 2 bis 3000.

Ausserdem wurden noch ~~wurden~~ in der Zeit von 6 Monaten etwa 3 bis 4000 "Goldene Zeitalter" aus der Tschechoslowakei durch W a g n e r über die Grenze geschmuggelt. Diese Zeitschriften brachte F e h s t mit zu den Treffs in Berlin, wo sie an die einzelnen Bezirksdiener verteilt wurden. Die gesamte Literatur ist in Bern /Schweiz gedruckt worden , von dort aus wurde es ~~xx~~ unentgeldlich nach Prag an das Zweigbüro der IBV geliefert . Auch wir in Deutschland erhielten diese Literatur ohne Bezahlung. F e h s t hatte lediglich eine Vergütung für die Schmuggler zu zahlen, die ihm von mir aus ausgehändigt wurde.

Bei meinen häufigen Zusammenkünften mit Daut befand sich die Glaubensschwester Ida S t r a u s s , die den Decknamen " M o r i t z" führte. Von Daut habe ich erfahren; dass die Strauss die Vervielfältigungen der Wachttürme herstellt.

Bezirksdiener W a n d r e s.

Meine Angaben auf Blatt 9 in der Vernehmung vom 15.4.37 habe ich wie folgt zu ergänzen:

Mit Wandres traf ich in Stuttgart 2 mal zusammen. Der erste Treff lag im November oder Dezember 1936. Wir trafen uns am Bahnhof und suchten die Wohnung einer Glaubensschwester auf. Den Namen der Glaubensschwester kann ich nicht angeben. Die Wohnung befindet sich schräg rüber vom Café "Olga" und zwar in der Strasse, die die Olgastr. schneidet. Die Hausnummer selbst kann ich nicht angeben. Die Wohnung ist aber im 2.Stockwerk gelegen. Soweit ich mich entsinnen kann sind in diesem Grundstück keine Geschäfte.untergebracht. Es handelt sich um ein reines Wohngrundstück. In der Wohnung, wozugegen waren: Bezirkdiener Wandres, sein Unterbezirkdiener Ludwig S t i c k e l aus Pforzheim, ich selbst, unterhielten wir uns über die Wahrheit und erörterten Fragen des Glaubens.Organisatorische Fragen , insbesondere , ob im Bezirk alles in Ordnung sei wurden schon auf dem Wege zu dieser Wohnung behandelt.

Bei dieser Gelegenheit möchte ich folgendes bemerken:

Gelegentlich des Haupttreffs im Mamtx Januar d.Js. in Berlin teilte mir W a n d r e s mit, dass er zur Vervielfältigung eine Schreibmaschine gekauft habe. Er legte mir eine Abrechnung vor, wonach er für 240.-RM eine neue Schreibmaschine, Marke unbekannt, gekauft habe. Den Lieferanten sowie den Lieferort vermag ich nicht anzugeben, da wir uns darüber nicht unterhalten haben. Ich vermute a-ber, dass Wandres die fragliche Schreibmaschine in Süddeutschland gekauft hat.

Bezirksdiener D i t s c h i.

Zu meinen am 15.4.37 über den Bezirksdiener Heinrich D i t s c h i gemachten Angaben ergänze ich noch folgendes: Mit Ditschi war ich im Oktober 1936 und dann noch einmal im Dezember 1936 in Dortmund zusammen. Wir trafen uns beide Male vorerst auf dem Hauptbahnhof in Dortmund und gingen dann zusammen nach der Wohnung d s Glaubensbruders B e i k e oder P e i k e in der Uhlandstr., Nr. unbekannt. Beike muss Inhaber einer im gleichen Grundstück gelegenen Stickerei sein, die sich im Erdgeschoss befindet. In beiden Fällen waren bei diesen Treffs anwesend: W a n d r e s, D i t s c hi, sowie der Unterbezirksdiener L ü n e n s c h l o s s vom Bezirk Ditschi und ich selbst. Bei diesen Treffs behandelten wir die Auslegung der Bibel und unterhielten uns über die Wahrheit. Der Wohnungsinhaber war nicht mit zugegen. Ich muss an dieser Stelle hervorheben, dass ich ausser den abgehaltenen Andachten michimmer überzeugen wollte, ob und wie die verschiedenen Bezirksdiener überhaupt noch für die IBV arbeiten. Es konnte ja möglich sein, dass in einigen Fällen Verhaftungen vorgenommen waren und der Bezirk dann ohne Leitung gewesen wäre. In solchen Fällen war es meine Aufgabe, einen neuen Bezirksdiener zu finden und einzusetzen.

D i t s c h i war bereits in Luzern als mein Nachfolger in dem Falle vorgeschlagen und bestimmt worden, wo ich als Reichsdiener verhaftet werde. Im Falle meiner Verhaftung hat sich Ditschi sofort in das Zweigbüro in Prag zu wenden, um weitere Weisungen entgegenzunehmen. Nebenher möchte ich noch erwähnen, dass Ditschi nach seinen Äusserungen Beziehungen zu Glaubensgeschwistern in Holland hat und mit diesen in ständiger Verbindung steht. Näheres hierüber weiss ich nicht anzugeben. Mir ist nur bekannt, dass Ditschi wiederholt mit Glaubensgeschwistern über Sterkrade ~~in~~ Holland in Verbindung steht. Ich halte es für sehr wahrscheinlich, dass Ditschi wiederholt persönlich in Sterkrade war.
Die Vernehmung wird abgebrochen .

Ad. II B   Berlin,den 26.April 1937.

V e r h a n d e l t.

Vorgeführt erscheint Erich F r o s t, Personalien bereits aktenkundig, und erklärt:

Am 6.März 1937, also am Tage des letzten Haupttreffs in Berlin, war Siebeneichler nicht zugegen. Weil wir über ihn besorgt waren, schickte ich die Ilse U n t e r d ö r f e r sofort nach München, um über Siebeneichler Erkundigungen einzuziehen. Ich übergab der Unterdörfer eine mir von Siebeneichler genannte Münchener Telefonnummer. Nach Anruf beim Inhaber dieser Nummer traf sich die Unterdörfer in München mit einer mir unbekannten Glaubensschwester, die mit Vornamen "Gertrud" hiess. Mir ist in Erinnerung, dass die Gertrud personengleich ist mit der Elfriede L ö h r aus München . Ich vermute das wenigstens so, eine nähere Begründung habe ich allerdings hierzu nicht.

Der in Prag im Zweigbüro der IBV tätige B a h n e r, Josef, ist Sudentendeutscher , schätzungsweise 34 Jahre alt, Bahner befindet sich für die IBV dauernd auf Reisen in der Tschechoslowakei , sein Wohnort ist Brünn, in der CSR,, Strasse unbekannt. Bahner war früher Offizier im Heere der CSR, er ist etwa 1,63 m gross, hat blasses Aussehen, blondes Haar. Bahner muss früher zeitweilig im Bibelhaus der Wachtturmgesellschaft in Magdeburg beschäftigt gewesen sein. Von Beruf ist er m.W. Kaufmann.

Heinrich D w e n g e r ist der frühere Leiter der Dienstabteilung der W.T.-Gesellschaft in Magdeburg gewesen. Er war dort viele Jahre tätig und ist Reichsdeutscher. Ich schätze ihn auf 45 Jahre, er wird 1,70 m gross sein, trägt kurzgeschnittenen Schnurrbart, hat Haare von bräunlicher Farbe, gescheitelt. Dwenger ist unverheiratet und in seiner Art ein Sonderling

Bei dieser Gelegenheit möchte ich angeben, dass die bei mir gefundenen schweizer Francs, es können etwa über 50 gewesen sein, von dem Bezirksdiener W a n d r e s stammen, der sie mir imFebruar dieses Jahres in Berlin beim Haupttreff übergeben hatte. Wandres erhielt diese Francs von süddeutschen Glaubensgeschwistern, die zum Kongress in Luzern waren und das Geld nicht restlos verbraucht hatten Die Francs hatten die Glaubensgeschwister als G.H.-Gelder dem Deutschen Werke zur Verfügung gestellt. Wenn ich nicht verhaftet worden wäre, hätte ich die Francs bei der Reichsbank eingetauscht. Bisher hatte ich dazu noch keine Gelegenheit gefunden,

v. g. u.

Erich Frost

geschlossen.

DOCUMENT G4-B
(English Translation)

Ad. II B

Berlin, April 2, 1937

Proceedings!

Brought for questioning: Erich Frost, born at Leipzig on December 11, 1900, of no fixed abode, states:

I am now 36 years old and [have been] a Jehovah's Witness since 1922. I was baptized by them on March 4, 1922. At present I am no longer able to give the name of the person who baptized me. I would like to add that my parents, too, had been Bible Students, as we were called at that time.

After Balzereit was arrested, and Brother Winkler was placed in charge of the German work of Jehovah's Witnesses instead of him, I was away in Czechoslovakia showing the Photo Drama [of Creation]. I attended the Lucerne convention in September 1936 and was entrusted by Judge Rutherford with the German work in place of the arrested Winkler, following the instructions by the office in Prague headed by Brother Dwenger. Thereupon a conference took place at Lucerne, dealing with the continuation of the German work only. The districts in Germany were newly divided up and taken over by the following brothers:

Georg Rabe, District Servant for

1. East Prussia,
2. West Prussia,
3. Pomerania,
4. Mecklenburg.

Artur Nawroth. District servant for

1. Eastern Silesia,
2. The Marches.

August Fehst. District Servant for

1. Western Silesia,
2. Saxony (west of the Elbe river), after the arrest of District Servant Wilhelm Engel in December 1936 or January 1937.

Otto Dauth. District Servant for

1. Berlin,
2. The Mark Brandenburg.

Fred Meier. District Servant for
1. Western Saxony including Anhalt.

Walther Friese. District Servant for
1. Thuringia,
2. the Harz,
3. Hannover.

Heinrich Ditschi. District Servant for
1. Schleswig-Holstein,
2. Oldenburg,
3. the Ruhr, Westphalia.

Albert Wandres. District Servant for
1. Rhineland,
2. Baden,
3. Wurttemberg.

Karl Siebeneichler. District Servant for
1. Bavaria.

I am not informed exactly as to a detailed division of the districts into so-called sub-districts. I merely know that in the major districts of Ditschi and Wandres fellow workers or so-called sub-district servants were active.

For Ditschi these persons possibly are:
1. Lüdenschloss, presumable given name: Ernst.
2. Fennhofen. I do not know the [proper] spelling of his name or his given name; his presumable given name is Erich; Ditschi used to speak of an Erich.

For Wandres these persons possibly are:
1. Schlümer, presumably Hermann.
2. Stickel, Ludwig.

As far as the individual districts are concerned, no sub-districts have been established in them; these districts were organized as groups, and the groups as cells.

I have known district servant August Fehst since 1931. In the past I was active in Czechoslovakia as a Bible Student together with him. I do not know his whereabouts. I suppose he has been living in Germany with no fixed residence for at least 1 year. He also was in Lucerne; since then he has been the district servant for Western Silesia and Eastern Saxony. At the well-known meetings in Berlin, Fehst either handed me very little money or none at all; on the contrary, he tendered me requests for the greater sums of money he needed to pay the smugglers that had transferred banned, illegal IBSA literature from Czechoslovakia to Germany. Moreover, he needed a lot of money to send that literature to the cover address of each individual district servant. Only in one case, on March 6, 1937, at Berlin, did Fehst hand over a sum of approximately 500 marks to me – No receipts were given in confirmation of the sums handed to me. This is true in any case: Fehst himself obtained the literature from Czechoslovakia, from Brother Wagner who lives in Warnsdorf, Czechoslovakia. Through Wagner, Fehst used to keep in contact with the [Watch Tower] branch office in Prague regarding the supply of IBSA literature. Wagner brought approximately 40,000 IBSA books and booklets across the border at Spindlersmühle (Riesengebirge) as well as at Warnsdorf (Zittau mountains). Fehst took these consignments and sent them to the individual cover addresses of the 6 other district servants. Fehst kept part of the literature for his own district.

In all, the consignments contained the following books and booklets:

1) The book 'Riches,' roughly 900 copies.
2) The booklet 'Judgment,' some 35,000 copies.
3) The booklet 'Supremacy,' some 2,000 copies.
4) The booklets 'Health and Life,' 'The Final War,' 'Good News' etc., some 2,000 to 3,000 copies.

Besides, within 6 months some 3,000 to 4,000 'Goldene Zeitalter' [*Golden Age* magazines] from Czechoslovakia were being smuggled across the border by Wagner. Fehst took those magazines with him to the meetings in Berlin, where they were handed out to the individual district servants. All of the literature was printed in Bern, Switzerland, from where it was consigned to the Prague office of the IBSA free of charge. We in Germany, too, got the literature without payment. Fehst merely had to pay the smugglers; that sum was handed over to him by me. His frequent meetings with Daut were attended by Sister Ida Strauss who had the cover name of 'Moritz.' From Daut I learned to know that Strauss made the copies of the *Watchtower* magazines.

District Servant Wandres.

I would like to add to my statement on page 9 of the interrogation of April 15, 1937, as follows:

I met Wandres twice in Stuttgart. The first meeting was in November or December 1936. We met at the railway station and went and saw a sister in her apartment. I cannot say what the sister's name is. The apartment is diagonally opposite the café 'Olga' in the street that crosses Olga Street. I cannot give the house number. The apartment is on the third floor. As far as I can remember, there are no shops on the site. It is a purely residential site. In the apartment, these persons were present: District Servant Wandres, his sub-district servant Ludwig Stickel from Pforzheim, I myself. We talked about the Truth and discussed religious items. Organizational points, especially as to whether things were all right in the district, had already been dealt with on our way to that apartment.

On this occasion I would like to remark: On the occasion of the major meeting in January of that year in Berlin, Wandres told me that he had bought a typewriter for reproducing literature. He showed me a bill for 500 marks for a new typewriter, trademark unknown. I cannot tell the supplier or the location of the firm, as we did not speak about it. However, I suspect that Wandres bought the typewriter in question in South Germany.

District Servant Ditschi.

I would like to add to my statement about district servant Heinrich Ditschi, made on April 15, 1937, as follows:

I met Ditschi in October 1936 and once more in December 1936 in Dortmund. On both occasions we first met at the Dortmund central station and then went to the apartment of Brother Beike or Peike in Uhland Street, house number unknown. I suspect Beike to be the owner of the embroidery firm on the first floor of the same site. On both occasions were present: Wandres, Ditschi, the sub-district servant Lönenschloss from Ditschi's district, and I myself. During those meetings we dealt with the interpretation of the Bible and talked about the Truth. The owner of the apartment was not present. Here I have to emphasize that – besides the prayers held – I used to see for myself whether the individual district servants were still working for the IBSA. For it might have been possible that in some cases arrests had taken place and that no one at all was in charge of the district. In such cases my task was to find and appoint a new district servant.

As early as at the time of the Lucerne convention, Ditschi was proposed and appointed as my successor as Reich Servant in case I should be arrested. In case of my arrest, Ditschi has to turn to the branch office at Prague to receive further instructions. Besides, I want to remark that according to his own statement, Ditschi has relations with brethren in the Netherlands and keeps in touch with them. However, I cannot say more about it. I merely know that Ditschi keeps in touch with the brethren in the Netherlands via Sterkrade. I think it is quite possible that Ditschi was repeatedly in Sterkrade.

The interrogation is broken off.

Berlin, April 26, 1937.

Proceedings!

Brought for questioning: Erich Frost, particulars already on record, states:

On March 6, 1937, the day of the latest major [IBSA] meeting in Berlin, Siebeneichler was not present. Since we were worried about him, I at once sent Ilse Unterdörfer to Munich so that she might make enquiries about Siebeneichler. I gave Unterdörfer a Munich telephone number which I had been given by Siebeneichler. After having called the holder of the number, Unterdörfer met a sister in Munich unknown to me, alleged Christian name of 'Gertrud'. I remember that Gertrud is the same person as Elfriede Löhr from Munich. At least I suspect but cannot substantiate this.

Josef Bahner, who works in the [Watch Tower Society] branch office in Prague, is a Sudeten German, approximately 34 years old. Bahner constantly travels throughout Czechoslovakia for the IBSA, his domicile is Brünn in the Czechoslovak Republic, unknown street. In the past, Bahner was a Czech officer, his height is 1.63 m. He is of pale complexion, fair hair. In the past Bahner must have worked temporarily at the Watch Tower Society Bible House in Magdeburg. He is a merchant by profession.

Heinrich Dwenger was in charge of the field service department of the Watch Tower Society in Magdeburg. He was busy there for many years. He is a citizen of the German Reich. I think he is some 45 years old. He must be 170 cm in height, has a short-trimmed moustache and brownish hair with a part. Dwenger is unmarried and odd in a way.

On this occasion I would like to state that the Swiss Francs – there might well be more than 50 – that were discovered with me, come from the District Servant Wandres who gave them to me in February of this year on the occasion of the major meeting at Berlin. Wandres got those Francs from South German brethren who were present at the Lucerne convention and were not able to spend all the money. As 'Good-Hope-Money,' the brethren had put the money at the disposal of the German work. If I had not been arrested, I would have changed the Francs at the German National Bank. Up till now I have not had the opportunity of doing this.

(Signed) Erich Frost

Questioning closed.

In many ways, Jehovah's Witnesses perplexed the Nazis. The overwhelming majority of Witnesses in Germany were ordinary, working-class Germans whom governmental officialdom expected would happily integrate into the *Volksgemeinschaft* or German racial community. After all, the vast majority of Germans – whether members of the great churches or of the various sects such as the Mormons, and even the Mennonites – showed themselves willing, and sometimes enthusiastic when it came to submitting to the demands of the Third Reich. The Nazis wondered why the Witnesses were so different. So, instead of trying to exterminate them (with the Jews and the Gypsies), beginning in 1938 the Nazis frequently offered Witnesses the option of signing a declaration whereby they would abjure their faith, sever all association with the Internationale Bibelforschervereinigung or IBV (the International Bible Students Association), and agree to fight for the Fatherland.

DOCUMENT G5-A

The Declaration Whereby Jehovah's Witnesses Could Abjure Their Faith and Be Released from Prisons and Concentration Camps

(German Text)

Konzentrationslager
Abteilung II

ERKLÄRUNG

Ich, - der - die . . . . . .

geboren am: . . . . . .

in: . . . . . .

gebe hiermit folgende Erklärung ab:

1. Ich habe erkannt, daß die Internationale Bibelforschervereinigung eine lrrlehre verbreitet und unter dem Deckmantel religiöser Betätigung lediglich staatsfeindliche Ziele verfolgt.

2. Ich habe mich deshalb voll und ganz von dieser Organisation abgewandt, und mich auch innerlich von dieser Sekte freigemacht.

3. Ich versichere hiermit, daß ich mich nie wieder für die Internationale Bibelforschervereinigungen betätigen werde. Personen, die für die Irrlehre der Bibelforscher an mich werbend herantreten oder in anderer Weise ihre Einstellung als Bibelforscher bekunden, werde ich unverzüglich zur Anzeige bringen. Sollten mir Bibelforscherschriften zugesandt werden, so werde ich diese umgehend bei der nächsten Polizeidienststelle abgeben.

4. Ich will künftig die Gesetze des Staates achten, insbesondere im Falle eines Krieges mein Vaterland mit der Waffe in der Hand verteidigen und mich voll und ganz in die Volksgemeinschaft eingliedern.

5. Mir ist eröffnet worden, daß ich mit meiner erneuten Inschutzhaftnahme zu rechnen habe, wenn ich meiner heute abgegebenen Erklarung zuwiderhandle.

den. . . . . .

Unterschrift

DOCUMENT G5-B
(English Translation)

Concentration camp
Department II

DECLARATION

I, the . . . . . .

Born on: . . . . . .

In: . . . . . .

I herewith give the following declaration:

1. I have come to know that the International Bible Students Association disseminates false doctrines and under the guise of religion promotes aims dangerous to the state.

2. Therefore, I have completely left this organization and have freed myself entirely from the teachings of this sect.

3. I herewith give assurance that never again will I participate in the activities of the International Bible Students Association. Should any persons come to me with the teachings of the Bible Students or who in any way show their association with them, I will immediately report them [to the police]. Should any Bible Student literature be sent to me, I will immediately take it to the nearest police station.

4. In the future I will respect the laws of the state, and especially in the event of a war will I defend the Fatherland with weapon in hand, and I will fully and completely join myself to the racial community of the [German] people.

5. I am informed that I will again be immediately taken into protective custody should I act contrary to the declaration given today.

Dated . . . . . .

Signature . . . . . .

APPENDIX H
Character Descriptions of J.F. Rutherford

During his years as president of the Watch Tower Society, J.F. Rutherford ruled that organization – and, eventually, Jehovah's Witnesses – with a rod of iron. Despite recent Witness claims to the contrary, he was an extremely harsh, willful person who would brook no criticism from his brethren. He was quite willing to use his office for personal self-gratification and was guilty of behaviour that was questionable from a moral standpoint, and he attempted to shield his private life from ordinary Jehovah's Witnesses and the general public. In addition, he used his ever-changing 'doctrinal system,' if it can be called that, in such a way as to enhance his own position and that of the Watch Tower organization. To say it was non-political – as Jehovah's Witnesses would like to insist today – is to give that term a very narrow meaning. In fact, Rutherford was a masterful church politician who attempted to play politics in the political arenas of the United States, Germany, and other countries. This was shown clearly by his involvement in the Bonus Army affair and in the events of the summer of 1933 in Germany. So his claim that he and his followers were politically 'neutral' was in many ways a charade, as was his life and administration.

Two of his close associates have left clear pictures of 'the Judge,' as he liked to be called. The first of these was Walter F. Salter, for many years Watch Tower Canadian branch overseer and, also, a close associate and confidant of Rutherford. The second was Olin R. Moyle, Watch Tower attorney at the Brooklyn Bethel, the headquarters of Jehovah's Witnesses, from 1935 to 1939.

There is evidence that Salter was involved with Rutherford in activities that would have shocked the Witness community had they been known.[1] In addition, Salter quite evidently was present with Rutherford at gatherings where a lot of liquor was consumed. So he was well aware of the latter's personal habits. He remained quiet about these facts, however, until after he began to question certain Watch Tower teachings in 1936, was removed from his position as branch overseer, and was excommunicated in a congregational trial that had all the characteristics of a spiritual lynching.[2] Thus, on 1 April 1937 he wrote an open letter to Rutherford, chastising him in sharp language for his teachings and especially for his style of life. Salter was somewhat open to the charge of dishonesty, however, for he sent copies of his letter to Rutherford to many Jehovah's Witnesses in envelopes marked with the return address of the Watch Tower Society in Brooklyn. Even so, it is doubtful that he deserved the bitter attacks that were to be levelled against him in *The Golden Age.* Not only was he damned as lazy, a traitor, and an 'evil slave,' but it was hinted – perhaps with some justification – that he was sexually immoral.[3]

Much of what he wrote relates specifically to doctrinal differences. However, only those parts of his letter that deal directly with Rutherford's conduct are reprinted below.

1 On 27 April 1926, George H. Fisher wrote a letter to W. Nieman of Magdeburg, Germany, accusing Rutherford of attending Al Jolson's Winter Garden Theater to see the Paris Edition of the then notorious show 'Artists and Models' on the evening before the Bible Students' annual celebration of the Lord's Supper. Fisher wanted to bring Rutherford, as an ex officio elder of every Bible Student congregation, before the individual churches for discipline. Fisher claimed he had the necessary witnesses to do so. Evidently, Rutherford had gone to the show with two elders (one of whom seems to have been Salter) and a young woman. But in July of the same year Fisher died at his desk and the matter never went any further. Nieman did, however, publish Fisher's letter and an analysis of it in a German leaflet titled 'Bruder George Fisher.' Rutherford's lame answer to Fisher's charge was that he was too busy in the Lord's work to be bothered replying to such criticism and, anyway, had never seen Al Jolson in his life and did not know what he looked like. See *The Golden Age,* 4 May 1927, 505, 506.

2 WT, 1937, 141, 159, 160.

3 For the specific articles attacking Salter in the crudest fashion, see *The Golden Age* of 5 May 1937 and the issue of 16 June 1937.

DOCUMENT H1
Salter's Letter to Rutherford

P.O. Box no. 404
Toronto, Canada
April 1, 1937

Hon. J. F. Rutherford
4140 Braeburn Road
Kensington Heights,
San Diego, California

. . . .

So much for doctrine: now a word regarding what I feel constrained to state concerning the corruption otherwise of the Society.

As the scales by the Lord's grace, have fallen from my eyes I have been astounded to see how blinded I have been to your actions, through a superstition that the WATCHTOWER was the Lord's channel of meat in due season for the household of faith and that you as President of the Society were God's chief servant amongst His people, and that you being responsible we should be submissive to whatsoever you required done, foolishly thinking that I had no responsibility in the matter and that anything you did that was wrong, or that I did as ordered by you, the Lord would overrule. It was with this thought in mind that I, at your orders would purchase cases of whiskey at $60.00 a case, and cases of brandy and other liquors, to say nothing of untold cases of beer. A bottle or two of liquor would not do; it was for THE PRESIDENT and nothing was too good for THE PRESIDENT. He was heaven's favorite, why should not he have everything that would gratify his desires for comfort. True, I had a part therein for I partook of your hospitality, or shall I say the Society's hospitality for it was the Society's money but I partook, as above stated, being blinded with the idea THE PRESIDENT was in charge and therefore responsible and not I. Today I see that the thought was absolutely wrong and that the squandering of the Society's money in that respect was a mis-appropriation of funds, and I should have taken no part therein whatsoever. I confess my wrong before the friends and before the Lord and ask their forgiveness and His.

Often as I thought about this extravagance and waste and then thought of the lot of the pioneers I was puzzled, but my conscience was lulled by the belief that the Lord was using you to serve His cause and people and therefore I did not and dared not say anything that I thought would cause the friends to lose confidence in you as a servant of the Lord. True, I have humorously said to those whom I thought were our mutual friends things regarding your idiosyncrasies that all MEN between friends say one of another, just as you have said of me, which things I know have been traitorously (Matthew 24:10, John 16:1, 2) reported to you not alone out of their setting but so out of their spirit that none who wanted to know the truth would recognize them as the original statements, and before my God I can state I have never to my knowledge done anything intentionally to injure you, the work of the Society, or its interests, in my life. In that betrayal you joined hands – not that I mind in point of fact I thank God that He permitted it and assure you I would do good to any of the conspirators had I the opportunity.

....

The squandering of the Society's money on liquor was only one thing I had cause to wonder over; there were other things. I could not help but contrast with the lot of the pioneers the luxury that you surrounded yourself with and the comfort that I enjoyed, and among these luxuries I cannot refrain from mentioning the following:

1. Not one but two 16-cylinder cars, one in California and one in New York.

One would not suffice for THE PRESIDENT nor would a 6 cylinder car be big enough for THE PRESIDENT, but a 4 would do for a pioneer, or a bicycle or a hand-sleigh, or trudging along without any vehicle at all.

2. Your New York apartment, easily worth a rental of $10,000.00 a year. And its luxurious furnishings.

3. Your palatial residence on Staten Island, camouflaged as essential to the broadcasting station WBBR.

4. As though that residence were not sufficient, a further small place of seclusion in the woods of Staten Island where you can go and rest your weary body while the pioneers and others trudge from door to door.

5. Your further abode at San Diego, for which you yourself told me you were offered $75,000.00, but of course it could not be sold and the funds used to help the pioneers because it was deeded to David – what hypocrisy!

6. Commodious and expensive quarters in Magdeburg, Germany, for the convenience of THE PRESIDENT, to say nothing of the provision made for your comfort in London.

And what is your mental attitude toward all this? Why you glory in it and brazenly advertise it to the friends. 'Who dares find fault therewith? Am I not THE PRESIDENT?' Yes, you glory in it, glorying in your shame.

. . . .

Now a word regarding the financial progress of the Society. You inform the friends and the public that the books and booklets are placed with the public at cost – they surely are and more!! You well know that the price to the pioneers until recently covered all costs including all appropriate overhead charges and even now the loss is only slight on some items, while on the other hand the price to the companies and public nets the Society at least 100%! What is this 100% if it is not profit? Poor gullible friends. How they believe everything you tell them!!! Where do they think the millions of dollars invested in buildings, machinery, stock, etc, at Brooklyn, Magdeburg, London, Toronto and other places, to say nothing of your own dwellings, etc, come from if not from profit on the books? You know and I know that the gain the Canadian office alone during the past few years was a hundred thousand dollars. And at the time I was relieved of my duties there was not only a large sum in the bank as customary but also over $25,000.00 in cash was lying in the Society's vaults at 40 Irwin Avenue and had for years, which could be used for the needs of the President or those whom he might designate in case of an international emergency – and the dear pioneers? Well, of course they could go hungry. Poor gullible friends!! My, were we not blind, and how blind the friends still are! And yet the annual reports tell of our great losses and how it is hoped the Lord will make it up. Well, it is said, 'figures don't lie, but liars do figure.'

. . . .

Sincerely,

W. F. Salter (signed)

Moyle's description of Rutherford's behaviour was made under very different circumstances. Salter had broken with the Watch Tower Society and had been excommunicated from the Witness community at the time he wrote the letter quoted above. Moyle, in contrast, was still a loyal Witness, and according to his own testimony he had a good relationship with the judge prior to chastising him for his conduct. Furthermore, there was no basis for accusing Moyle of any type of moral laxness; in many ways he was puritanical in his personal conduct. But following the delivery of the private letter that appears below, Rutherford called him before the boards of directors of both the Watch Tower Society of Pennsylvania and the New York Watchtower Society and had him expelled from the Brooklyn Bethel on the same day. After Moyle returned to his home state, Wisconsin, Rutherford had him labelled a 'Judas' and an 'evil slave' in *The Watchtower*, caused him to be excommunicated by fiat despite his desire to remain a loyal Witness, and proceeded to destroy his business with his Witness clients. In response, Moyle sued Rutherford, his fellow directors, and the two societies. After a long and revealing trial, he was ultimately able to collect more than $15,000 damages – a sizable amount in 1944, when the case and its appeal were concluded. By then Rutherford was dead.

Significantly, Moyle made many of the same charges against Rutherford that Salter did. Thus it is difficult to deny them. Interestingly, the Watch Tower Society deals with those charges by ignoring them. There is no mention of Moyle or of the trial's outcome in either of the Watch Tower's official histories, *Jehovah's Witnesses in the Divine Purpose* and *Jehovah's Witnesses: Proclaimers of God's Kingdom.*

DOCUMENT H2

Moyle's Letter to Rutherford

OLIN R. MOYLE Counselor
117 Adams Street. Brooklyn, New York
Telephone TRiangle 5-1674

July 21, 1939

Judge J. F. Rutherford,
Brooklyn, N. Y.

Dear Brother Rutherford:

This letter is to give you notice of our intention to leave Bethel on September 1st next. The reasons for leaving are stated herein and we ask that you give them careful and thoughtful consideration.

Conditions at Bethel are a matter of concern to all of the Lord's people. Nowhere among imperfect men can there be perfect freedom from oppression, discrimination and unfair treatment, but at the Lord's headquarters on earth conditions should be such that injustice would be reduced to the minimum. That is not the case here at Bethel and a protest should he made against it. I am in a good position to make such protest because your treatment of me has been generally kind, considerate and fair. I can make this protest in the interests of the Bethel family and of the Kingdom work without any personal interest entering into the matter.

ILL TREATMENT OF BETHEL FAMILY

Shortly after coming to Bethel we were shocked to witness the spectacle of our brethren receiving what is designated a 'trimming' from you. The fact, if memory serves me correctly, was a tongue lashing given to C. J. Woodworth. Woodworth in a personal letter to you stated something to the effect that it would be serving the devil to continue using our present calendar. For that reason he was humiliated, called a jackass, and given a public lambasting. Others have been similarly treated. McCaughey, McCormick, Knorr, Prosser, Price, Van Sipma, Ness and others have been publicly called to account, condemned, and reprimanded without previous notice.

This summer some of the most unfair public reproaches have been given. J. Y. McCauley asked a question which carried with it a criticism of the present method of Watch Tower study. For that he was severely reprimanded. Your action constituted a violation of the principle for which we are fighting, towit [*sic*], freedom of speech. It was the action of a boss and not that of a fellow servant. Securing a sufficient mode of study with imperfect study leaders is no easy task, and no method yet produced has proved to be one hundred per cent perfect. You stated that no complaints had come to you concerning this method of study. If that be the case you have not had all the facts presented to you. There is complaint in various places that the Watch Tower studies have degenerated into mere reading lessons. It may be that the present method is the best that can be used, but in view of known limitations honest criticism should not be censored nor honest critics punished.

Brother Worsley received a public denunciation from you because he prepared and handed to brethren a list of helpful Scripture citations on fundamental topics. How can we consistently condemn religionists for being intolerant when you exercise intolerance against those who work with you? Doesn't this prove that the only freedom permitted at Bethel is freedom to do and say that which you wish to be said and done? The Lord certainly never authorized you to exercise such high handed authority over your fellow servants.

Since the Madison Square Garden meeting there has been a distressing condition of restraint and suspicion at Bethel. The ushers were placed in a tough spot but did an excellent piece of work. They exercised care and diligence in watching arrivals at the Garden, and prevented a number of suspicious characters from entering. They were on the job immediately when the disturbance started and quelled a disturbance which would have otherwise reached serious proportions. But for two weeks following the convention there has been constant criticism and condemnation of them from you. They have been charged with dereliction of duty and labelled as 'sissies'. To see some of these boys break down and cry because of your unkind remarks is, to say the least saddening.

The brethren at Bethel have thoroughly demonstrated their loyalty and devotion to the Lord, and do not need to be berated for wrong doing. A suggestion of kindly admonition from you would be more than sufficient to check any wrongful action, and would eliminate resentment and induce greater happiness and comfort for the whole family. You have stated many times that there are no bosses in the Lord's organization but the undeniable fact cannot be evaded that your actions in scolding and upbraiding these boys are the actions of a boss. It makes one sick at heart and disgusted to listen to them. If you will cease smiting your fellow servants Bethel will be a happier place and the Kingdom work will prosper accordingly.

DISCRIMINATION

We publish to the world that all in the Lord's organization are treated alike, and receive the same as far as this world's goods are concerned.

You know that is not the case. The facts cannot be denied. Take for instance the difference between the accomodations [*sic*] furnished to you, and your personal attendants, compared with those furnished to some of the brethren. You have many homes, towit [*sic*], Bethel, Staten Island, California, etc. I am informed that even at the Kingdom Farm one house is kept for your sole use during the short periods that you spend there. And what do the brethren at the farm receive? Small rooms, unheated thru the bitter cold winter weather. They live in their trunks like campers. That may be all right if NECESSARY, but there are many houses on the farm standing idle or used for other purposes, which could be used to give some comfort to those who work so long and so hard.

You work in a nice air conditioned room. You and your attendants spend a portion of the week in the quiet of country surroundings. The boys at the factory diligently work thru the hot summer months without such helps, or any effort made to give them. That is discrimination which should receive your thoughtful consideration.

MARRIAGE

Here again is shown unequal and discriminatory treatment. One brother left Bethel some time ago for the purpose of getting married, and, so I am informed, was refused the privilege of pioneering in New York, apparently as an official disapproval of his action in leaving Bethel. On the other hand when Bonnie Boyd got married she didn't have to leave Bethel. She was permitted to bring her husband into Bethel in spite of the printed rule providing that both marrying parties should have lived there for five years.

Harsh treatment of one and favored treatment of another is discrimination, and should not have a place in the Lord's organization.

FILTHY AND VULGAR LANGUAGE

The biblical injunctions against unclean, filthy speaking and jesting have never been abrogated. It is shocking and nauseating to hear vulgar speaking and smut at Bethel. It was stated by a sister that was one of the things you had to get used to at Bethel. The loudest laughter at the table comes when a filthy or near filthy joke goes through, and your skirts are not clear.

LIQUOR

Under your tutelage there has grown up a glorification of alcohol and condemnation of total abstinence which is unseemly. Whether a servant of Jehovah drinks alcoholic liquor is none of my business, except in giving a helping hand to a brother who is stumbled thereby. Whether I am a total abstainer is nobody's business but my own. But not so at Bethel. There appears to be a definite policy of breaking in new comers into the use of liquor, and resentment is shown against those who do not join them. The claim is made, 'One cannot be a real Bethelite without drinking beer.' Shortly after we arrived it was arrogantly stated, 'we can't do much with Moyle, but we'll make a man out of Peter.' A New York brother intimated that I was out of harmony with the truth and with the Society because I didn't drink liquor. A New York sister stated that she had never used liquor or served it until some of the Bethel boys insisted upon it. A brother who used to drink liquor to excess became a total abstainer after getting the truth. He knew that a single drink of liquor would start him off to his former drinking habits, but in spite of that brethren from Bethel insisted upon his imbibing liquor and inferred that he was out of harmony with the organization through refusing. Total abstainers are looked upon with scorn as weaklings. You have publicly labelled total abstainers as prudes and therefore must assume your share of the responsibility for the Bacchus like attitude exhibited by members of the family.

These are a few of the things which should have no place in the Lord's organization. There are other more grevious [*sic*] injustices but I have had no personal contact with them and therefore do not discuss them.

It hasn't been an easy or pleasant task to write these things to you, and its still harder to make this protest effective by leaving Bethel. We sold our home and business when we came to Bethel and fully intended to spend the rest of our lives at this place in the Lord's service. We leave in order to register most emphatically our disagreement with the unjust conditions related in this letter. We are not leaving the Lord's service but will continue to serve Him and His organization as fully as strength and means will allow.

Neither am I running away from battling the Devil's crowd in the courts. I expect to return to the private practice of law, probably in Milwaukee, Wisconsin, and hope to be in the fight in every way possible. With this letter I am enclosing a statement of the major cases now pending in which I am actively participating. It would be unreasonable and unfair to drop these matters into your lap without further assistance or consideration. I am ready and willing to press these issues in the courts just as vigorously and carefully as though I remained at Bethel, and will do so if that is your desire.

We have considered this action for some time, but this letter is delivered to you just as we are leaving on a vacation trip for very specific reasons. First: It is desirable that you take time for thought and consideration of the matters herein set forth before taking any action. Hasty and ill considered action might be regrettable. Second: Frankly I have no desire for a verbal argument with you over these matters. I have had plenty of occasion to observe that a controversial matter does not receive a calm and reasoned discussion of the facts. Too often it turns into a denunciation of some person by you. I am not interested in that kind of a wordy battle. These statements are the reasons presented by Sister Moyle and myself for leaving Bethel. If we speak erroneously or wrongfully we are responsible before the Lord for so speaking. If we speak truthfully, and we stoutly contend that everything here related is the truth, then there is an immediate responsibility on your part to remedy the conditions necessitating this protest. May the Lord direct and guide you into fair and kindly treatment of your fellow servants is my wish and prayer.

Your Brother in the King's service,

Olin R. Moyle

P.S. Should you desire to write to me concerning these matters during vacation a letter will each me at Ticonderoga, New York, General Delivery after July 29th.

APPENDIX I
An Analysis of the Numbers of Jehovah's Witnesses Imprisoned and Killed in Nazi Germany

The statistics given for the numbers of Jehovah's Witnesses in Germany who were imprisoned and who were either killed or died of mistreatment in the prisons and concentration camps of Nazi Germany vary greatly. This is true of both those given by the Watch Tower Society and those by independent scholars. Some variation is, of course, quite understandable. Many factors make it difficult to ascertain just how many were actually imprisoned and how many perished. Among these is the fact that the borders of Germany were far from static during the years between 1938 and the collapse of the Third Reich in the spring of 1945. It is true that Austrians have apparently never been counted as among German Witnesses for the purposes of those statistics, even though that country was part of the Third Reich for some seven years. It is more difficult to decide whether Jehovah's Witnesses from such places as Sudetenland, Danzig, Memel, Alsace-Lorraine, and large areas of prewar Poland should be counted as part of the German Witness community or not. Then there is the question of documentation. As Detlef Garbe makes clear, many of the records from the concentration camps were destroyed at the end of the Second World War, so a fully accurate count of prisoners and fatalities is impossible.[1]

Nonetheless, it is instructive to look at some of the data that have been published over the years. Following the regular Watch Tower practice of counting only active Jehovah's Witness publishers or per-

1 See Detlef Garbe, Zwischen Widerstand und Martyrium: Die Zeugen Jehovas im 'Dritten Reich,' 4th ed. (Munich: R. Oldenbourg Verlag, 1993), 491–500.

sons, according to the *1974 Yearbook of Jehovah's Witnesses,* from 1932 to the spring of 1933 they grew from 12,484 to 19,268, and their spring Memorial attendance grew from 14,453 to 24,843 over the same period.[2] Of course, what this means is that the total Witness community would have at least amounted to around 25,000 – a figure often quoted in Watch Tower and other publications. Beyond these basic figures, which are undoubtedly too conservative,[3] things become very murky.

Throughout the period from the end of the Second World War until the publication of the *1974 Yearbook of Jehovah's Witnesses* in late 1973, Watch Tower statements were, from a historical standpoint, quite useless. For example, *The Watchtower* of 15 May 1950 stated on page 153: 'The most notorious case of persecution for living up to the name [of Jehovah] is that of the witnesses in Germany. They were banned by Hitler soon after he signed the concordat with the Vatican in 1933. Their property was confiscated. Ten thousand ministers were placed in concentration camps. Only eight thousand were released after World War II; two thousand had been murdered.' In fact, the Witnesses were banned throughout Germany on 24 June 1933, whereas the concordat between the Nazis and the Vatican was not signed until the following 10 September. Also, there were never anything like 10,000 Jehovah's witnesses in concentration camps.

Taking much the same tack, *The Watchtower* of 15 December 1950 stated on page 500: 'Already during the Hitler regime about 1,000 Jehovah's witnesses were executed as traitors, because they not only refused to serve in the war but openly opposed Hitler's authority. Another 1,000 of Jehovah's witnesses died in prisons and concentration camps.' Then, only two months later, *The Watchtower* of 15 February 1951 asserted much the same thing on pages 105–6: 'That is why during the Nazi regime in Germany from 1933 to 1945 Jehovah's witnesses in that land refused to heil Hitler! as their Fuehrer or Leader, and went to concentration camps and prisons, where 2,000 died cruel deaths, and of the 8,000 that came out alive, 2,000 were invalided for the rest of their lives.'

2 *1974 Yearbook,* 109–10.

3 Despite counting Memorial attenders as members of the community, these statistics would not have included everyone associated with the German Witness movement at the time. The Watch Tower Society has had a tendency to count only active persons as 'ministers' as members of its community, especially since J.F. Rutherford began his campaign to transform every Bible Student–Jehovah's Witness into a door-to-door 'publisher.' Thus children and certain others would not have been listed as members of the community in 1933.

The Watchtower of 1 June 1960 also played on the theme that ten thousand had been imprisoned. On page 327 it declared: 'Hitler failed to break them in prisons and concentration camps where he tortured 10,000 of them, and the Communists are failing to do it in their frightful prisons and slave-labor camps.'

The Watch Tower Society had come to claim that only some 2,000 Jehovah's Witnesses died under Hitler; curiously, though, in 1964 it arbitrarily decided to double that figure. At the same time, it returned to the theme of blaming the Catholic Church for their persecution. On page 13, *The Watchtower* of 1 January 1964 declared: 'Hitler, a Roman Catholic, the arm of his church in Germany, forbade Jehovah's witnesses to preach the kingdom of God, and these modem-day Christians had to say to Hitler's Gestapo police: "Whether it is righteous in the sight of God to listen to you rather than to God, judge for yourselves." They kept preaching even though 10,000 of them were put in concentration camps and over 4,000 died there. The rest nearly starved to death. The war's end aided their survival.'

Evidently, in order to make it seem as though the vast majority of Jehovah's Witnesses had remained loyal to their faith during the Third Reich, *The Watchtower* of 1 January 1971 stated on page 16: 'In 1932 when the last report was received from Germany and before the ban was placed on Jehovah's witnesses, there were 14,453 sharing in the Kingdom declaration. By 1946, following the collapse of the German war machine and the opening of the gates of the concentration camps – but not the graves – there were 11,415 dedicated Christians still in the great contest.' However, this statement was at best a half-truth. As quoted above from the *1974 Yearbook,* the Watch Tower Society in Brooklyn received the last report on the number of Witness publishers prior to the total ban on their work in June 1933 in the spring of that same year. By then there were 19,268 publishers.

A major change in Watch Tower statements about what happened to Jehovah's Witnesses under the Third Reich occurred with the publication of the *1974 Yearbook of Jehovah's Witnesses.* Quite evidently, through a desire to publish a formal history of what had happened, the German branch office of the Watch Tower had, for the first time, done some serious research. The *Yearbook* account skirts over some embarrassing facts and wrongly blames Balzereit rather than Rutherford for some of the statements sympathetic to Nazi policy; that said, it generally presents fairly accurate history. So, its statistics probably represent a close approximation to the truth. On page 212 it states:

> But despite the hard conditions [in May 1945], how those who worshiped Jehovah rejoiced! They had been privileged to prove their integrity to the Sovereign Ruler of the universe. During Hitler's rule 1,687 of them had lost their jobs, 284 their businesses, 735 their homes and 457 were not allowed to carry on their trade. In 129 cases their property had been confiscated, 826 pensioners had been refused their pensions and 329 others had suffered other personal loss. There were 860 children who had been taken away from their parents. In 30 cases marriages had been dissolved due to pressure by political officials and in 108 cases divorces had been granted when requested by mates opposed to the truth. A total of 6,019 had been arrested, several two, three or even more times, so that all together, 8,917 arrests were registered. All together they had been sentenced to serve 13,924 years and two months in prison, two and a quarter times as long as the period since Adam's creation. A total of 2,000 brothers and sisters had been put into concentration camps, where they had spent 8,078 years and six months, an average of four years. A total of 635 had died in prison, 253 had been sentenced to death and 203 of these had actually been executed. What a record of integrity.'

The Watchtower of 1 February 1976 repeated these data by saying on page 82: 'A total of 6,019 had been arrested, several of them two, three, or even more times, so that, all together, 8,917 arrests were registered; and these persons served sentences amounting to 13,924 years in prison. Many of these faithful men and women were put into concentration camps and thus collectively spent 8,078 years undergoing vicious treatment there. A total of 635 died in prison, 253 were sentenced to death, with 203 of these actually being executed.'

The Watchtower of 1 July 1979 continued to publish the same data. It said on pages 7 and 8: 'By way of illustration, please consider the years 1933 to 1945, when Adolf Hitler's "Third Reich" tried to exterminate [*sic*] Jehovah's Witnesses in the German Reich. Their activities were banned and 6,019 were arrested, several of them two, three or more times. Two thousand suffered in concentration camps. A total of 635 Witnesses died in prison, 203 being executed.' But over the next decade, the Watch Tower Society began to inflate the number of Witnesses who were imprisoned and died under Hitler by quoting Christine King and old statistics generated by Michael Kater. On page 8, *The Watchtower* of 1 October 1984 emphasized: 'Most outstanding among Dr. King's findings are the figures of deaths and imprisonment of Jehovah's Witnesses. These indicate that the figures previously published by the Witnesses were greatly underestimated. Dr. King's source for these statistics was a volume [*sic*] published in Munich, Germany, by Michael Kater. "My own perusal of Court and Gestapo records," she declared, "would certainly support these higher figures."' Then the Witness magazine went on to say: 'What are these figures? Some *10,000* were imprisoned, and together they received sentences totaling 20,000 years. *One out of every two German Witnesses was imprisoned, one in four lost their lives.*' As I have pointed out earlier, The *Watchtower* did no analysis of King's data, nor is there any evidence that King did any in-depth research on just how many Witnesses actually suffered imprisonment and perished from Nazi persecution.

A few years later *The Watchtower* of 1 January 1989 used a similar device to inflate the sufferings of German Witnesses. It stated on page 21: 'The book *Mothers in the Fatherland* [Jehovah's Witnesses]: were sent to concentration camps, a thousand of them were executed, and another thousand died between 1933 and 1945.'

By the early 1990s the Watch Tower Society was busy promoting the idea of Witness martyrdom. To that end it began to quote statistics that it, itself, had shown to be inflated. For example, on page 22, *The Watchtower* of 1 February 1990 quoted Friedrich Zipfel in *Kirchenkampf in Deutschland* (Church Struggle in Germany) regarding the persecution of Jehovah's Witnesses under the Third Reich. There, Zipfel is recorded as having written: 'Ninety-seven percent of the members of this small religious group were victims of National Socialistic [Nazi] persecution. One third of them were killed, either by execution, other violent acts, hunger, sickness or slave labor. The severity of this subjection was without precedent and was the result of uncompromising faith which could not be harmonized with National Socialistic ideology.'

Yet in 1993 the book *Jehovah's Witnesses: Proclaimers of God's Kingdom* presented statistics only slightly higher than those found in the *1974 Yearbook*. It stated on page 720 under the year 1933: 'Jehovah's Witnesses are banned in Germany. During the intense persecution down to the end of World War II, 6,262 are arrested, and their combined time of imprisonment totals 14,332 years; 2,074 are sent to concentration camps, where their confinement totals 8,332 years.' Curiously, this 'history' gave no statistics for the number of Witness deaths from persecution.

Published in 1995, the German Watch Tower brochure *Jehovas Zeugen–Menschen aus der Nachbarschaft: Wer sind Sie?* quotes an official German government document on page 16 as follows: 'About 10,000 were imprisoned. Some 1,200 members of this religious community suffered death for their resistance.'[4] Interestingly, the figure 1,200 seldom if ever appears in English Watch Tower publications.

Quotations from Watch Tower publications show an amazing lack of consistency and, often, lack respect for historical accuracy. Not only have statistics been tossed around with abandon, but often no attempt has been made to distinguish the fact that while a relatively large number of Witnesses were jailed, often several times, a much smaller number ended up in the concentration camps. It is quite true that following arrest and while being held in jails or prisons, many were severely beaten, tortured, and even killed; but in general, the privation experienced by those who were not sent to concentration camps was less severe than that experienced by those who were. What can therefore be said about the Watch Tower statements made above is that many of them were published more for shock value than for a desire to report facts accurately. They demonstrate, too, just how unreliable Jehovah's Witness publications and statements often are. This is clearly evident: despite what they have stated in publications such as the *1974 Yearbook, Jehovah's Witnesses: Proclaimers of God's Kingdom,* and *Jehovas Zeugen – Menschen aus der Nachbarschaft: Wer sind Sie*? at the Holocaust Museum in Washington, D.C., they continue to publish the old canard that 2,000 Witnesses died as a result of Nazi persecution.

Until Detlef Garbe completed his in-depth study of concentration camp records for *Zwichen Widerstand und Martyrium,* independent scholars gave statistics that were even more varied than did those of the Watch Tower Society. As pointed out earlier, Friedrich Zipfel held that 5,911 Jehovah's Witnesses were imprisoned and more than 2,000 killed between 1933 and 1945. But because he claims that there were only 6,034 in the Reich at the time, he wrongly states that 97 per cent suffered persecution and more than one-third perished.[5] Unfortunately, John Conway based his appraisal of the persecution of German Jehovah's Witnesses under the Third Reich on Zipfel, and therefore

4 These data are taken from *Informationen zur politischen Bildung* (Nr. 243, 2. Quartal 1994) on page 21 but seem to be from Detlef Garbe's research, discussed below. The above statement reads in German: 'Circa 10 000 kamen in Haft. Etwa 1 200 Todesopfer fordete der Widerstand dieser Glaubensgemeinschaft.'

5 Friedrich Zipfel, *Kirchenkampf in Deutschland – 1933–1945: Religionsverfolgung und Selbsbehauptung der Kirchen in der Nationalsozialistischen Zeit* (Berlin: Walter de Gruyter, 1961), 176n5.

came to a wrong conclusion.[6] Using Watch Tower statistics for the number of Witnesses in Germany in 1933, Michael Kater held that 10,000 were imprisoned and some 4,000 to 5,000 – roughly one-quarter of the Witness community – perished.[7] Christine King simply followed Kater and his sources.[8]

Garbe shows rather clearly that the number of killed was about 1,200, although he tends to agree with Kater that probably 10,000 were imprisoned. He admits that this is just an estimate, however, and he states correctly that many of the documents necessary for an accurate count are simply missing, as many were destroyed in the Second World War. Despite these caveats, it is useful to look at some of Garbe's data, which are undoubtedly the best that have been generated to date. According to him, the following concentration camps held the following numbers of Witness prisoners at one time or another: Auschwitz (circa 150), Buchenwald (477), Dachau (circa 150), Flossenbürg (250), Mauthausen (circa 150), Neuengamme (circa 100), Ravensbrück (close to 600), Sachsenhausen (500 to 600), Wewelburg (306). In addition, there were small numbers in Majdanek, Natzweiler Stutthof, and Vught (Herzogenbisch).

It must be noted that not all of these were German Jehovah's Witnesses. Garbe lists 445 from Austria, 282 from Poland, around 250 from the Netherlands, 60 from France, 7 from Belgium, and 2 from Italy and Luxembourg. In addition, there were small numbers from such countries as Yugoslavia, the Soviet Union, and Czechoslovakia. Accordingly, Garbe calculates that there were roughly 1,000+ non-German and more than 2,200 German Jehovah's Witnesses in the camps.

How many were killed or died from cold, hunger, overwork, physical punishment, and lack of medical treatment? Again, the number must remain indeterminate, but it was certainly lower than 2,000. In all probability the figure of 1,200 given by Garbe and the German

6 John S. Conway, *The Nazi Persecution of the Churches – 1933–45* (New York: Basic Books, 1968), 196. Barbara Grizzuti Harrison comments on Conway's statistics and calculates from them that if Conway and Zipfel were correct, over 3,000 Witnesses died in the concentration camps. She was evidently unaware that Zipfel had grossly underestimated the number of German Witnesses n 1933. See Barbara Grizzuti Harrison, *Visions of Glory: A History and a Memory of Jehovah's Witnesses* (New York: Simon and Schuster, 1978), 283.

7 Michael H. Kater, 'Die Ernsten Bibelforscher im Dritten Reich,' *Vierteljahrshefte für Zeitgeschichte* 17:2 (April 1969): 181.

8 Christine Elizabeth King, *The Nazi State and the New Religions: Five Case Studies in Non-Conformity* (New York and Toronto: Edwin Mellon Press, 1982), 169.

governmental *Informationen zur politischen Bildung* (Nr. 243, 2. Quartal 1994), as cited in note 5 above, is much closer to the truth. On the other hand, around 10,000 Jehovah's Witnesses may have been arrested. However, on the basis of Watch Tower figures published in the *1974 Yearbook* and in *Jehovah's Witnesses: Proclaimers of God's Kingdom*, that number seems excessive *unless non-German Witnesses are counted.* After all, the Witness community was and is a tight-knit one that would have known its own members and, in general, what had happened to them. Furthermore, if *The Watchtower* of 1 January 1976 quoted above is correct in stating that only 11,415 were active publishers in 1946, a year after the war, this indicates that there must have been a sizable apostatizing on the part of many Witnesses for various reasons during the Third Reich. So if only 11,000 remained loyal during the dark days of persecution, were practically all of them imprisoned? That may have been the case, but it seems unlikely. We know that there were some Witnesses active outside prisons and concentration camps even during the Second World War.

Although as Garbe says, we will never know totally the extent of what happened to Jehovah's Witnesses between 1933 and May 1945, much could be cleared up if the Watch Tower Society itself would open its files to any and all non-Witness historians. Unfortunately, that does not seem to be about to happen.

BIBLIOGRAPHY

Watch Tower Society Publications

All of the works listed below in this section have been published directly by the Watch Tower Bible and Tract Society of Pennsylvania (under its various names) or by subsidiary organizations such as the International Bible Students Association and the Watchtower Bible and Tract Society of New York. All have been published under the direction of the Pennsylvania corporation. Some, such as the *Convention Report Sermons,* have been reprinted by the Chicago Bible Students.

Published Works of C.T. Russell

Convention Report Sermons. Chicago: Chicago Bible Students, undated.
'Jews Not to Be Converted to Christianity.' *Overland Monthly* 58 (August 1911): 171–5.
Studies in the Scriptures, 7 vols. 1886–1917. Numerous editions
- Vol. 1: *The Divine Plan of the Ages.* 1886.
- Vol. 2: *The Time Is at Hand.* 1889.
- Vol. 3: *Thy Kingdom Come.* 1891.
- Vol. 4: *The Battle of Armageddon.* 1897.
- Vol. 5: *At-one-ment Between God and Man.* 1899.
- Vol. 6: *The New Creation.* 1904.
- Vol. 7: *The Finished Mystery.* 1917.

Although designated the posthumous work of Pastor Russell as taken from his various writings, Volume 7 was actually the edited work of C.J. Woodworth and G.H. Fisher with many of their personal ideas added to quotations from Russell. Many Bible Students refused to recognize it as an authentic work of the first Watch Tower president.

Published Works by J.F. Rutherford

Comfort for the Jews. 1925.
The Crisis. 1933.
Cure. 1938.
Enemies. 1937.
Favored People. 1934.
Judge Rutherford Uncovers Fifth Column. 1940.
Prohibition; The League of Nations: Of God or the Devil – Which? 1930.
Preparation. 1933.
Restoration. 1927.
Vindication. Vol. 1, 1931, vols. 2 and 3, 1932.

Anonymous Watch Tower Publications

[Franz, F.W.] *'Babylon the Great Has Fallen!': God's Kingdom Rules*. 1963.
Jehovah's Witnesses in the Divine Purpose. 1959.
Jehovah's Witnesses: Proclaimers of God's Kingdom. 1993.
'Let God Be True.' 1946.
'Let God Be True,' 2nd ed. 1952.
[Franz, F.W.] *Life Everlasting in Freedom of the Sons of God*. 1966.
[Franz, F.W.] *'The Kingdom Is at Hand.'* 1964.
[Franz, F.W.] *The New World*. 1942.
Organization for Kingdom-Preaching and Disciple-Making. 1972.
[Franz, F.W.] *The Truth That Leads to Eternal Life*. 1969.
[Franz, F.W.] *'The Truth Shall Make You Free.'* 1943.

Yearbooks of Jehovah's Witnesses. Various years from 1934 to the present. The earliest copies were styled *Year Books* rather than *Yearbooks*.

Magazines

The magazine now known as *The Watchtower Announcing Jehovah's Kingdom* began publication in July 1879. Devoted largely to doctrinal matters, since its beginning it has been published under the following titles:

Zion's Watch Tower and Herald of Christ's Presence – 1 July 1879 to 15 December 1908.

The Watch Tower and Herald of Christ's Presence – 1 January 1909 to 1 October 1931.

The Watchtower and Herald of Christ's Presence – 15 October 1933 to 15 December 1938.

The Watchtower and Herald of Christ's Kingdom – 1 January 1939 to 15 February 1939.

The Watchtower Announcing Jehovah's Kingdom – 1 March 1939 to the present. (Where the German edition of this magazine is cited or quoted, it is simply referred to as *Der Wachtturm.*)

On 1 October 1919 the second president of the Watch Tower Society began the publication of a second journal called *The Golden Age* (German: *Das Goldenes Zeitalter*).

Beginning on 6 October 1937, the title of *The Golden Age* was changed to *Consolation.* (German: *Trost*).

A second name change for that magazine occurred on 22 August 1946, when it became *Awake!* (German: *Erwachet!*).

Legal Cases Involving Jehovah's Witnesses

American Cases

Cantwell v. Connecticut 310 U.S. 296 (1940).

Lovell v. City of Griffin 303 U.S. 444 (1938).

Minersville School District v. Gobitis 310 U.S. 586 (1940).

Rutherford v. United States (May 14, 1919), 258 F. 855.

Schneider v. New Jersey 308 U.S. 147 (1939).

West Virginia Board of Education v. Barnette. 319 U.S.

British Cases

Walsh v. The Lord Advocate (1955) S.L.T. 393; [1956] All E.R. 129.

Canadian Cases

Brodie and Barrett v. the King, [1936] S.C.R. 118; 65, C.C.C. 289; 3 D.L.R. 81.

Duval et al. v. the King, (1938) 64 Quebec K.B. 270.

Saumur v. The City of Quebec [1953] 2 S.C.R. 299; 106 C.C.C. 289; [1953] D.L.R. 641.

Other Sources

Anthony, Dick. 'Tactical Ambiguity and Brainwashing Formulations: Science or Pseudo-Science?' In Benjamin Zablocki and Thomas Robbins, eds., *Misunderstanding Cults: Searching for Objectivity in a Controversial Field.* Toronto: University of Toronto Press, 2001.

Arnold Liebster, Simone. *Facing the Lion: Memoirs of a Young Girl in Nazi Europe.* New Orleans: Grammaton Press, 2000.

Aveta, Achille. *I Testimoni di Geova: Un'ideologia che logora.* Rome: Edizioni Dehoniane, n.d.

Bainton, Roland H. *Christian Attitudes toward War and Peace: A Historical Survey and Critical Re-evaluation.* Nashville: Abington Press, 1960.

Beckford, James A. *The Trumpet of Prophecy: A Sociological Study of Jehovah's Witnesses.* New York: John Wiley and Sons, 1975.

Beit-Hallahmi, Benjamin. '"O Truant Muse": Collaborationism and Research Integrity.' In Benjamin Zablocki and Thomas Robbins, eds., *Misunderstanding Cults: Searching for Objectivity in a Controversial Field.* Toronto: University of Toronto Press, 2001.

Berenbaum, Michael. *The World Must Know: The History of the Holocaust as Told in the United States Holocaust Memorial Museum.* Boston: Little, Brown and Company, 1993.

Bergman, Jerry. *Jehovah's Witnesses: A Comprehensive and Selectively Annotated Bibliography.* Westport, CT: Greenwood Press, 1999.

– 'The Jehovah's Witnesses' Experience in the Nazi Concentration Camps: A History of Their Conflict with the Nazi State.' *Journal of Church and State* 38 (Winter 1996): 87–113.

Bettelheim, Bruno. *The Informed Heart.* Glencoe, IL: The Free Press of Glencoe, 1961.

Beverley, James A. *Crisis of Allegiance.* Burlington, ON: Welch Publishing, 1986.

Blackwell, Victor V. *O'er the Ramparts They Watched.* New York: Carleton Press, 1976.

Bornkamm, Heinrich. *Luther's World of Thought.* Translated by Martin H. Bertram. Saint Louis, MO: Concordia, 1965.

Brendon, Piers. *The Dark Valley: A Panorama of the 1930s.* New York: Vintage Books, 2002.

Bromley, David. 'A Tale of Two Theories: Brainwashing and Conversion as Competing Narratives.' In Benjamin Zablocki and Thomas Robbins, eds., *Misunderstanding Cults: Searching for Objectivity in a Controversial Field.* Toronto: University of Toronto Press, 2001.

Burleigh, Michael. *The Third Reich: A New History*. New York: Hill and Wang, 2000.

Burns, James MacGregor, and Susan Dunn. *The Three Roosevelts: Patrician Leaders Who Transformed America*. New York: Grove Press, 200.

Bullock, Alan. *Hitler: A Study in Tyranny*. London: Penguin Books, 1990.

Cadoux, John C. *The Early Christian Attitude to War*. New York: Seaburry Press, 1982.

Canonici, Guy. *Les Témoins de Jéhovah face à Hitler*. Preface by François Bédarida. Paris: Albin Michel, 1998.

Castro, Americo. *La realidad histórica de España*, 4th ed. Mexico: Editorial Porrua, 1971.

Cetnar, William, and Joan Cetnar. 'An Inside View of the Watchtower Society.' In Edmond C. Gruss, ed., *We Left Jehovah's Witnesses – A Non-Prophet Organization*. Phillipsburg, NJ: Presbyterian and Reformed Publishing, 1974.

Cículo europeo de antiguos deportados e internados Testigos de Jehová, eds. *Memoria de un Testimonio: 1933–1945*. Madrid: published by the editors, undated.

Cole, Marley. *Jehovah's Witnesses: The New World Society*. New York: Vantage Press, 1955.

Conway, Flo, and Jim Sliegelman. *Snapping: America's Epidemic of Sudden Personality Change*. Philadelphia: Lippincott, 1978.

Conway, John S. *The Nazi Persecution of the Churches – 1933–1945*. New York: Basic Books, 1968.

Cornwell, John, *Hitler's Pope: The Secret History of Pius XII*. New York: Viking Penguin, 1999.

Coulter, Carol. *Are Religious Cults Dangerous?* Dublin: The Mercier Press, 1984.

Cumberland, William H. 'A History of Jehovah's Witnesses.' Doctoral dissertation, University of Iowa, 1958.

– 'The Jehovah's Witness Tradition.' In Ronald L. Numbers and Darrel W. Amundsen, eds., *Caring and Curing: Health and Medicine in the Western Religious Traditions*. New York: Macmillan, 1986.

Davidson, Eugene. *The Making of Adolf Hitler: The Birth and Rise of Nazism*. Columbia: University of Missouri Press, 1997.

Dawn Bible Students Association. *When Pastor Russell Died*. East Rutherford, NJ: Dawn Bible Students Association, n.d.

Daxelmüller, Christopher. 'Solidarity and the Will to Survive: Religious and Social Behavior of Jehovah's Witnesses in Concentration Camps.' In Hans Hesse, ed., *Persecution and Resistance during the Nazi Regime: 1933–1945*. Bremen: Edition Temmen, 2001.

Fetz, August. *Weltvernichtung durch 'Bibelforscher' und Juden.* Munich: Deutscher Volksverlag, 1925.

Finkelstein, Norman C. *The Holocaust Industry: Reflections on the Exploitation of Jewish Suffering.* London and New York: Verso, 2000.

Foerster, F., and M.M. Wintrobe. 'Blood Groups and Blood Transfusions.' In Maxwell M. Wintrobe et al., eds., *Harrison's Principles of Internal Medicine,* 7th ed. New York: McGraw-Hill, 1974.

Franz, Raymond. *Crisis of Conscience: The Struggle between Loyalty to God and Loyalty to One's Religion,* 3rd ed., 3rd. printing. Atlanta: Commentary Press, 2000.

Frend, W.H.C. *The Rise of Christianity.* Philadelphia: Fortress Press, 1984.

Friedländer, Saul. *Nazi Germany and the Jews: Volume 1: The Years of Persecution, 1933–1939.* New York: Harper Perennial, 1997.

Gager, J.G. *The Origins of Anti-Semitism: Attitudes towards Judaism in Pagan and Christian Antiquity.* New York: Oxford University Press, 1983.

Garbe, Detlef. 'Social Disinterest, Governmental Disinformation, Renewed Persecution, and Now Manipulation of History.' In Hans Hesse, ed., *Persecution and Resistance during the Nazi Regime: 1933–1945.* Bremen: Edition Temmen, 2001.

– *Zwischen Widerstand und Martyrium: Die Zeugen Jehovas im 'Dritten Reich,'* 4th ed. Munich: R. Oldenbourg Verlag, 1993.

Gebhard, Manfred. *Geschichte der Zeugen Jehovas: Mit Schwerpunkt der deutschen Geschichte.* Berlin: Libri Books on Demand, 1999.

– *Die Zeugen Jehovas: Eine Documentation über die Wachtturmgesellschaft.* Leipzig, Jena, Berlin: Urania-Verlag: 1970.

Graffard, Sylvie, and Leo Tristan. *Les Bibelforscher et le nazism 1933–1945.* Paris: Editions Tirésias, 1990.

Grizutti Harrison, Barbara. *Visions of Glory: A History and a Memory of Jehovah's Witnesses.* New York: Simon and Schuster, 1978.

Gruss, Edmund Charles, and Leonard Chretien. *Jehovah's Witnesses: Their Monuments to False Prophecy.* Clayton, CA: Witness, 1997.

Guse, Martin. 'The Little One ... He Had to Suffer a Lot: Jehovah's Witnesses in the Moringen Concentration Camp for Juveniles.' In Hans Hesse, ed., *Persecution and Resistance of Jehovah's Witnesses during the Nazi Regime 1933–1945.* Bremen: Edition Temmen, 2001.

Harder, Jürgen, and Hans Hesse. 'Female Jehovah's Witnesses in Morningen Women's Concentration Camp: Women's Resistance in Nazi Germany.' In Hans Hesse, ed., *Persecution and Resistance of Jehovah's Witnesses during the Nazi Regime 1933–1945.* Bremen: Edition Temmen, 2001.

Hassan, Steven. *Combatting Cult Mind Control.* Rochester, VT: Park Street Press, 1988.

Hébert, Gérard, S.J. *Les Témoins de Jéhovah: Essai critique d'histoire et de doctrine.* Montreal: Les Éditions Bellarmin, 1960.

Hellmund, Dietrich. 'Critical Reflection on the Video Documentary "Stand Firm against Nazi Assault": Propaganda or Historical Documentation.' In Hans Hesse, ed., *Persecution and Resistance of Jehovah's Witnesses during the Nazi Regime 1933–1945.* Bremen: Edition Temmen, 2001.

– 'Geschichte der Zeugen Jehovas (in der Zeit von 1870 bis 1920) mit einem Anhang: Geschichte der Zeugen Jehovas (bis 1970). Doctoral dissertation, Evangelical Theological Faculty of the University of Hamburg, 1972.

Helmreich, Ernst Christian. *The German Churches under Hitler.* Detroit: Wayne State University Press, 1979.

Hesse, Hans, ed. *Persecution and Resistance of Jehovah's Witnesses during the Nazi Regime 1933–1945.* Bremen: Edition Temmen, 2001.

Hislop, Alexander. *The Two Babylons or the Papal Worship Proved to Be the Worship of Nimrod and His Wife.* 2nd U.S. ed. Neptune, NJ: Loizeaux Brothers, 1959.

Hitler, Adolf. *Hitler's Table Talk: 1941–1944.* Translated by Norman Cameron and R.H. Stevens with an introduction and new preface by Hugh Trevor-Roper. London: Phoenix Press, 2000.

– *Mein Kampf.* Translated by Ralph Manheim. Boston and New York: Houghton Mifflin, 1971.

Höhne, Heinz. *The Order of the Death's Head: The Story of Hitler's SS.* Translated by Richard Barry. London: Penguin Books, 2000.

Horowitz, David. *Pastor Charles Taze Russell: An Early American Christian Zionist.* New York: Philosophical Library, 1986.

Höss, Rudolf. *Death Dealer: The Memoirs of the SS Komandant at Auschwitz.* Edited by Steven Paskuly and translated by Andrew Pollinger. New York: De Capo Press, 1996.

Jiménez, Jesús. *Los objectores de consciencia en España.* Madrid: Editorial Cuadernos Para El Dialogo, 1973.

Johnson, Eric C. *Nazi Terror: The Gestapo, Jews, and Ordinary Germans.* New York: Basic Books, 1999.

Johnson, Paul. *A History of Christianity.* Harmondsworth, Middlesex: Penguin Books, 1978.

– *A History of the Jews.* London: Phoenix, 1998.

Jonsen, Albert R., and Stephen Toulmin. *The Abuse of Casuistry: A History of Moral Reasoning.* Berkeley: University of California Press, 1989.

Kamen, Henry. *Inquisition and Society in Spain in the Sixteenth and Seventeenth Centuries.* London: Weidenfeld and Nicolson, 1958.

Kaplan, William. *State and Salvation: The Jehovah's Witnesses and Their Fight for Civil Rights.* Toronto: University of Toronto Press, 1989.

Kater, Michael H. 'Die Ernsten Bibelforscher im Dritten Reich.' *Vierteljahrshefte für Zeitgeschichte* 17:2 (April 1969).

Kennedy, David M. *Freedom from Fear: The American People in Depression and War. The Oxford History of the United States,* Volume 9. New York and Oxford: Oxford University Press, 1999.

Kershaw, Ian. *Hitler 1889–1936: Hubris.* New York and London: W.W. Norton, 1998.

King, Christine Elizabeth. 'Jehovah's Witnesses under Nazism.' In Michael Berenbaum, ed., *A Mosaic of Victims: Non-Jews Persecuted and Murdered by the Nazis.* New York and London: New York University Press, 1990.

– *The Nazi State and the New Religions: Five Case Studies in Non-Conformity.* New York: Edwin Mellon Press, 1982.

Kogon, Eugen. *The Theory and Practice of Hell.* New York: Berkley Medallion Books, 1958.

Kostelniuk, James. *Wolves among Sheep: The True Story of Murder in a Jehovah's Witness Community.* Toronto: HarperCollins, 2000.

Lalich, Janja. 'Pitfalls in the Sociological Study of Cults.' In Benjamin Zablocki and Thomas Robbins, eds., *Misunderstanding Cults: Searching for Objectivity in a Controversial Field.* Toronto: University of Toronto Press, 2001.

Lemhöfer, Lutz. 'Between Historical Documentation and Public Promotion of One's Image.' In Hans Hesse, ed., *Persecution and Resistance of Jehovah's Witnesses during the Nazi Regime 1933–1945.* Bremen: Edition Temmen, 2001.

Lewy, Guenter. *The Catholic Church and Nazi Germany.* New York: Da Capo Press, 2000.

Lietzman, Hans. *A History of the Christian Church.* Translated by Bertram Lee Woolf. Guildford and London: Lutterworth Press, 1961.

Lifton, Robert Jay. *Thought Reform and the Psychology of Totalism: A Study of 'Brainwashing' in China.* Chapel Hill: University of North Carolina Press, 1989.

Manwaring, David R. *Render unto Caesar: The Flag Salute Controversy.* Chicago: University of Chicago Press, 1968.

Macmillan, A.H. *Faith on the March.* Englewood Cliffs, NJ: Prentice Hall, 1957.

'The Martyrdom of St. Polycarp, Bishop of Smyrna.' Translated by Kirsopp Lake. In *The Apostolic Fathers.* Vol. 2 Loeb Classical Library. Cambridge: Harvard University Press and Heinemann, 1970.

Mattera, Ray. '"This Generation Shall Not Pass Away": Eschatology, Ecclesiology, and Ethics in the Theology of Jehovah's Witnesses with Special Reference to Jesus' Eschatological Discourse.' Master's thesis, Northern Baptist Theological Seminary, 1999.

Milton, Sybil. 'Jehovah's Witnesses as Forgotten Victims.' In Hans Hesse, ed., *Persecution and Resistance during the Nazi Regime 1933–1945.* Bremen: Edition Temmen, 2001.

Novick, Peter. *The Holocaust in American Life.* Boston: Houghton Mifflin, 1999.

Parker, J. *The Conflict of the Church and the Synagogue: A Study in the Origins of Antisemitism.* New York: Atheneum, 1974.

Pellechia, James N. 'Teaching Tolerance: A Case Study.' In Hans Hesse, ed., *Persecution and Resistance of Jehovah's Witnesses during the Nazi Regime 1933–1945.* Bremen: Edition Temmen, 2001.

Penton, M. James. *Apocalypse Delayed: The Story of Jehovah's Witnesses.* 2nd ed. Toronto: University of Toronto Press, 1997.

– 'The Eschatology of Jehovah's Witnesses: A Short Critical Analysis.' In *The Coming Kingdom: Essays in American Millennialism & Eschatology.* Edited by M. Darrol Bryant and Donald Dayton. Barrytown, NY: International Religious Foundation, 1983.

– 'Jehovah's Witnesses and the Secular State: A Historical Analysis of Doctrine,' *Journal of Church and State* 21(1) (1979): 55–72.

– *Jehovah's Witnesses in Canada: Champions of Freedom of Speech and Worship.* Toronto: Macmillan, 1976.

– 'A Story of Attempted Compromise: Jehovah's Witnesses, Anti-Semitism, and the Third Reich.' Christian Quest 3(1) (Spring 1990): 33–45.

Peters, Shawn Francis. *Judging Jehovah's Witnesses: Religious Persecution and the Dawn of the Rights Revolution.* Lawrence: University of Kansas Press, 2000.

Raines, Ken. 'JWs and the Nazis: The Watchtower Responds to Critics.' *JW Research Journal* (January–June 1999): 3.

Reynaud, Michel, and Sylvie Graffard. Jehovah's Witnesses and the Nazis: Persecution, Deportaion, and Murder. Translated by James A. Moorhouse with an introduction by Michael Berenbaum. New York: Cooper Square Press, 2001.

Rich, Norman. *The Age of Nationalism and Reform, 1850–1890.* New York: Norton, 1977.

Rogerson, Alan. *Millions Now Living Will Never Die.* London: Constable, 1969.

Rothchild, Silvia. *Voices from the Holocaust.* New York: New American Library, 1981.

Schnell, William J. *Thirty Years a Watch Tower Slave: The Confessions of a Converted Jehovah's Witness.* Grand Rapids: Baker Book House, 1956.

Sevenster, J.N. *The Roots of Pagan Anti-Semitism in the Ancient World.* Leiden: E.J. Brill, 1975.

Shein, Edgar. *Coercive Persuasion.* New York: Norton, 1961.

Shirer, William L. *The Rise and Fall of the Third Reich.* New York: Fawcett Crest, 1983.

Singelenberg, Richard. Review of *Persecution and Resistance of Jehovah's Witnesses during the Nazi-Regime,* edited by Hans Hesse. *Journal of Law & Religion* 18(1) (2002–3): 101–19.

Singer, Margaret. *Cults in Our Midst: The Hidden Menace in Our Everyday Lives.* San Francisco: Jossey-Bass, 1995.

Stevens, Leonard A. *Salute! The Case of the Bible vs. the Flag.* New York: Coward, McCann & Geohegan, 1973.

Stroup, Hebert Hewitt. *The Jehovah's Witnesses.* New York: Columbia University Press, 1945.

Sulpina, Wolfram. 'Persecuted and Almost Forgotten.' In Hans Hesse, ed., *Persecution and Resistance during the Nazi Regime 1933–1945.* Bremen: Edition Temmen, 2001.

Tal, Uriel. *Christians and Jews in Germany: Religion, Politics and Ideology in the Second Reich, 1870–1914.* Translated by Noah Jonathan Jacobs from Hebrew. Ithaca and London: Cornell University Press, 1975.

Twisselmann, Hans-Jurgen, *Der Wachtturm-Konzern der Zeugen Jehovas: Anspruch und Wirklichkeit.* Giessen: Brunnen Verlag, 1995.

Whalen, William J. *Armageddon around the Corner.* New York: The John Day Company, 1962.

Wheaton, Eliot Barculo. *The Nazi Revolution 1933–35: With a Background Survey of the Weimar Era.* Garden City, NY: Doubleday, 1968.

White, Timothy. *A People for His Name: A History of Jehovah's Witnesses and an Evaluation.* New York: Vantage Press, 1968.

Wrobel, Johannes. *Die Videodokumentation 'Standhaft troz Verfolgung: Jehovas Zeugen unter dem NS-regime' Eine Stellungnahme.* Stelters/Taunus: self published, 1997.

– 'Die Videodokumentation 'Standhaft trotz Verfolgung' – Propaganda oder zeitgeschichtliches Dokument?' In Hesse, Hans, ed., *'Am mutigsten waren immer wieder die Zeugen Jehovas': Verfolgung und Widerstand der Zeugen Jehovas im Nationalsozialismus.* Bremen: Edition Temen, 1998.

– 'The Video Documentary "Jehovah's Witnesses Stand Firm against Nazi Assault."' In Hans Hesse, ed., *Persecution and Resistance during the Nazi Regime 1933–1945.* Bremen: Edition Temmen, 2001.

Yonan, Gabriele. 'History, Past and Present: Jehovah's Witnesses in Germany.' In Hans Hesse, ed., *Persecution and Resistance during the Nazi Regime 1933–1945.* Bremen: Edition Temmen, 2001.

– Jehovas Zeugen – Opfer unter zwei deutschen Diktaturen 1933–1945; 1949–1989. Berlin: Numinos, 1999.

– Spiritual Resistance of Christian Conviction in Nazi Germany: The Case of the Jehovah's Witnesses. *Journal of Church and State* (Spring 1999), as posted by the Encyclopedia Britannica at www.britannica.com.

Zablocki, Benjamin. 'Towards a Demystified and Disinterested Scientific Theory of Brainwashing.' In Benjamin Zablocki and Thomas Robbins, eds., *Misunderstanding Cults: Searching for Objectivity in a Controversial Field*. Toronto: University of Toronto Press, 2001.

Zinn, Howard. *A People's History of the United States, 1492–Present*. Revised and updated. New York: HarperCollins, 1995.

Zipfel, Friedrich. *Kirchenkampf in Deutschland – 1933–1945: Religionsverfolgung und Selbsbehauptung der Kirchen in der Nationalsozialistischen Zeit*. Berlin: Walter de Gruyter, 1961.

Zürcher, Franz . *Kreuzzug gegen das Christentum*. Zurich and New York: Europa-Verlag, 1938.

INDEX